Preface

This book is aimed at university and polytechnic students who expect to work in industry but who as yet have only limited experience. In particular it is for engineering and science students doing management as a joint, subsidiary, or additional subject. There is nothing about the way the book is written, or its content, which will preclude other student groups or managers on post-experience courses reading it and gaining both enjoyment and insight, but engineering and science students are the main intended audience. This group usually has to make do with 'hand-me-down' books meant for the main-line business studies student, which is an important reason for our writing this book as an alternative.

With the undergraduate reader in view we mean to give an idea of 'how you will find it when you get there', and to provide background and understanding. We have written about the reality of industry as we see it, not about particular techniques or specialisms. So although we discuss influence and leadership, for example, this is done without going into the intricate details of psychological processes; or when it comes to a subject such as statistical quality control we are content to say what it is and where it fits in, rather than reproduce existing specialist literature. There will be some concepts and some theory but nothing esoteric, only readily absorbed ideas to help make sense of experience.

There are plenty of academics who think of managers, when they think of them at all, as a bunch of flying-by-the-seat-of-their-pants, crisis-mongering pragmatists, so engrossed in daily fire-fighting as to lack an overview of the organization, how it works, and where it is going. Many managers on their side think of academics, even those specializing in management subjects, as being too involved in systems and theories and not enough aware of what it is like 'at the coalface'. There is no doubt some truth in both views, but as academics who have been in industry we hope to bridge the gap. This means being frank about industry, and not pretending that everything happens according to some highly rational masterplan. At the same time it means being aware of the real life constraints, the challenge of uncertainty and imperfection, and having some feel for what managers do, and have to do, to get results.

In pursuing these aims we have tried to avoid especially the approach which simplifies reality by imposing too much order, reason and rightness. This is what might be called the 'wouldn't it be nice if industry were like this' genre of textbook writing: it bores the pants off the not-so-naive student. Instead we are aiming at something more lifelike, and oriented to British (not American) management, in the 1980s.

Loughborough   P.A.L.
August 1983   R.A.L.

Acknowledgements

This book owes a lot to our contacts with and experience in industry, and we would like to take this opportunity to thank all the companies who have extended their hospitality to us, and all the managers who have talked to us about their work.

Peter Lawrence would like to express his thanks to a former student, John Mansfield, whose undergraduate project on the work of salesmen produced valuable material for the chapter on sales in this book.

We are both conscious of the stimulus we received from our colleagues and students in the Department of Management Studies at the University of Loughborough in the period during which the ideas for this book were generated, and we would like to record our thanks to them. Finally, we would like to thank our secretary, Mrs Chris Derbyshire, for a fast and friendly handling of our manuscript.

To
Virginia Ann Lawrence
and
Sandra Louise Lee

Contents

Outline structure   xi

1. The emergence of the modern business organization   1
The business organization in its environment—Pre-industrial production—The Industrial Revolution—The factory system—The legacy of change—The structure of the business organization in the nineteenth century—The structure of the business organization in the twentieth century—Changes in the business environment; trade unions; industry and government; technology; Britain's changing place in the world economy—The recession and management

2. The corporation   27
Organization structures; family firm; semi-independent unit; a complete company; motor car factory; chemical works—Structure and technology—From the Battle of Britain to company structure—The finance link; financial accounting; cost and management accounting; financial ratios—Beyond the bottom line

3. Understanding and influencing; from principles to people   48
The classical view; shop floor management; formal organization—The human relations view; motivation and behaviour; job design—Leadership; Blake and Mouton's studies, Hersey and Blanchard's studies

4. Understanding and influencing: from systems to politics   73
The systems view—The political view; power

5. Purchasing   90
Strikes, costs, and the common cold; what purchases?; raw materials; components or bought-out parts; subassemblies, routine consumables; energy; capital equipment—Is purchasing important—Where does purchasing fit in to the company?—For whom does purchasing purchase?—What do companies demand from their suppliers?; reliability; punctuality; quality; price; flexibility—Vendor analysis: formal and informal—When is purchasing difficult?; Genuine scarcity of goods; goods purchased on commodity markets; genuine shortage of manufacturing expertise; conflict with other departments;

company reputation; limited market intelligence; material with a short shelf life; typical plight of the small firm—How to get the best out of a weak hand—How to play a strong hand—Who should control purchasing—How the purchasing manager can fight back

6. Production   116
Who are the production managers—What is it about?; supplies, new products—What about the workers?; overtime; keep the cog wheels turning—Information is control—End play—The work pattern of production managers—Who hates who?—Industrial relations—Manufacturing policy

7. Sales   134
Sales and marketing—The marketing mix; the four Ps; images and distinctions—The Salesman—Targets of opportunity—What do you want to know?—The game of selling—Closing the sale

8. Personnel management and industrial relations   154
The development of the personnel function: the welfare phase; the scientific/systematic phase—Selection—Appraisal—The industrial relations phase; trade union structure; union recognition; management and unions; key issues—The systems phase; manpower planning—The practice of personnel management

9. Contemporary issues in British industry   171
Unemployment—impact and prospect; the causes of unemployment; the consequences of unemployment; what it is like to be unemployed; the future—Japan—lessons to be learned?; Japanese industry; What can British management learn from Japan?—Male and female roles; the future—Management and social responsibility—The impact of new technology—Discussion

Index   197

Outline structure

A word about the structure of the book. There are nine chapters all of which, apart from Chapters 3 and 4, can stand alone. Nevertheless there is a logic in the ordering of the material.

Chapter 1 deals with the development of the modern business organization from its pre-industrial counterparts to the present day. This historical focus enables simple organizational concepts such as the main management functions to be introduced and placed in the context of a changing environment.

In Chapter 2 the management functions and their relationships are further developed and some financial aspects of business are explored. This ensures that the reader has a good grasp of the way the basic systems of a business enterprise are put together.

Chapters 3 and 4 provide an overview of the development of ideas on how organizations should be run and how people should be managed. These are outlined simply and practical insights are drawn so that by the end of Chapter 4 the reader has a solid picture of organizational life on which the next four 'functional' chapters can build.

Chapters 5 to 8 provide not an abstract appreciation of management in Purchasing, Production, Sales and Personnel, but a taste of the real thing. Not just the rational, neat way things could be if people were unthinking automatons, but the problems, the tensions, the conflicts, and the politics too.

In Chapter 9 some of the interesting issues which the contemporary manager is facing are discussed. By looking at questions surrounding the new technologies, sex roles, management ethics, and other areas of change the reader will hopefully be stimulated to face the challenge of management into the twenty-first century.

One final note, at the end of each chapter will be found a 'topic web' summary of its major subject areas. At first glance these may appear a little complex but the reader is invited to start in the core box and follow the connections between topics and sub-topics. It is a useful learning exercise to recall what is the nature of the links as suggested in the chapter and a useful creative exercise to develop new links and perhaps new topics.

This book is conventional in that it is written in linear form, but we do not think linearly and topic webs are a useful device for stimulating memory and creative thought. Students often find them helpful for purposes of exam revision.

1 The emergence of the modern business organization

Introduction

The world is changing fast—some say at an ever-increasing rate. There is much discussion about the problems faced by today's managers living in a hostile, turbulent, and confusing environment. The world, and in particular the world of business, is a complex place but it is by no means beyond us to make some sense of it, sufficient sense so that we can pursue our own objectives more effectively and help to influence the nature of the changes which are to come.

History is the place to start with this process of gaining understanding—not, of course, the history of kings and queens, battles and dates that we may recall from our early school days. We need to examine the development of the business organization and its environment—changing people, changing economy, changing technology, changing society.

Why a historical perspective? Think about someone you have just met. You may get to know them by experiencing with them a range of new situations and events. But it is their past which has made them what they are and you will not know them well and be able to fully understand their attitudes and actions until you know about their family, their schooling, and their other experiences—in short, their history.

In the next few pages we shall be surveying some 300 years of history using the business organization as our focal point. This exercise involves a great deal of abbreviation and omission and moves at a dizzying pace. Hold on to your seat! First, however, we need to be aware of one simple model which represents the business organization in its environment.

The business organization in its environment

All contemporary business organizations of any size are subdivided into departments which perform particular functions for the whole organization. We shall be examining the different functions in much more detail in later chapters, but let us briefly familiarize ourselves with the terms that we shall be using:

Production   is concerned with making the organization's products.

Marketing	is concerned not just with sales but also with establishing what customers want, what products should be made, how they should be packaged, branded, advertised, priced, and distributed through wholesalers and retailers to the final consumer.
Finance	is concerned with where the money comes from and goes to. Money is the most commonly used measure of organizational activity and a vast array of financial information is used in decision-making. Finance departments are also involved in endless calculations to ascertain how much profit the company is making.
Purchasing	is concerned with what companies buy and for whom.
Personnel	is concerned with the people, how should we select, train, pay and promote them. It also embraces management and union relationships.

There are other functions which are performed within many modern complex organizations (see Chapter 2) but these five functions are basic. Already we can see that there is much to be learned before we can understand the business organization. But it is not enough simply to know what goes on in each of the basic functions, we also need to understand how they relate to each other. We do not understand the motor car if we just know about suspension, ignition, transmission, brakes, steering, and so on; true understanding requires a knowledge of how these systems interact so that the car can operate.

If we look at Fig. 1.1 we can see the business organization represented in the central box. This diagram indicates that we must not only understand the sub-systems and how they interact, but also how the organization interacts with its environment. This will require a knowledge of our competitors, customers, unions, and suppliers. Better still if we can understand the wider environment—how our organization is influenced by the state of the economy, by the culture of our society and by government policy and so on. Some of these notions may sound a bit vague, the culture of society for instance, but we will take them up again at various points in the book and show what they amount to in practice.

One important point about Fig. 1.1 is that we could use it to represent the business organization of today or of 50, 100, or 300 years

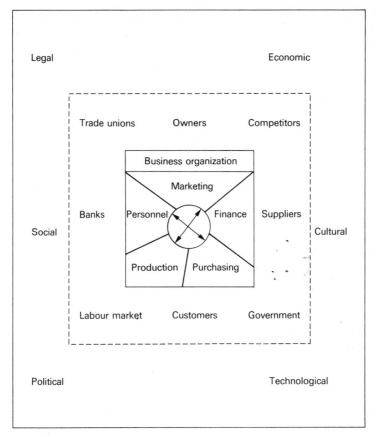

Fig. 1.1   The business organization in the environment.

ago. The basic functions would still be carried out but in very different ways. The important variables in the environment might have similar labels but they would be very different in character. Let us try to outline some of the key changes.

Pre-industrial production

If we go back to the seventeenth and eighteenth centuries we see that Britain was emerging from the post-feudal system. The idea of the king owning all the land in his kingdom and parcelling it out to his followers in return for their services had disappeared. No longer were serfs working for the lord of the manor in return for small plots of their own from which they could scrape a living.

The economy was, however, still predominantly agricultural with a number of different landowner–worker relationships in existence; the idea of the paid worker was becoming more common. There was no sharp division between manufacturing on the one hand and agriculture on the other, and many farm workers were plying other trades such as textile manufacture or metal-working to supplement their income.

Towns, a few very large, and villages existed throughout the country in which craftsmen carried out their business. Half a dozen groups of crafts—textiles, clothing, leather, metal-working, building, and the processing of food and drink—provided employment for roughly three-quarters of the urban workforce and also accounted for most of the non-agricultural occupations in the country regions.

The basic unit of production was the craftsman—a skilled man working with perhaps a few 'journeymen', or qualified assistants, and apprentices. The craftsmen joined local craft guilds which maintained craft standards and regulated trade in both raw materials and manufactured products. Manufacturing by craftsmen tended to be small-scale, using labour-intensive methods with little fixed capital. Since production techniques involved little use of bulky machinery there was rarely any need for specialized premises in which to house.

The largest employers of labour at this time were manufacturers who put work out to employees in their own homes. This is known as the 'domestic system' or 'putting-out', and it was most common in the woollen, metal-working, and leather goods industries. The domestic employers provided the out-workers with raw materials on which they would work. Sometimes they would also provide machinery and instruction. The employer would arrange for distribution and collection of the raw materials 'in-progress' at each stage of manufacture.

The 'domestic-system' replaced the 'craftsman' system in some industries because the craftsman and his methods were more expensive and inefficient. The domestic system too, however, had its limitations. In the late seventeenth and eighteenth centuries the population was growing and markets were expanding. New technology was emerging, which required bulky plant and power-driven machinery to be used with close supervision. The new technology was of processes as well as machinery, often requiring work to flow without interruption from one stage to another.

Thus technical and market forces led to the increasing use of specialized premises for manufacture. These early manufactories were often located close to a convenient source of water power; if this was not near a centre of population then, in some cases, a town was built to house the new work-force. The first genuine factory was a silk-throwing mill which produced yarn for weaving. This was put up on the river Derwent in Derby in 1719 by Thomas Lombe. The mill employed 300 people, mainly women and children.

The Industrial Revolution

Britain was the first country to 'industrialize'. Over a period of 50 or so years from the mid-eighteenth century a predominantly agricultural economy gave way to a predominantly industrial one. The major industrial sectors to develop were cotton, iron, coal, copper, glass, paper, and building. The building of canals and better roads, and later railways, helped to provide the communications network so essential if industries are to feed off each other's products, capital, and labour.

Economic historians have debated at length the nature and causes of the Industrial Revolution. We are not concerned with the finer points of their discussion, but we can learn from their insights. They write about the importance of economic resources such as capital, raw materials (coal and iron, for example), and labour. The development of more efficient agriculture fed a growing population, the development of new technology provided cheaper and more efficient methods of production. The social structure and prevailing social attitudes enabled factories to be set up and created demand for their output. Related to these social forces was the ready supply of entrepreneurial talent which emerged to exploit the opportunities presented by the new circumstances. The Industrial Revolution did not take place overnight. It is only by considering the structure of the economy and the nature of people's lives in the early eighteenth century, and then again several decades later, that we can see the change from agricultural domination supplemented by skilled craft production and domestic employment to smoking, humming, dynamic industry with ever-increasing numbers leaving the land in order to live in the rapidly growing towns and work in the new factories.

The factory system

Between the mid-eighteenth and the mid-nineteenth centuries the factory method of production superseded its earlier rivals. Agriculture, even in 1851, still employed almost a quarter of the workforce, but by then manufacturing, processing and mining employed almost half.

6 The emergence of the modern business organization

The 'factory system' with which we are so familiar involved drastic changes from the earlier methods of production. Previously, the independent craftsman decided when and where and how much to produce. He owned his own tools and workplace, he chose his own production methods and was generally his own boss. The out-worker was not strictly an employee, although he was often economically dependent on his domestic work. Frequently the workplace was his own and perhaps the machinery too. He could work when and in the way he chose, without close supervision or fixed hours. By contrast the worker in the factory was totally dependent on the factory owner economically. He worked, frequently in appalling conditions, for long hours under strict supervision and discipline, with no legal or welfare or union protection. Poorly paid child labour was common, there was no health and safety legislation, no security of employment, few holidays and no prospect of improvement. The reader is recommended to dip into some of the references at the end of the chapter to gain a picture of nineteenth-century Britain which will enrich his appreciation of the relatively comfortable lives most of us now lead.

One important effect of the factory system was that it separated home from work. No longer was the home the centre of a range of productive activities in which the whole family took part. In the new era the home became a dormitory; for the whole of the working day—the very long working day—men, women and children toiled to scrape a living at the premises of their employer.

The production logic of the factory was inescapable. The new technologies were more capital-intensive. The machines had to be fully utilized and they required a power source. The most efficient processes involved an elaborate division of labour and a high degree of supervision. Labour was plentiful and thus cheap—trade unions were almost non-existent. The prevailing economic doctrine was '*laissez-faire*'—non-involvement by the government—which meant there were few legal restrictions on the employers' activities.

The legacy of change

This story of the change from post-feudal society to fully fledged industrialization has been told many times before, usually in more detail than here. It is important to realize that it is not 'just a history lesson', not just a set of facts about the past which some people think are worth knowing for their own sake. This feudal–industrial transition has had all sorts of effects on the present.

It has affected the regional pattern of modern Britain, giving us 'traditional' areas of heavy industry clustered round coalfields and flowing water, most of them now in decline. Similarly, it had a displacement effect on a later wave of industrialization, powered by electricity and oriented to consumer goods, settling these in the Midlands and South-East rather than in the heavy industry areas. So in the long run, events that happened in the eighteenth and early nineteenth centuries have caused later regional differences, and often social and political attitudes to go with them.

Or again, the fact of Britain having the first Industrial Revolution, briefly described in the last few pages, is one of the factors which led to Britain's economic eclipse since the Second World War. Early industrialization meant in the long run an over-commitment to 'unfashionable' branches of industry with old equipment and methods. Or to look on the brighter side, early industrialization and urbanization is one of the factors which led to the consolidation of farm land and its energetic exploitation. Today Britain has the biggest farms in the Common Market. British agriculture has been a big success story with a massive increase in output since the eve of the Second World War, and an even bigger increase in productivity.

Yet perhaps the most important effects are the ones which are difficult to weigh and measure, the ones that are 'all in the mind'. The traumas of early factory life do much to explain the anti-industrial element in British life. Say 'industry' to an English schoolboy and the most likely image is of ten-year-olds slaving in a Lancashire cotton mill of the 1830s. When British trade unions are accused of living in the past this is a way of saying their actions today are sometimes over-determined by folk memories of the early industrialization. The strength of the environmentalist movement in Britain clearly owes something to the same folk memory. So in outlining part of Britain's economic past one is charting the present too.

The structure of the business organization in the nineteenth century

Throughout the nineteenth century the fundamental units of business were the sole proprietorship and the partnership.

In these types of company the sole proprietor or *any* of the partners is liable for the *whole* of the debts and obligations of the firm. Partnerships terminate on the death of a partner, although new partnerships can, of course, be formed. Partnership shares can only be transferred with the consent of all partners.

It was not until towards the end of the century that 'limited liability' became legally possible and widely taken up. A 'limited' company is a legal entity in its own right, separate from its owners.

8 The emergence of the modern business organization

The liability of the owners is limited to the amount of money each has invested—and no more. Thus by buying shares in a limited company you are only risking the price of the shares, whereas if you invest even a small amount to join a partnership then, should it fail, you are legally liable to the limit of your wealth.

Surprisingly, so effective was the partnership system that for most of the nineteenth century there was simply no demand for limited liability. Partnerships were based on professional and commercial skills and investment. Often an engineer would combine with a financial backer to start the firm. If new skills or more finance were required then the partnership could be increased in size. By unifying ownership and control the partnership system reduced the dangers inherent in trusting the business, or part of it, to others.

If the firm became so large as to require more managers, then trusted employees could be made partners, ensuring that their own fortune was dependent on the firm's success. With the risks involved in being a partner you had to be very sure of a manager's commitment!

Clearly, with this system firms were likely to remain fairly small. There was a vast amount of subcontracting in which large jobs tended to be split into smaller more manageable tasks and passed on to other small firms.

The Limited Liability Statutes of 1856 and 1862 made possible investment in industry by ordinary people (with money of course!) who did not want to be bothered with management but who did want to share in the profits of a successful enterprise. However, the partnership system gave way slowly so that by 1885 less than 10 per cent of all companies were limited. It was the high capital cost industries—steel, shipbuilding, chemicals, brewing—which were most keen to exploit this new source of funds.

In the last two decades of the nineteenth century there were several Stock Exchange booms, so that by the turn of the century the industrial pattern was beginning to take on the shape with which we are familiar. There were limited liability companies, a reducing proportion of partnerships and owner-managed firms but still more substantial family businesses than we see today. There was, however, no nationalized sector, all industry still being in private hands. And there were none of the large multinationals that are such a vital part of our modern economy.

The structure of the business organization in the twentieth century

Throughout the nineteenth century most manufacturing companies had simple management organization. Managerial tasks were performed by members of the owning family or by partners in the business, assisted by relatively few foremen and clerks. Figure 1.2 represents this situation for a hypothetical firm.

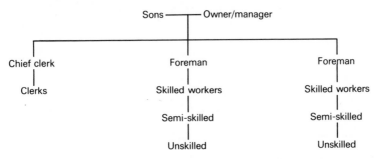

Fig. 1.2   A hypothetical owner-managed firm.

This sort of structure was common right up to the First World War. Not all of the functions which exist in large modern organizations were likely to be found. Market Research, Personnel, Research and Development for example are all fairly recent developments as management specialties. Nevertheless within this simple structure all the basic functions of any business enterprise were carried out. The owner was responsible for policy and probably for sales. The clerks were responsible for the accounts and wages and routine purchasing. The foreman was in charge of all production-related activities and also the hiring and discipline of the employees.

In general, companies were small. Large sites of over 200 or 300 employees were comparatively rare—nowadays most cities have several sites on which more than 6000 or 7000 workers are employed—and these are often only part of a much larger organization.

Even by the turn of the century it was becoming obvious that there were inadequacies in the type of structure portrayed in Fig. 1.2. Larger organizations were found to be better able to cope with the sort of changes that were taking place in the business environment. They offered considerable advantages in terms of increased productivity, market share, and profit. Capital could be obtained on the now thriving Stock Exchange by selling shares to the general public, so why subcontract potentially profitable work? Increasing size has been one of the major themes of organizational change during the twentieth century.

A comparison of Fig. 1.3 with Fig. 1.2 helps us to identify the sort of developments which had occurred in company structure by the mid-twentieth century. Management functions such as marketing, personnel, finance, production and purchasing have emerged or been differentiated, and larger companies employ professional specialists in each of them. We can see from Fig. 1.3 that the proportion of employees actually engaged in production has declined. Hopefully

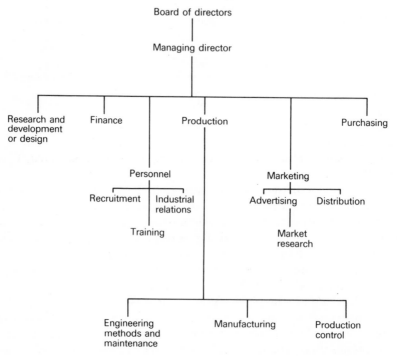

Fig. 1.3   A hypothetical limited liability manufacturing company.

this smaller number of 'blue-collar' workers are more productive because of the 'back-up' from the management specialists and their growing army of 'white-collar' technical and administrative staff. In Britain in 1907 administrative personnel represented 8.6 per cent of production workers. In 1948 they were 20 per cent, by 1966 they were 24.3 per cent—and with the spread of computerization since that time the proportion now must be considerably higher.

Changes in the business environment

Having looked at changes in organizational structure we must spend some time considering the context within which these changes have occurred.

The major stimulus for organizational change is a change in environment. Figure 1.1 (p.3) indicates some of the major features of the business environment that we should examine in order to try to understand the changes which have taken place.

Trade unions

The trade union movement can trace its origins back to the trade guilds of medieval times, but for us it is sufficient to go back to the mid-nineteenth century.

It was in 1851 that the Amalgamated Society of Engineers was formed by a group of engineering craft unions. They can be distinguished from earlier unions in that their policy was to work within the capitalist system for better wages and working conditions. Many earlier unions had been fundamentally revolutionary in spirit, working *against* rather than *with* the grain of capitalism, in consequence of which they were opposed by both industrialists and government.

The ASE paved the way for many other unions of skilled workers. They had full-time leaders and a national executive who became expert in industrial and political activity. These unions worked hard on both fronts to increase their power and also their legal and social respectability. Successive acts in the later part of the nineteenth century gave unions the right to own property and to strike without fear of prosecution.

The next leap forward in trade union history came during the 1890s when, protected by the new legislation, unskilled workers began to form unions. The power of these unions did not lie in the indispensability of their scarce skills but in the large numbers of their membership. They have developed into the vast 'general' unions of today, such as the Transport and General Workers Union and the General and Municipal Workers Union.

The trade union movement has a long and colourful, often dramatic, history of battles with government and employers. Their fight for legal and social acceptance and industrial and economic influence has been and continues to be a story of two steps forward and one step back. The figures on union membership reflect their progress: (Table 1.1).

During the First World War the trade unions cooperated with

government. They permitted their members to be conscripted or moved around within the economy as the war effort required. They permitted 'dilution' of skilled labour—in other words, deskilling jobs so that less trained workers could do them, and they permitted strikes to be made illegal. Factors such as these increased union popularity and help to explain the high membership figure for 1921. During the

TABLE 1.1.
Union membership (per cent of working population).

Year	Membership
1892	11.2
1911	17.9
1921	37.6
1931	22.5
1938	29.9
1948	45.1

1920s, however, the economy suffered. The war had damaged industry and many skilled men were lost. Many of Britain's overseas customers had gone elsewhere for goods while we could not provide them. Britain had been losing her prominent world trading position for decades and this was hastened by the war. Add to these problems the massive world recession and we can see how difficult life was for businesses during this period. With the survival of their firms threatened, managers sought to cut wages, and when unemployment is high and order books are low the unions are in a weak position. The union movement suffered a crushing defeat in the General Strike of 1926. It is not surprising that the membership figures even by 1931 were considerably down on the high of ten years earlier.

The 1930s was a period of retrenchment. Gradually the unions regained credibility and, as the Second World War approached, almost one worker in three was a union member. The effects of the Second World War on the union movement were similar to that of the First World War. Once again union cooperation was rewarded by a vastly increased membership. This time, however, the gains were not quickly lost. During the 1940s and 1950s industrial relations departments in firms became common. Bargaining over pay and conditions became a routine feature of industrial life and many companies developed joint management/union procedures and committees to deal with grievances, health and safety, job grading and other matters of mutual concern. The by now established managerial class had, in large measure, accepted the unions as the legitimate voice of the workers in these matters and was intent on creating an institutional framework for working out problems.

During the last 20 or so years a new type of union has become prominent—the 'white-collar' union. The number of white-collar workers has become so large that it is no longer possible for managements to accord them the privileged status of the earlier part of this century. Their differentials in terms of pay and other special conditions were deeply eroded by the success of the blue-collar unions in the 1950s so that the emergence of white-collar unions to protect and further their interests was only to be expected.

Nowadays about half the working population are trade union members. More than this, over three-quarters of us benefit from trade union-negotiated collective bargaining agreements. There is no doubt much more to come in the fascinating story of trade unions, managements and government—one thing is certain, however, anyone who fails to follow developments and be aware of union attitudes is unlikely to be an effective manager.

Industry and the government

The government, following the economic doctrine of *laissez-faire*, tried not to influence greatly the nature of industrial life during the nineteenth century. Circumstances forced some involvement—Factories Acts, Truck Acts, etc. were passed to curb the worst excesses of the exploiting owners. The gradual legal recognition of trade unions was also important. However, the considerable involvement of the state in industry with which we are familiar is largely a twentieth-century phenomenon.

The situation now is that the modern business enterprise has to collect and pay National Insurance and Value Added Tax as well as other government taxes. It is influenced by a number of government departments—the central one being the Department of Employment. In recent years companies have been subject to government guide-lines and restrictions on pay and other industrial relations activities. There are an enormous number of government-related bodies which may be important—training boards, the Equal Opportunities Commission (EOC), the Advisory Conciliation and Arbitration Service (ACAS), and so on.

Legislation, although much less prominent than in many of our European neighbours, has also affected organizational activities— laws on health and safety, industrial relations, pollution, consumer protection and equal opportunities to name but a few, restrict management freedom in order to protect society as a whole. But of equally great significance has been the emergence of the state as an employer in its own right.

In 1926 the government established the Central Electricity Generating Board, in 1927 it established the British Broadcasting Corporation, in 1933 it created the London Passenger Transport Board. In 1936 15 sugar beet companies were amalgamated into the British Sugar Corporation. In 1939 the British Overseas Airways Corporation was established. The Bank of England was formally nationalized in 1946, and in the same year was passed the Coal Industry Nationalization Act. The Gas Act of 1948 nationalized the gas industry, and in 1951 it was the turn of steel.

There is much more, of course. The development of the welfare state and the education system has meant that millions more workers are basically in government employment. What these nationalized industries have in common with the front runners from the private sector is size. Few would argue that the problems of how to structure and manage the huge organizations that have been created have been solved. They remain one of the great challenges for future managers.

Technology

One of the most important factors in an organization's environment is technology. Two excellent examples of how technological changes have significantly affected economic and industrial development are given by the cotton industry, and by the iron and steel industry. These key sectors were fundamental to the industrial revolution and we shall sketch the landmarks in their history.

Cotton Cotton was the first major industry to replace hand methods of production with machinery and when power was harnessed to the machines the factory system developed. By 1815 cotton had replaced wool as the major export from the United Kingdom, by the 1830s it provided over half the total value of export trade.

All the words describing nineteenth-century industrialization describe the cotton industry: factories; child labour; gruelling toil; vast profits; entrepreneurial talent; slums, poverty and disease amongst great wealth; and technological development.

In tracing industrial changes we have to beware of cause-and-effect assertions; some of the main factors that assisted the development of cotton were the new markets being opened up in the colonies and tropics, and the availability of raw material supplies from the cotton plantations of the southern states of the United States. Labour with the right skills was available in the established wool industry and, in the early days at least, capital requirements were fairly low. The transport network of roads and canals was improved as the cotton industry required. The humid climate of Lancashire and parts of Yorkshire and Derbyshire (cotton thread is less likely to break if spun in a moist atmosphere), and the availability of sources of power in the form of streams and coal were also important factors. But none of this could have been so effectively exploited without the major technological innovations.

The technological revolution in cotton involved the successive overcoming of bottlenecks between spinning and weaving. In 1733 John Kay of Bury had invented the 'flying shuttle', which enabled the more efficient weaving of a wider cloth. This meant that spinners could not provide sufficient yarn to meet the needs of weavers.

The breakthrough came in the 1760s when James Hargreaves of Blackburn invented a successful spinning machine—the 'spinning jenny' which could spin several threads at once.

In 1759 Richard Arkwright of Preston patented his 'water frame'. This device spun the thread by means of water-powered rollers, and it could spin a stronger thread very rapidly. Arkwright's invention is sometimes credited with a key role in the development of the factory system. It could not be worked by hand and was too bulky and expensive for the home worker.

Those responsible for technological innovation do not always benefit financially—John Kay was very unpopular with weavers because, in the short term, he reduced their income. He had to move home several times before fleeing to France where he died in poverty. Richard Arkwright was the patentee of the water frame not its inventor, but he was driven from Lancashire by the resentment of the hand-workers. Arkwright, however, was an organizer. He started many factories and on his death left £500 000, an incredible sum for those days.

Samuel Crompton of Bolton managed to combine the principles of both the 'jenny' and the 'frame' to produce a fine and strong yarn—Arkwright's yarn, though strong, was coarse. This meant that fine cotton no longer had to be imported. Crompton, unlike Arkwright, was not a manager. He took out no patent and did not exploit his new idea to the full; he died poor.

These inventions meant there was a reversal of the weaving–spinning bottleneck. In 1785, the same year that Arkwright's patent was cancelled, Edmund Cartwright invented a power loom. Early versions of the power loom were crude and ineffective, but their development was essential, especially when Watt's steam engine was used to run the 'mule' in the 1790s.

And so the story continues. The technological improvements

affected the organization of the industry. Factories became essential, high output became possible, people required training, large profits were made, raw materials had to be obtained, production systems to best exploit the technology had to be designed—in short, management was required.

The cotton industry continued to expand, although it began to lose its pre-eminence throughout the nineteenth century. However, due mainly to competition from overseas, there has been a progressive decline in cotton exports since the 1970s.

The development of the British cotton industry is one of the great business history stories of all time. The coincidence of supply and demand, talent and technology, and opportunity and response make it an epic. And if one concentrates for a moment on the technology it is also highly instructive: we see a series of self-motivating inventions, where each development puts a premium on the next, where imbalances and bottlenecks cry out for inventive remedy. This pattern is classic, but it is easier to see how it operated in the past, than to see it happening in the present. And in the present the pattern is complicated by new demands, for safety or environmental harmony or taking pressure off materials in short supply. But the pattern exists in the present none the less, and it offers the most poignant research challenge.

Iron and steel Few industries can develop on their own. The cotton industry required improved shipping and internal transport industries. It made demands on the construction industry for the building of factories and also the 'textile towns' to house workers near remote sources of power. It required engineering for the construction of machinery, and later the steam engines to power it. All these industries require, effective iron and steel production. The fact that this in turn requires a thriving coal-mining industry serves to illustrate further the level of industrial interdependence which must exist for any economy to industrialize. We shall outline below the important technological breakthroughs in iron and steel manufacture to show how the dynamic works in practice.

The iron and steel industry has three main stages: 'smelting' to produce basic pig iron, 'working' to produce ingots of wrought iron or crude steel, and 'finishing processes' such as casting, forging, drawing and extrusion.

In the middle ages furnaces for smelting were charcoal-fired and 'hammer working' was used. By the beginning of the eighteenth century the timber forests had been so heavily exploited to produce charcoal that timber was in short supply. It is difficult to imagine what sort of industrialization could have taken place if Abraham Darby of Coalbrookdale had not discovered a method of using coke from coal for smelting iron. Previously, it had been impossible to use coal freely in the smelting process, since its sulphur content combined with the iron to make it too brittle.

The Darby family used their process secretly at first in order to maximize financial advantage. The widespread diffusion of the coke smelting methods, therefore, took almost half a century!

Many foundries were established during the second half of the eighteenth century. These required considerable capital but, as was the pattern, this was found by small partnerships. Samuel Walker's Rotherham Works in Yorkshire had £200 000 worth of capital tied up in them. Walker was exploiting the secret of making tempered steel first discovered by Benjamin Huntsman in 1750, a secret acquired by dubious means.

In 1783 Henry Cort devised the process of 'puddling' or stirring pig iron to remove impurities. The more pure metal was then passed between grooved rollers to make it more malleable. These processes reduced production costs considerably and meant that many more uses of iron could be found; hence they were prerequisites of the vast expansion of output in the nineteenth century.

One of the great technical problems of the eighteenth-century foundries was to raise temperature sufficiently using a minimum of fuel. The Darbys and another great iron family, the Wilkinsons, found ways of using Watt's steam engine to produce a blast of air; this was widely used after 1800, also providing the power for rolling mills. In 1828 J.B. Neilson discovered that by heating the air-blast, coal could be used in place of coke, thus economizing on fuel and accelerating the smelting process.

In 1839, James Nasmyth invented a steam 'shingling' hammer for use in the forging process. This was used to rid the puddled iron of slag before it passed to the rolling mill.

Steel is an alloy of iron and carbon which can be more malleable, stronger and cheaper than malleable iron. Until the mid-nineteenth century steel was hard to produce because of the level of carbon and the problems of controlling impurities. But demand for more and better material with these properties was very high. Industrialization meant buildings and machinery; from 1830 the railways developed rapidly, and ships, bridges and a whole range of engineering applications cried out for steel. Furthermore, exports grew rapidly from the middle of the century, for the world was dependent on Britain for supplies of finished iron for transport equipment.

In 1856, Sir Henry Bessemer developed a process for producing steel in a 'converter'. A very powerful blast was used, instead of puddling, to burn out the impurities from molten pig iron. Carbon was added, in an iron alloy of known composition, to produce the required steel. The properties of this material proved far more suitable than wrought iron for products such as rails, boiler plates and applications where great strain occurred. In 1868 the Siemens–Martin open-hearth process, using pig iron and steel scrap as well as iron ore, was developed.

By the 1880s other processes of steel-making had become established which overcame a problem with both the Bessemer Converter and Siemen–Martin processes. Most British ores contain phosphorus which reduces the quality of the steel, and these processes failed to remove it. But in 1878 Sidney Thomas and Percy Gilchrist showed that if either type of furnace was lined with a basic (as opposed to acidic) material, this would take up the phosphorus from the iron.

Once again the story progresses, encompassing further improvements. The electric furnace and the discovery of the special alloy steels were vital advances at the turn of the century. Other developments took place in production technology; it was found to be economical to place the coke–ovens, blast–furnaces and steel works close together so that molten iron could pass between them and coke–oven gas could be used to generate electricity for operating the rolling mills.

In recent years there have been technical innovations such as the 'oxygen blast' which increases the productivity of open-hearth furnaces and can produce steels with very low carbon content. Steel-makers can now use natural gas, oil or electricity as fuel.

These two industries are key examples. Industries rise in terms of economic significance and then decline relative to newer industries which better serve the needs of the times. Currently we are witnessing massive development in the oil industry which is helping to protect us from the decline in the motor industry and other older 'staple' industries, such as those described. Who knows where the future direction of the British economy lies?—perhaps in the new 'sunrise' industries which are based on microprocessor electronics, autorobots, laser technology and genetic engineering as the technological 'spurs' of the moment. These are discussed in more detail in Chapter 9.

One thing is sure: the technology of products has developed rapidly. It is necessary for leading companies in almost all markets to invest vast sums in research and development in order to keep one step ahead of their rivals. Product life-cycles in general have been steadily reducing as better replacements for existing products result from engineering improvements and breakthroughs.

Equally rapid has been the development of technology in the area of production management. At the turn of the century the design of jobs, workplaces and production processes was often an *ad hoc* affair with few methods available for the systematic pursuit of efficiency. This situation changed between the wars as new techniques for timing jobs, improving work methods, rationalizing workplace and factory layout, and controlling and scheduling production activities, were developed. Machines employed became more complex and industries tended to become more capital-intensive.

Since the Second World War production processes have become increasingly sophisticated with the division of labour being taken to new limits, with thousands of individuals, in dozens of departments, undertaking highly specialized activities, each highly dependent on the others, requiring a high degree of coordination if the potential benefits are to be achieved. The development of new techniques such as operations research and the use of computer systems has added considerably to both the efficiency and the complexity of the modern business organization.

Other environmental factors

What other environmental influences have affected the activities of twentieth-century companies?

The market environment of most organizations is now ruthlessly competitive. The days when a product could be conceived, developed and manufactured at leisure and then proudly revealed to an eager market are no more. In the modern business it is a specialist job to find a gap in the crowded marketplace. High capital cost and aggressive competition make it necessary to be very sure before the investment is made. Marketing has to be well thought-out and dynamic.

Large modern enterprises employ legal specialists to help them interpret and cope with legislation. They employ financial specialists and economists to help them predict and plan for economic changes which may affect demand for their products or the price of raw materials, labour, loans and so on. A more subtle but equally important aspect of the environment for which they rarely plan is the social aspect.

During this century the expectations of employees, owners, customers and even the managers themselves, have changed consider-ably. Our organizations are no longer the 'hire-and-fire' exploiters of the working people they once were. They often provide canteens, sports clubs, holidays, pensions, good working conditions, training, and even planned promotion prospects. We cannot explain all these changes as forced on unwilling managements by such pressures as legislation, economic forces, and trade union power. There has been a social change which has brought with it the expectation of these benefits on all sides. It would be unthinkable for a modern manager to treat employees in the way that his nineteenth-century counterpart did.

The emergence of the managerial class   Limited liability means that people can invest in industry simply by buying shares on the stock market, perhaps through a bank or directly through a broker. Most people who buy shares do so in order to benefit from the profits of the company, some of which are distributed to shareholders as dividends. They may also benefit if the share price, and thus the value of their investment, rises. These shareholders are not particularly interested in the day-to-day running of the company except where it affects these two variables. The control of the company, in most firms of any size, rests with the management, a group of technical and administrative specialists who do not own a significant proportion of the shares.

This 'divorce of ownership and control' started slowly. Many of the first businessmen using the Stock Exchange to raise extra capital still retained a majority interest by issuing shares to their friends, family, and themselves. But as they passed away and divided their shares amongst their offspring—many of whom sold them in order to pursue other interests, and as new share issues were made to finance further expansion, the dispersion of ownership became widespread. In fact over a third of all UK shares are now held by institutions such as insurance companies and pension funds. These large holdings are a potential source of power over the management, but are only likely to be used if dividends become unsatisfactory.

The power vacuum, as owners became remote from the business, was filled by professional managers as an emerging 'managerial class'. At first this new group had no identity and was insecure about both its expertise and its right to power. Everybody knew where the owner's right to power originated—the rights of property—but what of the unpropertied manager? Some argued that he was simply a servant of the owners, carrying out their will. Others argued that a manager's rights to power came from society—he was the trustee of the nation's resources, an impartial arbitrator between 'capital' and 'labour'. This somewhat philosophical debate seems almost forgotten now as we simply recognize the manager's job as an essential economic function, but it re-emerges from time to time in different forms. The debate over 'worker participation' and 'industrial democracy' is closely related to discussion of the rights of managers to manage.

The central concern of the new industrial élite, however, was to develop technical expertise. Organizations were growing, markets were becoming more competitive, technology was changing more rapidly, the trade unions were becoming a force to be reckoned with, and legislation and government policy were starting to affect their freedoms. They needed new and better ways of understanding and managing in order to cope with these problems. Our present society and the business organization which is its most distinctive feature are largely a direct result of the activities of this very recently developed managerial class.

In Chapters 3 and 4 we shall examine how their activities have been reflected in, and perhaps influenced by, the different approaches to management which have been developed alongside the changes already described.

The contemporary business organization There are over 50 000 manufacturing establishments employing more than ten people in Great Britain, two-thirds of them employing less than 100 people. Let us not run away with the idea that all business organizations have become large. But in terms of economic importance we must look first to the larger enterprises, for they provide most of our goods and services, wealth and employment. We must not, however, forget the great contribution of our small businesses, they must be supported and nurtured because it is from these that the giants of tomorrow may emerge.

The story of British industry since the Second World War has been one of mergers and takeovers. In many industries managements have seen advantages in merging with rivals to take a larger share of the market and perhaps reduce administration, distribution and research costs. There are often advantages in combining with suppliers of raw materials to ensure supply, or with distributors or retailers to ensure access to the market place. Many mergers or take-overs have been to obtain patents, or expertise, or access to a new market, or to acquire a product range which complements an existing line. Another form of growth has been 'diversification' or acquiring businesses with distantly related or unrelated products—often simply to avoid 'putting all the eggs in one basket'. If one product line fails others will still keep the business afloat.

Thus our economy is now a complex web of 'groups' of companies, many of them part of vast 'multinational' corporations such as Ford or IBM or Philips with businesses located all over the world. These multinationals have enormous resources and power, their activities can influence national economies, but they are difficult for any single government to control because they can switch people and resources from country to country. Multinationals represent another challenge for the manager of the future.

Britain's changing place in the world economy

In this section we shall briefly review the changes which have taken place in Britain's position in respect to the rest of the world. This will help to show the importance of the wider economic environment and is complemented by the next section, in which we shall note the effects of the current recession on management in business organizations.

In looking at Britain's changing position in the economic world the pattern that emerges is one of *relative* decline accompanied by (increasingly modest) absolute growth. And, of course, there has been some offsetting of the decline of staple industries by the success of new ones.

Britain was a powerful trading nation long before the Industrial Revolution. Colonial trade had grown to one-third of the total by the mid-eighteenth century, and then military victories in India and Canada opened up new markets. The existence of overseas markets was a powerful stimulus to manufacturing industry and with the new, more efficient factory system producing large quantities of cheaper goods, overseas trade was further boosted.

Because she was the first nation to industrialize, Britain had a head start in international trading. The apparent abundance of entrepreneurial and engineering talent, the availability of raw materials, the availability of the necessary capital, and her relative political stability, were among the factors which enabled Britain to dominate world trading until the third quarter of the nineteenth century. Thereafter, her overseas competitors narrowed the gap and in some areas took the lead. Table 1.2 shows British industrial output as a percentage of the world total in comparison with France, Germany and the United

TABLE 1.2

Britain in the world: National industrial outputs (as per cent of world total).

Year	Britain	France	Germany	United States
1800	35	28	11	4
1850	27	18	13	13
1900	16	9	13	34
1950	9	4	9*	37

*Federal Republic only

States. This figure marks a relative decline but it is important to remember that the total volume of world output was increasing rapidly as more and more countries, particularly the United States and some European countries, industrialized.

These later industrializing countries had the benefit of British technological advances and often British capital and talent. The latecomer sometimes starts with the most up-to-date equipment and may not have the historical problems Britain had, such as small self-financed partnerships which could not exploit economies of scale. They often had natural resources in plentiful supply at a time when British reserves were depleting, and cheap labour at a time when British unions were gaining strength.

By the last quarter of the nineteenth century our best coal seams were worked out and both America and Germany had surpassed our iron and steel output. Nevertheless, right up to the First World War Britain was still second only to the United States as a major industrial power.

The First World War and the interwar years were times of great change in British industry. During the conflict all efforts were geared to war production. Often long-term maintenance was sacrificed so that capital equipment became worn, obsolete and less efficient. While the war continued, export customers had to look elsewhere, often to the United States or Japan; also in many cases they developed home industries to replace the lost British product. These markets could not be won back after the war. The new unstable political and economic climate discouraged the earlier faith in free trade, and many nations tried to build up domestic markets and erect trade barriers to protect themselves from competitors. Britain's prosperity was highly dependent on expanding world trade, and she was particularly hard hit by the depression.

Although the 'staple' industries such as heavy engineering, textiles and iron and steel may have declined in world importance, their output in total has increased this century in line with the general trend of economic growth. They are still important to the British economy even if greater vitality has been shown in new sectors such as electrical engineering, chemicals and plastics, aircraft and aero-engines, motor vehicles and consumer engineering, and recently the development of North Sea oil.

As we suggested at the beginning of this section, Britain's decline has been relative. The economy has continued to grow only modestly in recent years, but Britain has done badly compared with other industrial countries. In 1950 Britain was the richest country in Europe; by 1980 all the north-west European countries except Ireland had a higher GNP per capita than Britain, and some east European countries were catching us up as well.

This has given rise to much soul-searching in Britain, especially in the last decade, and a variety of explanations and causes have been canvassed. This, in fact, may be the most encouraging sign. The world has seen great powers, even great empires, decline before. But it has not happened before to a literate, educated, industrialized country in the age of mass communications. So it may be that awareness of the problems will produce a reaction and reverse the trend.

The recession and management

The recession which began in 1980 with its persistent inflation, high interest rates, very low economic growth and, above all, high unemployment, is causing management severe problems. There are vast differences between the experience of companies, and between industries for that matter, but some generalizations can be made.

Many companies are feeling the pinch. They are finding it difficult to maintain sales levels in contracting markets. Fierce competition both from home and overseas companies means that prices have to be cut to the bone in order to survive. This has led to strenuous efforts to contain labour costs, and to a new, cost-cutting interest in the purchasing function (see Chapter 5). Profit levels are reduced, in many cases a firm will take orders at minimal profit just to keep the factory open. In these circumstances managements have no choice but to try to improve productivity and cut costs, as well as redoubling their marketing effort.

Productivity is a ratio between output and manpower, so improving productivity involves a close scrutiny of production systems and manning levels. Paradoxically, if productivity is increased the firm may require even less employees to fulfil declining orders. But increase productivity you must, or you may end up with no orders at all.

How else can costs be cut? By skilful purchasing, perhaps squeezing suppliers who, after all, are in the same difficult position as you, is one important way. By looking hard at materials and parts, looking for cheaper alternatives, or for gains through value engineering. By seeking to reduce scrap and wastage, and saving fuel and energy costs. It is surprising how many companies have started turning off the lights during the lunch break.

In many companies labour costs are a major component of overall costs, so in a recession there is heightened interest in trying to use labour more efficiently by redesigning jobs and work systems.

Another area in which we have all witnessed managements cutting back is the price of labour itself. In the 1920s recession wage cuts led ultimately to the unsuccessful General Strike. In the 1980s wage cuts are less obvious because inflation means that employees can actually receive an apparent increase at some level below the rate of inflation, experiencing an actual drop in real income.

In a recession trade unions are basically weak. They know that firms are fighting for survival and a strike will simply weaken their position further. One of the authors was recently discussing this situation with the Industrial Relations Director of a large group which has decided to use these years of relative union weakness to rationalize its collective bargaining agreements and make various changes in work methods which it could not make in more prosperous times without tough union opposition.

The finance and accounting function is, of course, responsible for keeping the score in what is, in many cases, a losing game. It is difficult to estimate costs with inflation, exchange rates and interest rates either high or difficult to predict. In the years of recession so many firms have had to borrow to survive, and the current high interest rates are now often proving the final blow, particularly for smaller firms.

Management at any time is difficult. It has become harder during this century as the rates of economic, technological and social change have increased. The recession has added a new dimension, or a new challenge.

It has also become clear that a recession has its own dynamics. In 1980 there was horror at the sharply rising rate of unemployment, and this continued in 1981. By early 1982, however, it was clear that 'the end of the beginning' had been reached. De-stocking, postponing repairs and equipment purchase, and similar short-term manoeuvres with which many companies had responded to the recession, had run their course. One could observe an increase in intercompany trading. More money was around, and productivity had gone up.

Not only can one not predict the future, but it is also difficult to foresee the extent of man's adaptation to it. A recession is not only bad news, but a flux of adverse circumstances. It calls for resourceful adaptation, and this may well be forthcoming.

Recommended reading

Allen, G. C. (1970). *The structure of industry in Britain*. Longman. London.
Hobsbawm, E. J. (1969). *Industry and empire*. Pelican, Harmondsworth.
Mathias, P. (1969). *The first industrial nation*. Methuen, London.
Wright, F. (1957). *The evolution of modern industrial organisation*. Macdonald and Evans, London.

Questions

1. What is the long-term importance of Britain having had the first Industrial Revolution?
2. What can be learned about the nature of economic activity and technical advance from the development of the cotton industry in the eighteenth and early nineteenth centuries?
3. What is to be understood by the phrase: the environment of the business organization?
4. What are the key changes in the business organization over the last 100 years?
5. Does it make any sense to speak of a recession as offering managers a challenge and opportunity?

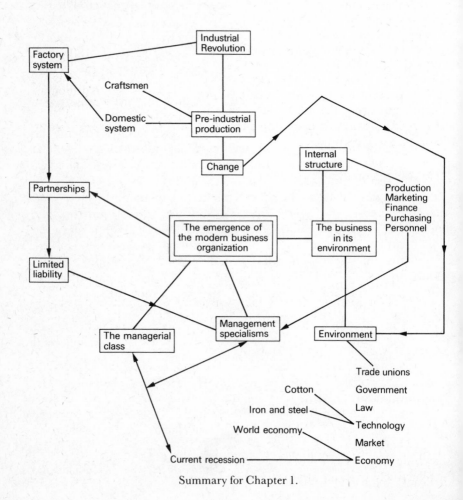

Summary for Chapter 1.

2 The corporation

A major purpose here is to take up and develop a theme from the previous chapter, that of the structure of the business firm. The earlier discussion showed the transition from owner-managed workshop to modern corporation (see Figs. 1.2 and 1.3 in Chapter 1). We now want to enlarge on this theme of the structure of the firm, and offer some illustrations, with three objectives in mind:

(1) to show how complexity increases with size;
(2) to show what range of entities may be part of a modern company;
(3) to show the variety of forms and organizational arrangements.

At least in a superficial way the first point is common knowledge, but considerations of range and variety are less readily appreciated. Textbooks themselves may be partly to blame for this in that they often present a single and idealized organization chart for 'a typical firm', and give the impression that is all there is to say. We will proceed by example using the formal organization charts from several companies we know.

Organization structures

Family firm

The company depicted in Fig. 2.1 is a small family firm employing 90 people. It belongs to the mechanical engineering sector, makes a range of hydraulic equipment and is located in the north of England. The most striking overall characteristic is a lack of definition and formalization typical of the small firm.

Take, for instance, the homely board of directors: the managing director and the technical director are brothers, the sons of the founder; the non-executive director is the founder's widow; and the Chairman is the family solicitor. But note the lopsidedness of the board where the only function represented is the technical, and the reasons are probably quite accidental. If one of the founder's sons had become an accountant there would probably have been a financial director, if one had trained elsewhere in sales there would be a sales director, and so on. Note, too, the lack of clarity and hierarchy at the top where the whole board (in practice the managing director and technical director) are shown as controlling the next level of managers collectively without any proper line of command.

This second line down, ranging from sales manager on the left to chief draughtsman on the right, also conceals real differences of status and influence. At this level the export manager and the new product manager are in fact a cut above the others. These two are both young, university graduates, and obviously going places; what is more, the success of the firm is conceived primarily in terms of marketing a new product range abroad.

Small private company
90 employees
Complete unit
Hydraulic equipment

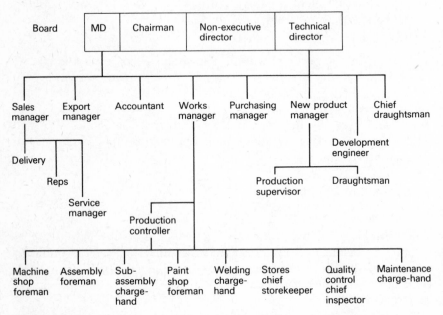

Fig. 2.1   Small private company, 90 employees, complete unit; manufacturing hydraulic equipment.

This company again exhibits the short chain of command typical of the small firm. There are only two ranks between the managing director at the top and the production workers at the bottom, those of foreman and works manager. The production controller is naturally reporting to the works manager; he is a one-man band, and the control system consists of magnetic blocks on a datelined blackboard showing the progress of jobs through the works against target finishing dates. To have quality control as well as maintenance under the works manager is unusual and violates a basic principle, namely that someone responsible for producing the goods should not control those who inspect them as well. But then such anomalies are common in small firms, especially where one is discussing individuals and very small groups rather than sections or departments.

Semi-independent unit

The company, part of whose organization is depicted in Fig. 2.2, brings us straight away to a new consideration. This is that most industrial and commercial organizations, above the level of the smallest, do not stand alone but are part of some larger entity. This company is a semi-independent unit employing 160 people; it belongs to a larger works consisting of five manufacturing divisions and the head office paraphernalia all located on a central site three miles away.

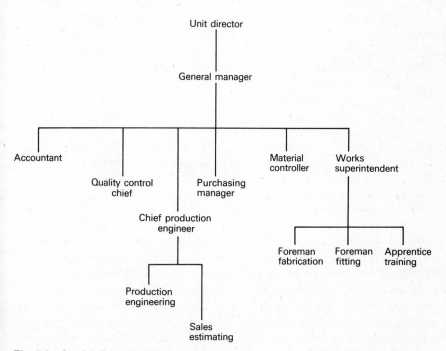

Semi-independent unit employing 160 people
3 miles from rest of works
Heavy fabrications

Fig. 2.2   Semi-independent unit employing 160 people, 5 km from rest of works; manufacturing heavy fabrications.

This unit is tied into the main works by the fact that the unit director is also the main board finance director, and by the fact that most of the work undertaken by this unit (heavy metal fabrications) is in the form of sub-contracts for various of the other five manufacturing divisions. The money the unit earns for this work is a matter of internal pricing policy: the unit is not free to fix its own prices for the five divisions.

On the other hand, the unit is independent in several ways. It is a profit centre, that is to say it has to show a profit on its own operations independent of the profit of the company as a whole. It is also geographically separate (vastly important this); the unit director is absent most of the time (at the main works) and the general manager enjoys considerable autonomy in practice. Among other things he acts as his own salesman getting orders on the open market to utilize that part of the manufacturing capacity not taken up by the requirements of the main works.

We can also see here the effect of increasing size. There are now three ranks between the board and the production workers—those of general manager, works superintendent, and foreman. Quality control (inspection) has now become a separate function reporting directly to the general manager, not to a production manager as in the case of the previous company. Maintenance is not shown, but the facility is provided by the main works where the personnel department is also located (the previous company was too small to have a personnel department).

But we are not yet out of 'anomaly land'. For the unit director to have the general manager as his only subordinate is an odd arrangement. It reflects the desire of the company to tie the unit in, although it is geographically separate; it also reflects somewhat the fact that the general manager is a production man by background (in Britain it is usually people from finance and marketing who get to run companies).

The way 'sales' is organized is also very instructive. The commonsense view that any manufacturing entity must have a sales department is often simply untrue. Many manufacturing establishments are simply producing for the benefit of some related works or division, for some other part of the group. In such cases the level of demand and the price paid are established internally, not in the market place. With the company discussed here there is spare capacity, so the general manager goes out to get orders from outside the company, backed up by a small sales/estimating group who do the costings. This again brings up a more general issue, which is that chief executives (the general manager in this unit is almost a *de facto* chief executive) do become involved in selling, even where the company has a well-organized sales team. To put it bluntly, if the deal is big enough, and the customer important enough, the chief executive will front it.

A final point about this second company concerns production control. As in the previous example, manufacturing establishments generally have a production control section, which establishes and monitors production schedules—in other words, decides what jobs will be done in what order to which deadlines, and tries to make it happen. In this second company there is instead a materials controller. There is no hard and fast rule about it, but production control is sometimes called materials control if, as in this case, the lining up of the materials to do the job is more important than scheduling an array of disparate orders. Another variation is that the purchasing function, acquiring the necessary materials and components (see Chapter 5), and the production control function as described above, are sometimes put together under the label of materials control.

The complications of the last paragraph have a more general importance. This is that although in discussing firms we talk about ranks and job titles, rules and departments, procedures and functions, and so on, companies are not like the army or the civil service. There is endless variation in industry and commerce, in the ways operating units and companies are put together, and there is not even any standardization of job titles or names of departments.

A complete company?

The company depicted in part in Fig. 2.3 is different in kind from the two others already discussed. It employs 460 people, manufactures a range of specialized industrial equipment, and is located in Scotland. This is an independent company, yet it is part of a larger group. But in this case there is no connection between the company depicted and the other companies in the group. These several companies provide widely different goods and services, have different markets, and do not trade with each other (as in the case of the last company discussed): they form, in other words, a conglomerate. The company's affiliation with the group is financial: the company passes on (much of) its profit to the group, may be allowed to borrow money from the group, and in certain circumstances (commercial failure!) may find that the group head office will interfere with policy and appointments. Otherwise the company shown in Fig. 2.3 will follow the golden rule: as long as you are making money you can do what you like.

Setting aside for the moment the question of independence within

32 The corporation

the conglomerate, this company is the first in the series with a visible and comprehensive board of directors. There is a managing director and he has a deputy; production and engineering have been separated; all the major functions are represented at board level (the

Independent company, part of larger group
460 employees
Fluid handling equipment

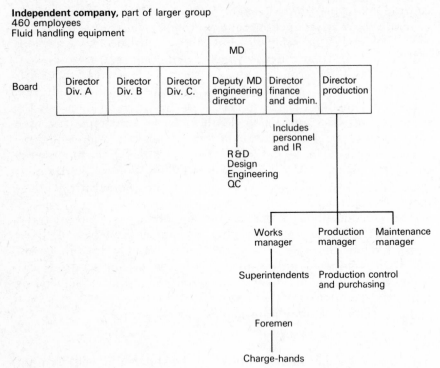

Fig. 2.3   Independent company, part of larger group, 460 employees; manufacturing fluid handling equipment.

three divisional directors on the left of the chart are all sales directors responsible for the sales of three different ranges of products from the three manufacturing divisions). What is more, everything is fitted in neatly with, for example, managers responsible for personnel and industrial relations reporting to the finance director. All this reflects the greater formalism of a larger company that is also complete in itself although part of a conglomerate.

There are other manifestations of this. Here we have a company with its own research and development (R&D) and design capability. Quality control is not only taken out of the control of any production manager but is separate up to board level. There is a personnel section. The hierarchy is lengthening, so that between the managing

director and the shopfloor workers come the production director, the
works manager, superintendents, foremen, and chargehands.

Motor car factory

Moving sharply up the size scale the company whose organization is
depicted in Fig. 2.4 is a motor car factory, employing some 4000
people, and located in the Midlands. This factory is part of a large

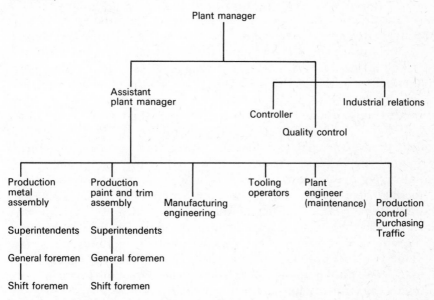

Fig. 2.4   Complete manufacturing unit, part of US multinational, over 4000
employees; car factory.

American multinational corporation, which is why there are so many
things missing from the organization. Sales and marketing (see
Chapter 7 on differences), design, research and development, central
planning, and so on, are all located elsewhere. The works represented
by this organization chart is purely a manufacturing site; the
non-manufacturing functions are geographically separate, the UK
headquarters is elsewhere, the European head office is in a different
country, and world headquarters are in the United States.

Note some of the titular differences. Because this is just one works
among many its head is not in the formal–legal sense a managing

director—hence the titles 'plant manager' and 'assistant plant manager'. The title 'controller' is an Americanism; in a British company this manager would be chief accountant or head of finance. And the fact that there is an industrial relations manager rather than a personnel manager is a motor industry-ism. Industrial relations tend to be precarious in the motor car industry, so the emphasis is on industrial relations troubleshooting and averting strikes, rather than on the conventional personnel functions (see Chapter 8).

The functions which report directly to the plant manager rather than to his assistant are also typical of the automobile industry. These are: industrial relations, because of the disruptive effects of industrial action for a mass production assembly line industry; quality control, because quality is desperately important in the production of high cost, highly visible consumer goods; and the controller because Americans are very hot on financial planning and budgetary control.

The structure indicated in the organization chart for this works again shows the effect of increasing size. All the necessary functions are present, or to put it another way, there is high specialization. Production is divided into the two main lines of metal assembly on the one hand, and paint and trim assembly on the other. Plant engineering (normal maintenance) is separate from manufacturing engineering, which is concerned with devising, maintaining, and improving manufacturing methods, and this in turn is separate from tooling operations, the tool-making preparations for very long production runs of particular models. And in a works with 4000 employees the chain of command from the plant manager at the top to the shopfloor workers is long, ranging through the ranks of assistant plant manager, production manager, superintendent, general foreman, and shift foreman (this double level of foreman is typical of the motor car industry, and not just in Britain).

Chemical works

As a last example of the endless variation in the way companies are structured consider the chemical works whose organization is depicted in Fig. 2.5. This works employs a little over 1000 people and is located in the south. Again this works is part of a much larger entity, so the manager in charge has the title 'works manager' not managing director. In fact this company is organized into a number of divisions, differentiated by product or product group, and the divisions are in turn broken down into works. Figure 2.5 shows one of the works, in a leading division.

This works shows clearly how one can read off what is important from the organization chart. As with the motor car factory this chemical works is a pure manufacturing unit. What is important is making the product on the one hand and maintaining, repairing, and on occasion replacing and installing the complicated equipment for making it on the other hand. So the works manager has two principal subordinates: an assistant works manager in charge of production, and a works engineer in charge of repair and maintenance functions. And these two are paralleled all the way down the hierarchy, so that the various section managers in charge of subdivisions of production have opposite number section engineers responsible for maintenance

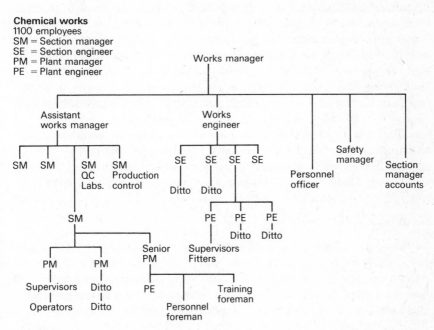

Fig. 2.5   Chemical works, 1000 employees. SM = Section manager; SE = section engineer; PM = plant manager; PE = plant engineer.

back-up; the plant managers in charge of yet smaller production units are matched by plant engineers in the other hierarchy, and so on down to production operators versus maintenance fitters.

As with most of the works or companies given as examples in this chapter, it is part of a larger whole, so some functions, R&D for example, are missing; these will be at separate establishments, or at divisional or even national headquarters. But this is not the whole story. In this works there is no purchasing section either, but this is because the principal raw materials come from another division in the same company; so there is no problem of supply as prices are internally fixed. And to complete this story there is no sales department either because the output of this works goes in turn to another works as a raw material, prices again being a matter of internal policy not market negotiation.

There is a further point of interest concerning the companies depicted in Figs. 2.4 and 2.5. In Chapter 6 on production it is argued that production tends to be a rather low status function, typically avoided by younger, better qualified and more ambitious managers. But this is not always the case. The car company and chemical corporation discussed here are big outfits organized into a number of manufacturing sites supplemented by a few special establishments (such as for R&D, testing, and so on), and various levels of head office administration. So to run one of these manufacturing sites is a top job, and the way up is via the lower line production management posts. So that in the case of the chemical works the ranks of the plant managers will provide the next generation of works managers, which means that production is a high status function and a good career choice!

There is a wider moral. The generalization about production being a bit of a 'Cinderella function' is true, but it is not everywhere or always true. Very few generalizations about British industry are, and this is part of the variety that it has been our purpose to illustrate.

Structure and technology

So far in this chapter we have treated structure as that which can be read off company organization charts. This focuses attention on particular things: ranks and titles, the presence or absence of functions and the way they are put together, and relations between the parts and the whole. That is a perfectly legitimate approach, but there are others; or to put it another way, there is more to company structure than a plan of the formal organization.

One can go beyond questions about the number levels in the hierarchy and what they are called, and also check on the spans of control (number of people directly reporting to someone) of managers, chief executives, or even foremen. These two simple measures, length of hierarchy and span of control, when they are combined, enable triangular depictions of companies, so that a tall slim triangle, for instance, indicates a company with a long hierarchy, but one where the managers and supervisors have only narrow spans of control (few people reporting to them).

Other questions about the personnel employed by a company might concern skill levels, job or departmental specialisms, relative proportions of direct and indirect labour, managers and non-managers, technical and non-technical staff, and so on.

Or it is possible to characterize a company structure in terms of how flexible it is, how bureaucratic, and how specialized. The relative importance of different functions will vary, so that in one company sales is everything, but in another company manufacturing whatever it is in volume is what counts. Or companies can be analysed in terms of their decision structure, along the lines of who decides what at which level, the time span of decisions, their frequency, the relative proportions of policy decisions and problem-solving decisions, and so forth.

The observations of the last two paragraphs are not meant to constitute a comprehensive list of everything that might be looked at under the heading of company structure; but the important thing is that there is a lot of variation in all these aspects as well. This endless variety in the way companies are organized and structured has been a challenge to management theorists, who have tried to make sense of it in some way, tried to find patterns and causes.

In a modest way we have been doing this already. The five examples discussed earlier illustrate three propositions about company structure:

(1) Size is an important determinant of structure.
(2) So is the fact of whether the unit of analysis stands alone or is part of a larger entity.
(3) Particular operating exigencies will be reflected in the structure (e.g. for example, the importance of tooling up in the automobile industry, or of process plant maintenance in the chemical industry).

But there are other theories to explain the differences, and one of these approaches takes the technology-cum-production system as the key to understanding company structure. The classic study of the way technology is associated with different structural features is the work of an English sociologist, Joan Woodward (1958). Taking a sample of over 100 firms in South-East England she constructed a ten-point scale of technical complexity, and then simplified it into three basic types:

(1) Unit (or small batch) production, where only one (or a few) of a kind are made at a time, and design to meet customer requirements is important, for example, bespoke tailoring, or shipbuilding.
(2) Mass (or large batch) production, where the emphasis is on tooling up for long production runs at low unit cost, for example, motor car manufacture.

(3) Process production, where complex plant is capable of the near continuous production of what is usually a dimensional product (one which can be measured rather than counted), for example, petroleum, chemicals, much of the food processing industry.

Where the companies were put under these three headings many of the other features fell into place. So that, for instance, as one moves up the scale of technical complexity from unit production through mass production to process production the number of levels in the hierarchy increases and so does the ratio of managers and supervisors to total personnel; in other words, they come to constitute a higher proportion of the total workforce. Similarly the ratio of direct to indirect labour increases, and the proportion of graduates engaged in production management goes up. These patterns are summarized in Fig. 2.6.

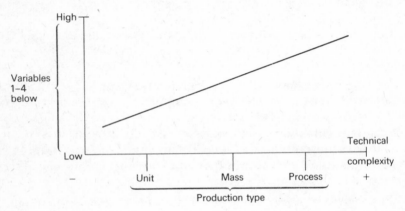

Fig. 2.6   A number of the organizational variables relate to the technologies in this progressive way: 1 : number of levels in management hierarchy; 2 : ratio of managers/supervisors to total personnel; 3 : ratio of indirect to direct labour; 4 : proportion of graduates among supervisory staff engaged in production.

But not all the variables form this progressive pattern. Unit production and process production companies turn out to have some common features, while mass production companies differ from both the other types by being organizationally inflexible, emphasizing written rather than oral communication, having first-line supervisors (foremen) with large spans of control, and by compartmentalizing the functions of management in the sense of clear-cut boundaries between them, and separating technical expertize out from the line management hierarchy. Some of these differences are summarized in Fig. 2.7.

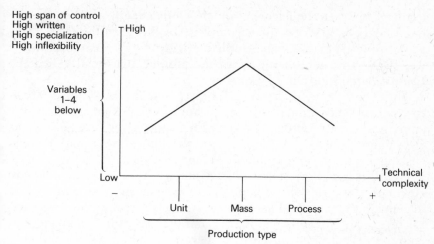

High span of control
High written
High specialization
High inflexibility

Variables
1–4
below

Fig. 2.7   A number of the organizational variables relate to the technologies in this way : i.e. increase up to mid-point in the complexity scale and then decrease : 1 : span of control of first-line supervisors; 2 : organizational flexibility; 3 : amount of written as opposed to verbal communication; 4 : specializations between functions of management and technical expertise functions, manifest in a line-staff structure.

These comments on the role of technology are not a full summary of Woodward's study, still less of the debate it engendered, but enough has been said to give the flavour, and to show that technology or production systems do seem to be associated with other features of the company organization. But equally important is the fact that Woodward's study does take us beyond commonsense opinions about size and so forth by showing that it is possible to see some pattern and order to it all.

From the Battle of Britain to company structure

Another theory which is not as comprehensive as that of Woodward, but has more patriotic elan, is the idea of Burns and Stalker (1961). This is that there are two basic structures, which they call mechanistic and organic, appropriate respectively for companies in stable and changing contexts. In a way, it all starts with the Battle of Britain.

An important reason that we won the Battle of Britain is that we had a home radar chain which enabled us to spot most incoming aircraft formations and concentrate our own fighters accordingly. This radar system had been developed in the late 1930s, and what fascinated Burns and Stalker was how participative and democratic this development had been, with a lot of contact, exchange and feedback between the scientists and development engineers on the one hand, and Air Ministry officials and RAF officers on the other. This was in contrast to the (later) German attempt to develop radar, which was a bureaucratic charade centring around an official called the Plenipotentiary for High Frequency!

This contrast is the germ of Burns and Stalker's ideas about mechanistic and organic structures, later developed on the basis of a study of some 20 Scottish and then English firms in, or entering, the electronics industry. The mechanistic structure is one where there is clear division of labour among the managers; each one knows exactly what his job is and sticks to it. Channels of communication are clear-cut and vertical, with orders coming down and reports and information going up. The chief executive is a real authority figure, assumed to be virtually omniscient, and the subordinate managers all enjoy clearly defined authority and responsibilities. Information is concentrated at the top, and that is where the decisions are made. The gist of the mechanistic structure is summarized in Fig. 2.8 in the form of an (oversimplified) organization chart.

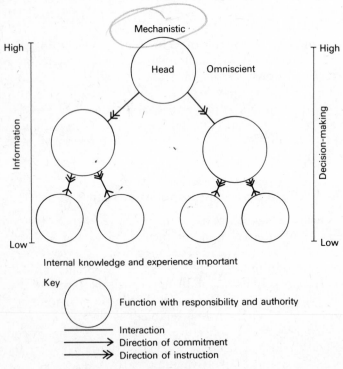

Fig. 2.8   Mechanistic structure.

The mechanistic structure is appropriate for companies operating in a stable environment, making established products by means of well-known methods for a stable market. The organic structure on the other hand is marked by fluidity and lack of definition. Jobs are not clearly defined, there is much lateral communications, and relevant knowledge is more important than rank. The organic structure, basically the reverse of the mechanistic, is again summarized in Fig. 2.9 in the form of a simplified organization chart.

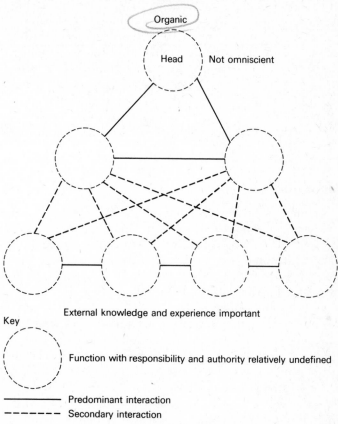

Fig. 2.9   Organic structure.

The organic structure according to Burns and Stalker is suitable for companies facing change, particularly where they are innovating as to product, on the basis of a new body of knowledge, the output oriented to a new market—exactly the position of electronics firms in the 1950s, the period of the study. There is a limitation to Burns and Stalker's theories which should be made clear, namely that firms which ought to be mechanistic generally are, but firms which find themselves in a change situation and which ought to move according-ly towards an organic structure do not always do so. The change-stimulated transition to an organic structure is sometimes frustrated by the chief executive and by the political and status considerations of other managers.

We have introduced these ideas of Burns and Stalker because again they go beyond a commonsense appraisal and show a more imaginative patterning of structural features. Their work is interesting in another way, however, which is that it demonstrates that there is no cutoff point for organizational structure. Structural features blend with behavioural ones. In the mechanistic model, for instance, formal structure is affecting attitudes and behaviour, while the organic structure is in part a set of generalizations about the behaviour of managers involved in it. Thus the study with which we end the present discussions of structure looks forward to the more systematic exploration of the behaviour of people in organizations presented in Chapters 3 and 4.

The finance link

Besides forming a bridge to Chapters 3 and 4 the discussion of company organization will also hopefully set the scene for the treatment of particular management functions—sales, production, personnel, and so on—later in the book. In fact we have left out one non-technical function from this later single-chapter treatment, and that is finance. This is based on the assumption that finance is the area of management work which intended readers are least likely to enter, unless of course they retrain as accountants, in which case they will not need this section as an introduction. So in these later chapters it has seemed sensible to put the emphasis on any connections between the function discussed and finance, rather than on having a detailed analysis of the finance function itself.

It may, however, be helpful to give a brief overview of what, to put it in homely terms, accountants in industry do all day. This will round out the notions of structure that have been explored by showing that companies have a financial structure too. This is so not only in the sense that a company needs capital at its inception and profit for its continuation, but also that all operations have a financial purpose and may be subject to review in these terms.

Financial accounting

Firstly, accountants in industry are involved in the provision of legally required documents, at fixed though infrequent intervals. These are principally:

(1) the balance sheet;
(2) a profit and loss account;
(3) a statement of the sources and uses of funds;
(4) the directors' report.

To these four one should really add the provision of an annual report to employees, a document which serves to explain the performance of the company to the people who work in it. This information includes, incidentally, a value-added calculation (value of sales minus cost of bought-out parts and services) which enables employees to see what the contribution of their efforts has been. This employees report is not a legal requirement but it has become increasingly common.

The provision of these various documents and statements naturally requires a lot of systematic record-keeping, including records of sales made, of the cost of parts and materials, of bad debts, of the wages bill, of overhead costs of other kinds, as well as records of the purchase of the firm's fixed assets. It also requires calculations of the depreciation of these assets and some mechanism for assigning this depreciation to accounting periods. So even if the balance sheet and profit and loss accounts are only produced annually, they are based on a continuous monitoring and information-gathering process.

The basic proposition of the profit and loss account is that sales minus all costs equals profit. This profit is then variously allocated between dividends to shareholders, interest on loans, retained earnings (profits kept for reinvestment), and corporation tax. Corporation tax is paid at the basic rate of 52 per cent (or 42 per cent for small companies).

The balance sheet is a summary of assets and liabilities at a point in time. Under the heading of liabilities come:

(1) funds from shareholders in the form of share capital;
(2) retained earnings;
(3) money owed but not actually paid, for example, to suppliers;
(4) unpaid corporation tax.

The assets are usually:
(1) the plant, machinery, buildings, land, works;
(2) unsold stock;
(3) work in progress;
(4) cash in the bank;
(5) debtors—people who owe money to the company.

Actually paying suppliers (see Chapter 5) and credit control (deciding who may be allowed credit) are also generally counted as part of financial accounting as opposed to cost and management accounting.

Cost and management accounting

One might say that the essence of cost and management accounting is that it is like producing a balance sheet and profit and loss account every month. Cost and management accounting involves analyses which are both more detailed, and more frequent, than simply knowing how much profit the company has made each year.

This operation involves focusing on internal transactions. So one wants to know, for instance, how the total labour will breakdown for the production of different products or services, and the same for the cost of purchased parts and materials. It is not enough to know that the company is making a profit (hopefully); one wants to know where that profit is coming from—which works, divisions, products, and operations are generating most profit?

Two approaches used in this connection are job costing and process costing. Job costing is straightforward and simply involves ascertaining the cost (and therefore profit) of any particular job. A shipbuilding company, for example, will want to know the cost of the five oil tankers it built for a particular customer, as distinct from its overall operating costs and profits. Process costing is the alternative used where one is concerned with the production of, say, a long stream of homogeneous products. Take, for example, a company producing among other things tins of baked beans. It will not be helpful to establish the cost of a single tin, or of a dozen, or even of a crate of 200 tins. The technique is to cost the process over time; to establish, that is, the cost of running that canning line for a week or a month, and then dividing the resultant figure by the number of tins produced in the period.

In practice job costing and process costing are interlinked, where different things are made on the same equipment, or the same thing is made in different ways—the same component, for instance machined on a conventional machine or on an numerically-controlled (NC) machine. But in principle the two approaches do differ.

The results of these calculations and analyses are used in two ways. The first use is budgetary. The information enables a forward planning of expenditure associated with products and services. To put it simply, it enables the company to work out in advance the probable cost of making a million goods. The information also facilitates the allocation of departmental budgets; one needs to know, for instance, how much the personnel department will need in the coming year to do its job properly. And of course budgets are not only attempts to anticipate costs and expenditures; they are also used to control expenditure and monitor performance. It is this fact that makes establishing (particularly departmental) budgets such a tricky political act. Production managers are especially apt in piling on the agony in this connection, anticipating everything from an exceptionally severe winter to a rise in world copper prices that may push up their operating costs.

The second use of this cost information is to facilitate and sustain *ad hoc* decisions. Pricing decisions are a good example: how should a new product be priced, what price rises should be made on existing products, is there a need for differential pricing (say different prices in different territories, or one price for trade buyers and another for DIY purchasers). Then there are 'make or buy' decisions regarding components, and occasionally equipment, which need to be supported by cost analyses. And there are strategic decisions about what products to emphasize, and which markets to go for, which can only be based on analyses of cost and profitability.

Financial ratios

Finally, appraising business operations involves the analysis of financial ratios. The profit and loss account only yields the absolute profit, and the balance sheet indicates the position at a particular point in time. But the real test is an adequate return on capital employed. So the primary ratio is that of profit: capital employed. And this in turn may be reformulated in terms of two secondary ratios:

$$\frac{\text{profit}}{\text{sales}} \quad \text{and} \quad \frac{\text{sales}}{\text{capital employed}}$$

These ratios are used diagnostically to see if the company is doing as well as in the past, as well as other comparable organizations, as well as it ought to. So the analysis of these ratios may highlight problems or inefficiencies. This is all part of the work of the accountant in industry.

Beyond the bottom line

This outline of the financial structure of the company has implications going beyond the scope of the present book. And although we do not intend to explore these issues it is appropriate to indicate their existence.

Finance is forward-looking, but it is not *very* forward-looking. It is about how to get next year's cash/budgets/profit, etc. right on the basis of a painstaking analysis of the recent past. But what must a company do to be sure of being profitable in ten years time?

This question opens up issues of corporate strategy, or in English, of business policy. It raises questions of product replacement and regeneration, of the anticipation of changes in demand, the exploitation of new markets and the realignment of market shares, of diversification, acquisitions, and research strategy. Finance has a major contribution to make to all these decisions, and some of them are also conditioned by organizational structure. But questions such as these go beyond both management accounting and organizational design, belonging as they do to the realm of business leadership.

References

Burns, T. and Stalker, G. M. (1961). *The management of innovation*. Tavistock Publications, London.
Woodward, J. (1958). *Management and technology*. HMSO, London.

Recommended reading

Ansoff, H. J. (1968). *Corporate strategy*. Penguin. Harmondsworth.
Drucker, P. F. (1968). *The practice of management*. Pan Books Ltd., London.
Lammers, C. J. (ed.) (1979). *Organizations alike and unlike*. Routledge and Kegan Paul, London.
Sizer, J. (1969). *An insight into management accounting*. Penguin, Harmondsworth.
Woodward, J. (1965). *Industrial organization theory and practice*. Oxford University Press, Oxford.

Questions

1. What does it mean to say that companies are structured in an infinite variety of ways?
2. What sort of factors determine the way companies are put together?
3. Is there any pattern about the connections between
   (a) technology and structure?
   (b) market situation and structure?
4. What is the difference between financial accounting and cost and management accounting?
5. Suggest a viable business policy for the British shipbuilding industry.

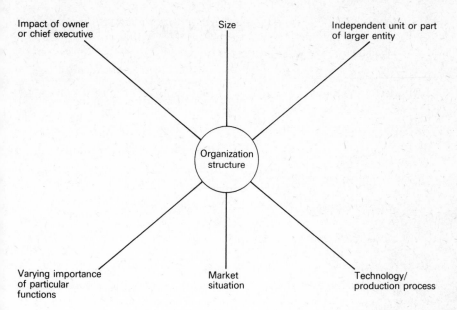

Summary for Chapter 2.

3 Understanding and influencing: from principles to people

Imagine the problems of someone from an entirely different culture to our own, where there are no business organizations, if they were suddenly placed in charge of one of our companies. They simply would not know where to start, they would have no concept of what business is like, what it should be striving for, and how the people in it should act. It would take a long time to build a picture in their minds, what we call a model, which would guide them so that they could make wise decisions. Fortunately for us, we have been brought up in a business-oriented society so that we all have in our heads some model or models of the business organization. These models are basically the way we think; they influence our interpretation of the events which occur and they influence our personal behaviour. If our picture of organizational life is not well developed then we will be confused by what we experience; if it is naive then we will have great difficulty in achieving the objectives we set ourselves.

The purpose of this chapter and Chapter 4 is to describe a range of useful models which have emerged through the years, influencing the behaviour of managers and providing different insights into organizations. We will be examining each model in outline and the contribution it has made to our understanding. The stance we will maintain will be the healthy scepticism of those concerned with the real world in all its demanding complexity. Furthermore, we are not concerned merely to understand what happens, we need to know enough to influence that real world, dare we say, manipulate it?

The classical view

In Chapter 1 we noted the contextual changes which fundamentally affected the character of the business organization during the late nineteenth and early twentieth centuries. In particular limited liability and increasing size led to the emergence of a new 'managerial class' who, while not owning a significant part of the organization, had the power to control it. It is the managerial class which nowadays, by its cumulative actions, exerts perhaps the greatest influence over the nature of our society. Just as the emergence of the managerial class is largely a twentieth-century phenomenon, so is the development of sophisticated ways of thinking about the business organization. This is no doubt unfair to the many successful managers of the eighteenth and nineteenth centuries who must have had implicit models or theories which they used to guide their actions, but since there is little systematic writing and no development of a body of knowledge from that time, we must start by analysis of 'management thought' with those who were managing around the turn of the century.

The first view of organizations which we must examine is that put forward by their earliest spokesmen. In part it reflects the needs of the day and the different environment of organizations in the first quarter of this century; this makes the model appear oversimple but it is where our forerunners started, and it is where we must start, not just for historical reasons but because the past has had a formative effect on the present.

The early 'spokesmen' for the new managers were usually experienced and successful managers themselves. They were aware of the problems of their colleagues in coping with the new circumstances we have outlined and they attempted to synthesize their experience systematically into an easily learned model of the organization, and a simple set of rules for improving its performance.

We often refer to these writers as belonging to the classical 'school of thought'. This simply means that their ideas are in many ways similar; they tend to have attitudes in common and make comparable assumptions about such things as the goals at which the organization should be aiming, and the motives of the people who work in it. This is an oversimplification because often these writers were at odds on many points; nevertheless, we have to structure our thinking somehow and 'schools of thought' is a reasonable way to do it.

What we then tend to do is to talk about the ideas of the classical school as though they were one single body of thought. This we will tend to do here, although we will also be discussing the work of some major writers. The basic classical view of organization is represented in Fig. 3.1.

Fig. 3.1   The classical model.

The classical view portrays the organization as an instrument for making profit for the owners. The purpose of management is to convert inputs—men, money, materials, and so on—into profit via good managerial practice. There are two main aspects to 'good managerial practice' according to the classical writers; these are 'administration' or 'formal organization', which will be discussed in the next section, and shop floor management.

Shop floor management

One of the earliest writers in this area was an American, Frederick Winslow Taylor. Taylor was an apprentice machinist who rose to foreman and finally became a management consultant. He had a chequered history in which he became perhaps the most influential management theorist ever, and to many, the most unpopular. The unpopularity of his ideas, or as he believed, their misuse, led to a Congressional Enquiry at which Taylor had to testify. We shall pick out the most important features of Taylor's work.

The underlying philosophy of Taylor's model goes like this: Employees come to work primarily to maximize wages, management need to design the organization and the payment systems so that if people work hard they will do just that. If management has done its job properly then the increased efforts of the workers will mean higher productivity, higher profits and ultimately higher dividends to the owners. Everybody wins, workers get high wages, owners get high dividends and managers are happy because they have done their job well. This is known as a 'consensus' model, the organization is seen as a team, fundamentally all parties are on the same side. But how does Taylor believe that consensus can be achieved?

His first major idea is 'the divorce of planning from doing'. Employees are neither suited to make decisions nor do they want to do so. Planning and decision-making should be passed up the hierarchy to the better qualified, more broadly motivated managers.

This leads directly to the second major idea, job design. Taylor believed in the maximum fragmentation of work. Tasks should be divided into their simplest possible constituent elements and each worker should do as few elements as can be conveniently combined into a job. This deskilling process was seen to have advantages such as minimizing training time, making recruitment easier, making it easier to organize work into flow lines and removing undesirable decision-making from shopfloor workers. There would be less problems to cause errors and workers could become incredibly quick at their simple tasks.

Simplifying jobs paves the way for perhaps Taylor's greatest contribution to management—time study. Time study involves a number of different techniques for calculating how long a qualified worker of average ability and motivation should take to do a job. Nowadays it has been developed into a very fine art and is combined with method study aimed at finding the best method for doing the job. Times from time studies are useful for calculating such things as costs, delivery dates, and machine loading, as well as for balancing the work done by each operator on a flow line. For Taylor, however, the main purpose of these times was to form the basis of payments-by-results systems.

If we know how long the average worker should take, then we can pay people more if they work faster and less if they work slower. In terms of motivation, the assumption is that people will work as fast as they can to earn as much as they can.

Formal organization

Most of the classical writers were more concerned about the higher levels of the organization than they were about the shopfloor. It is to their ideas that we now turn.

Ask most people to draw a diagram representing the business organization and they will usually draw something close to the classical administrative model—a 'hierarchy', probably fairly similar to that shown in Chapter 1 Fig. 1.3. Though most people will draw a hierarchy, only a few are clear about what the hierarchy represents.

Hierarchy, or formal structure, is a classical idea and it represents the *authority* relationships within the organization. Authority may be defined as 'the right to get things done'. For the classical writers this right originates with ownership—the rights of property. The owners delegate their authority to the board of directors who in turn delegate it to the managing director. And so it goes right down to the worker on the shopfloor who has authority over his tools, equipment and so on. Authority carries with it the obligation to carry out the duties over which the employee has authority, this obligation is known as one's 'responsibility'. Good management practice involves ensuring that responsibilities are met, thus the concept of 'accountability' is introduced, being the measurement of responsibility.

Already we have the outline of the classical model. People in organizations are seen as part of a hierarchy, a network of interlinking jobs, defined by detailed job descriptions which specify the tasks required and the authority and responsibility of the jobholder. We know that the purpose of this hierarchy is to make profits and that jobs at the bottom end should be simple and repetitive. The decision-making and planning should be carried out at higher levels in the structure. The man recognized as the pioneer of this view of organizations was a Frenchman, Henri Fayol. Fayol, like Taylor, was a successful manager. He became a coal-mine manager at the age of 25 and by the age of 47 was managing director of a large but almost bankrupt French mining combine. He held this position for 30 years, during which time it became highly successful and more than doubled in size. When he retired Fayol set out to summarize the basic principles he had used so that they could be passed on to the new breed of managers. His synthesis of his experience into a list of 'principles of management' set the pattern for most of the classical thought which followed.

Fayol believed his principles were just useful guides for managers; however, later writers have often presented their principles as universal prescriptions for success. We have already discussed the ideas of hierarchy, authority, responsibility, delegation and account-ability which form the basis of many principles, so let us now look at some of the others.

Unity of command	No member of an organization should receive orders from more than one superior.
Exception principle	Decisions which recur frequently should be reduced to a routine and delegated to subordinates and only those which are non-recurring should be referred to superiors.
Span of control	No supervisor should have more than five subordinates reporting to him.
Unity of objective	The objectives of each organizational unit should integrate with and contribute to the achievement of the organizational objectives.
Organizational balance	The relative size and importance of each department should remain consistent with its desired contribution to organizational objectives.

And so on. Many classical writers give the impression that there is no need for the manager to understand the true complexities of organizational life, as these have been worked out by the writer and taken into account when designing his particular principles.

Looking down the examples given the reader may be struck by their commonsense logic. Unity of command will avoid conflicting loyalties for subordinates; the exception principle will allow higher managers to use their time more economically, and they may be more capable than subordinates in dealing with non-routine matters; a limited span of control will allow closer and more effective supervision; if departments are 'balanced' and 'integrated' they will be more effective.

But it is possible to argue with the logic on a variety of grounds. Our secretary has several bosses, we work out between her and ourselves what the work priority should be with no difficulty (usually!); the exception principle may lead, like Taylor's view on job design, to boring, routine jobs down the hierarchy. Furthermore any passing on of decisions may cause costly delays, for example, when a good customer complains about faulty goods and wants action, and the best information for making the decision is often located at the operational level; the appropriate span of control for a supervisor will depend on his capabilities, the nature of the task, the ability and motivation of subordinates and other such factors; finally the idea that departments *should* be balanced and integrated is a prescription which does not allow for reality. Organizations do not have objectives, only people do. Different people pursuing their own objectives, or their view of what the organization's objectives should be, will build empires, compete with other departments and generally engage in the range of political behaviours which make organizations so interesting.

Despite these criticisms it is important not to entirely dismiss classical principles. The important thing is to understand that any approach has both strengths and weaknesses—there is no *right* model which will be useful in all circumstances. The classical ideas form the basis of most organizations in which people work. The principles are very useful first approximations to what goes on, and one merit that was particularly important at the time is that they are easy to understand.

On the debit side it can be seen that the classical view is about how these writers think an organization *should* behave. We are more concerned with how it does. The idea of a machine-like business in which people form cogs, performing according to their job descriptions, using their prescribed authority, working in carefully balanced departments to achieve carefully worked out goals, is not a bad simple model, but it provides only the bare bones of understanding. In particular the reader may be unhappy about the treatment of people by the classical writers. They are portrayed crudely as money-motivated automatons who are happy with repetitive, unskilled work. Further, there are seen to be two classes of people; the managers are more broadly motivated than the rest, they are prepared to take on challenges, to plan and make decisions, these are the people who should co-ordinate and control the activities of the majority—a 'them and us' philosophy.

The human relations view

It was discontent with the classical treatment of people which led, in the 1920s, to a change of direction. The 'human relations' writers focused not on structure but on people as their central feature of the organization. The insights they provide help to put flesh on the classical skeleton.

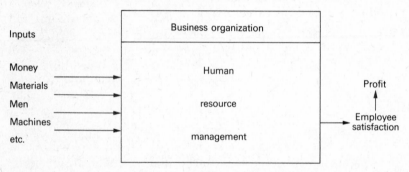

Fig. 3.2   The human relations model.

In the classical model the organization is viewed almost as a machine, all we have to do is design the parts and fit them together correctly and it will perform according to plan. The reaction against this by the human relations writers was to view the organization as a network of human relationships. If managers want to make profits they will need to persuade people to be productive. Let us consider how difficult a problem this is.

First, a few classical assumptions about people:

(1) People are basically lazy and will not work unless they have to.
(2) People are motivated primarily by money, and knowing this is the key to human resource management.
(3) People prefer simple, routine, repetitive jobs involving a minimum of decision-making.
(4) People do not like problems, they are not interested in taking responsibility or earning promotion.

How appropriate are these assumptions? How well do they apply to you? Hopefully not too well! If you look at each statement in turn you will probably find yourself saying: Yes, this applies to some people in some situations, but it isn't the whole story. Consider the scenario below:

John, a recent graduate, had just taken over as supervisor in the plating shop; it was his first management post. He discovered within a few days of arriving that almost all the 20 young men in the shop were going home early, sometimes by as much as 15 minutes. John knew that his department was beating all its work targets and he didn't want to do anything to upset things. How should he react?

The classical approach would be for John to use his authority to demand adherence to the formal rules, but if he is too heavy-handed and productivity falls his career may be in jeopardy.

John will need to know much more about people in general and his new subordinates in particular if he is going to sort out this situation without problems. He needs information about the individuals and the group he is now supervising. Groups tend to develop 'norms' or patterns of behaviour which are difficult to change. Is leaving early an established norm or is it just taking advantage of a 'green' supervisor? Is the norm more complicated? The previous supervisor may have allowed it to develop in return for high productivity. If John is to change things he must break down barriers; he is new and thus anything he does now sets a precedent. If he is too tough or too soft he may destroy a productive group. Information can only be obtained and barriers be broken down by getting to know the individuals. Within the group there may be 'informal leaders', 'hard workers', 'rebels', 'time servers' and others. Knowledge of the roles people play in the group will be vital if it is to be managed. More than this, if John is going to create a good working atmosphere of hard work and loyalty then he needs to know how each individual sees himself, his circumstances, his ambitions, his fears and the range of factors making up personality and motivation. Only with this knowledge can he act wisely.

Consider another scenario:

Simon, a production engineer, has been charged with developing a new computer-controlled system for scheduling jobs between the machines on the shopfloor. He is having problems because old Joe, the progress chaser, keeps feeding him incorrect information about the whereabouts of jobs in the system, and because the machine operators prefer to select their own order for doing jobs. How should Simon proceed?

The classical approach here would be for Simon to design the system and to try to discipline Joe and the operators if they do not use it properly. A more 'human relations-oriented' approach might include letting Joe play a part in developing the system and also involving the operators. Keeping people informed, letting them make suggestions and participate in decisions, being aware of the insecurity related to change—these are commonsense human relations ideas.

In neither of the scenarios is the formal classical approach, relying on 'authority' and 'rules' likely to be the best. Managers need human relations insights and skills if they are to be effective. We shall examine three of the key areas on which human relations writers have focused: 'motivation and behaviour', 'job design', and 'leadership'.

Motivation and behaviour

Here we are concerned with why people act as they do, and how we can change their actions; the manager is concerned with both understanding and influencing.

Earlier we looked at a list of classical assumptions about people. Douglas McGregor, a human relations writer, labels such assumptions 'Theory X'. He believes that supervisors and managers who follow such assumptions are not getting the best out of their subordinates, in fact they may be creating problems for themselves. If people are treated as though they are lazy, irresponsible, and money-motivated, then that is how they will act. McGregor contrasts 'Theory X' with 'Theory Y' in which people are viewed more positively. The assumptions below characterize this approach:

(1) People are not basically lazy, they do want to work and will do so if they are treated right.
(2) People are able to develop, to take responsibility, to use initiative and to make decisions.
(3) People can be self-motivated and self-controlled and will work towards organizational goals if management create suitable conditions and opportunities.

In Theory Y people are viewed as more mature and capable than in Theory X. Both are generalizations, of course, but they serve as a useful thought-provoking introduction to a survey of human relations ideas. They demonstrate the fundamental change from the classical view to a perspective in which people are studied in much more depth. Probably the best known theory of motivation is that of Abraham Maslow. Maslow postulated a 'hierarchy of needs' (Fig. 3.3). Maslow investigated the nature of what he calls 'peak experiences'. Reports were obtained in answer to the request to think of the most wonderful thing that happened in one's life. On the basis of these reports Maslow developed his hierarchy. The lowest level of needs are physiological: air, water, food, etc. Until they are satisfied the next level of needs does not operate; that is, lower levels on the hierarchy are prepotent over high levels.

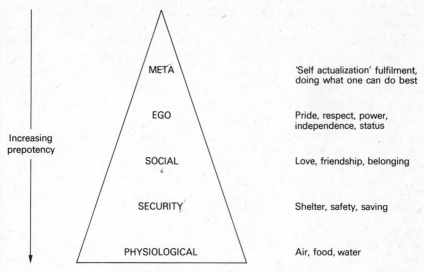

Fig. 3.3   Maslow's hierarchy of needs.

Let us imagine we have survived a shipwreck on a desert island. The first needs which we will try to satisfy are hunger and thirst. The next level of needs are 'security' needs; we will probably make or find a shelter from the sun and any dangerous animals. Also on this level we will try to ensure a continuing supply of food and water and perhaps find a weapon to protect ourselves. We may stay at this level long enough to construct a stockade and maybe even capture some animals within it. Eventually, however, we will probably find our life rather lonely, and here the social needs are beginning to operate. If we are lucky our explorations around the island will turn up some fellow survivors, and for a while the group will satisfy our needs for company, friendship and belonging. In any group, however, people strive to be individuals, this is the ego needs operating. Some want to lead, others want just to be respected for the qualities they bring to the group. Everyone wants to be seen as important to the group in some way.

At the top of Maslow's hierarchy are 'self-actualization' needs. These are different for each of us. They are expressed in such ideas as self-fulfilment, life purpose, being fully stretched, giving our best and achieving a sense of meaning and accomplishment. For our group on the desert island self-actualization, the ultimate motivation, may be to work towards discovery and return to civilization. According to Maslow, even the most untalented individual will, given the right conditions, seek self-actualization. We should note, however, that once this state is achieved a new goal will replace the old one, and our motivation will continue.

Maslow's model provides a useful view of motivation. The idea of people responding to a hierarchy of needs shows the range of need satisfactions which organizations can usefully provide. Money can operate at any level on the hierarchy, for some it is an indicator of status, and for others its pursuit is a lifetime goal. For most people, however, it operates most directly at the lower levels, providing the means for buying food, clothes, housing and so on, and providing savings to ensure a secure future. Thus money is likely to be a useful motivator for management to use—particularly where the lower order needs are not yet satisfied, but also at higher levels.

What are the other management implications of Maslow's hierarchy? To satisfy security needs management may offer security of employment, sick pay and pensions. Social needs are largely a challenge to the skill of the first-line supervisor but could include sports and social facilities too. Ego and self-actualization needs involve opportunities for training and promotion, creating levels for people to progress up and systems to show them how they are doing and to encourage and help them to do better. The first-line supervisor can be involved here too, giving praise and recognition for work well done and allowing subordinates to take responsibility.

It is believed by the followers of Maslow that most people will voluntarily choose self-actualizing goals which are in line with effective organizational performance.

One writer in the human relations tradition whose ideas follow Maslow's closely is Frederick Herzberg. Herzberg's method for studying motivation was to ask people to talk about things which caused changes in their level of satisfaction with their job. In order to quantify his results, Herzberg noted what was said and how long was spent saying it. He then categorized the major factors that people said caused both job satisfaction and dissatisfaction, and weighted them according to the length of time they were talked about by the subjects.

Herzberg discovered that the factors which, when positive, lead to satisfaction do not, when negative, tend to lead to dissatisfaction. Conversely the factors which, when negative, lead to dissatisfaction do not, when positive, tend to lead to satisfaction. Take pay for example: when people perceive pay as too low it tends to make them feel dissatisfied; when it is perceived as high, however, it does not lead to particular satisfaction.

The 'dissatisfiers' Herberg renamed 'hygiene factors' and the 'satisfiers' were called 'motivators'. The 'two-factor' theory can be represented thus as shown in Fig. 3.4.

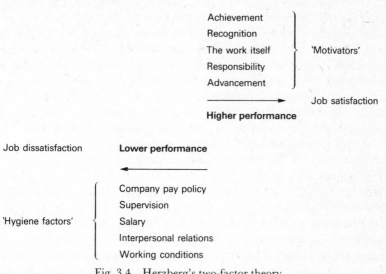

Fig. 3.4   Herzberg's two-factor theory.

Herzberg believes that in most modern organizations the hygiene factors are well catered for. His research indicates that, this being the case, further improvements in salary, social relationships, working conditions and so on will not motivate workers to higher performance. This can only be achieved by attention to the motivators.

It should be noted that the hygiene factors refer primarily to the environment of work, whereas the motivators are related to the things people can control, or at least try to influence, themselves. This implies for management that they should focus on providing opportunities for training and promotion, and providing feedback to employees on how well they are doing. It also throws particular emphasis on the way jobs are designed. Herzberg saw this as a key area, and we shall return to it shortly.

The 'motivators' relate closely to Maslow's higher order needs, and up to the 1960s most human relations writers concerned themselves with identifying the needs which motivate behaviour. Edgar Schein has outlined a set of assumptions about human nature which may be where this line of thinking was bound to end up; this is known as the theory of Complex Man.

(1)   People are both complex and highly variable. They have many motives which are arranged in some sort of hierarchy which is specific to the individual. This hierarchy is subject to change from time to time and situation to situation.

(2)   People are capable of learning new motives through organizational experiences.

(3)   People may achieve different need satisfactions in different places. For example, they may work to satisfy physiological and security needs, but satisfy social needs at home and ego and self-actualization needs by running marathons, or joining a union, or doing voluntary work.

(4)   People may respond to many different kinds of managerial strategy, depending on their own motives and abilities, and the particular circumstances; in other words, there is no one correct managerial strategy that will work for all people at all times.

How do you feel about the complex man assumptions? Probably you feel they are basically right, but not a lot of use to the practising manager. This is perhaps fair comment in that it is not too helpful to merely tell the supervisor 'everyone is different'. In some ways the generalized models of Maslow and Herzberg are more useful. They indicate the sort of organizational and supervisory practices which will allow most people a reasonable degree of job satisfaction and perhaps motivate them to higher performance. But in many situations as in the scenarios of John and Simon discussed earlier, the supervisor is dealing with specific individuals and particular circumstances. He must tailor his actions with much more precision than just working out where people are on Maslow's hierarchy.

The complex man model emphasizes the need for supervisors to learn human relations skills, not just simple theories. There is a range of exercises and techniques, which cannot be described in detail here, that are designed to teach to supervisors two major qualities. The first quality is diagnostic ability. The supervisor must have the sensitivity to appreciate the personalities and motivations of all his subordinates. Training in this area often involves the supervisor being placed in a range of subordinate situations so that he can learn to 'empathize', put himself in their shoes. It will involve case studies and perhaps 'T' groups at which particular supervision problems are discussed with other supervisors and trainers. One of the aims of these sessions is for the supervisor to gain an impression of how he is seen by other people—often a somewhat traumatic process.

The second quality is that of personal flexibility. By exposing the supervisor to a range of different problems calling on different types of behaviour, it is hoped to develop the adaptability required to cope with the different demands that 'complex man' will place upon him.

Before leaving the subject of motivation, we need to note the new direction many writers are taking. No longer are they simply trying to find out what people's needs are and how they are ordered. This view of people is rather patronizing. It sees people as being essentially reactive, waiting to be motivated by management. In the newer approaches people are seen as active, not responding to needs but pursuing goals, deciding between options, weighing up the pros and cons. These approaches are knows as 'Expectancy' theories or 'VIE' (valence, instrumentality, expectancy) theories. The model outlined in Fig. 3.5 below is a simplified version.

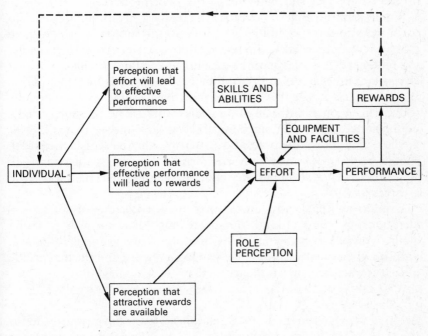

Fig. 3.5   Expectancy theory.

Expectancy models such as that shown above try to identify the thought processes underlying motivation, satisfaction and performance. They separate out the basic components of these thought processes and in doing so help to provide us with insights into possible problems.

Figure 3.5 is best explained with the help of an example:

Fred, a development engineer, is told by his boss, Jane, that he has a good chance of being promoted by the end of the year. However, she tells him that he will have to perform well on the two projects he is currently involved with. How is Jane's statement likely to affect Fred's motivation?

Expectancy theory tells us that Fred will not simply respond to a need for advancement, he will make a calculation—although this may well be subconscious. First he will assess whether hard work on his part will lead to good performance in the two projects. Fred's ego will play a part here, does he believe he's good enough? What about the people he works with, will they negate his extra efforts? Does he have the right facilities and training to do a good job?

Next Fred will assess whether good performance will lead to promotion. Is it possible that Jane is exaggerating her power to promote him? Has she made others the same promise?

Finally, Fred will decide whether he really wants promotion. Is the extra work and responsibility worth the commitment he would have to make? Does he want more money, status, power? Here is where the various 'need' theories may help us to understand Fred's choice. If any of the three factors are zero, then Fred will not increase his effort. If they are not, then they will act together in some way to produce some effect on Fred's input to his work. The output, Fred's performance, will only improve if Fred has the right skills and facilities and if his 'role perception', that is, what he sees as the job he should be doing, accords with that of Jane. Finally, at the end of the year, Fred will re-evaluate his effort depending on the rewards he receives.

Expectancy theory provides management with some useful generalizations. People will tend to expend more effort towards reaching goals (a) when they are reassured that they can accomplish the task, and (b) when the probability of receiving a reward and the magnitude of that reward are known in advance.

Job design

An area in which many human relations writers have contributed is the study of job design. It is only too easy to design jobs in accordance with some technical or economic criteria and then to discover that there are problems because people are demotivated by the work in some way. It may be that failures in job design will not manifest themselves as complaints about the work itself, but will instead emerge as excessive wage demands or petty industrial relations problems. Let us take a closer look at the subject of job design.

The 'traditional' approach, following the ideas of Taylor, we have already discussed. The objective here is to improve productivity by the use of 'time and motion' techniques and job simplification. This is the classical principle of division of labour—maximum work efficiency will be achieved if jobs are simplified and specialized to the greatest extent practicable. Taylor, and those who have come after him, the industrial and production engineers, have made a massive contribution to industrial efficiency. Job simplification has reduced costs and made a wide variety of goods available to all. This approach is widely used to the present day, it is common in all industries. Without a doubt, division of labour is essential, it is not desirable for one person to build a whole car or television set, the question is one of degree.

If carried too far jobs may be boring and unchallenging, offering none of the motivations which Herzberg suggests are important. Demotivated workers may be very hard to manage, there may be problems of lateness, absenteeism and high labour turnover; in extreme cases workers may restrict output. One problem of simple, routine, repetitive jobs is that they do not train the jobholder for promotion, offering no outlet or prospect for satisfaction of higher order needs.

However, let us not be too emotional about this. The engineering logic of job simplification is often inescapable. If one firm tries to make jobs more interesting but reduces productivity as a result then those doing the better jobs are likely to soon find themselves ex-employees of a bankrupt company. The human relations approaches to job design aim to achieve high productivity without incurring the human costs of the traditional approach. Early suggestions included 'job enlargement', which involves more tasks of a similar nature to the original one (such as putting all four wheels on a car instead of just one), and 'job rotation', periodically moving workers from one job to another. Both these approaches offer some increased challenge to the employee, but only at a low level.

Herzberg, in line with his two-factor theory, suggests 'job enrichment' (Fig. 3.6). Job enrichment involves building into the job factors such as variety, challenge, interest and responsibility. If possible the enriched job should allow for the learning of new skills, to cope with new problems; it should provide the employee with a sense of personal worth and individuality. The task should contain an open end in its description to allow for taking on more responsibility and for changing and improving work methods.

As an example of 'enriching' a job, consider the people who clean a college hall of residence. The classical way to design their jobs would be to make them specialists, one person makes the beds, one vacuum-cleans, one polishes floors, etc. In an extreme case the cleaners would be told where they should be working and when and

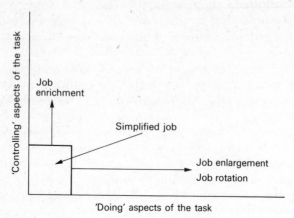

Fig. 3.6   Approaches to job design.

with what equipment. To ensure good performance a supervisor would make regular checks.

There are a number of steps which might be taken to enrich these jobs.

Task identity and variety By making the cleaners responsible for particular areas they could be involved in all the different cleaning tasks. This would provide variety and make them feel they are doing a 'whole' job.

Responsibility and independence Instead of checking up, why not just leave it to the cleaners? The students they serve will complain soon enough if they are not satisfied. Making a task somebody's independent responsibility is much more likely to encourage conscientiousness and pride than is close supervision.

Establishing client relationships Making cleaners more independent and assigning them to particular rooms might lead to them forming relationships with the 'customers'. This may be a motivator in itself and it could encourage the cleaners to meet special needs of some students—like not knocking at the door too early on a Monday morning!

Job-based feedback Since the cleaners do a 'whole' job they will know when they are doing a good job.

There are further possibilities of course, it may be feasible to allow the cleaners to choose what sort of cleaning equipment they wish to use and to make suggestions for improvements.

Another approach to job design which needs to be mentioned is the idea of 'autonomous work groups'. This involves delegating some managerial aspects of the work not to the individual but to the work group. The group may be given responsibility for assigning people to tasks and shifts, for deciding and meeting output and quality targets, for deciding training needs, for some aspects of discipline, and so on. In some cases the group is given a say over recruitment, and perhaps even how the pay which the group receives should be divided among its members.

This approach could be used for our cleaners if they were a sufficiently cohesive group that was committed to the task in hand and was interested in this form of independence. One problem with autonomous work groups is that of connecting them to the rest of the organization. What happens to the conventional supervisor, and how is the group dealt with when productivity or industrial relations problems occur?

The idea of job enrichment is an important one if two assumptions are accepted:

(1) It is important for a business organization to take responsibility for the satisfaction of workers' higher order needs (as Maslow calls them).
(2) Enriching jobs need not reduce productivity.

It is, of course, possible to argue with both assumptions. One point which has to be made when considering job design concerns individual differences. One man's meat is another man's poison. As an impecunious postgraduate student, one of the authors was obliged to 'moonlight' for a few months in a brickworks. He got to know the other labourers very well, but found the work, stacking bricks, mind-bogglingly dull. On commenting to this effect to his colleagues he was amazed to be given a long lecture on how interesting the work was. To add insult to injury, the group of labourers then expressed amazement that anybody could find university work interesting! It is dangerous to assume that everybody wants 'enriched' jobs. What is enrichment to some might simply be hassle to others. There is an argument that people, to some extent, self select. They only apply for jobs which they want to do. However, in times of unemployment people are likely to take any job that is available and, in any case, people can be conditioned to expect boring jobs, but this does not mean they would not prefer something more challenging.

We will touch upon this subject again in Chapter 9. High unemployment may become a permanent feature of our society unless new industries, job-sharing, shorter hours and other industrial changes are made. New technologies based on microprocessors, robotics, genetic engineering and laser optics are emerging. Such developments may have far-reaching implications for the jobs that people do.

Leadership

Motivation is the very broad field of study concerned with understanding and influencing the behaviour of people at work. Leadership is a closely related area which focuses on the ways a supervisor should act in order that his subordinates should be motivated to work for him.

What are the qualities of a good leader? Some of the classical writers sought to answer this question. They were aware of the need to justify selection to membership of the managerial elite. They tended to answer in terms of personality traits: a good leader displays intelligence, confidence, initiative, ruthlessness, and so on. The reader might add to this list such characteristics as decision-making ability, verbal skills, determination, integrity, energy and perhaps compassion.

One problem with this approach is that there are so many potentially desirable qualities that the ideal leader might possess. Such qualities are very hard to measure and it is even harder to prove that people possessing them are more effective leaders than those who do not. If any particular quality or trait is mentioned it is always possible to find some acknowledged great leader who did not possess it.

Most human relations writers believe behaviour rather than personality is the key to successful leadership. This takes some of the emphasis away from selecting people with particular characteristics and focuses attention on the possibility of training people to behave in more effective ways. The early writers tended to be looking for the one best leadership style so that people could be trained to use it.

One classic study carried out in 1939 by Lewin, Lippitt and White, examined the effects of different leadership styles using groups of 10-year-old boys that were roughly matched in terms of economic background, intelligence and so on. The adult group leaders adopted three different styles in trying to get the boys to work. In the 'authoritarian' groups the leaders made decisions and told the boys what to do. They supervised closely, checked on their behaviour frequently, and demanded obedience. In the *laissez-faire* groups the leaders gave the boys little or no direction. They allowed them almost complete freedom to do what they wanted and simply answered questions when asked. In the '*democratic*' groups the leaders encouraged the boys to discuss group decisions and objectives and jointly assign tasks. The democratic leaders operated between the authoritarian and *laissez-faire* extremes, they did give direction to the group but within prescribed limits freedom was allowed. The leaders invited criticism of their ideas and welcomed suggestions.

The highest performing groups were the authoritarian and democratic groups, but in the former the boys' motivation was low and they only worked when the leader was present. The boys in the democratic groups kept working when unsupervised and showed more originality and interest. Morale and 'group feeling' was lowest in the *laissez-faire* group, while the members of the autocratic group were often hostile to particular 'scapegoat' individuals. The democratic leaders were most popular.

On the basis of this, and similar studies, the idea of 'democratic leadership' (an American misnomer) has often been seen as the answer to all industrial ills. More recent work, however, has suggested much greater scope for differences in style. The modern view is that the style which serves best will be contingent on the situation. There are a range of 'contingency' studies which place emphasis on different factors when choosing between styles (Fig. 3.7).

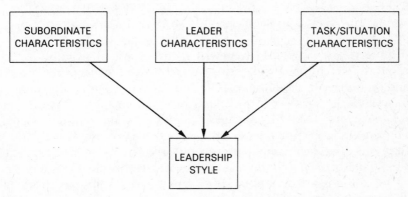

Fig. 3.7   The contingency approach to leadership.

It does not seem unreasonable to suggest that a different leadership style will work in a university department than on an assembly line or in a clerical office, but what clues are there as to which style is best?

Blake and Mouton's studies

Blake and Mouton draw attention to the fact that there is more variety in leader characteristics than the autocratic–democratic–*laissez-faire* continuum indicates. They have developed a 'management grid' and a related questionnaire in order to classify the leadership style a supervisor uses (Fig. 3.8).

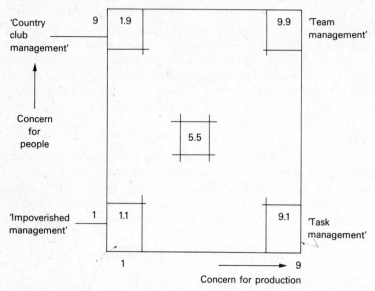

Fig. 3.8   The Blake and Mouton 'management grid'.

Supervisors are placed somewhere on the grid depending on the extent to which they display two characteristics, 'concern for people' and 'concern for production'. The '1.1' manager shows no commitment either to the task or to the subordinates; hopefully there are few 1.1 managers! The '9.1' manager is highly task and output-oriented. He believes in getting the job done and people are simply a means to that end. The behaviour pattern of a production-oriented manager should not be seen as undesirable, it is just that he only focuses on one aspect of the work situation. He assigns tasks, emphasizes deadlines and stresses the need to be ahead of the competition. The '1.9' manager is much more concerned with people, he sees his role primarily as one of creating a pleasant social environment. The people-oriented manager also concentrates too much on only one part of the work situation. He is friendly and approachable and finds plenty of time to listen to subordinates and help them with problems. He probably stands up for them against the rest of the organization.

The '5.5', or 'middle of the road', manager pushes for production but not too hard. He is prepared to accommodate people and make production sacrifices, but for Blake and Mouton the best style of leadership is '9.9'. This manager is highly concerned both with people and production, and sees no conflict between the two concerns. He has learned the skill of integrating task and employee requirements to get the best of both worlds, his people are hard-working and efficient, yet he has motivated them to see their own goals and high production as compatible.

Blake and Mouton, although they expand our concept of leader behaviour, were still trying to find the one best leadership style. Hersey and Blanchard build on their model to introduce a new contingent variable which may affect which is the best style—the subordinates (Fig. 3.9).

Fig. 3.9   Hersey and Blanchard – subordinate maturity and leadership.

Hersey and Blanchard's studies

The grid is simplified to four basic styles of leadership. Superimposed on the grid is the development sequence which employees who are skilfully motivated should follow. This introduces the idea of 'maturity' of subordinates which Hersey and Blanchard see as the major influence on leadership style. 'Immature' employees tend not to be committed to the task at hand, they are unwilling or unable to take responsibility and set their own goals. For employees such as these, Hersey and Blanchard see the 'Telling' style of leadership, the '9.1' quadrant as appropriate. As employee maturity increases in terms of motivation, commitment and competence, the supervisor may move to a 'Selling' or '9.9' style in which employees are still assigned tasks and supervised, but further benefit can also be gained from working at the human relationships. Hersey and Blanchard see it as an important part of the supervisor's task to try to increase employee maturity over time so that supervisory style may eventually change. 'Selling' they see as likely to remain the most commonly effective approach, but if maturity is greater then employees will not need so much task supervision, and they can be involved in goal-setting and decision-making using a 'participative' style. The most committed and capable of employees will need very little relationship with their supervisor either of a task or social nature; in this situation a 'delegative' style is appropriate.

Other researchers have emphasized the nature of the work being done as a key factor affecting leadership style. If the task is tightly structured and has to be done in a particular way, then there seems little point in 'participative' style. If the time-scale for decisions is very short then 'delegation' or 'telling' may be appropriate depending on employee 'maturity'. If the work is creative it may be necessary to 'give employees their heads' so that they can develop ideas without being inhibited by close supervision.

The contingency approach to leadership involves a supervisor in thinking through his own personality and capabilities and the characteristics of his subordinates, their task and the situation to determine in broad terms which general approach is best. How much involvement in decisions is he going to allow? How much will he set deadlines and targets? How hard will he try to befriend subordinates and build up work group morale? The study of leadership directs thought to these issues.

Leadership training for supervisors attempts to develop the same qualities as motivation training—diagnostic ability and flexibility of behaviour. It usually involves some exercise like the Blake and Mouton grid so that supervisors can see themselves as they are, and compare their own behaviour with other possibilities. A range of case studies, exercises and group discussions will encourage them to think through their work situation and their own style, and hopefully to see where they can make desirable changes. Some courses start with feedback of results from a survey of the actual subordinates of the supervisors, in which they have been asked to comment on particular behaviour patterns and attitudes of their boss. This helps to overcome the 'I'm already a good leader' attitude which is very common; indeed it can be a traumatic revelation!

Our brief review of three areas of human relations writing by no means does justice to a rich and rewarding view of organizations. If we do not understand people we will certainly never understand the world in which they work. It is important, however, that we do not become over sold on any one model of the business organization. Just as the classical principles and assumptions only provide a partial understanding, so do the human relations studies of motivation, job design, leadership and other areas such as communications, group dynamics and participation.

Recommended reading

Handy, C. (1976). *Understanding Organizations*. Penguin, Harmondsworth.
Hunt, J. (1979). *Managing people at work*. Pan Books, London.
O'Shaughnessy, J. (1976). *Patterns of business organization*. George Allen and Unwin, London.
Pollard, H. (1974). *Developments in management thought*. Heinemann, London.
Robbins, S. (1979). *Organizational behaviour: concepts and controversies*. Prentice-Hall, Englewood Cliffs, NJ.
Sofer, C. (1972). *Organizations in theory and practice*. Heinemann, London.

Questions

1. What implications do the differences between the classical approach and the human relations approach have for shop floor management?
2. Draw a simplified, hypothetical organization chart ('hierarchy') for a large single-site manufacturing enterprise. What does this chart represent? How useful is it likely to be as a guide to understanding the behaviour of individuals within the organization?
3. On taking up a supervisory position you discover that, although output levels are high, your subordinates are very bad timekeepers. You decide that the bad timekeeping cannot continue. How would you proceed to correct this situation?
4. How useful is it likely to be to a practising supervisor to be aware of Maslow's theory?
5. What do you see as the major insights which a supervisor may gain from a study of human relations?

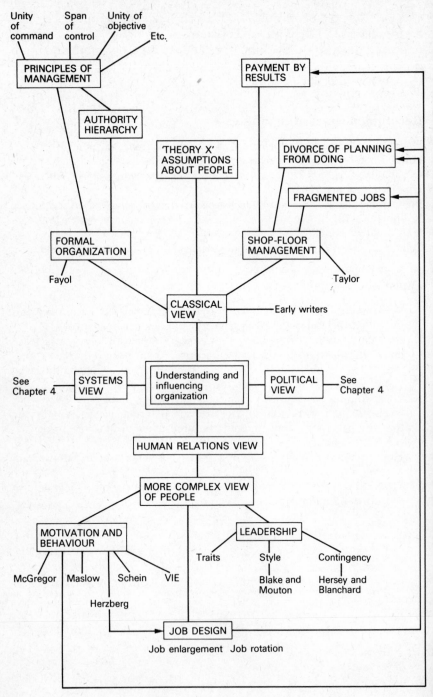

Summary for Chapter 3.

4 Understanding and influencing: from systems to politics

How convenient it would have been if the student of management just had to learn a set of classical prescriptions and principles. If only they accurately reflected reality. Introducing people with all their unpredictability and complexity is, however, a necessary step if we are to learn to manage effectively. Each different way of thinking about organizations helps us to explore some new important dimensions. But we have to beware of the idea that *this* is the *right* model. Each approach offers insights that may be valuable, but they all have their limitations too and it is important to keep these in mind.

Just as the behaviour of managers is not wholly described in terms of classical authority and responsibility, so is it not wholly described in terms of human relationships and management of people. Other matters have an important influence, matters like:

1. What products should we make?
2. What are our competitors doing?
3. How can we cut costs?
4. How reliable are our suppliers?

The two models discussed so far have taken such considerations for granted. The impression has been given that organizational activities are all about 'principles' or 'people' respectively. In fact, of course, much organizational activity can only be understood by using a model which incorporates the management functions such as production, marketing, personnel, purchasing and accounting. Such a view is provided by the idea of the organization as a 'system'.

The systems view

This way of thinking about organizations is so valuable that it was introduced in a basic form at the very beginning of Chapter 1 in order to provide a framework for a historical look at the emergence of the business organization. In this section we will expand the earlier description

The world in which we live can be viewed as consisting of an enormous number of interlinked 'systems'. These 'systems' may be very small as are the atoms of which we are composed, or they may be very large as is the solar system of which our planet forms a part. The systems may be tangible as is the motor car, or intangible, as are concepts like the legal system. The systems may be natural like plants and animals, or manmade like a gas fire.

So what makes all these things systems? Most things can be viewed as systems provided they fulfil some simple criteria. They must be composed of interdependent parts or subsystems. These subsystems must combine together in some way to form a unit. The unit or system must perform functions for some greater system of which it is a part.

The early origins of systems theory lie in biology. The human body, as much else in nature, is composed of parts which can be viewed as systems and subsystems, the respiratory system, the digestive system, the nervous system, the skeletal system and so on. These systems interact together to produce a living, breathing, thinking human being, who is much more than just the sum of the parts. Each subsystem of the body has its own subsystems which perform functions for it, so that it can survive and perform its functions for the body. It is possible to analyse and subdivide the subsystems down to the very parts of the atom.

The individual whose body has just been viewed in system terms can be viewed as a subsystem of many wider systems. He is a subsystem performing functions for his family, for the economy, for the rugby team, and so on. He may also be a subsystem performing useful functions for a business organization.

Some systems, like manmade machine systems, are known as 'closed systems'. This means that the inputs, such as petrol, oil, water and electricity are known, and the system can be arranged to use them in some hopefully predictable way to produce the desired outputs. Other systems, like the business organization, are 'open systems'. This means that the inputs and outputs cannot be easily predicted or controlled. There are, as Fig. 4.1 shows, many sources of inputs to the business organization. The classical and human relations models both operate as though the organization is a closed system whose inputs and outputs are simple and controllable, but in reality many of the things which cross the organizational boundary, new laws, people, changes in technology, competitors' price cuts, interest rates and so on, are neither easily predicted nor controlled, yet they are ignored at the manager's peril.

Already we have started to build a systems view of the business organization. It is an open system with a range of complex and changing features in its environment which have to be managed. It has interdependent subsystems such as accounts, marketing, production, personnel, and purchasing, which have to be integrated so that the organization can continue to function.

The systems view shows us how much there is to learn if we are to

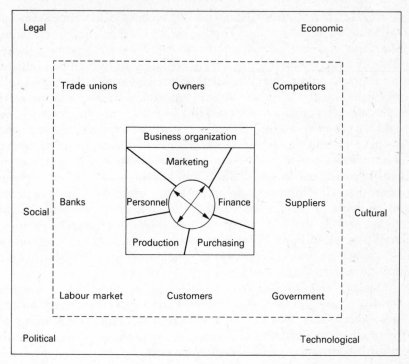

Fig. 4.1 The systems model.

understand the business organization. We have to understand each of the subsystems and how they operate, beyond this we have to understand how the subsystems interact with each other to produce an organization which is greater than the sum of the parts.

We also have to understand the different aspects of the organization's environment, the economy, the technology, the law, the society, competitors, customers, suppliers, trade unions; all these things will have to be coped with as part of the routine of management. The different subsystems will take responsibility for particular aspects of the organization's environment; for example, purchasing relates to suppliers, marketing to customers and competitors, personnel to the trade unions and much of the legal environment.

As we will see in later chapters, each of the management subsystems has its own subsystems. Marketing consists of integrated activities in the areas of sales, branding, packaging, market research, product development and so on. Personnel may be subdivided into industrial relations, training, recruitment, manpower planning and so on. The degree of subsystem creation will depend partly on the size of the organization and partly on the business it is in, but there will always be work groups and, finally, individuals as the basic system units.

The systems approach provides a good descriptive model and the important reminder that classical structure and human relations ideas are by no means all that we need to know about. The systems approach offers much more than this but it cannot be examined in depth here. Suffice to emphasize one key area of improvement from the new model—information. If organizations are to cope with changes in their environment, if they are to operate as integrated units rather than separate subsystems, then information flow will be of vital importance. The information network is the organization's nervous system without which none of the functional subsystems could operate. Much 'systems' work is about monitoring changes, improving information flow and improving decision-making and responses to change. A couple of examples should help to show how organizations can be viewed as adapting systems.

Suppose, for example, we are a cigarette manufacturer. Over the past few years a number of changes have been occurring in our environment and our planners can only see the trend of these developments continuing. Due to government pressure we have had to drop television advertising altogether, and severely curtail advertising in other media. The adverts have to carry a government warning and are limited in a number of ways to prevent us building a desirable image for the product. The product has been subject to a very high level of taxation and this, combined with considerable antismoking propaganda from many quarters has increased customer resistance.

This information crosses the organizational boundary primarily through the marketing function and higher functions such as 'corporate planning' where medium and long-term company plans are formulated. The survival of the system is threatened, how should it respond? The first level of response comes from the marketing function which sees its powers threatened by the elimination of TV advertising. It increases investment in other forms of communication, such as sports sponsorship (for example, the John Player Special Formula 1 car), and in creating clever poster, press and film adverts. Beyond this the company responds by expanding in overseas markets. The third world is being opened-up by the cigarette manufacturers using marketing methods which would no longer be allowed in the United Kingdom. And beyond this, many tobacco companies looking to the long-term future are making efforts to diversify away from tobacco into other products.

The organization, or system, perceives a threat to its survival and, much as a human being would when threatened, it responds in order to mitigate the negative forces. This can only happen if information is properly received and processed, and if the right decisions are made and implemented. The subsystems have to cooperate in order to produce the required new products, recruit the required new people, generate the required finance and so on.

The second example of an organizational system adapting to change is taken from the motor industry. Let us suppose we are a major family car manufacturer. In recent years there have been a number of changes in the environment, the price of petrol has increased greatly, the status symbol desirability of a large car has declined, and the onset of recession has made purchase price of prime importance, as people can no longer afford large, thirsty, expensive cars. How does the system respond? In this industry, as in many others, environmental trends must be spotted early because there is a long the 'lead time' before a new product can be developed. If we are to survive we will have to develop a low-cost family car with very good fuel consumption. Having identified this need the different subsystems must cooperate, perhaps in the form of cross-system project teams, or new cross-system departments in order to bring about the required changes. Research and development engineers, design engineers and marketing managers will work together on the new product. They may be developing new technology or adopting technology which has developed outside the organization.

At each stage the new product will be tested in marketing terms, there is no point making it if it will not sell—and at the right price. Accountants will be involved in costing both the product and the production system, and finding the necessary funds. Industrial and production engineers will estimate production times and develop work methods and plans for machine layout and scheduling the work through the production system. Purchasing managers will be confirming the availability of and negotiating contracts for 'bought-in' parts and raw materials. Personnel will be assessing the needs for people in terms of numbers and skills, they will be monitoring the labour market to check that the required manpower is available, and if not they will be setting up training systems to produce people who can fill the gaps. Personnel will also be working with the trade unions to set up a job grading system, payment systems and other procedures for the new employees. The unions may need to be involved at every stage of the changes to ensure their acceptance of the new situation. And so it goes on, departments working together, individuals, resources, information, skills and effort all crossing subsystem boundaries in order to ensure that the overall system, the organization, survives and prospers. At the end of the day out pops the new Mini Metro, or Ford Fiesta or whatever, the system's attempt to adapt to its new circumstances.

As with the earlier models of the organization it is as well to consider limitations. The major problem with the idea of 'system' is that it introduces too much *order* into our thinking. The assumption is that the system *should* survive and make profits and produce goods and services for society and that the subsystems, the management functions, *should* perform their part in the system operation and work together to achieve system objectives. In fact there are no system objectives which can be divorced from the people specifying them. If we ask one senior manager what the objectives of the firm should be and he says X, and we ask others and they reply a, b, c and d then what *are* the objectives of the firm? And so far we have just asked managers. Objectives the shareholders would like the firm to pursue may be high dividends and high share prices, the workers might be interested in high wages, interesting work and long holidays, the government might like to see high exports, high employment and high taxes. Whose objectives should be taken as the goals of the system?

With a closed system whose objectives are known, as is the case with most machines, it is just a technical matter, albeit often a very complex one, to design the system towards the given ends. But when the system is open so that inputs are hard to control or predict, and when there are a range of interest groups pursuing different and often conflicting objectives within it, then it is important not to oversimplify by creating an impression of a neat and tidy 'system'. Organizational life is much more interesting that that! People are servants of the system but they also create it. Different people pursuing different goals use the system and try to change it in different ways. The final model of organization which we are about to examine encourages us to think about these considerations.

The political view

A major limitation of all the approaches so far described is that they overlook the existence within organizations of individuals and groups pursuing different interests. This blinkers them in that they tend to ignore the conflicts which are often a feature of organizational activity.

Consider the following examples from the authors' experience:

A young man worked hard for several years, trying to gain promotion to higher management. He took evening classes to improve his qualifications, achieved all the targets set for him at work and was well liked by his colleagues. How dismayed he was when a newcomer with no experience and few qualifications was appointed to the post he sought. Why had *he* not thought of marrying into the owning family?

A new appointee was asked by his production manager to follow up a directive from the board and investigate the possibility of introducing a new computerized stock control system. It was made clear by the production manager that if the report was unfavourable then there was a good chance of a merit bonus at Christmas. The report was unfavourable.

A researcher trying to find out why companies introduced a new flexible working hours system was told, while in the office, about hoped-for savings in overtime pay and reductions in absenteeism and lateness. After getting to know the managers involved much better he learned, in the pub, how they were trying to make a name for themselves or increase the responsibilities of the personnel department. In one case the system was originally considered by the personnel manager so that he could agree to drop the idea in return for cooperation on another issue.

These cases would seem to indicate that there is a side to the business organization which has not yet been explored.

If we do not accept the idea, underlying the models so far examined, that organisations have preset objectives and tasks, and if we do accept that there are many interest groups which will try to get their own way within the organization then we have the beginnings of a political model. Figure 4.2 represents the major interest groups both inside and outside the organization which try to influence its behaviour, or rather the behaviour of the other interest groups. We could add to this list such groups as employers' associations, banks, consumer pressure groups, local councils and others, depending on the circumstances.

Fig. 4.2   The political model.

This is a 'pluralist' model, it does not see the organization as a unitary whole but as a loose and dynamic 'coming together' of sectional groups and individuals. Each party will be pursuing sectional objectives which will often conflict. There will be conflicts of interest between workers and owners, government and boards of directors, marketing managers and production managers, industrial relations managers and trade unions. Individuals may belong to a number of interest groups; as the group gets large the affiliation will tend to be looser because the coincidence of goals between the individual and the group will tend to diminish. Thus at one level the organization comprises a large number of competing and compromising interest groups and yet at another level it is itself an interest group. It should be noted also that many of the aspects of Fig. 4.2 can themselves be seen as political coalitions, trade unions, suppliers, competitors, and governments are all forms of organizations with different interest groups within them. It is often a mistake to think in terms of 'the union wants this', 'the government wants that'; these are rarely united bodies and it may be important to identify the different factions within them.

The Marketing Manager was judged on sales volume so he was prepared to offer product variations to customers and quick delivery in order to make the sale. He was always at odds with the production manager who was judged by cost of production. He wanted long runs of standardized products with no pressure on delivery.

There are three managers with potential for promotion to the executive position. They are always trying to outdo each other, sometimes this stimulates them to terrific achievements, other times there is a lot of duplication of effort and waste of energy. Which ever one is appointed the others will either leave or cause problems.

The trouble with the accountants and personnel managers is that they won't let us get on with the job. They are there to give us advice when we need it, not to make the decisions.

There are two key questions to be answered relating to the political model—Why do organizations not disintegrate with so many interest groups pulling in different directions? and What determines the things that happen in organizations and the directions they follow?

The answer to the first question centres on the stabilizing forces at work. One major factor is that each party has a stake in the survival of the system, if the organization goes out of business nobody wins. There may sometimes be some coincidence of objectives between the different groups or, more often, they can achieve their different goals by working and cooperating together. An important point here is that the objectives people pursue may be partly conditioned by what they see as achievable within the political framework. Equally important as a stabilizer is the 'socialization' process, people are brought up with a view of what the business should do, how people should act and what they should expect which leads them not to 'rock the boat' but to accept the goals which they are 'supposed' to accept.

Perhaps the most important stabilizing factor in all business organizations is the extreme influence of one particular interest group—the top management. These people can create rules, systems, policies and procedures to ensure the general conformity of most people within the organization to their idea of desirable behaviour. In this view the recruitment system can be seen as a method of pre-vetting, recruiting only those who support the top management's view of the world. The appraisal and promotion systems ensure that only those who accept this view will be promoted to powerful positions, the training system is about informing people what is expected of them, and the payment system rewards them for staying in line. A wide range of control systems are used by managements to integrate the different sectional groups; budgets, management by objectives, policy statements and manuals, job descriptions, rules and regulations, and direct orders all help the organization to cohere, albeit in the direction favoured by one particular interest group. The top management group, in political terms the 'dominant coalition', may well not be a united group although they may support the management control systems described; many of the most dramatic political battles take place as senior executives fight for promotion, or empires, or to try to change the direction which the organization is taking.

This concentration of so much control of organizational activity into the hands of the top management means that they tend to create the 'rules of the game' which govern most political behaviour. Conflict most often occurs within these 'rules', only rarely does it involve some party in trying to 'change the system'. Often managers pursuing some interest on behalf of themselves or their department will try to justify their behaviour as 'best for the organization', which usually means 'in line with the interests of the dominant coalition'.

Having looked at the political model in outline we must now examine its most fundamental variable, one neglected by the other views of organization. This key variable is POWER.

Power

Power is what makes things happen. Its strength and direction, the obstacles and counterforces in its way determine the direction of the organization and chart the course of events in all our lives.

Power is real life. It is an unpopular word because it implies restrictions on individual liberty, making people do things they would not otherwise do. But that is the nature of all societies and most definitely of all business organizations.

When discussing the classical approach we encountered one of their key variables, authority, and said it was the *right* to make people do things. For the classical writers authority and power are the same thing. We, however, distinguish between them, power is the *ability* to make people do things. People can have authority without power and power without authority; the management scrapheap is full of people who have failed to appreciate this fact.

Power is not purely a property of an individual. We tend to say he is a powerful man or she has great power but this is to overgeneralize. What we are really saying is under these circumstances, with regard to this type of decision, she has great power. A managing director may have great influence in the boardroom but none at all on the golf course or in the pub. Thus power, like leadership style and motivating force, is a *contingent* variable.

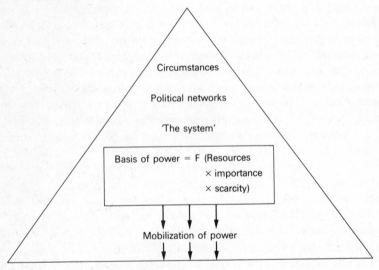

Fig. 4.3   Power: sources, uses and context.

The political view of the manager sees him not as a servant of the owners, or as a technocrat serving the system, but as a manipulator trying to compete and cooperate with others in order to pursue his own ends. The political manager needs to understand power. Figure 4.3 represents three important and related aspects of this vital factor. Power must have some source or basis, the stronger an individual or group's powerbase the stronger is their position. But a strong powerbase may be ineffective against a weaker one if it is not used or mobilized skilfully; this is the second aspect of power. The third aspect we have already drawn attention to, all power interactions take place within particular circumstances and an established political context such as the systems which management have set up to control activity towards their ends. This context may place major constraints on the alternatives open to the parties in a political struggle and may also influence their bases of power.

Let us draw on your own experience to illustrate these three precepts. Most of the time when you were a child you did not question the context of your life, the way your activities were influenced and controlled. You just accepted the way things were. Children dress this way, behave that way. Parents can do different things, talk differently, act differently.

Occasionally you would push against the system, not usually to try and change it but just to obtain some short-term improvement for yourself. You found it hard to get anywhere. Why? Was it because your father was bigger than you and could physically coerce your obedience? Was it because you respected your parents and believed in their legitimate right to give you instructions? Perhaps you were sometimes bribed by offers of more pocket money? Certainly when it came to bases of power, yours were limited.

Sometimes though you could successfully do things your parents disapproved of. How? Maybe by persuading them to your way of thinking with good arguments? More often by withholding information about your activities. Sometimes you could get one parent on your side and form a coalition against the other. As you grew older of course your parents began to recognize your independence and your right to disagree with them. The political situation between you had changed. In the meantime, however, you had to act cleverly to use your weak power base to get your own way.

Several writers have tried to categorize the potential bases of power which people can use. One classification is that devised by French and Raven. They have identified five main power bases.

Reward power This is the ability to provide things which people want, the 'carrot', People may do what their boss tells them because he offers them promotion or higher pay.

Coercive power This is the ability to punish or at least do things which people do not want, the 'stick'. A supervisor, for example, may be able to discipline people or prevent their promotion or give them unpleasant tasks.

Legitimate power This is the acceptance by those being influenced of the right of the powerholder. Subordinates may obey a supervisor because they believe he is the one who should tell them what to do irrespective of his ability to reward or coerce. Legitimate power is similar to the classical idea of authority, except that it does not come from the top down, but is given by the subordinates. In some situations subordinates may give legitimate power to someone other than their formal boss, a shop steward perhaps, or an informal leader.

Referent power This is based on people 'identifying' with the powerholder, responding to their feeling that this is the way he should act and that they would act in the same way if they were him. Referent power in the extreme would be hero worship, but in other forms may be comradeship or respect.

Expert power This is based on special abilities or knowledge. A supervisor may be obeyed because of respect for his technical knowhow.

These bases of power may or may not be real, in many situations it is enough that the person we are trying to influence believes that they are, or may be real. It should be interesting for the reader to consider someone they have power over, or who has power over them, what are the power bases at work?

In almost all situations there are power bases on both, or all, sides. Workers can reward a good supervisor by working well or a technician may have expertise which his boss does not. But we must go beyond these simple 'vertical' relationships. Much organizational life is about managers interacting with other managers. Departments may compete for a larger share of the budget. Major projects such as new products or new factories offer opportunities for political activity. Competition for promotion or trying to introduce new systems or machines, are further areas where different power bases may be brought to bear.

David Mechanic (1962) has a slightly different way of looking at sources of power which complements that of French and Raven. For him one has power if one has, or controls access to: *Information* which people want, *people* who can get things done or who have power and/or *instrumentalities*, things that people need or want. A point which follows from this is that the same power base may be useful in some cases but not in others, depending on two factors, 'importance' and 'scarcity'.

The 'importance' of a power source relates to the degree that it is needed by the parties we are trying to influence. This factor is sometimes called 'dependence'. The 'scarcity' or 'irreplaceability' of a power source relates to its availability elsewhere, if there are several other sources of a particular reward or piece of information, then its usefulness as a power base diminishes. Thus power is given by an equation, it is a function of the resources at our disposal, their importance and, in some cases, their availability elsewhere.

Crozier (1964), researching in a French tobacco plant, discovered that the maintenance engineers appeared to possess inordinate power, which they exploited to their advantage. He concluded that this was largely because the only major unpredictable uncertainty at the plant was machine breakdowns, the rest of production was routine. The engineers kept their irreplaceability level high by refusing to allow documented repair procedures and by training new engineers verbally.

Two protagonists whose objectives conflict may have equal power but one may have more success than the other because he mobilizes his power more effectively. Consider the combatants in a chess game, the outcome will be determined by the strategic ability of each player, furthermore if a more skilful player takes over a game in a weak position he may still be able to win. So it is in organizations: clever mobilization of apparently weak power sources may be more effective than poor mobilization from strength.

The most obvious method of converting a power base into action is the use of *force*. In organizations this will rarely take the form of physical bullying, it is more likely to be economic threat 'do it or I'll fire you', 'pay us more or we'll strike', or, 'promote me or I'll resign'. Force is a crude method of getting your own way. It may be initially effective, but it tends to have long-term negative effects due to built-up resentment. The defeated party may just be waiting for a chance to get even.

Perhaps a more desirable means of influencing people is *persuasion*. In its pure form this would simply involve convincing people that a particular course of action is best, relying on expertise and logic. Often, however, a manager who tries this method is backing it up, albeit not openly, with potential coercion or perceived legitimate or referent power.

A common strategy involves *exchange* of services or favours for the desired behaviour. In the case of union/management negotiations there may be a formal exchange of increased productivity for increased pay. Between managers exchange may take the form of favours, such as the personnel manager agreeing to support a production request to the capital expenditure committee if he is supported on the job grading committee. On a less obvious level a subordinate may be loyal to his boss in order to get a pay increase or a promotion.

Perhaps the most subtle method of mobilizing power is by creating the *ecology* to make it difficult for people not to do what you want. This is the method used by the dominant coalition, but it is often also possible for lower managers to create systems, rules and procedures within their own departments. Manipulating the situation may also take such forms as setting up a large committee in order to delay a decision, or loading it with people who support your view.

The authors have witnessed a situation in which management set up the ecology rather unwisely and had to pay the price. They organized an entire foundry around the output of one machine operated by a small, cohesive group of semiskilled workers. These workers soon discovered how indispensable they were and managed to acquire skilled rates for their semiskilled work and very favourable bonuses.

Successful strategy usually involves forming coalitions with like-minded people, or with people who are prepared to support you on this issue because it suits them or so that you will support them later. The organization is a complex network of coalitions, some formal like departments or trade unions, but many of which are short-term and informal. The idea of forming a coalition may remain unspoken even while it is actually happening.

To conclude this brief insight into the political nature of organizations let us suppose that we want to change the organization in some significant way and build up a picture of how we might do it.

As a production manager we have decided that we need a new microprocessor-controlled robot. This we hope will make our department more productive and help us to get promotion. The first step is to assess the decision situation. Who makes the final decision? Is it one person or a committee? How will the decision be made? Democratically? Upon what criteria will the decision be made? Is our decision in competition with others for scarce resources?

Having answered questions such as these, the next step is to carry out a 'force field analysis'. Of those involved in the decision situation, who is for us, who is against us and who is likely to be neutral or indifferent? Our political behaviour may involve preparing a report to justify the purchase in terms which will appeal to the dominant coalition and the decision-making body. This will provide information as a power base. We need to influence those who are against us, can they be persuaded to change their views? Are they likely to fight fiercely? What strategies are available to them and can they be countered?

Those who are involved in the decision process but not committed may be candidates for exchange strategies, If you help us on this we will help you on that. Those who are likely to be on our side are candidates for a coalition. A combination of our talents and power bases with theirs may increase our strength out of all proportion.

Conclusion

If this all seems a long way from the neat classical model of workers accepting authority and carrying out their responsibilities, then it just goes to show how far our view of organizations has advanced during this and the previous chapter. The political approach is the last we shall examine, but we must not see it as a replacement for the other approaches. In many situations a political insight is invaluable but the insights of the classical, human relations and systems models will also throw useful light on any organizational experience.

The classical school introduced important concepts like authority, responsibility and delegation and emphasized the importance of managements' formal structure of the organization. The human relations school provided a new language for managers. Motivation, participation, leadership and group dynamics offer invaluable assistance to the manager trying to get things done with and through people.

The systems approach draws attention to the wide range of problems faced in managing the business organization. It demonstrates how the different parts of the organization interact and cannot be understood in isolation any more than can the organization be understood except with a knowledge of its external environment. The systems approach shows how the study of management information sciences and the use of computers to provide data and assist communications flow and decision-making will be essential in the increasingly dynamic and difficult environments most businesses face.

The political approach reminds us once again that organizations are about people. It encourages us to think in terms of our own objectives and our own view of what the organization's objectives should be. Management is often about making changes and competing in what can be a tough world. The study of politics and power may take too much attention away from the possibilities for cooperation and harmony, but it is as well for the manager of the future to be aware that all is not going to be sweetness and light.

References

Crozier, M. (1964). *The bureaucratic phenomenon.* Tavistock, London.
Mechanic, D. (1962). Sources of power of lower participants in complex organizations. *Admin. Sci. Quart.* **7**, Dec.

Recommended reading

Emery, E. (Ed.) (1969). *Systems thinking*. Penguin, Harmondsworth.
Handy, C. (1976). *Understanding organisations*. Penguin, Harmondsworth.
Hunt, J. (1979). *Managing people at work*. Pan Books, London.
Kast, F. and Rosenzweig, J. (1974). *Organization and management: a systems approach*. McGraw-Hill, New York.
O'Shaughnessy, J. (1976). *Patterns of business organization*. George Allen and Unwin, London.
Pfeffer, J. (1981). *Power in organizations*. Pitman, London.

Questions

1   How can viewing the organization as a system help us to understand it?
2. As managing director of a medium-sized engineering company you have become aware that your major product is gradually losing its place in the market. What insights would the systems view provide which would help you manage this problem?
3. The classical approach to understanding organizations sees authority as the major part of power. How might such a view cause problems for the practising supervisor?
4. How would you, as a recent appointee, attempt to maximize your power and accelerate your career progress?
5. When you are a manager how will you cope with the conflict between 'system' and 'politics'?

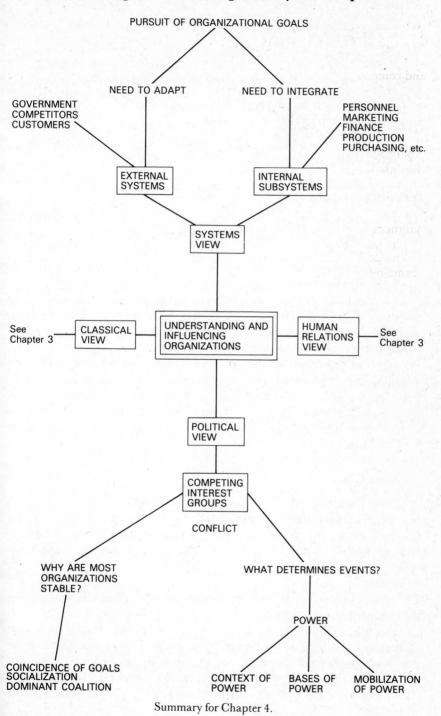

Summary for Chapter 4.

5 Purchasing

In 1980 the British Institute of Management issued a report on the purchasing function (Farrington and Woodmansey 1980). In the Introduction appears the coy remark:

It is a fact that in manufacturing industry the cost of purchased materials and components can account for 50–60% of sales revenue.

Strikes, costs, and the common cold

There was a time when liberal-minded lecturers liked to argue that the abolition of the common cold would do more for output, productivity, and profits than would the abolition of the right to strike. It is probably true, but this claim is not very helpful since it balances two impossibles against each other.

The purchasing operation is different. It is direct and tangible. It is about deals and negotiations for things companies need in the here and now, and it is very much susceptible to man's control, especially to the control of someone who knows what they want. So to say that a 10 per cent reduction in the cost of bought-out parts and materials would do more for profits than a 10 per cent reduction in the days lost through strike action is not only true but realistic. Reductions in purchasing costs can be achieved, and how to do it is a main theme in this chapter. But first it will be helpful to set the scene, operationally and organizationally.

What purchases?

Business companies all have to buy things to carry on their operations; these vary infinitely, but for our purposes they can be grouped into six basic categories: raw materials, components, subassemblies, routine consumables, energy, and capital equipment.

Raw materials

Everyone knows what raw materials are, yet there is no agreed definition. If one calls to mind the commonly accepted examples, such as iron and copper, cotton and cocoa, rubber and clay, it turns out that they have little in common: some come from temperate Europe and some only from the third world; some are mined and some are grown; and they may be animal, vegetable or mineral. All they really have in common is the fact that they are seminatural and unfinished:

they are valued for what can be done with them, for what in manufactured or processed form they may become. Many companies, in fact, are not concerned with anything as primary and unformed as raw materials; their purchases fall in the second category.

Components or bought-out parts

Just about every manufacturing company in existence buys in some parts or components, and the variety is infinite. Some will be in ones and twos, some in large batches; some will be simple, some amazingly complex; some will be bog-standard, others elaborately modified. To give some idea of the scale of the purchasing operation in a small commercial vehicle plant visited by one of the authors, the head of production control spoke of needing 14 000 bought-out parts, and some 300 subassemblies—which leads to the next category.

Subassemblies

These are a special case of bought-out parts, separated from mere components by their greater complexity and finishedness. The automobile industry offers good examples; where car-making or car-assembling plants buy in, or bring in, a ready made gearbox, transmission system, or engine, they are dealing in subassemblies rather than components.

Routine consumables

The next category is what might be termed routine consumables. All companies need such items as light bulbs and carbon paper, and something to clean the windows with. This unexciting group of products is distinguished from components in that they are not central to the manufacture of particular products, but just to the maintenance of the works and offices.

Energy

The need for energy to drive machines or power manufacturing processes is also universal. And this energy, whether oil, gas, electricity, or coal, has to be bought too. Its absolute and relative cost has risen in the last decade and so have the constraints and options. Buying energy has become more important, and more difficult, than it used to be.

Capital equipment

Finally, companies are involved in capital equipment purchases, in buying machines, plant, transport, handling gear, manufacturing sites and systems. These purchases are different in kind from the others; by definition they are intermittent or occasional, massively expensive, and require extensive expenditure justification, especially in Britain where the usual philosophy is 'don't buy a new one if you can make the old one work somehow'.

These six represent the range of things which companies do or may purchase. We have mentioned them all for the sake of completeness, but what this chapter is concentrating on is the recurrent, production-linked purchases in the first three categories—materials, bought-out parts, and subassemblies.

Is purchasing important?

For most companies most of the time it certainly is. It accounts for a large share of the typical company's resources, and it is often an area where economies can be made. The purchasing operation is an indispensable preliminary to manufacturing, the efficiency with which it is managed is an important determinant of the company's ability to keep to its product schedule and send out finished goods on time, and purchasing decisions may also affect product quality.

There are, however, two cases where the purchasing operation is much less critical, and both cases concern (some) big companies. The first is where a given company has achieved a high level of vertical integration (see Chapter 2). Vertical integration is the phrase used to describe the process whereby a company extends its operations 'backwards' to control the supply of raw materials and components, either by starting to manufacture them itself or by acquiring firms which already do, or 'forwards' by acquiring transport, distribution networks, retail outlets, or even by buying an advertising agency to praise its own products. Where backward vertical integration has been achieved the company concerned is, by definition, its own supplier (and only has itself to blame if it runs out of something).

The second exception also involves some large companies. Where a company manufactures a lot of different things, and does so in different plants, works and manufacturing divisions, there is often a lot of internal trading, with one part of the company supplying another which in turn sells (some of) its product to yet another part. To give an example, some of the ICI works buy all their raw materials from another ICI division, and sell their entire output to a different ICI division which needs them as an ingredient to its own manufacture. In such cases the company's control over its source of supplies is much more secure, because it is 'all in the family', and the cost is a matter of company policy on transfer pricing, not as is usual in purchasing, a free marketplace negotiation.

Where does purchasing fit in to the company?

One of the themes of this book has been that although it is convenient to speak of 'industry' and 'management' as though they are everywhere and always the same, there are in fact many differences. The way the purchasing function is fitted into the company organization is a case in point. The most straightforward setup is where the purchasing department reports direct to the managing director (Fig. 5.1).

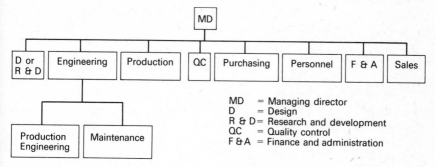

Fig. 5.1   The independent purchasing function.

The British Institute of Management Report we cited at the beginning says that for most of the 200 or so companies in its survey the purchasing department is independent, in the sense of reporting direct to the head of the firm or works, as in Fig. 5.1 above. The bigger the company in terms of number of employees, and the larger its sales turnover, the more likely it is to have an independent purchasing department. It is clear that independent departments have become the fashion in the last ten years, and heads of independent

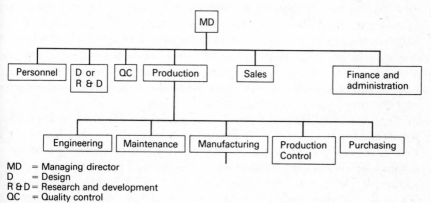

Fig. 5.2   The production-integrated purchasing function.

departments have on average higher salaries than purchasing managers reporting to the head of some other department, even where the firms are the same size.

When purchasing is not independent it may be integrated with production (Fig. 5.2). We will consider later the pros and cons of having purchasing under the control of a senior production manager: it is one of those situations where the advantages are more obvious than the things that may be lost.

A variation on this theme of purchasing being integrated with production is where purchasing and production control are linked in a materials control unit within production (Fig. 5.3).

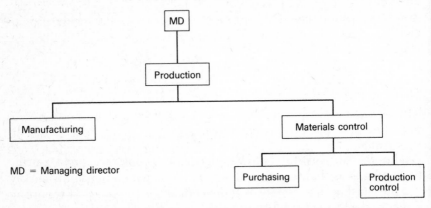

Fig. 5.3   The materials-control integrated purchasing facility

Production control devises and administers a production schedule, deciding what manufacturing jobs will be done in what order and numbers to which deadlines. This enterprise invariably depends to some extent on purchasing getting all the requisite components on time, but this 'to some extent' varies. Where a company makes a limited range of products, and makes them in large batches and long production runs, production control should be relatively straightforward. If, however, these products depend disproportionately on a large number of bought-out parts then the control of production depends much more on lining up all the parts and materials on time. In these circumstances the type of organization depicted in Fig. 5.3 above may be best.

It also occasionally happens that purchasing is a subdepartment within sales. There is a certain logic to this since purchasing is 'sales in reverse'; buyers need to deal with suppliers' salesmen, wheel and deal, and talk discounts and deadlines, for which tasks actually being a salesman is not a bad qualification. In practice, however, companies where purchasing is handled by sales are probably ones where the purchasing operation is not thought to be either complicated or critical for manufacturing.

The same is true of yet another organizational arrangement where purchasing comes under finance, or finance and administration. Again there is a plausible rationalization for this setup in that there may be cases where the purchasing operation is largely contractual and needs even-handed administration rather than an aptitude for doing deals.

Finally, in small owner-managed firms the owner himself is quite likely to act as his own buyer, and indeed some small firms depend on keen buying more than anything else to show a profit. There are also some corresponding difficulties which small firms in particular face in trying to buy the supplies they need; these are discussed later in the chapter.

For whom does purchasing purchase?

This is not a silly question because the obvious (and right) answer is not the only one. This obvious answer is that the purchasing department buys for and on behalf of production those things that production needs for the manufacturing programme to go ahead. This is quite true, but there is both a major and a minor qualification.

The minor qualification is that purchasing quite often buys materials for R&D, design and engineering departments as well as for production. These other departments may well want materials and components to play with—for experiments, prototype construction, mockups, and testing—and the purchasing department will probably get them what they want.

The more important qualification is that quite often it is design or engineering departments which place the orders for parts with purchasing on behalf of production. This may sound like nonsense, but there are many cases where it is a sensible arrangement. If design have after all actually designed a product, or if engineering have translated the design into a set of manufacturing methods, then they should know better than anyone else what components and materials are required. So they will place the orders with the purchasing department, giving the technical specifications and sometimes stipulating, or recommending, particular suppliers.

So although purchasing departments exist primarily to buy things for production, they may do this either on the orders of a production or production control manager, or at the direction of someone in design, engineering, or methods.

The system varies from company to company depending on policy, tradition and accident; and on how complex the products are, and whether they are new, modified, or customized, factors which favour the control of designers and engineers. The origin of the orders lodged with the purchasing department also affects its power and discretion. Production managers tend to have a 'where's my bits' mentality; most of all they 'want it now'. If the parts are there on time, and are usable, the average production manager will not ask too many questions; how, where, and at what price they were obtained is secondary. But designers and engineers tend to be perfectionists: they know exactly what they want, are more likely to insist on high quality, and give very narrow specifications that do not allow buyers to shop around. And designers often have strong convictions about who are the right suppliers, emphasizing quality and precision, rather than price and punctuality. All this will tend to restrict the purchasing manager's room for manoeuvre.

What do companies demand from their suppliers?

Companies vary in what they attach most importance to in choosing suppliers and negotiating with them, but 'the mix' is made up of six elements:

(1) availability;
(2) reliability;
(3) punctuality;
(4) quality;
(5) price;
(6) flexibility.

Availability

Availability is the most basic consideration. A company must have what it must have or it cannot make anything. The simplest way of ensuring a supply of any given item is to have several suppliers of it, on the grounds that if one lets you down the others will keep you going. This may also be a way of avoiding supply failures caused by strikes. West Germany is a good example where companies will often have suppliers in different parts of the country knowing that wage negotiations occur at different times in different regions so that even if the negotiations lead to strikes, the strikes will not be simultaneous, and there ought to be some suppliers in business when the goods are needed.

Suppliers, of course, have their pride. They like being sole suppliers to their customers, it gives them security and the whiphand, and they do not like being used as stopgaps and second-strings. One way round this for the buyer is to do 90:10 deals, getting 90 per cent of the amount needed from a tried and trusted supplier, and placing an order for the remaining 10 per cent with a subsidiary supplier. The latter can be talked into it with the argument that in the middle term the buyer intends to increase the amount purchased from the secondary supplier, and if for any reason the main supplier defaults the minor supplier will get all the business. From the buyer's point of view the guiding principle is 'the more the merrier'.

There are some cases where it is genuinely difficult to find alternative suppliers—where the supplier has a monopoly, or where the component is highly specialized. But buying companies are sometimes too ready to admit defeat on this. When a purchasing manager says 'there really is no one else we can buy it from' this should be taken to mean 'I have not found anyone else yet'.

Finding new suppliers is an important part of the purchasing function, or should be. And there are several ways of going about it. The formal way is to cultivate market intelligence, consult trade manuals and directories, like *Kompass* which lists all firms with their products by region in one volume and all suppliers by product in the second volume. The informal way is 'keeping your ear to the ground' at trade conferences and business lunches, in hotel bars and airport lounges, keeping tabs on who makes what for whom.

Sometimes, figuring out alternative suppliers can be helped by a question and answer game. Ask yourself where your company's rivals get their supplies from, and if you do not know, find out. Maybe you cannot call them up and ask, but Uncle Albert in Sunderland could work out an innocent pretext and do it for you.

Let us go further, and take a contrived but expanding example. Suppose your company needs to buy Volkswagen door handles. The obvious place to go is to Volkswagen's own official and accredited supplier in West Germany, whoever that may be. This is guaranteed to give you quality, reliability, and the right specifications. But hold on, perhaps there is a cheaper way that does not lose anything. There are probably pirate suppliers in Germany, who supply the second-hand and DIY trades: these are bound to be cheaper, and may be just as good—perhaps Volkswagen itself uses them in a crisis! Or think again: Germany is a high wage economy, its GNP per capita is nearly double that of Britain, but Volkswagens are made (or assembled) outside Europe too. They are made in Mexico, for instance, and the chances are there will be a network of local Mexican suppliers of some components that may be cheaper still. Or again if you can find a country where Volkswagens are made and driven in considerable numbers, say Brazil, then once more there will probably be local pirate suppliers for some components; a pirate supplier in a non-European low wage economy will take a lot of beating for cheapness.

Another approach to the problem of availability is the method known as consignment stocking. This is the system where the supplier provides a large quantity of a commodity, on the premises of the buyer, who pays for small quantities as and when they are used. This gives the buyer instant availability and low stock costs, while the supplier gets free warehousing on the buyer's premises, and a nice even production throughput. In practice, consignment stocking is only common for petrol, oil, bulk-containerized fluids, gases, and some chemicals in fluid or powder form. But in principle the method can be extended to other commodities. If an engineering firm uses five million screws a year why should it not ask GKN for a consignment stocking deal? After all, both parties benefit, and the most durable relationship is one based on mutual exploitation.

Reliability

A good supplier is a reliable one: a supplier who never lets you down, and never says no, deserves this accolade. Suppliers who always deliver the goods, even when there is some scarcity because of strikes, closures, or a run of the market, are like gold dust. And it is worthwhile for a company to keep a list of them, a proper systematic filed list.

Another aspect of this reliability is sending the right goods. This observation is not facetious. The Red Star parcel service is kept in business by exasperated production managers sending back the wrong goods and pressurized suppliers (hopefully) sending out the right goods second time around. This aspect of supplier reliability is also important enough for the buyer to keep records.

There is a similar point which again may sound facetious, though it is seriously meant. It is that suppliers often send the right things in the wrong numbers. If they send too little it may impede the production programme; if they send too much it may cause the buying company ordering, accounting and storing problems (as well as costing them money they do not need to spend). Sending the wrong number is so common it cannot be explained by supplier forgetfulness; there is a deeper plot. The tendency is for suppliers to send more than was ordered, and to invoice the buyer for the higher number sent, rather like the grocer who always cuts off too much cheese. This tactic offers considerable advantage to the supplier who has the nerve to do it. If a supplier systematically sends say 5 per cent more on all orders he has the chance to increase annual turnover by that proportion without incurring any additional sales costs, spending on advertising, or on product development. This is a good deal.

A further refinement is for the supplier to confuse the buying company by mismatching dispatches and invoices. Imagine a company which places an order for 18 of a particular component. The practised oversupplier will send first 13, then an invoice for 11, then send another eight, and follow it up with an invoice for ten. With a bit of luck the purchaser will feel so pleased at making the invoices and deliveries match (eventually) that he will pay for 21 without demur.

It should be said that oversupplying is much less common since the onset of the recession in 1980, because everyone is striving to cut costs and this has led to greater vigilance. There are also some cases where oversupplying and undersupplying by small amounts are quite legitimate. A lot of supply contracts, typically for large numbers of small and cheap items, have a plus or minus 5 per cent clause, the idea being that with repeated consignments it will all work out right in the long run. Again there are occasions when the buyer will be quite happy to get more than he ordered, if, say, the item concerned is easily breakable in the course of further manufacture. The situation where the financial controller (see Chapter 2) limits the size of orders placed, out of a general concern for economy or cash flow management, and buyers then collude with suppliers to send more than the order demands, and invoice it in small helpings, is also by no means rare.

Finally in this litany of supplier malperformance it may be added that a reliable supplier is one who sends a complete order, not just in the sense of the right number, but in the sense of making sure that any necessary accessories are there. Imagine the annoyance and inconvenience caused to a company buying 1000 of a component, each of which should come with four fixing screws, if for each of the 1000 one of the screws is missing.

So far we have discussed reliability in terms of readiness to meet orders, sending the right thing, in the right number, in a complete form. But reliability may also be understood financially. A reliable supplier is one who is sound financially. One who will not go out of business, or let you down because he cannot pay his own suppliers, and if he can offer good credit terms to his customers better still. When it comes to the critical issue of payment for goods supplied, large companies are usually most at fault, and small suppliers most vulnerable. Such abuses have often come to light in recent months when small companies have been declared bankrupt, a receiver has taken over, and then discovered the little firm was owed thousands of pounds by some household name company. There is a moral in this; if you want your supplier to be sound financially, pay your *own* bills on time, especially if your company is bigger than his.

Another factor which tends to make suppliers reliable in the earlier senses is the development of institutional links between a company and a supplier. The basic pattern is where the supplier does something original and distinctive for the buying company, such as doing research for it, designing something specially for it which no one else will buy (and no one else can make), or solving a manufacturing methods problem for it; such services take the supplier out of the ordinary category of firms with which a simple trading relationship exists. It is another example of mutual exploitation which will tend to render the buyer grateful and the supplier dependable.

Punctuality

The reputation which British industry has for delivery punctuality is frankly awful. There is not very much hard evidence, but what there is, regrettably, confirms the popularly held opinion. The question of how to get goods out to the customer on time is obviously important, and the causes of the frequent failure to do so are complicated: these will be discussed in more detail in Chapter 6 on production, but we may make here the simple point that the late arrival of bought-out parts is a frequent problem for production managers and a common cause of their failure to meet production deadlines. So the good supplier is a punctual one, and many suppliers are not punctual. Again the issue of the punctual delivery of goods by suppliers is so critical for the buyer's own production schedule that it is worth keeping records of the performance of suppliers in this respect.

There are also some things the purchasing manager can do to facilitate supplier punctuality. If the first rule is to keep records and favour the punctual supplier, the second rule is do not order late. This is a counsel of perfection; often the purchasing manager cannot order at all until someone in another department has given him the specifications and the go-ahead. And people in these other departments have their own problems; they run into unexpected difficulties sometimes, get orders from higher management to change direction, and face capricious demands from customers. So there will be times when a buyer just has to place an order late. But recognizing that should not lead to a sloppy ordering policy. Most of the time the things needed for the manufacturing programme can be ordered on time, and it is the purchasing manager's responsibility to see that they are.

It is possible to give a more precise meaning to the phrase 'place orders late'. Suppliers themselves typically quote lead times (the time it takes to make particular components) and undercutting these lead times is to be avoided at all costs. So if a supplier says it takes 8 weeks to make it, do not place an order 6 weeks before your company needs it.

A third rule would be not to ask for the impossible. If a company wants something new, or something significantly modified, or singularly difficult, then the supplier should be allowed time enough. The supplier's representative may say 'Sure, we can do it in 4 weeks' just to keep you happy in the here and now, but if the 'it' is something the supplier has not made before, maybe something that requires a bit of design work or some experimentation as to methods, then it will probably take longer and the buyer should anticipate this.

In fact an ability to anticipate, to foresee snags and to allow for foulups, is important for the whole purchasing–production operation. There are so many things that can go wrong that most of the time some of them actually will. This is not necessarily disastrous if buyers in the first place and production managers in the second have allowed for it. We can all make adaptations; it just needs a little time and imagination.

This anticipation is good for both sides. The best supplier is one who delivers on time. The second best supplier is one who tells you in good time if he cannot deliver. And the worst supplier is one who tells you the day before a consignment is due that everything is on time, and then calls you three days later to announce a 4-week delay.

Quality

The importance of quality is obvious. If bought-out parts prove to be of unsatisfactory quality when checked by the manufacturer who is going to use them then they have to be returned or rectified, delay is unavoidable, and the production schedule may suffer. It damages the credibility of the supplier, and makes it less likely that he will get subsequent orders. So it is worth the dispatching firm getting things right, and the receiving firm making sure they are.

From the standpoint of the purchasing company there are various ways of ensuring the quality of bought-out parts. One way is to check the supplier's quality control procedures; if these turn out to be satisfactory then inspection by the receiving company is in the nature of a double check. This option is not always open to the buying company; suppliers naturally do not relish visits from their customers' engineers where the latter poke around, find out all the supplier's defects, and write wordy reports about it for their technical director. But where the buying company is appreciably bigger than the supplier, or accounts for a substantial portion of the supplier's business, and this is a common buyer–supplier relationship, then it is usually possible for the buyer to insist on access to the supplier's works and on the opportunity to check out his inspection procedures.

All companies carry out their own inspection on incoming parts and materials. The goods inwards section in companies not only does the paperwork on incoming supplies, it also inspects them, and this inspection (theoretically) decides whether the goods are released to the production department, or are sent back if they are judged defective. What happens in goods inwards is, for most companies, the principal guarantee of the quality of the parts they have bought.

There are several things to add to this simple goods inwards formula. The first point is theoretical. Depending on what the goods are, and on how many there are in a consignment, you do not necessarily (have to) inspect them all. There are statistical sampling methods which yield various levels of probability that the ones not inspected are as good (or bad) as the ones which are inspected, and there is a specialist literature on this statistical quality control.

The second point is that it is necessary to unpack a little the idea of quality. Quality, after all, is just a nebulous word suggesting that something is good, or good for the purposes intended; that the components are suitable for the manufacture of given products with which the company is concerned. This notion of quality is translated into the practical via 'specifications', dimensional and technical requirements that the component has to meet. And when the parts are inspected in goods inwards they are checked against the specification. This operation may lead to dispute, especially between inspectors in goods inwards on the one hand and production bosses who need the parts on the shop floor on the other. Mostly that is because the specifications are often in terms of tolerances not absolutes; to give a crude example, the specifications may say an item has to be between 100cm and 102cm, rather than 100cm dead on. When an inspected item is on the boundary of one of these tolerance specifications, or is just a little bit 'out of spec', goods inwards will want to reject it, and production will claim it is, 'good enough' and in any case 'we want it now'.

A related problem is that it will just so happen that the specifications include some inessential stipulation. Again to give a crude example, the specifications may say the component has to be triangular, with six 18mm holes, and be painted green. Then one will turn up in goods inwards that is the right shape, with the right number of holes, but is painted grey. Here again goods inwards will tend to stick to the letter of the law and want to reject it, while a production manager will argue that the colour does not matter. In short, specifications are not, in practice, as cut and dried as they might sound, and are often the subject of argument and compromise.

The third point is that if there is one area of the typical company which is understaffed it is goods inwards. The most common dispute between goods inwards inspection and production is not about the accept or reject decisions, but about the speed of these decisions, with production clamouring to have bought-out parts inspected and released fast. So a concomitant to having suppliers who deliver goods of acceptable ('in spec') quality, is having a goods inwards section staffed and on the ball to ensure a fast throughput of parts into production.

A final consideration in this connection concerns new suppliers. In the earlier discussion of availability we urged dual or multiple sources, having several suppliers for any given item, as the best way of maintaining availability. This implies that the enterprising company will be seeking potential new suppliers continually, and in fact commissioning some of them. This has implications for goods inwards inspection. When a company has dealt with a supplier for 15 years, and has checked out the supplier's quality control procedures, there may be a case for taking the decisions on trust. But with new and untried suppliers inspection in goods inwards should be rigorous. And that is particularly true where the new supplier has been signed up on the initiative of a purchasing manager rather than an engineer.

Price

The best way of keeping the price of bought-out parts within reasonable bounds is to have several suppliers in competition. Most often this happens naturally; and sometimes the item concerned is so specialized that very few companies can make it at all. Between these two extremes there is sometimes a grey area, where the purchasing company can use its initiative to bring other suppliers into the market, especially if it is a huge company with big money to spend. The usual tactic is to approach companies who make something similar to the item sought, or who already make other things for the buyer, and try to persuade them to make what is needed. Potential new suppliers can be helped with technical advice, big company knowhow, and subsidized development costs. A firm order for the given item, over a medium-term period, can induce a potential supplier to break new ground and make something new for an attractive customer.

Negotiation plays a central part in getting a good price, and this theme will be taken up later in the chapter. A basic point is that one seldom loses by bluff and boldness. Do not be afraid to say 'that is too

dear' and start to walk away; with luck you will be called back before
you reach the car park and offered something better (and if not you
can always go back next week and accept). Big orders can be put out
to tender, and then the results can be used as a springboard for
another round of tendering. One of the present authors had to place a
big order for a government department, and put it out to tender to six
companies. When the results came in the best offer (cheapest) was
taken as standard and the other five were invited to re-tender in the
light of it.

Price negotiations are often bedevilled with discount calculations.
Discounts are a kind of commercial jungle through which the buyer
has to hack his way. First, they are genuinely complicated. Different
companies will work different systems on different percentages.
Second, there is usually a sliding-scale system whereby the more one
buys the lower the unit price becomes. And third, there is often an
element of pure conmanship in discount quoting in the sense that the
'basic price' that the supplier quotes and from which the discount is
deducted does not really exist. All customers, that is, will get *some*
discount, the amount varying with the size of the order and the extent
to which the salesman regards the buyer as open to being conned by
enormous discounts off inflated starting prices. So where discounts are
being bandied around the starting price is best regarded as fiction and
the discounted end-price as fact. There is no golden rule for handling
all this; discounts are there to be evaluated, and have to be evaluated
for rival suppliers to be compared.

Lastly it is worth remembering that 'suppliers are human too'.
They share with the rest of humanity a concern over cash flow, and a
buyer with a reputation for prompt payment has a strong bargaining
weapon.

Flexibility

One of the themes of this book is that industry is not 'a clean
well-lighted place' where everything happens according to a rational-
ly conceived and systematic masterplan. Companies have problems,
face crises, get things right by the skin of their teeth, go bankrupt with
a full order-book because a major customer has defaulted, change
their minds, rejig production schedules, and vary their supplier needs.
Suppliers who are so helpful, and so well-organized themselves, that
they can adapt to the changing, fluctuating, sometimes even stop–go
needs of the customers are at a premium. So a very good supplier is
one who will do favours and adapt without (too much) complaint; a
supplier who will, for instance, process late orders, or take on oddball
orders ('specials'), or handle immediate orders, or accept orders for

unusually small quantities, or cope with changes in the 'call-off' rate (the number taken per time-period where a supplier has a running contract with a customer). And the supplier who can afford to wait and be paid has achieved an all-time popularity since the onset of the recession.

Vendor analysis: formal and informal

Vendor analysis is the term given to a company's evaluation of other companies who sell to it. Since the term is rather grand it may create the impression that this is an administrative luxury for giant multinationals only. It is not. In practice, vendor analysis means keeping records on how good a service suppliers provide, including several of the things we have been highlighting in the last few pages. And it is comparatively easy to keep a log on whether suppliers deliver the right things in the right number at the right quality at the right time. It is comparatively easy, and it is worth the effort.

Vendor analysis also has an informal aspect. All the buyer objectives we have discussed in the present chapter are facilitated by contact with suppliers. The more buyers and purchasing managers visit their suppliers the more they will know about a given supplier's capacity, methods, trading position, commitments, financial stability, eagerness for extra work, and the quality of its management. It is also one of the facts of life that it is harder (for suppliers) to refuse favours to people they know personally. So every visit to a supplier should be another increment of goodwill which may get your production manager out of a fix one day. Personal contact between buyers and suppliers occasionally leads to corruption; it often involves what the morally severe might think of as venal (free lunches, gin and tonics forever, and tickets to Lords), but such risks are vastly outweighed by the potential gain in information, understanding and commitment.

When is purchasing difficult

A lot of the operating difficulties affecting a company's purchases have come up in discussion already, and in some cases possible remedies have been canvassed. It may be helpful, however, to group together the factors and or circumstances that make purchasing difficult, and hint at countermeasures if there are any.

Genuine scarcity of goods
Purchasing is difficult if there is a genuine scarcity of goods. The

common cause is industrial action; lorry transport was hard to come by in the winter of 1979, engineering components in the autumn of 1979, steel in the winter of 1980, and so on. Whether or not a company gets the supplies it needs in such circumstances is a matter of willpower and ingenuity. It very seldom happens that none of the commodity at all is available; it is usually a case of there being some but not enough to go round. So the first thing is to tell yourself that your company has a divine right to have what there is, and the second thing is to figure ways of getting it. One way is to think, imaginatively and constructively, about other sources of supply and then try to tap them before anyone else does. And the other way is to put pressure on your regular suppliers to give preference to your company if there is not enough for everyone. In pressurizing suppliers threats are not a good tactic; threats you cannot carry out weaken you, and mild threats alienate people without forcing them to do what you want. It is better to remind the supplier of all the favours your company has done him in the past; everything from having made payments in advance to having given his delivery drivers free meals in the works canteen is grist to the mill here. And from past favours one moves subtly to future favours; how much more highly your company will esteem the supplier if he does his best for you in the present crisis, how the managing director only last Tuesday remarked that we should up our order with Hodgkins and Co., and so on.

Goods purchased on commodity markets

A particular case of intermittent shortage is where goods are purchased on commodity markets—for coffee, cocoa, tin, rubber, and so on. Here natural disasters can drastically reduce world supply, and all customers get roughly the same amount of warning. There is not much an individual purchasing manager can do about this, and commodity market trading in any case is a specialist operation involving forward buying and option buying (buying or buying rights to commodities that have yet to be mined, produced or grown).

Genuine shortage of manufacturing expertise

Purchasing may be difficult where there is a genuine shortage of manufacturing expertize; when, that is, there are simply not many companies who know how to make what the buyer needs. A good example in Britain is castings. Getting castings of good quality is often a problem for small and medium-sized companies: the big foundries which are geared up for it do not want small orders, and the small foundries which will jump at the order do not always have the facilities and expertize. There are only two ways out. Find alternatives, foreign if necessary, or tempt other suppliers into the market in the way discussed above.

Conflict with other departments

Purchasing may be difficult where the purchasing department finds itself in conflict with other departments. We have already mentioned that there may be differences of opinion and priority as between purchasing on the one hand and design and engineering departments on the other. There is also plenty of scope for disagreements between purchasing and quality control (purchasing wants it uncomplicated, quality control wants it perfect), between purchasing and production (purchasing wants it cheap, production wants it now), and even between purchasing and sales (purchasing wants a good deal, sales want to soften up the market by favouring potential customers or their associates). In such conflicts the purchasing manager does not always have to give way to superior force; there are some counter-tactics, and these will be outlined in the last section of this chapter.

Company reputation

The purchasing operation will be complicated if the company has a reputation as a bad payer. There is not much the purchasing department can do about this, since it is a matter of overall company performance and economic climate. But it is the duty of the purchasing manager to advise higher management on priorities when it comes to outstanding debts to suppliers. The two basic priorities are to pay suppliers who will go bankrupt if you do not, and to pay suppliers who have threatened to cut off deliveries if existing debts are not settled.

Limited market intelligence

Purchasing is unnecessarily difficult if the buyer has limited market intelligence. This issue has been raised in the earlier discussion of availability. Too often buyers do not know enough about who else does, could, or might make what the company needs. This is an eminently solvable problem.

Materials with a short shelf life

If a company's products require for their manufacture materials with a short shelf life (things that go off, go bad, degenerate, or experience a change of chemical state with the passage of time) this makes the purchasing–production operation even more of a knife-edge affair than it usually is. There is no absolute answer; what helps is for salesmen to anticipate orders, production bosses to anticipate volume needs, having small buffer stocks, and multiple sourcing. It is one of the unfortunate facts of life that companies which have a daily input of (perishable) materials for current manufacture can be closed by a 15cm snowfall.

Typical plight of the small firm

The most pervasive problem in purchasing, however, is the typical plight of the small firm in buying the things it needs. Its basic problem is that its order is small and from the point of view of the larger manufacturer especially, probably not worth bothering with in normal times. This problem is compounded by the fact that big manufacturers often will not deal direct with small buyers at all, so the small firm has to buy from a trade stockist. A stockist is an intermediary warehouse cum onselling institution; the stockist buys big lots cheap from the manufacturer, and onsells them dear in small lots to small firms or other consumers. Stockists exist to exploit the poor bargaining position of the small firm. Add to these disadvantages the facts that the small firm is unlikely to be able to help its suppliers with technical resources, managerial back-up, or development money, and it will be clear that it may face real problems in getting good, and especially cheap, service from its suppliers. We turn to this problem next.

How to get the best deal with a weak hand (or the small company bites back)

There are three precepts:

1. Use your imagination.
2. Bargain tirelessly.
3. Play from strengths.

Let us take them together, assuming for argument's sake that the price of bought-out parts is important for our putative small company, and that buying these more cheaply will affect profit margins and is worth some effort. The problem looks bad, but imagination may suggest ways round it. First, it may be possible for small companies with similar purchasing needs to combine in their dealings with larger suppliers or stockists. This is not as novel as it sounds; farmers have been forming combines for years both to sell their produce and to buy feedstuffs and agrochemicals on better terms. Second, a small company may be able to get a bigger company (which deals direct with a manufacturer) to order for it, out of pure good nature or in return for some favour. Third, the small company's customer may well be big enough to get a better deal than the company itself can get from its suppliers. If the company's bought-out parts contribute to the particular customer's product, then the customer may well find it worth while to use its superior bargaining power to help. Fourth, there is a refinement on this deal. Imagine a small company which has 100 customers, 99 small and one large. The company asks its one large customer to negotiate better deals with suppliers on its behalf, induces the big customer to do this by passing on all the benefits to the big customer in the form of lower prices, but still increases its profit margins with its 99 small customers.

In view of what was said at the end of the last section it may be thought that the small company does not have any strengths to play from. Think again:

(1) It is one of the paradoxes of the business world that small companies are often good payers. It does no harm to remind their suppliers of this fact, and try to cash in on it, especially in a recession.

(2) Similarly, small companies quite often have plenty of money, relative to their size; some are practically drowning in liquidity, if only because they are not expansionist and have nothing to do with their profits. A company that can pay fast, make down payments with the order, or even make forward payments, has a potent bargaining weapon.

(3) When small firms buy it is usually the owner himself who does the deals. This gives him a tactical edge over the big firm buyer (a mere 'hired managerial hand'); he speaks for himself, can commit the company, and does not have to ask anyone back at head office before doing a deal.

(4) A lot of small companies have a simple product range and very little in the way of product development. This means they may have nice stable demand for purchased materials over respectable periods of time: this is worth something to suppliers, especially as a formalized commitment, even if the amount in a given month is small.

(5) Small companies can buy, so to speak, in the reject shop. It was suggested above that a lot of argument surrounds the question of quality and conformity to specifications, so that much stuff which somebody can use, gets officially rejected. Now suppliers who have such stock on their hands cannot unload it on Rolls Royce, but they might on Grab All and Son of East Tree Stump. So if a small company is in the market for

items a supplier might find it difficult to dispose of this can be
a lever for getting better terms than the next man.
(6) The small firm owner is invariably a local man with good local
contacts. This is good for favours, handshake deals, and the
various combine initiatives mentioned above.

The list is not meant to be exhaustive. It just serves to show that
everyone has some cards to play, you just have to figure out what they
are. The points made here are simply real-life applications of the
'power' and 'influence' concepts discussed in Chapter 3.

Finally, it is worth stressing the value of tireless bargaining.
Sometimes a company can get what it wants, not because it deserves
it, can pay for it, or give something in return, but because the supplier
finds it easier to give in. So if the other side gets tired first, you may get
what you want without even paying the market price.

How to play a strong hand

Now let us consider the other extreme, the position of a big company
with high prestige, big money to spend, and large orders to confer. A
buyer representing such a company holds all the trumps; everyone
wants to deal with blue chip companies, multiple sourcing is easy, and
the buyer can go for years without ever paying for his own lunch. But
how exactly can the big company use such power? It is a combination
of negotiation, multiple sourcing, and using power beneficently—
which means helping others to help you.

To set the scene, let us note that everyone aims at multiple sourcing
but big companies find it particularly easy to obtain since there is
readiness and competition to sell to them. This multiple sourcing, and
the big company's attractive customer status, mean that its worries
about availability, flexibility, reliability, quality, and punctuality are
reduced (or jolly well ought to be). So it is freer to concentrate on
price, and has more to gain by price reductions wrung from its
suppliers.

The advantage of multiple-sourcing in price negotiations is
obvious, and the big company often enjoys a further advantage in this
connection in that it can play off not only British suppliers against
each other, but British against foreign, and European against
Asian—and they do. What is more the big company is likely to have
running contracts with its suppliers which are renegotiated annually;
so it has a chance to flex its bargaining muscles at the beginning of
every contract and once a year thereafter. When the two things are
combined, multiple–multinational sourcing and annual renegotiation,
the big company has formidable bargaining strength.

But perhaps the most distinctive thing about the big company is that it can influence its suppliers positively. It can sometimes get them to reduce prices by showing that it really is cheaper to produce large numbers for a big buyer. Everyone understands this in principle, but calculating *how much* cheaper it is to make 1000 rather than 50 is much more demanding, and the big company is better placed to demonstrate the point. Similarly, the big company can often get the supplier to show its costings and these may well be wrong; costing is difficult, but big companies have more time and expertise to throw into the battle. Again big companies are often buying from suppliers things they already make themselves, or used to make, or could make if they felt like it; so they are often in a position to help suppliers with manufacturing methods. This leads to another consideration which is that the big company has more of everything so it can also choose to help suppliers with technical information, tooling-up costs, hand-me-down machinery, R&D back-up, and development costs—all or any of which may enable the supplier to reduce the price. It is perhaps less obvious, but the big company can help the small supplier with quality management. Imagine, for instance, a supplier who has trouble interpreting safety legislation, does not know how to introduce a proper bonus system, and does not know how to computerize its stock control; big companies can do all this and employ specialists whom they can lend out. So small suppliers may benefit from a 'free' consultancy service.

The big firm can also help its suppliers to reduce their prices by doing deals for them, or bringing them in on bigger deals. First, and we mentioned it earlier from a different angle, the big company can do its supplier's buying for it on more favourable terms. Second, it can piggyback its small suppliers by getting its big suppliers to supply its small suppliers on cut price terms. Third, it can simply use its influence to put other business in the way of its suppliers. A variation of this theme is that the big company, in placing an order with supplier A can nominate supplier B as supplier A's supplier, thus increasing B's turnover without raising A's costs. Fourth, the big company buyer can sometimes help suppliers with aggregate deals: it can, that is, make a supplier supply to the group or division, rather than to just the works or section part of the firm, again increasing the supplier's turnover.

When it comes to transportation the big company is again more favourably placed to get it more cheaply, especially if it is question of nice regular shipments and there is time to shop around. The worst deal is rushing in an emergency consignment of raw materials in a chartered Boeing 707.

This calls to mind a last consideration. For the big company, buying some supplies abroad may have a commercial and tactical advantage, but it also renders the company liable to import duty. But if the company can convince Customs and Excise that what they are importing is unobtainable in the United Kingdom they may be exempt from the import duty. Yet again the big company is more likely to have the time and resources to do so.

Who should control purchasing

We showed at the beginning that purchasing departments may be independent (reporting direct to the managing director), controlled by a senior production manager, by sales, or by finance, and in the case of small firms the owner-manager is typically his own buyer. The two dominant types are the first two, independent or production controlled, and it is worth spending a minute on their rival merits.

There is no absolute answer, it depends on circumstance and priorities, but at least we can point to what each is good for. If the company is most concerned with volume of production, continuity of production, and completing its orders on time then there is a lot to be said for having purchasing production-controlled. But there may be a price to be paid: buyers in a production-controlled regime will come to espouse the works manager's 'where's my bits' mentality; this is good for the punctual arrival of the bits but not for price negotiations. Another effect is that production managers are in a certain sense conservative; they will never change from a satisfactory supplier, and indeed their instinct is often justified in that new suppliers sometimes bring horrendous and unanticipated problems with them. So production-controlled purchasing is not likely to be innovative with regard to new suppliers or multiple sourcing: it is likely to run a good and where necessary patched-up operation using the suppliers to hand. So to approach the question from the opposite direction it would be fair to say that if cost reduction and multiple availability of bought-out parts are the priorities they will be better pursued by an independent purchasing department. Again the idea could be expressed differently by saying that purchasing has two functions:

(1) basic: getting the bits on time; and
(2) qualitative: generating the market intelligence, advising higher management and other interested departments, making clear to designers and engineers what is possible in known market terms, cost reduction through keen negotiating, and the creative search for alternatives.

The basic function is best served by the production-controlled setup, while the qualitative functions are best served by independence.

This, in turn, raises the question: suppose that purchasing managers experience difficulty in carrying out the qualitative functions because their independence is restricted by demands and pressures from other departments, is there anything they can do?

How the purchasing manager can fight back

To set the scene there are two types of restriction on the purchasing manager's freedom to choose, negotiate, and emphasize the qualitative aspects of the job. The first is production or production control managers who want things quickly 'at any cost'. The second is designers and engineers, so concerned with quality and methods that they overspecify the items concerned and sometimes even specify the supplier, thus reducing the purchasing manager to a mail clerk.

For purchasing managers it is a problem that can be confronted with education! The higher the purchasing manager's level of technical education the better placed he is to argue with engineers and designers about materials and specifications. Even where purchasing managers do not have an engineering training or background they may well be able to master relevant tracts of knowledge thereby enhancing their power. And again educational preparation shades into pure persuasion. The purchasing manager has a legitimate viewpoint, his qualitative objectives are credible, even laudable—so why not convince others.

At a more crudely political level the purchasing manager may get some mileage out of playing various departments off against each other. Production and design are often at loggerheads, and so are production and engineering; the astute purchasing manager can do a deal with production over speed of delivery in return for support in having the specifications liberalized. Or again designers are not usually interested in cheapness, but the finance department will be, and it is a good cause on which to appeal to higher management if there is too much obstruction around. A self-confident purchasing manager is also free to indulge in defiance if there is not a better tactic; he can revise the specifications on his own authority, make the deal, claim it's a good one, and defy anyone to challenge him.

Or if a purchasing manager feels he has been put on too often he can sanction his tormenters. In extremes he can complain to a common boss, but this is a little crude. Better if he can catch one of his tormenters breaking some company rule first, like engineers person-

114 Purchasing

ally receiving the salesman from a supplier (accepting a present from him is better still) or maybe ignoring company policy requiring competitive tendering. Where production or production control ask too often for rush orders they can be disciplined by being asked, in writing, if they are willing to pay the supplier a premium price, or bear the emergency transport costs on their departmental budget. Finally, if the purchasing manager feels that production have cried 'wolf' too often ('we must have it tomorrow') he can always sanction them by conveniently failing to get something. This will remind them they could work better together.

If this chapter has a general moral it is that most situations do offer a choice, but sometimes this is not obvious.

References

Farrington, B. and Woodmansey, M. (1980). *The purchasing function, Management Survey Report No.* 50. British Institute of Management, London.

Recommended reading

Buckner, H. (1967). *How British industry buys.* Hutchinson, London.
Huitson, A. and Keen, J. (1965). *Essentials of quality control.* Heinemann, London.
Strauss, G. (1962). Tactics of lateral relationship: the purchasing agent. *Admin. Sci. Quart.* 7, September, 1962.
Turnbull, P. and Cunningham, M. (eds.) (1981). *International marketing and purchasing.* Macmillan Press Ltd., London.

Questions

1. Discuss the proposition that multiple-sourcing is the prerequisite for a successful purchasing operation.
2. What, in practice, are the obstacles to multiple-sourcing, and how may they be overcome?
3. Companies vary in what is most important to them in their dealings with suppliers; explain why this is so and give some examples.
4. What are the characteristic difficulties that small firms may encounter in buying the parts and materials they need? Is it possible to suggest solutions to these difficulties?
5. What is the case for and against having the purchasing department under the control of a senior production manager?
6. What advantages does a large company have in managing its purchasing and how may these be turned to good account.

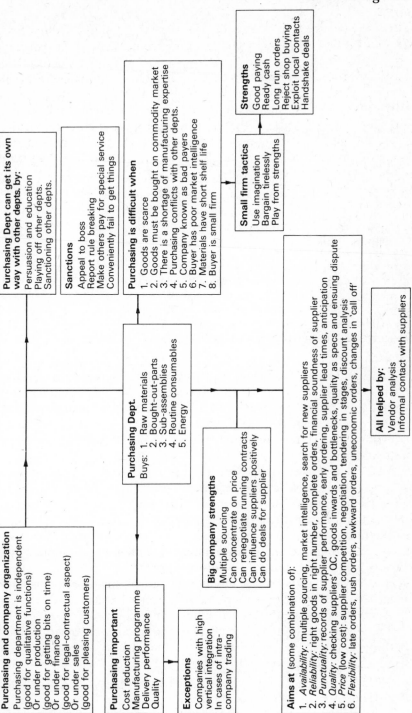

Purchasing and company organization
Purchasing department is independent
(good for qualitative functions)
Or under production
(good for getting bits on time)
Or under finance
(good for legal-contractual aspect)
Or under sales
(good for pleasing customers)

Purchasing Dept can get its own way with other depts. by:
Persuasion and education
Playing off other depts.
Sanctioning other depts.

Sanctions
Appeal to boss
Report rule breaking
Make others pay for special service
Conveniently fail to get things

Purchasing is difficult when
1. Goods are scarce
2. Goods must be bought on commodity market
3. There is a shortage of manufacturing expertise
4. Purchasing conflicts with other depts.
5. Company known as bad payers
6. Buyer has poor market intelligence
7. Materials have short shelf life
8. Buyer is small firm

Small firm tactics
Use imagination
Bargain tirelessly
Play from strengths

Strengths
Good paying
Ready cash
Long run orders
Reject shop buying
Exploit local contacts
Handshake deals

Purchasing important
Cost reduction
Manufacturing programme
Delivery performance
Quality

Exceptions
Companies with high vertical integration
In cases of intra-company trading

Purchasing Dept.
Buys: 1. Raw materials
      2. Bought-out-parts
      3. Sub-assemblies
      4. Routine consumables
      5. Energy

Big company strengths
Multiple sourcing
Can concentrate on price
Can renegotiate running contracts
Can influence suppliers positively
Can do deals for supplier

Aims at (some combination of):
1. *Availability*: multiple sourcing, market intelligence, search for new suppliers
2. *Reliability*: right goods in right number, complete orders, financial soundness of supplier
3. *Punctuality*: records of supplier performance, early ordering, supplier lead times, anticipation
4. *Quality*: checking suppliers' QC, goods inwards and bottlenecks, quality as specs and ensuing dispute
5. *Price* (low cost): supplier competition, negotiation, tendering in stages, discount analysis
6. *Flexibility*: late orders, rush orders, awkward orders, uneconomic orders, changes in 'call off'

All helped by:
Vendor analysis
Informal contact with suppliers

6 Production

Introduction

There is a joke in one of Gavin Lyall's novels that to get your case carried in Norway (on arrival at your hotel for instance) you need to be the king, and have a bad back (Lyall, 1982). There are, that is, some places where there is no respect for age or rank: manufacturing is like this. It is all hassle, hustle, and problems.

One of us once asked a production manager at a machine tools company to write a summarized note on how he spent the previous afternoon. This note contained the sentence:

Struggling manfully to keep head above water; pressing sister factory in north-east for promised tools, pressing purchasing department to get paint, demanding action from production control, and nagging repair crews at work all over the shop; also talking one of superintendents through his job list to make sure he *really* knows what the difficulties are going to be; and received small deputation of workers complaining they're not making enough on piece rates.

Funnily enough the hectic reality of manufacturing often does not come over in books about production management. A common reason is that such books are often written by engineers and tend to redefine production management as production engineering, zooming in on questions of factory design, machinery layout, production systems, and value engineering.

This tendency overlaps with another, namely that which depicts manufacturing as a set of operating contingencies which can all be handled by rational and numerate systems. This point of view sees production management as being all about planning the inputs, throughput, and output. So the questions which get treated in such books are things like materials requirements planning (organizing the flow of bought-out parts), inventory control (how many of what to keep in stock), production planning and control (how much of what to make in which order), shop loading (distributing jobs between available machines), theories of maintenance cover, and so on.

These two overlapping perspectives are important, but they have both produced an extensive literature which does not need adding to here. They also leave out something, namely what it is that production managers actually do. This is what the present chapter focuses on.

Who are the production managers?

Perhaps surprisingly there is no agreed answer to this question, but one can distinguish between the broad (and sloppy) view and the narrow (and precise) one. Consider this organization chart for a company with 1000 employees making domestic appliances (Fig. 6.1). Who, in this company, are the production managers? The broad view is that it is the works director and all those of supervisory grade and above who report to him, directly and indirectly. Looked at functionally this means not only manufacturing and assembly but also materials (purchasing and stock control), production control, maintenance, industrial engineering (setting rates for jobs), and quality control (inspection). This broad view is implied by many of the books, which tend to deal more with the scheduling–materials planning–inspection–maintenance type of topics than with actual direct manufacturing ones.

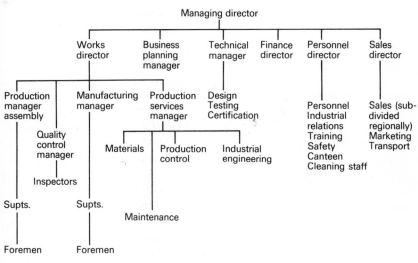

Fig. 6.1   Locating production manager.

This chapter takes the opposite, and narrow, view; that production managers are people whose ultimate subordinates make and assemble goods. In terms of Fig. 6.1 the production managers are the works director, the production manager assembly, the manufacturing manager, and their superintendents. All the others are in supporting roles, a fact symbolized in the organization chart depicted in Fig. 6.1 by grouping most of them under a production *services* manager. Materials planning, scheduling, devising job rates, inspecting, and keeping the works going are all activities which precede, sustain, or follow production; they do not actually constitute production. But production managers are people who run people who make things, and seek services and support from others.

What is production all about?

There is a good survey of the work of production managers where the majority describe their basic activity as 'urging supplies in and production out' (Gill and Lockyer 1979). In practice this in–out equation involves a whole range of manoeuvres, operations, and initiatives, but they have two things in common. They all involve other people, and they are usually done in a hurry.

Supplies

To start with there is the whole question of getting the parts and materials and sub-assemblies from suppliers which was explored in the last chapter on purchasing. It is the production manager who is at the receiving end of suppliers who send the wrong bits, defective parts, the wrong number of components, and who above all send them late. In the same way our production manager is at the receiving end of subcontractors who foul-up assignments or default on their obligations. And when the parts and materials actually arrive at the company where they are to be used in manufacture they have to pass through the eye of a needle in the form of the goods inwards section.

One cannot rely on goods inwards inspection being perfect, but one can usually rely on it being slow. So the typical production manager as part of the urging supplies-in role will pressurize buyers and purchasing managers, hassle suppliers directly, threaten and bully subcontractors, endlessly demand new consignments sent by the Red Star parcels service, and when other distractions fail will try to engender a sense of urgency in goods inwards—and, for a real challenge, talk them into accepting some consignment they have already rejected.

New products

But not all products are routinely made where the process begins with the acquisition of parts and materials. Some are new, or newly modified, for a particular customer, or made only intermittently to order rather than as a continuous flow from workshop to warehouse. This opens up a new range of possibilities. If the product is new it will come from design, and thus be subject to frustration's law. This states that however long design are allowed for the operation, it will always take longer. And when they have finished (the creative act of design) this does not necessarily mean the machine drawings will be ready, or that inconsistencies will not be discovered when one begins to work to the drawings. Those lovable perfectionists in design are also loath to stop even when specifications and drawings are delivered to production; designers have a tendency to try to finesse through further embellishments even when the product is going through the workshop (production foremen need to watch out for this!).

Again with new products it is not only a question of design, but of devising manufacturing methods. So production engineering staff may be involved to decide how the item is to be made and by what sequences; this may involve having special jigs or fixtures made, the preparation of parts lists, and perhaps some decisions on whether to make or buy particular parts. Similarly, people in industrial engineering or work study may need to draw up instructions for machine operations, or time manufacturing operations, and set pay rates for them. Production planning will schedule the product concerned and monitor its progress through the manufacturing process. But these are all preliminaries to manufacture, and may be points of intervention for the production manager if they are not done right or soon enough. While all these things are supposed to be happening the production manager may well have a completion date for the ensuing product: this will encourage him to reach back into these preliminary operations and get people moving.

What about the workers?

When manufacture begins it might be thought that all one needs is workers, and in a recession this is hardly likely to be a problem. Not so fast. Workforce size is highly inflexible. For years we have heard about overmanning, the need to slim, and reductions in the head count. When all this has happened the workforce may be scarcely adequate to the workload and downright inadequate when orders pick up. Many a managerial hatchet man has made his name by firing in January people who were sorely missed in March.

Then again, having the right number of workers on the books does not mean you will have the right number on the shopfloor at 8.00 on Monday morning. While general absenteeism is calculable, and so are seasonal fluctuations, there is no way of knowing who will be sick or absent at a particular time. And maybe it turns out to be two of the only three workers in the shop who know how to work the capstan lathes, or perhaps it is the one superintendent with whom the shop stewards will do business. So there are always short-term and particular manning and cover problems. The problem is at its most intractable in conveyor belt mass production works, where the assembly line cannot actually be started up until the work positions are manned; or at best there will be an agreement with the union that when it is started up management has only a few minutes grace to complete the manning—by instant transfers and juggling.

Overtime

Overtime working, which might be seen as the company's obvious resource when work builds up or there is a danger of 'slippage' (work falling behind schedule), may not be so easy to turn on and off in practice. At the heart of this difficulty is the fact that there are really two views of overtime. Management regards it as a rational and manipulable resource to be used on its own terms, but workers tend to regard it as an 'economic goody' which should be subject to norms of social justice and fair play. So in practice clashes often occur. Management will request a particular group, say welders, to work overtime, only to be told that some other group have a better claim because 'it's their turn'; or workers' representatives will attempt to do all-or-nothing deals with management on overtime (one in, all in!).

Another pervasive difficulty is that management has come to see that overtime working is difficult to turn off (so one is more reluctant to turn it on in the first place). Employees become accustomed to the disproportionate rise in income which goes with overtime, and understandably resist its cessation. If there is one thing which makes a workforce trigger happy it is the loss of overtime earnings when these have been there so long they have been taken for granted. People not familiar with industry might be surprised to know that when a new worker is taken on the critical point is often not the hourly rate or weekly wages but the amount of guaranteed overtime.

Keep the cog wheels turning

Not only does the act of production require adequate numbers and combinations of available workers, there is also a need for functioning equipment and working machines. There is no way this need can be taken for granted.

It is an odd fact about British industry that much of it is not well equipped. While British expenditure on R&D is similar to that of other advanced industrial countries, expenditure on production technology appears to lag. What is more those concerned are often morosely proud of the fact that many a British workshop is equipped with unreliable junk: it is more of a challenge to keep it all working, to get jobs through the system; it appeals to the 1940 spirit of the typical production manager.

Similarly, it has to be conceded that maintenance is not generally a British strength, and there are several factors involved here. First, maintenance is a cost, not something that directly generates income, so there is, if you like, a natural tendency to limit it. To this might be added the marked 'accountancy flavour' of higher management in Britain (see Chapter 2) with its penchant for cost-cutting. Unwillingness to spend on maintenance sometimes reaches epic proportions. One of the authors once attended a meeting in a big name engineering company chaired by the assistant managing director and attended by heads of manufacturing divisions. The latter were urging the importance of getting the roof repaired and cited as part of their case the fact that rain coming through the roof and onto the machinery had, on several occasions, caused electric fires! The assistant managing director responded by inviting them all to write him formal letters listing these atrocities so that he would have 'something to show the Board'.

Second, there is the associated point that maintenance is typically *corrective* rather than *preventive*. The maintenance section, that is, intervenes to put right things that have gone wrong (leaking roofs, machinery breakdowns, assembly line stoppages). It is an associated point because it derives, at least in part, from the fact that maintenance tends to be under-resourced. And of course it adds to the uncertainties of the production manager's life.

Third, there is often a command problem with regard to the maintenance section. Maintenance workers, that is, are generally tradesmen—fitters, electricians, and so on—and consider themselves a cut above ordinary production workers (machine minders, assembly line stooges). This distinction often finds organizational expression in the fact that these maintenance workers have a different chain of command, reporting ultimately to their technical director rather than to the production director. This may make it difficult for supervisors and production managers to get the quick response they want from maintenance when it comes to breakdowns and other urgent repairs. It is hardly surprising that a survey of production managers showed that those who did not control the maintenance function were avid to get their hands on it (Lockyer and Jones 1980). And perhaps it is also not surprising that a different survey of maintenance chiefs (Husband and Barker, 1976) revealed that they felt many production workers were systematically abusing their machines while their bosses showed a staggering failure to appreciate the needs and contingencies of maintenance!

Information is control

While all these struggles over supplies and drawings, biddable workers and workable machines are going on, the production manager can expect some enfilading fire from colleagues in finance and administration and perhaps from management services as well. The accountants will bombard him with computer printouts showing he has spent too much, that his wage bill is too high, that (the cost of) overtime working is rising, and that so far this month he is nowhere near meeting the target for overhead cost recovery. For an encore they will be happy to explain why he cannot have a new lathe (a) because the company cannot afford it, (b) because they have found an error in the production manager's 'pay back' calculation (pay back = how long it will take a machine to pay for itself in savings or profits).

The production manager may find that other interesting documents arrive on his desk—perhaps an analysis of shop loading, the utilization rates for various machines, showing that he is misusing capacity. Or calculations of the cost of work-in-progress or the loss to the company through downtime (periods when work has stopped for whatever cause) or analyses of faults prepared by quality control, all of which tend to suggest he is not doing a marvellous job.

The pressures created by such 'information flows' make it important for the production manager to develop some counter-strategies for his own protection. One general strategy is purely psychological; in the theory of criminal behaviour it is called 'condemnation of the condemners'. This means you define all the others who are producing annoying bits of paper as lacking your responsibilities, realism, practicality, and urgency (in their words, they are useless twits). This takes some of the sting out of it, but there are some other manoeuvres.

Production managers always like to be able to show that at any point in time their section has completed a lot of work and thereby generated considerable revenue for the company. And often production managers have a choice in the scheduling of different jobs and batches, as these have different prices for the customer. When this is the case it is common for production managers, and foremen for that matter, to do first the nice straightforward jobs with a high income value. The same tendency is even more acute when monitoring periods are approaching their end. Output and performance, that is, are monitored by time-period. So towards the end of such periods, and especially towards the end of the financial year, there is a rush to push the total up by finishing big jobs 'just in time' for their value to be added to the current year's figure (next year can take care of itself—by then you might have retrained as an accountant).

Tactical concealment (of completed work) is another ruse. Everyone knows that workers do this. The employee, for instance, who has to make 25 sprockets a day goes crazy and turns out 30 by lunchtime, but hides 15 so he can turn them in any time he wants an easy day. The practice is also common among managers who hold back completed jobs (that is, do not tell accounts) so they have some extras to throw into the battle whenever the figures need pushing up ('What do you mean, I can't have it because my section has only done £27 000 worth this month?')

Then there is collusion. Collusion with suppliers can be helpful these days when finance are inclined to tell you to break down big orders to suppliers into smaller lots spread over time. So if you need 20, but the order is to buy five now, then another five in April, and then ... you send out an order for five while phoning your contact at the supplier to make sure 20 are sent. There is also collusion for the mutual suppression of error. Those keen types in quality control, for instance, may not enforce the letter of the law (against you) when you have shown what a right-minded person you are by losing the breakdown of delays incurred in goods inwards.

This leads to a consideration of what might be called 'end play'.

End play

When the goods are made that is not the end of it. They have to be inspected, packed, and got out. Inspection may be a problem, not just in the sense that it is inconveniently rigorous (or an orgy of ritualistic nit-picking, depending on your point of view) but more often because it is slow. Nothing is more irritating for workers who have made an extra effort to do a job fast, or to the production manager that set them up, than to see the completed item languish in final inspection. The usual counter-tactic is for the production manager to invade inspection, bypass the quality control manager and give jobs his own priority.

The packing operation is a minefield. It is not just that one may run out of bottles, cans, and bailing wire, but packing is often in part mechanized and so is vulnerable to breakdowns. We have seen a brewery brought to a standstill because its only (old and decrepit) machine for washing out barrels broke down, a powdered milk factory knocked sideways when its can making line went awry, and an engineering works unable to dispatch an important consignment because it had run out of sticky labels with the skull and crossbones motif, mandatory (Board of Trade regulations) because the equipment involved cylinders of toxic gas.

Getting goods out is usually a matter of transport and logistics. And it sometimes involves dependency on others—the public transport system, a private haulier company, or some other part of the works providing return load space on their lorries bring goods to you. Where the dispatch of produce to customers is a continual and patterned event, as with say the supply of food products to grocery retailers, one speaks of *distribution* as a functional activity. In this case organizational feuding may add to the other hazards, because there is no set formula for who should control distribution. Production tend to claim that as they have made the stuff they ought to run distribution, and sales tend to argue that getting goods to the customer is the logical consequence of selling so that distribution should be part of their empire. We once witnessed a battle at a brewery where the production managers ganged up to take distribution away from sales; this was all in the interests of operating efficiency, of course, though one of the warring team explained that the takeover would increase the number of their subordinates enough to lift them all into the category qualifying for the next largest company car.

A common way of explaining what production is all about is to detail the sequence of activities between the company accepting an order and the dispatch of the completed product. This is usually done in technical and system terms, describing for instance design work, tooling up, and production control methods. We have used this model too, but done it in terms of describing the contacts and dependencies of the production manager, and indicating a lot of the working problems along the way. One of the things which comes out of this exercise is the fact that production management work is not solitary; it is all about talking to people, or in more formal terms, about liaison and coordination. This can be seen in breakdowns of how production managers spend their time.

The work pattern of production managers

A recent study of what production managers 'do all day' by one of us showed the following distribution of time (Table 6.1). This breakdown demonstrates beautifully the interactive nature of the production manager's job. Formal scheduled meetings are the ones which occur regularly, often on a same time–same place basis, such as daily production meetings (monitoring output, discussing working problems), daily supply meetings (chasing up the supply of bought-out parts) or periodic departmental meetings where a production manager gathers together his direct subordinates and they talk about everything of interest since the last meeting of the series. Convened

TABLE 6.1
A time budget analysis for a sample of managers.

Activity	Per cent of working time
Formal scheduled recurrent meeting	15.50
Convened special purpose meeting	14.46
Ad hoc discussions	17.93
Tours of the works	17.35
Telephoning	7.23
Desk work	11.16
Explanations to the researcher	12.08
Total proportion of working time accounted for under these headings	95.71

special-purpose meetings are ones which do not occur regularly but are convened as needed to deal with particular issues. Meetings, for instance, to discuss the introduction of a new product, or to organize a move to new premises, or to launch a drive on improved quality, would come under this heading. Together these two kinds of formal meeting account for nearly a third of the working time of the managers in this sample.

The *ad hoc* discussions are little chats with colleagues or subordinates either singly or in small groups, of a more or less spontaneous kind. They are not at all formal as are the scheduled and convened meetings, and are typically inaugurated by a phone call of the 'are you free now' kind. If these *ad hoc* discussions are added to the formal meetings the sum accounts for nearly half the production managers' working time.

The last category in Table 6.1, that referring to explanations given to the researcher, does not of course measure the normal work of production managers; it is just included as a check on how much the study itself affected the work of this group of managers—if there had been no researcher present they would probably have spent that time on even more *ad hoc* discussions with colleagues. The time spent telephoning is also interactive of course; telephoning is just 'the continuation of interaction by other means'.

The time spent touring the plant is interesting in that time spent on the shop-floor by production managers serves a variety of purposes. It is partly a way of exercising supervision and control. It is also an opportunity to check the working of machines or the functioning of the manufacturing process, perhaps to do little checks on quality, or get feedback on manufacturing methods. It is an information-gathering exercise too, seeing the progress of various jobs, doing a visual check on work in progress, noting absences and breakdowns, and so on. But above all, touring the works is an opportunity for more chat. It offers the chance to have 'a quick word' with inspectors and foremen, people from work study and engineering production, storemen, packers and drivers. It means making oneself available for employees and shop stewards who want to moan or explain or 'bring something to your attention'!

The time the typical production manager spends doing paperwork of some kind in his office is small. Some of this paperwork is just monitoring his own activities: writing reminders, lists of things to do, prompts for meetings, and so on. Another small portion concerns correspondence: reading it, writing it, dictating replies, and using correspondence files to build up a case (for example, finding a way of blaming someone else for something which has gone wrong). A third portion relates to reading and writing reports. Lower level production managers may have to do little routine reports—on absentees, employees coming late, lists of job rejects, and so on. Higher level production managers are often required to produce more complex documents at widely spaced intervals: a general appraisal of production over the past year; a forward-looking plan for personnel requirements; or predictive data on manufacturing costs which will help sales people decide on next year's price list. These demanding, non-routine writing jobs often get done at home rather than fitted into the hurly-burly of the working day.

Who hates who?

Two of the themes we have explored in this chapter, the highly interactive nature of the production manager's job, and the fact that because the manufacturing operation depends on so many other people there are numerous points of possible antagonism, come together in a comparative survey carried out at the Bradford Management Centre. One item in this survey required groups of finance, marketing, personnel, and production managers to class their relationship with a whole range of departments and functions as satisfactory or unsatisfactory or somewhere in between. The results are shown in Table 6.2 (taken from Lockyer and Jones 1980).

At a glance one can see what well-adjusted, irritation-free managers work in finance and personnel; their entries in the unsatisfactory column never reach double figures. The marketing managers are not quite so benign in their view of the rest of the organizational world. They have a certain hostility towards R&D, no doubt based on the view that researchers fail to generate customer-pleasing products;

TABLE 6.2
Who hates whom in British industry.

	Finance (%)		Marketing (%)		Personnel (%)		Production (%)	
	Satis-factory	Unsatis-factory	Satis-factory	Unsatis-factory	Satis-factory	Unsatis-factory	Satis-factory	Unsatis-factory
Sales	48	5	40	12	43	3	40	17
Marketing	47	7	—	—	43	3	36	20
Production	45	8	58	27	52	6	—	—
Personnel	47	3	39	3	—	—	57	13
Finance	—	—	49	21	54	6	50	13
Design	13	2	27	2	21	0	36	22
R&D	23	2	32	14	24	3	38	23
Top management	69	3	48	9	68	5	67	10
Work study	23	4	13	7	35	2	22	9
Production control	25	2	23	8	30	2	62	17
Maintenance	61	6	4	2	39	0	37	35
Purchasing	61	3	24	12	39	0	49	17

towards finance who cut the achievements of the marketing man down to size (and obstruct his claims for travel and entertainment expenses); but most of all towards production. This will reflect an irritation at the inflexibility of production from a sales point of view. Production managers are understandably not wildly keen to chop and change the production programme, make dramatic end-price lowering savings, build in endless customer-pleasing modifications, and have everything ready yesterday. Yet these are the factors which salesmen would like to help them get bigger and better orders.

When it comes to the responses of the production managers themselves it is quite clear that any hostility sales and marketing people have for them is amply reciprocated. Furthermore the production managers emerge as having many more irritations and hostilities than their colleagues from the three other areas of managerial work; indeed almost every entry in the unsatisfactory column reaches double figures. This is even more remarkable when the sample of managers is senior as in this instance. It is a survey of directors or senior managers reporting directly to a director; people at this level might have been thought to be better insulated against the daily hassle of shortages and breakdowns.

Table 6.2 does not mean, of course, that production managers are recruited from the most cantankerous 10 per cent of the human race. It is simply that the manufacturing operation is complicated and vulnerable and marked by a lot of dependency on others. The entries in the unsatisfactory column in Table 6.2 simply parallel the working problems of production managers described earlier in the chapter.

Industrial relations

The production manager's job generally includes an element of industrial relations work, but it is probably fair to say that this work differs a lot from the popular conception. First, it is not all about strikes. Strikes occur, of course, both official and unofficial, but from the standpoint of the individual production manager they are rare events however large they loom in the national statistics. Second, having put the pay claim and strikes nexus in its place, it has to be said that the industrial relations incidents with which production managers are involved cover a fascinating variety of issues from subcontracting to safety, overtime to teabreaks, and demarcation to discipline, with a sprinkling of pure personality clashes and exploding touchiness. And third, it is not all bad. Some of the production manager activity which comes under the industrial relations label is in fact constructive and harmonious dialogue rather than troubleshooting. Most companies of any size have some machinery for joint consultation, a works committee or works council, which meets regularly and routinely, not just in response to some crisis. Such meetings are frequently chaired by a production manager.

What is most striking when one gets on the inside of industrial relations is how many angles there are. Few of the issues seem to be black or white, and in many cases one could argue persuasively for both sides. Consider for instance this little story from a light engineering company where one of the authors worked.

In this company the chargehand in the heavy assembly section needed a tool made up to keep his section working. The tool-room said they would not do it for him, at least not quickly enough, so the chargehand got a pal in another section to do the job for him. The shop stewards objected and demanded a meeting with the production manager where they argued:

(1) Demarcation lines had been violated; only the tool-room can make tools.
(2) The fact that the tool had been made by a third party from another section added insult to injury (more difficult to overlook than if someone in heavy assembly had done it).
(3) Heavy assembly had been working overtime but the tool-room had not. In a small way, taking this job from them pushes back incrementally the chance that they will be offered overtime working.

What happened is that the production manager offered the stewards an apology, and begged leave to adjourn the meeting to investigate (at this point he was criticized for not having had tea served at the meeting, but nothing worse). He then checked the facts with the parties concerned and they are true; he told off the chargehand from heavy assembly in the presence of the tool-room superintendent (justice is seen to be done); reconvened the meeting with the shop stewards, reported back and gave assurances. The whole incident was over by mid-afternoon of the day on which it came to light; but consider some of the angles.

There is no question of a strike or any kind of a stoppage, and it is not about money in any direct sense. But in spite of this it has taken up the production manager's time and attention. Then there is what one might call 'grievance layering'; a complaint about demarcation is run into the triangular relations between these work sections and aligned with implicit complaints about overtime. There is also more than a hint of 'grievance conversion' about all this; if all sections had been working overtime would anyone have cared about the demarcation issue? Finally, as with so many industrial relations incidents, there is a clash between the working needs of the firm as perceived by management and supervision on the one hand, and the moral view of the workforce on the other. In this particular incident that tension was symbolized by the fact that the chargehand who started it all was not only reprimanded by his boss for causing a demarcation dispute, he was also personally congratulated by the managing director for his commendable initiative.

What can one learn from a review of industrial relations incidents? That such incidents are usually complicated. That quite unconnected things may be brought together for bargaining purposes: imagine you are a shop steward representing the welders, and management have just asked the welders to work overtime to clear a bottleneck—why not seize the chance to ask for a better car park or the sale of jam doughnuts during the morning teabreak? That issues may be redefined by those raising the grievance; there is a move towards the articulation of grievances which are tangible and conventional. Perhaps there is 'something about management in this company' that one dislikes; you cannot have a strike over that, but you can certainly hammer them for violating safety regulations. Which is another way of saying that management's vulnerability will probably be exploited; if management is weak, or ignorant, neglects safety, indulges in 'corner-cutting' mucking around with the rule book, or allows anomalies in pay and conditions to develop, it can expect to get clobbered sooner or later. The production manager is the best person to see that management does things straight.

Manufacturing policy

In talking about the work of the production manager we have tended to describe the world as it is, not the world as it ought to be. Production management is a difficult and demanding job involving endless hassle; any realistic account has to say that. This does not mean there is no chance for improvement, no place for systematic thought, for establishing objectives and deciding their priority, for a rational solution of operating problems. It is just that these things happen less than one would like, and it is only recently that the expression 'manufacturing policy' has emerged to cover them.

One of the funny things about production is not just that it tends to operate in a hand-to-mouth way, but that higher management takes this for granted. It is the natural state of things. One intervenes in manufacturing only if there is a threat of a strike or if those irresponsible idiots down there want to spend £2 million on new plant.

Otherwise you let them get on with it, and hope there won't be too many foul-ups. Not only is this not an ideal state of affairs; it is also inconsistent. After all, for years we have had the notions of corporate strategy and business policy which are all about where the company as a whole is going, but only recently have there been the beginnings of an attempt to develop a policy for manufacturing which will integrate it with overall company objectives.

There are several strands to the case for the evaluation of manufacturing policy. The first suggested above is logical; it is necessarily entailed by having a corporate strategy for the company as a whole in the first place. The second is what might be called arbitrational. Some of the classic conflicts, such as the conflict of interest between sales and production can in a certain sense be resolved at a higher level. One can think it through, that is, and decide what the primary objective is, and this will both show 'which side to favour' and justify it. If, for instance, the market is very competitive and salesmen can only compete by offering customers special modifications to suit individual needs, then this has to be recognized. Even then this does not just mean that production has to lump it: there are various things one can do to make handling modifications easier—lengthen the lead times, have a separate section for 'specials', employ more skills–versatile labour, and so on. The third reason in favour of developing a manufacturing policy is that it should illuminate key problems, the ones which are worth solving rather than tolerating. If, for instance, raising quality and reducing scrap is a really critical issue then one can pour in talent and resources to solve it—better equipment, more training, checking out the quality of suppliers, instituting medial inspection, setting up Japanese-style quality circles (see the discussion in Chapter 9), and so on.

Finally, we might introduce two ideas propounded by the American, Wickham Skinner, who is particularly associated with the emergence of manufacturing policy. Skinner speaks of the Equipment Process Technology (EPT), which is the technical and organizational system for making something. Skinner's basic point is that the EPT cannot do everything well, it cannot deliver fast, and cheap, and high volume, and high quality, and be very flexible all at the same time. So devising or utilizing any EPT involves trade-offs of the it-may-be-expensive-but-it-enables-us-to-introduce-new-designs-fast kind. One needs manufacturing policy to identify objectives and harmonize these with the EPT.

But perhaps Skinner's breakthrough is to expose the fallacy of some taken-for-granted wisdom. This is that it is always right to aim at low cost and high efficiency in production, isn't it? No, says Skinner, not always. Maybe the company is aiming at quality or flexibility or speed or excellence, and there will be a price to pay for them. The point of manufacturing policy is to identify manufacturing as a competitive resource, not just a candidate for cost cutting.

References

Gill, R. W. T. and Lockyer, K. G. (1979). *The career development of the production manager in British industry*. British Institute of Management, London.

Husband, T. and Barker, B. A. (1976). Maintenance engineering—the current state of the art. *Prod. Eng.*, February.

Lockyer, K. G. and Jones, S. (1980). The function factor. *Management today*, September, pp. 56–64.

Lyall, G. (1982). *Blame the dead*. Pan Books, London.

Further reading

Hill, T. J. (1984). *Production/operations management*. Prentice-Hall International, London.

Wild, R. (1980). *Operations management: a policy framework*. Pergamon, Oxford.

Skinner, W. (1978). *Manufacturing in the corporate strategy*. John Wiley and Sons, New York.

Lawrence, P. (1984). *Management in action*. Routledge and Kegan Paul, London.

Questions

1. What is meant by 'production is a central function'?
2. British industry has a poor record for delivering on time. What causes can be inferred from the discussion in this chapter?
3. Is it true to say that manufacture is best described as a variable sequence?
4. The who controls whom question is never more significant than in the relationship between production and associated functions.' Discuss.
5. What is manufacturing policy, and how may it be linked to overall corporate strategy?

(a) THE BATTLE OF THE PASSES

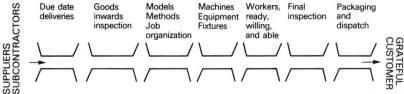

(b) THE MANUFACTURING CLOCK

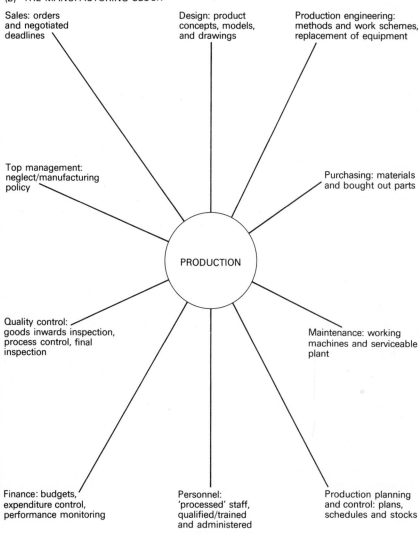

Summaries for Chapter 6.

7   Sales

Most introductory books have a chapter on marketing rather than on sales, and there are good reasons for this. Marketing is a bigger concept, it logically precedes sales, and it encompasses sales. Nonetheless, we want to talk primarily about sales rather than marketing in this chapter, and will give reasons for the choice. But the first thing to tackle is the difference between sales and marketing.

Sales and marketing

Marketing is a great idea. It is, by origin, an American business inspiration, and its practice marks off modern business from the crude 'we make it, you take it' philosophy of an earlier age.

The essential idea is that the market is king. The goods or services on offer are fashioned, designed, and oriented to a preconceived market in terms of actual or potential customers.

So the marketing concept involves a lot of things, and we try to show some of the range and indicate where sales fits into marketing in the next two sections on the Marketing Mix and the Four Ps. But the general consideration is that the business organization needs to be geared to marketing; after all, there is no point in making something the customer does not want, though in practice a lot of companies seem to be geared to production with the unfortunate salesman trying to sell whatever production happens to make. Marketing then is a big concept. Sales is part of it, but marketing is also about product image, branding, packaging, advertising and more besides.

Sales on the other hand is quite simply about selling, about getting someone else—a company, wholesaler, stockist, retailer, member of the general public, government department, local authority, public utility or whatever—to buy something.

Selling covers seeking out potential new customers and maintaining relations with existing ones; it involves calling, persuading, demonstrating, negotiating, and on good days actually taking orders.

Sales is active and tangible, whereas much of marketing is about thinking and planning, or has a 'back room' touch to it. Marketing, therefore, embraces sales strategy; gathering information helpful to salesmen; analysing sales results; making decisions on prices and distribution channels and advertising; gathering market intelligence (demand forecasts and the strength of the competition); and calculating which product lines, operating divisions, sales areas, customers, or types of deal are most profitable.

This difference between sales and marketing is reflected in the higher education system. Marketing can be divided up into topics, analysed and systematized, and as such is very teachable. So marketing is a standard subject in management and business courses in universities and polytechnics. Sales, on the other hand, hardly exists as a respectable academic subject. Courses in sales are provided by the private sector (consultants and entrepreneurial salesmen) in the form of high-fee one-day courses in London hotels, and not by the universities. Marketing has generated a vast literature, much of it theoretical in form; books on sales are far fewer, practical and exhortatory in tone, and are often along the lines of 'how to win friends and influence people'.

Having said all this the sales versus marketing distinction gets blurred in practice in several ways. First, except for companies or manufacturing units engaged in internal trading (discussed and illustrated in Chapter 2) all companies have sales, but they do not necessarily have a specialist marketing function. Second, where there is no such specialized marketing function, sales will tend to encompass some of the aspects of marketing referred to above, albeit in a random and amateur way. So salesmen will appraise customers and products for profitability, note the effect of advertising, feedback customer wishes which may eventuate in new products, and so on. And again in the absence of a specialized marketing department, top management may still be taking marketing decisions regarding prices, product range, and distribution methods, for instance. Third, there is the question of language cosmetics: the usual view is that marketing 'sounds nicer' than sales, so what appears on the organization chart of any given company as marketing may in fact be primarily sales; the (so-called) marketing manager may be running a fleet of salesmen.

This chapter is mostly about sales rather than marketing. It is about what salesmen are like, and what they do, how they go about it, and what problems they encounter. This choice does not detract from the importance of marketing, but is based on several other considerations, already hinted at. Sales is not well covered in the existing literature, unlike marketing, and in higher education courses it is hardly covered at all. What is more, concentrating on sales is in line with the philosophy of this book which is to focus on the 'sharp end' of management work. Nevertheless, we can helpfully set the scene with some ideas from the marketing literature, which should help to amplify our understanding of marketing, and where sales fits.

The marketing mix

An American, Borden, coined the phrase and developed the idea of the marketing mix (Borden 1964). It is really two ideas conjoined, simple yet revolutionary. The first is that companies do *a variety* of things to sell their goods and services; it's not just about price, or excellence of design, or the comprehensiveness of the guarantee, or whatever. So this variety of things is the mix. The second idea is that the mix is variable. To put it negatively this mix is not static; it is not a question of say three parts price and one part advertising, across the board. Or to put it positively, companies emphasize different things (part of the mix) at different times. It is quite clear in practice that this variation does occur, even though we cannot plot all the patterns and determinants. This leads to another question: what are the basic ingredients of the mix?

The four Ps

In fact there is no single answer to this question. Or to put it another way, various writers have formulated different mixes. But there is no doubt that the most generally accepted version is that popularized by another American, E. Jerome McCarthy, known as the four Ps (McCarthy 1964). These are Product, Price, Place, and Promotion, and they show well where selling and the salesman fit in.

The first two Ps are very straightforward. *Product,* of course, covers the notions of the excellence of design, the appeal and utility of the product, its reputation for quality and reliability, the availability of spares where relevant, as well sometimes as the nature of the guarantee and the after-sales service. *Price* is not only unit price but also on occasion the cost of things which have to go with the item purchased (underlay for carpets, high-reach forklift trucks for modern warehouses). Price may also be modified by reductions for quantity, discounts, special offers, particular deals, or according to a tiered market system (for example, sales at different prices to manufacturers, stockists, or the general public).

Place in McCarthy's formulation does not actually mean location, but distribution channel, the process whereby things made reach, or are made available, to the end-users. In the marketing literature the emphasis is not so much on physical distribution (loading, transporting, and storing), but on the institutional arrangements in the sense of the use of wholesalers and stockists, retailers and direct outlets (mail order or onsite selling), franchise arrangements and so forth. And finally, *Promotion* connotes both advertising and publicity on the one hand and personal selling (what salesmen do) on the other.

These ideas of the marketing mix and the four Ps are not perfect; there are, for instance, overlaps between the four Ps, and sometimes the distinctions break down. But they certainly capture some of the variation in practice. It is clear, for example, that steel is sold primarily on a product basis, that the sale of detergents owes a great deal to promotion, that forecourt petrol sales are heavily price-determined, and the sale of airline tickets is much affected by the system of outlets from airline office to bucket shop. These schemes are also helpful in showing where sales 'fits in' and in demonstrating that the salesman's work is contingent on these factors of price and distribution system, promotional advertising and product features.

Images and distinctions

One of the distinctive things about the salesman's job is that the general public does have a picture of it, in contrast to, say, the job of the buyer, personnel officer, or production superintendent. Like most of the general images we have it is partly right and partly wrong but above all it fails to differentiate—it tends to assume that all salesmen do much the same thing in the same way. A large part of this chapter goes along with the assumption by giving a general account and stressing common features, but it is important to make some of the distinctions clear too. A quick look at the patterned note summary at the end of the chapter (p.152) will help to orient the reader.

In the foregoing discussion of the marketing mix and the four Ps we have been pointing up these distinctions implicitly. These ideas show us that the sheer importance of personal selling varies a lot from case to case. So at the weak end of the scale the salesman may be simply taking orders generated by forceful advertising, towering product quality, or irresistibly low prices; at the strong end the salesman may bear the whole burden of introducing and exploring, negotiating and persuading for a single sale to take place.

There are some other distinctions.

First, there is the very simple one between selling capital goods and consumer goods. Consumer goods are destined ultimately for the general public, usually via the mechanism of wholesalers, and then retailers (stores, shops, and stalls). Capital or industrial goods are sold to other companies, utilities, public authorities and sometimes governments. This simple distinction is buttressed by some further generalizations. Personal selling is reckoned to be more important in the case of what we call here industrial selling: the salesman in this case will be dealing with well-informed professional buyers, other managers, or public officials, not (gullible) members of the general public. This consideration puts a higher demand on the salesman's knowledge of the product and its application, his preparation and skill. This is an important reason why we will tend to emphasize industrial selling in the present chapter. It is also reckoned that promotional advertising is more important for consumer goods, and it is more general in form and appeal. Advertising for industrial goods tends to be more specialized, and technical, and fact and capacity-based.

In the previous paragraph we glossed over the fact that consumer goods, destined for the general public, are often sold to wholesalers or retail chains in the first instance. This simple fact has important implications. It means that salesmen for consumer goods are also frequently dealing with professional buyers, and even if the product is simple the negotiations may be tough. And this setup illustrates the importance of the marketing mix idea, where the salesman is directing his efforts at retail buyers while his company is directing its promotional activities at the general public.

Second, there is an equally simple distinction between selling goods and selling services. In a way this distinction is not obvious because most of the marketing literature focuses on the sale of goods rather than services, and again many services seem so obviously a part of our daily lives as not to require much selling (hairdressing, car servicing, going to the swimming pool, pub or pantomime). But commonsense is not a good guide in this matter. As has been pointed out in Chapter 1, the service sector (or the tertiary sector as economists call it) has been expanding at the expense of the secondary or manufacturing sector, indeed this has been happening in pretty well all the rich industrial countries (apart from West Germany). What is more, some of the services now on offer are of considerable sophistication and complexity, especially those intended for industry—from consultants, banks, and computer bureaux for instance. Having said this it has to be admitted that the distinction between goods and services sometimes breaks down. Take computers. Although a computer is undoubtedly a product it tends to be sold as a service—in terms of its capacity to solve problems or manipulate information.

Third, it is important to distinguish between the salesman who is primarily concerned with getting new business and the one who is mostly involved in repeat orders. Again our popular image of the salesman includes the notion of doing deals and signing contracts, yet for many salesmen this is a pretty rare event. Imagine being a salesman for a paint manufacturer; the work will be almost entirely repeat-order business, visiting other manufacturers who must buy paint for their products, and the only question is how much of which kinds they need for the next week's production run. Or consider as an archetypal example of repeat-order selling the work of a yarn salesman (yarn for carpet manufacture). The salesman described the operation as follows in an interview: 'Really an account-minding operation, as distinct from an account-developing operation. You had no authority whatsoever to negotiate prices; they were fixed for given quantities so selling as such didn't exist. You were going once a month to a customer, and going through his planned take-off for the next month for each type of product they were taking'. In other words, no question of whether to buy, only of how much, when. At the other end of the scale a salesman for Telecoms Gold, the electronic mail system whereby incoming mail is stored at a central computer and accessed by 'the recipient' at any convenient computer terminal, will be operating almost entirely in terms of 'first-time buyers'. Of course there are intermediate positions, where new order and repeat-order business is mixed. A salesman selling tail-lifts for lorries, say, will expect to sell replacement and additional tail-lifts to present customers (transport fleet operators), take business from rivals, and also identify new entrants to the road haulage business who need this gear. There is also a variation on the theme where initial sales to a customer lead to further sales going beyond the simple replacement model. Imagine for example being a word processor salesman. You sell a word processor and some printers to a company, and immediately acquire a quite valuable service contract. The purchasing company will also buy paper and floppy discs and self-replacement parts from the selling company. But beyond this is also the possibility that the company which buys the word processor realizes that it really needs two of them, and that the six other works in the group should be similarly equipped. And if the company does not realize this spontaneously the salesman might help them along the road of greater understanding. This is called 'milking the customer base'.

Fourth, the power of the buyer is important in the salesman's way of going about his persuasive task, and even for the pattern of the marketing mix. This power consideration is relevant in industrial selling where the typical buyer is another company. Now clearly the bigger the potential buying company, the more it will expect and be able to get a good deal, especially with regard to price. But buyer power in this sense is not only a matter of size, but of the extent to which company purchasing is centralized. Some very large companies are divisionalized or decentralized or organized in a way which gives considerable autonomy to subdivisions or individual works, so that purchases may be made at works level and the great size of the parent company is negated. Or in another organization the phenomenon is reversed, where for instance the needs of a host of, say, tiny village primary schools are catered for by the centralized buying power of the county education authority, who get the cheapest cricket balls in Europe. Such considerations of size and centralization matter a great deal to salesmen.

There is another twist. The highly centralized (or large) institutional buyer is usually buying phased consignments rather than making a unique purchase. Thus such a company is likely to be entering into some contractual arrangement with its suppliers. A salesman representing one of these suppliers knows that he will have to offer a competitive price (or terms) in the first instance (the centralized power of the buyer works to his disadvantage), but thereafter the salesman may be able to finesse through price rises without a lot of difficulty, because it will simply be too much hassle for the centralized company to change to another supplier (the centralized power of the buyer works to the salesman's advantage).

Fuel oil is a good example of this phenomenon. The price varies a lot, even from day to day. Salesmen representing the oil companies do emphasize price to their customers, but the fluctuations are too numerous for it to be possible to quote a standard price. Instead the salesman will tell potential customers that his company's oil has never varied more than say 5 per cent of the mean market price over such and such a period; or better still has varied only within the limits of 2 per cent above and 5 per cent below! In this case the centralized buyer is likely to drive a hard bargain at the start of the contract, and whenever it comes up for renewal, but in between will be insensitive to price fluctuations and highly unlikely to change to another supplier. But the independent transport operation running three lorries may well change if the competition can offer him a better price on Tuesday than you did on Monday. Of course a good salesman knows all this: but what is a good salesman?

The salesman

If one checks the backgrounds and qualifications of salesmen and women there is incredible variety: a mix of graduates and non-graduates; people who have moved sideways from other jobs in the same company (costing, testing, customer support, field repairs, and so on); former manual workers and ex-professionals; people trained at business schools, on company schemes, or not at all. Indeed it is clear that selling has been a way up for people who began in some quite humble job but who 'had a bit of personality' and managed to catch somebody's eye. If one talks to salesmen one also finds some who had, or were trained for, old-fashioned professional jobs but gave them up for the excitement of sales work. When it comes to personality, however, there is a pattern—salesmen themselves are conscious of what makes a good salesman, and ready to list the features.

A salesman needs a high degree of self-discipline to be a success. Remember most of the time he is working alone, away from the company that employs him. He can 'hit the road' at 6.30 am or after lunch, play golf or talk to prospects. Of course there are some controls—sales reports, periodic sessions with the area sales manager, comparative breakdowns of calls or orders—but all this takes some time to bite. The successful salesman is going to be a self-starter.

He needs to be resistant too. After all 'you can't win them all'; selling is a job with built-in disappointment and intermittent failure. Sometimes failure to get an order will come after considerable time and effort has been spent, and the salesman has to be able to shrug it off and start again. He also needs to be strong-minded enough to walk away from a sales prospect when the signs are that the negotiation is not going to lead anywhere.

One of the effects of recession is to increase the salesman's need to be numerate. The recession means pressure on prices so the salesman will often be caught up in calculations of margins, discounts, subsidies, and rebates. Sometimes he will be drawn into costing purchases or operations for potential customers as well. To give a strong example, salesmen for companies making fertilizer may find themselves doing cash-flow forecasts for farmers to demonstrate both how quickly the purchased fertilizer will pay for itself, and how in fact the farmer does have enough money to buy it from current income.

Salesmen tend to stress the importance of general awareness, being wide-awake and on the ball. They are, after all, constantly seeking information about who might need what, evaluating possible sales leads, trying to find their way around someone else's company to talk to the right person, looking for clues as to what the prospect really wants and what will turn him on.

The need for technical competence and product knowledge varies a good deal, but is obviously most important in industrial selling to specialized users rather than to retailers serving the general public. But it is also fair to say that this requirement is rising generally as the industrialized countries move their manufacturing up market and leave the more routine stuff to countries with lower labour costs (the Third World) or zero strike records (USSR). The recession also has an effect here by making the search for new applications for existing products, rather than the development of new products, more attractive. This again puts a premium on the salesman's technical and product knowledge.

There are three other themes which come up regularly in discussions with salesmen. The first will surprise the more cynical reader: it is the importance of integrity. False claims for products are counterproductive, so are delivery promises which can't be kept. The salesman is also privy to all sorts of privileged information about his clients and their companies and this has to be respected. There is too the moral–tactical problem of the salesman's competitors. On this point both the textbooks and the salesman's folklore are in agreement: do not denounce your business rivals—just hope that the customer will do that for you.

The next thing is what everyone knows, that the salesman has to be good at getting on with people. Not only does the salesman deal with a lot of different people, in the sense of a whole series of retail managers, or buyers at different companies; sometimes he has to sell to different sets of people as part of the same operation. The industrial paint salesman, for instance, may deal with purchasing managers in a contractual sense but he also needs to convince people in production that his paint is right for the job. Someone selling tail-lifts for lorries will do business with fleet managers but needs to persuade fitters and mechanics as well. A fertilizer salesman is usually selling his wares to merchants while at the same time running a parallel sales campaign with individual farmers to get them to ask for his brand when they go to the merchant. Getting on with a variety of people is not just a matter of projecting his own personality, but of being sensitive to the needs and wishes of others. A salesman who talks all the time is a failure, whatever the popular image. When he is talking; he can't be listening, and listening is the key.

Lastly, the salesman needs, and is very conscious of needing, a positive attitude. He has to see doors opening not closing, to consider opportunities in a positive and confident way. Believing that something is going to happen is not usually enough to make it happen, but it certainly helps.

Targets of opportunity

Salesmen whose work involves a high proportion of what the American textbooks call 'missionary selling' (new orders as opposed to account minding) must begin by identifying potential customers. There is a range of ways to do this. Probably the most basic is the use of trade directories such as *Kompas* or *Dun and Bradstreet*. The purpose is to identify buyer–user possibilities: are there in the area any manufacturers whose products need painting, and premises that need heating, any administrative entities whose work could be speeded up using word processors, any retail outlets that could be brought into the existing chain, or whatever the selling company's interest is? When the possibles have been identified the next step is to 'mail shot' them (send them appropriate literature) or 'cold call' them (go and see them on the offchance).

Another method of attracting potential customers is by being represented at a trade fair or exhibition. Exhibition stands are so expensive these days, however, that this traditional method is probably in decline, especially for big well-known companies who will get talked about even more if they are not present at a major exhibition (consider the stir that would follow if British Leyland did not have a stand at the Motor Show). This has given rise to the growing popularity of the mobile display caravan, now common for instance for the sale of double glazing, cavity wall insulation, telephone accessories, and garden ware (some companies in West Berlin, where skilled labour is in short supply, use the trailer method for recruiting craftsmen!).

Seminars are another method which is growing in popularity. These are particularly appropriate for attracting, and warming up, possible customers for a new technology product or service, where there is a burden of explanation on the seller. So demo-seminars on, say, the role of the computer in materials requirements planning for production controllers are common, or sessions for estate agents showing the distinctive contribution the word processor could make to their business. Seminars, incidentally, appeal particularly to East European buyers, who see them as a chance to steal the west's technical secrets—and get free Scotch!

Advertising is the most fundamental method for stimulating actual or potential customers, even if this advertising is not handled by the salesman himself. Such advertising ranges from general TV adverts for consumer goods to more customer specific advertising in the trade press (or in executive magazines such as Management Today). Probably the most specific form of trade advertising is with magazines that offer a reader-reply service, whereby each advertiser is given a number, and the reader circles the number of some product or service in which he is interested on a grid on the back of the magazine. The reader might, for instance, have an interest in forklift trucks, and would then circle number 16 (Lift'em Ltd). The card grid would then be sent to the editors of the magazine, who collect together all the enquiries and send off the names and addresses of interested parties to the manufacturer concerned. These are passed on to the salesman, who has to decide whether they are:

(1) genuine enquiries;
(2) people who want pictures for the bedroom wall;
(3) competitors who want the latest specifications.

Word-of-mouth communication provides a miscellany of sales leads and is the most pervasive of the methods discussed here. This again ranges from the unprogrammable results of chat in hotel bars and airport lounges (undoubtedly the most important) to highly specific recommendations. In the case of the electronic mail system referred to earlier, a lot of the salesman's leads are the result of the parent company telling its subsidiaries to get themselves into the twenty-first century.

Sometimes, of course, identifying potential new customers is a matter of imaginative thinking or making reasoned connections, rather than the well-tried methods listed earlier. Imagine, for instance, you have hotel rooms to sell, weekdays, in a non-tourist area. To say that the customers will be 'businessmen' is true but unhelpful; it does not tell you how to get at them. In this case advertising and personal selling has to be directed towards those who arrange and assign rather than to the end-users. So the people to go for are personnel and training managers in companies who organize away from home training courses, or require job applicants to present themselves for interview; sales managers who organize travelling salesmen (and the individual salesman's secretary) are good hits in the same way, as are firms of consultants and accountants who are endlessly sending their staff out to advise and audit.

Or again imagine you are selling advertising space in a magazine; in this case you have to know the target market for the company you are trying to sell this space to. A magazine with say 75 per cent of the readership in what the advertisers call the AB socioeconomic groups (the top two) may well appeal to producers of quality cognac brandy or owners of fine art showrooms, but will not provide an effective showcase for a non-stick frying pan offer.

What do you want to know?

Selling is a constant struggle for information. The search for potential new customers discussed above is just the start. In his dealings with potential customers, indeed with everyone at the buying organization, the salesman is looking for clues as to the buyer's intentions. Are they serious or is he just playing around; what does he want; what will hold him back; what will be decisive?

The answers to some of these questions will be structured by organizational factors. So when the salesman visits the company of a potential customer he may have a desperate need to know their capital budget: this will be absolutely crucial for capital equipment sales such as machine tools or materials handling equipment. Similarly the salesman may need to know if the potential buyer has taken any decisions in principle as to how to spend the budget. Imagine again trying to sell magazine space to an advertising agency acting for a manufacturer. Knowing the agency's budget for this client is not enough. Suppose they have decided to concentrate on TV advertising; after a few 30-second adverts on London Weekend Television at £13 000 a time they will not have much left for you.

Another related piece of information is the customer's fiscal year. This gives the clue to when they have money to spend, and when they are soft-pedalling waiting for the next lot. This time-span of the budget may also indicate urgency on the part of the buyer—maybe they have to spend the money by the end of the budgetary period, say next month. This is good news: the salesman's favourite word is now.

The salesman will also be trying to find his way around the customer's organization. What is the hierarchy, who reports to whom, who is responsible for what? Above all the salesman is struggling to identify the MAN—the person with the Money to spend, the Authority to make the decision, and the Need for the product or service the salesman is offering.

Not all the information that is helpful to the salesman is to be obtained in this face-to-face interactive way at the client's organization. In some cases information about the state of the economy, or particular sectors, is important. Many goods which are the subject of industrial selling are conditioned by the demand and output of something else. Thus sales of sheet glass are heavily conditioned by the state of the construction and automobile industries, the sale of paint by the electrical goods industry, and so on. There may be regional differences too. For instance, a fall in mortgage interest rates is good for the sale of alcohol in the south (higher disposable income, let's celebrate), and not in the north where too many people live in council houses.

Companies also like to know their market share, though sometimes this is difficult to get hold of. Where it is difficult, one resort is to visit the customers of rivals, and to look at the serial or batch numbers of their latest consignment. The number of, say, machines or batches supplied in a year is often contained in this code. If, for example, one notes on two visits the codes 55/82 and 65/82 this suggests that 65 units have been supplied in 1982 and that ten units were sold in the period between the two visits. Market share analysis is not always an exact science. But it can be useful knowledge in two ways. If the market share is increasing, this itself can be used as a selling argument along the lines of: 'Our market share has increased over the last two years, which I think you will agree means we must have a superior product'. Or again, market share information provides not only a rough measure of a company's competitive success, but also gives something to aim at (for example, 15 per cent now, 18 per cent by 1986).

The game of selling

The marshalling of persuasive arguments is the crux of the selling operation, Having made this simple point it has to be said that there are a lot of angles.

We have suggested before that sometimes the salesman has to work on/sell himself to several people in different positions in the same organization in order to effect a sale. Consider, for example, selling lubricants. Here the salesman may have to sell himself to the

(1) machine shop foreman,
(2) machine operator,
(3) production engineer,
(4) production director,
(5) stores manager,

and then end up negotiating a formal supply contract with a purchasing manager. The point at issue is that the salesman needs adaptability as well as agreeableness. This problem is much less marked with repeat-order selling where the salesman has an opportunity to build up a stable relationship with many customers. Nevertheless, these interpersonal considerations structure the marshalling of relevant selling arguments.

In these struggles for acceptability and right communication the salesman is going to try to avoid alienating anyone. To a large extent this is done by negative precautions—by being well-groomed, polite, punctual, and moderate in speech and (implied) habit. It is said that IBM requires its salesmen to wear white shirts, dark suits, and no beards; this is not meant to suppress their individuality but is based on the belief that this is the sartorial formula least likely to offend anyone.

Again it is important for the salesman to talk to the right level and in an appropriate manner. A computer salesman, for instance, addressing a seminar where the audience consists largely of managing directors must use general terms like overall efficiency, reduction of cash-flows and improvement of customer service and dispatch levels. Data processing managers, on the other hand, will want to know about Megabytes, CPU's, and Modem capabilities.

Where there is a divorce in the client organization between the decision-maker and the buyer, the salesman will struggle to maintain contact with the latter. Consider, for example, a computer salesman who invites the managing director of another company to a seminar or presentation. The managing director probably sends someone from the management services department, but afterwards, in order to keep in contact with the managing director, the salesman may write to him along these lines:

Dear Mr So and So,
I was delighted to see your Mr X at our presentation. I understand that he believes the system could have advantages for your company which I would like to take further. May I suggest that we meet on ...

In the earlier discussion of the personality and attributes of the good salesman we have referred to the importance of product knowledge. Demonstrating technical competence will help the salesman to sell himself and his product, though the degree of latitude varies. In some industries if the salesman is asked questions to which he does not know the answer, the honest reply 'I don't know, I'll find out and come back on that one' will be acceptable and the salesman will maintain his credibility. In other, usually less technically complex, industries the salesman is expected to know all the answers. The buyer does not want to know that the salesman is not a systems specialist or auto-electrician; he wants to know the answer.

The persuasive argument may well take the form of a related or even unrelated service. We mentioned earlier that the fertilizer salesman may well produce cash-flow calculations for farmers. Among those who sell to farmers, whether directly or indirectly, such services may include soil analysis, yield estimate, and various species of agro-counselling. Unrelated gifts may also have a positive effect. A photocopier salesman told one of the authors that for years he told prospective customers that this month the company was making a special offer of some particular camera to anyone who bought a photocopy machine (as soon as someone placed an order he would go round the corner to Boots and buy the camera).

Again it may be critical not so much to stress the product as the desirable consequences which will follow its acquisition—greater efficiency, lower operating costs, fast payback, or the solution of hitherto intractable problems. But the consequences may be more lyrical than these, as is suggested by the Revlon executive who claimed that the company was 'selling hope'. To take a middle-of-the-road example, a hotel in central Birmingham may be sold on the grounds that it will facilitate pleasant excursions to Stratford-upon-Avon and Shakespeare country.

A potential customer may only be persuaded of the rightness of the salesman's claims by a visit to the premises of another customer who has already acquired the product in question—this is almost *de rigeur* for the sales of machine tools in West Germany for example. This can be made more compelling by building in a 'fun' factor, too. We know of one British equipment manufacturer who arranges demo weekends for potential American customers and their wives—they include Saturday morning shopping in London for the wives, and 'an evening in a real English pub' for the husbands, as well as the hard sell.

An appeal to patriotism may be a lever the salesman, or company, can use. Some British Leyland plants have segregated car parks for visitors who arrive in foreign cars, and indeed national economic interest has come to figure large in some car advertising. Perhaps the best case is that of Volvo who sell in the United Kingdom on the argument that most of the components are British. Salesmen for (indigenous) oil companies may well use 'Why do you buy from the Americans?' as a starter in the battle to get established users to change suppliers.

There are also cases, as was suggested in Chapter 5 on purchasing, where the seller is able to undertake some development or design work for the buyer, or perform very well on technical liaison. If this is the buyer's need, it may be the best argument at the salesman's disposal.

In cases where several companies offer a very similar product or service there is likely to be price competition among them. But precisely because the product or service is similar it is likely to be difficult for any one supplier to win the price war outright. This may mean that they seek some other form of differentiation, that these salesmen urge some other consideration. Again oil offers a good example. In the 1973–74 oil crisis, BP among the oil companies in Britain did very well in maintaining continuity of supply to its customers. This fact is still used by BP salesmen to mark off their company from rivals.

Early in the present chapter we propounded McCarthy's notion of the four Ps, involving a discussion of the relevance of price in marketing. Although the salesman does not usually fix the price, it is up to him to do all he can with the price structure, discounts, and differentials at his disposal. It is a sad fact in Britain that the Chancellor of the Exchequer regularly raises the duty on alcohol at each budget. In anticipation salesmen encourage their customers to place bumper orders in March at the old (pre-budget) prices. More frequently, however, manufacturers determine price and price changes, and their salesmen use price to help them get a sale where they can. Some sales to farmers are again a good example. Fertilizer is a seasonally used product—used mainly in the spring and autumn. Since storage costs are high, an early delivery rebate system is used to get farmers (via their merchants) to purchase their fertilizer in June and then store it themselves, rather than the manufacturer having to store it until autumn. And if a farmer lives near to a store he may be able to collect the fertilizer himself, save haulage costs, and thus enjoy a further price reduction.

If the price is wrong, or simply uncompetitive, a salesman can work 24 hours a day and still have little to show for it. Alcohol again provides an illustration where a salesman of our acquaintance made a concerted effort to increase sales of spirits at cash and carry stores calling every week to ensure that the shelves were always full. Sales did not increase because the main rival brand was slightly cheaper. In fact sales only increased when the rival's product was sold out, and was off the shelf for three days.

But to offer a final example of a more positive kind it should be said that companies are sometimes ingenious in the quasi-price manoeuvres they engage in. A Scottish hotel chain operates a scheme aimed at business travellers. When a businessman stays at one of this company's hotels he is given a blank card which is ruled off into squares. Every time he stays at one of the company's hotels a square is stamped. When the card is full he and his family are entitled to a free weekend at any of the company's hotels.

Throughout what we call here the game of selling, however, the salesman's most important function remains the alert quest for clues as to the real needs of the buyer. These may not be obvious. Consider here our favourite example, paint. Suppose a manufacturing company uses 100 000 litres of paint every year, and the paint buyer is unhappy about using this volume of paint. The salesman may think that the buyer is dissatisfied on account of the expense, and may suggest a price reduction. While this will undoubtedly be accepted, the buyer may still not be satisfied. The approach should be to propose a paint that will do the job with only two coats instead of three. Even if this new paint has a higher unit cost, it will still satisfy the buyer's need—to reduce paint volume.

Closing the sale

If we were all perfectly rational there would be no need for salesmen to develop techniques for closing a sale—but we are not, and there is. Throughout, the salesman is struggling against the customer's natural human reluctance to spend money, actually make a decision, exclude other options, and perhaps find he has made a mistake.

Salesmen have learned to cope with these human proclivities. Sometimes they prepare for the hurdle of the sales-close by inserting a trial close into the dialogue, something along the lines of which of these models would most fully meet the needs of your company? When it comes to it the salesman may simply adopt a direct approach and invite the potential customer to sign the order form feeling that all the groundwork has been done and there is little to fear.

A variation on this is to use what is called the assumptive close. In this the salesman speaks as though the order has already been placed, along the lines of 'you'll be surprised how much our word processor will speed up the work in your office' or 'would you like us to do installation for you as well'.

The alternative close is like the assumptive close but it offers the customer some choice while presupposing that the crucial decision to buy has already been taken. This is conveyed by a question like: 'Would you like it delivered straight away, or at the end of the month?'

A very common method is what the textbooks call the suppositional close. The salesman sets up the customer to commit himself while the salesman shoulders the burden of proof. It takes the form of a leading question in the form: 'If I can show you that our computer really will solve your production scheduling problems, are you ready to place an order?'

Salesmen who find this too bold may prefer a step-by-step approach where the customer is worked up to the final decision by being asked to confirm that all the ancillary questions have been settled:

'You agree that our price is competitive?'
'Our credit terms suit you?'
'You've agreed you like the de luxe model best?'
'And you feel the 2-year guarantee is a definite plus?'
'OK, let's sign!'

A lot of these are standard closes, appear in the textbooks and are taught on sales courses. What is more, they can be used for persuasive purposes other than those of commercial selling. Yet there is room for individuality. One salesman described to us what he called the puppydog close; it is based on a pet shop analogy where the potential customer is invited to hold the puppy (try out the product) which he will then find too endearing to relinquish. Where there is a will, there is an appropriate manoeuvre.

References

Borden, N. H. (1964). The concept of the marketing mix. *J. Advertis. Res.* 2–7.
McCarthy, E. J. (1964). *Basic marketing: a managerial approach*. Richard D. Irwin, Inc., Homewood, Ill.

Further reading

Cannon, T. (1980). *Basic marketing*. Holt Rinehart and Winston.
Cowell, D. (1984). *An introduction to the marketing of services*. Heinemann in conjunction with the Institute of Marketing, London.
Davidson, J.H. (1974). *Offensive marketing*. Penguin, Harmondsworth.
Enis, B. M. and Cox, K. K. (eds.) (1977). *Marketing classics: a selection of influential articles*, 3rd edition. Allyn and Bacon Inc., Boston.
Lund, P. R. (1974). *Compelling selling*. Macmillan Press Ltd., London.

Questions

1. 'Selling is selling; it is the same everywhere'. Do you agree?
2. To what extent is the idea of the four Ps
   (a) helpful?
   (b) watertight?
3. What qualities are needed for repeat-order/account-minding selling?
4. What does it mean to say that information and persuasion are the essence of personal selling?
5. How would you go about selling accommodation in a national hotel chain:
   (a) weekdays?
   (b) at weekends?

152 Sales

The Four P's

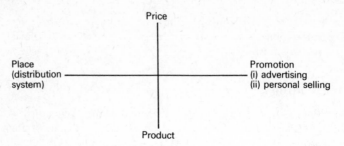

Sales situation variables

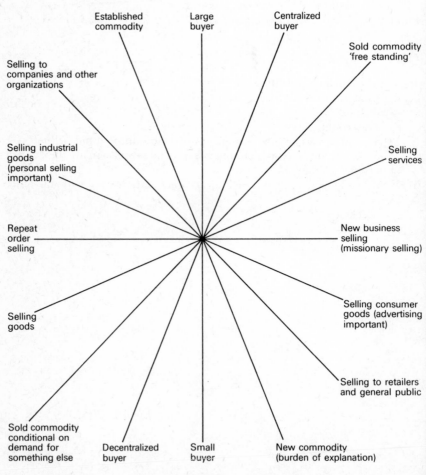

Summary for Chapter 7(a).

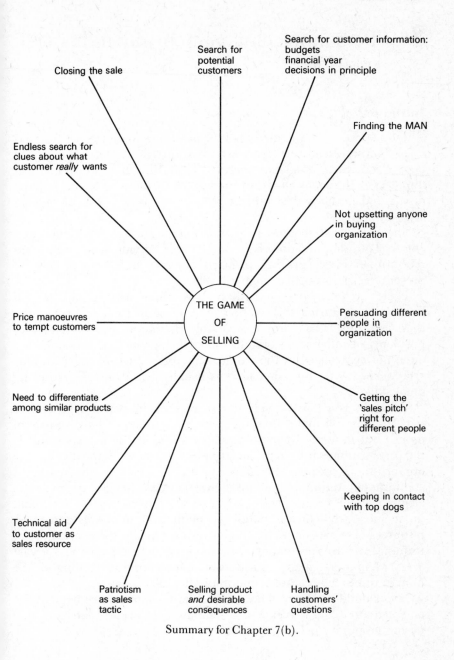

Closing the sale

Search for
potential
customers

Search for customer information:
budgets
financial year
decisions in principle

Finding the MAN

Endless search for
clues about what
customer *really* wants

Not upsetting anyone
in buying
organization

THE GAME
OF
SELLING

Price manoeuvres
to tempt customers

Persuading different
people in
organization

Need to differentiate
among similar products

Getting the
'sales pitch'
right for
different people

Technical aid
to customer as
sales resource

Keeping in contact
with top dogs

Patriotism
as sales
tactic

Selling product
and desirable
consequences

Handling
customers'
questions

Summary for Chapter 7(b).

8 Personnel management and industrial relations

Introduction

There are two main stereotypes of the personnel manager. In one he is a soft, rather ineffective figure who is primarily trying to be nice to people on the company's behalf. Often he has to implement unpleasant decisions made by managers in more powerful departments and he finds this difficult because he sees his role as looking after employees.

The second stereotype is a 'bureaucrat', a record keeper and enforcer of rules, an administrator who also attends negotiations and recruitment interviews but primarily to take notes or, at best, to present decisions taken at higher levels.

There are elements of truth in both these descriptions as will become clear during this chapter. The personnel department, more than any other, has problems of role definition and even greater problems of influencing organizational behaviour. Its functions are often not centralized in the hands of the personnel manager and his relationship with 'line' managers is usually a difficult one requiring great skill.

Yet there is a positive side to the work of the personnel manager too. He may not make anything, or sell anything, or have control of money but in many ways the resource for which he is responsible is the most important. Without people not much happens in any organization, success or failure is often related to the qualities, commitment and motivation of the workforce. They are the dynamic element which create goods and services, profits, wages, taxes and much more from lifeless buildings, plant, raw materials and other resources. The personnel function is responsible for their recruitment, training, welfare, promotion, pensions, payment systems and a vast array of matters, many routine but many more as exciting as the human resource is complex and unpredictable.

Let us build a picture of how the modern personnel department has emerged after over 80 years of development and return later to study its contemporary behaviour.

The development of the personnel function

In Chapter 1 we mentioned the changes in the nature of employment which the factory system brought about. The employee was, for many of the employing owners of the eighteenth and nineteenth centuries, simply a commodity to be bought as cheaply as the market would allow and worked as hard and for as long as possible. Working conditions were usually appalling by today's standards and there were none of the benefits we now expect, such as canteens, sick pay, pensions and training. Most employers were unconcerned about the welfare of those who toiled in their factories and it was not until trade unions became stronger, from the mid-nineteenth century onwards, and legislation began to emerge governing matters such as health and safety and the employment of children, that their treatment began to improve.

Even up to the First World War most owner-managers held the ethic 'a man has the right to do what he will with his own' and while in his employ labour was part of an owner's property. However, there were exceptions. Some employers such as Rowntree and Cadbury felt that employee welfare was their responsibility and emphasized the need for a 'living wage' and shorter hours to leave time for 'betterment and family life'. These men were motivated by religious belief, they were Quakers. In 1896 Seebohm Rowntree appointed the first welfare officer, a woman, to look after his employees in the confectionery industry. This was the acorn from which the personnel function grew.

Figure 8.1 represents the way the personnel function has developed

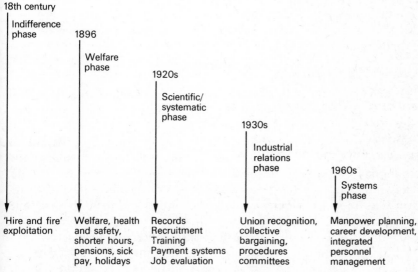

Fig. 8.1   Phases in the development of the personnel function.

through a number of identifiable phases. All the arrows continue to the present day to indicate the important point that there are still many firms which have not progressed beyond each phase and in fact only a small proportion would claim to have entered the systems phase. The factor not included in Fig. 8.1 is employment legislation. Unfair dismissal, redundancy, equal opportunities and a wide range of other areas are now influenced by law and even the least concerned company cannot be as exploitive as its earlier counterparts.

The welfare phase

By 1913 there were sufficient welfare workers for Seebohm Rowntree to call a conference in York which was attended by nearly 60 people. At this meeting the Welfare Workers' Association was formed, which has developed, through a number of names and formats, into the modern Institute of Personnel Managers, the professional body serving specialists in the personnel field.

The welfare tradition in personnel is concerned primarily with the physiological but also to some extent with the psychological and social needs of employees. The personnel manager may be responsible for ensuring that his premises comply with health and safety regulations, and in larger organizations for the provision of canteen facilities, and in better-off companies for the provision of sports and social amenities. Companies often offer their own sick pay and pension schemes which improve on those provided by the state. Many companies still employ a welfare officer who, on top of the responsibilities outlined above, is available to provide advice and practical help to employees who have problems, not necessarily directly related to work.

The scientific/systematic phase

The need to make the best use of available labour during the First World War helped to bring about the 'scientific' or, more accurately, 'systematic' phase of development.

In 1915 the government had established the Health of Munitions Workers Committee to investigate the influence of hours and conditions on output and health in the munitions industry. In the following year they had set up the Industrial Welfare Department, directed by Jesse Boot, in order to introduce new welfare and personnel practices into factories whose work was important to the war effort. These bodies and others also concerned themselves with job design, working conditions and training and selection for 'dilutees', those people, often women, who undertook the jobs of skilled workers who had been sent to the war front. Their efforts provided great impetus, and by the 1920s there were significant advances being made in areas such as selection and training. The aim was to develop techniques which would improve the effectiveness of these activities so that better people were chosen and training times reduced. This same tradition in personnel management has led to ideas such as job evaluation and personnel appraisal.

The scientific/systematic aspects of its work are so fundamental that we must explore some of them in more detail before progressing to the next phase of personnel's development. We shall focus on selection and appraisal because they are two of the major systems likely to affect the reader.

Selection

The long-term ability of an organization to survive and prosper depends not only on its financial assets and tangible resources but also on the quality and commitment of its work force. The human resource, however, is different from other organizational resources in that it does not readily submit itself to objective evaluation. Herein lies one of the major obstacles to 'scientific' techniques in many aspects of personnel management, and particularly the selection process that all of us have to go through at various stages in our lives.

In an attempt to improve the quality of new employees *systematic* procedures have been worked out which attempt to reduce the inevitable subjective element to an acceptable level. Furthermore they try to ensure that whatever subjective elements remain in the procedure are as visible as possible.

All selection procedures involve a number of stages from the following list:

(1) job analysis,
(2) job description,
(3) jobholder specification,
(4) recruitment,
(5) application form,
(6) short-listing,
(7) testing,
(8) interviewing,
(9) references,
(10) medical,
(11) analysis and selection.

There is no space here for describing the theoretical details of each stage, but let us consider them in outline as potential candidates for a particular job.

Most jobs will not involve each stage in the process; if we need a floor sweeper we may not bother with short-listing for example, we may simply take the first able-bodied applicant. And for some jobs the various stages will be more detailed than others. The application form for our new floor sweeper will be much briefer than that for a new production manager. Let us consider the latter case.

Before the job is advertised someone in the personnel department will have liaised with production on three related activities. Job analysis involves identifying the component parts of the job, the authority and responsibility it carries and the circumstances in which it is performed. For the production manager position much of this has probably already been written into a job description which will be sent with the application form when we respond to the advertisement. One problem here is that jobs change over time and a new jobholder may be expected to do the job in a different way. Job descriptions give an impression of accuracy and permanence which does not reflect reality. When reading them we have to remember the difficulties of measuring and describing such ambiguous concepts as skill and responsibility. 'What sort of person are they looking for?' is the question we are asking ourselves and the personnel department may ask it too, and draw up a jobholder specification. As an applicant, you would not see this, but you must attempt to work it out so that you can respond well to the application form and interview.

The jobholder specification is an interpretation of the job analysis and description in terms of the kind of person suitable for the job. One of the simplest formats used is to specify 'essential' and 'desirable' qualities of the jobholder; these may be fairly clear cut like academic qualifications or level of previous experience, or they may be more nebulous like level of self confidence or initiative.

Many organizations develop detailed specifications using a number of categories such as:

Physical attributes	Such as smart appearance conforming with the traditional expectations of the workforce.
Attainments and education	Such as good engineering background preferably to HND level, several years' experience with Widget machines, super-vision in a unionized situation, apprecia-tion of budgeting, costing and work study techniques.

Special aptitudes	Such as ability to cope with anticipated major production method changes and computerization, experience of robot-controlled machines useful.
Personality	Such as high ambition tempered by human qualities, need to be sympathetic to those affected by major changes and able to help deal with union resistance, but must not lose sight of targets.

By developing a clear picture of the desirable jobholder there is a much better chance of making a favourable appointment. The specification can be used when assessing applications in order to short-list, and later after the interviewing stage when making the final selection.

The first we know about the vacancy is when we come across the advertisement. The personnel manager will have already considered the option of recruiting internally and indeed there may be internal candidates against us. For the post of production manager he will have chosen the advertising medium with care, specialist journals perhaps or the quality press. The advertisements may tell us something about the jobholder specification: do they emphasize the need for someone with experience or for someone with drive and ambition? What do they say about wages, are they 'middle of the road' or 'high flyer' level?

The application form stage is often the hardest of all, especially in today's labour market. There may be over 100 applicants for a job and probably only four or five will be short-listed. The application form is not merely designed to obtain basic information about your experience and qualifications, it is the key to the short-list. If you cannot be bothered to spend the hours it requires getting it right at this stage then you are unlikely to reach the next. When you are asked to describe your previous achievements and your personal qualities and interests this is your chance to shine. You can do best if you have managed to deduce what the jobholder specification looks like so that you can emphasize your strong points and play down any weaknesses in advance. For example, if the advertisement asks for ten years' experience with Widget machines plus a knowledge of the new robot-controlled type it is possible that your wide experience of the new technology in non-Widget applications will earn you an interview in place of the applicant with 20 years' experience of the old technology only—if you fill in the form skilfully.

For many manual jobs the applicants would be subjected to a series of physiological tests designed to assess their eyesight, dexterity, coordination or whatever is required. For managerial jobs some firms have developed psychological tests designed to assess the factors which make a good manager.

If you recall the section on leadership in Chapter 3 you will already have identified the problems with such tests. What makes a good manager? Self-confidence, aggression, maturity, initiative, verbal skills, friendliness, ambition? How do we measure such qualities? How do we compare individuals who have different measures of each quality? The problems are enormous but many firms have their pet tests to which they subject all applicants even though they have no proof of their efficacy.

Selection tests are the idea of 'scientific selection' taken to the extreme. Tests of physiological qualities and certain mental skills are well tried, but beyond that the tests should at best be considered experimental. Selection is much more complex than simply measuring the size and shape of the organizational hole and specifying and identifying the right size and shape of employee to fill it. First, individuals mould jobs to their own personalities, jobs also change due to interaction with a dynamic environment. Furthermore, it is often not an objective matter as to what qualities are required to do a job well, and finally the individual himself interacts with his surroundings and will grow and change with time; the very fact of being selected for a job may change him.

At this stage, since we are considering practicalities rather than theory, we should also note the political background to the selection process. If the theory of a rational assessment of job and jobholder is carried through into the actual process it will help to remove the worst excesses of political behaviour and this is the main advantage of being systematic. But politics cannot be eliminated entirely. There are two main parties involved in the 'rational assessment', the personnel manager and the prospective superior. Who should have the major say in the selection process? The personnel manager stands apart from the internal politics of the recruiting department and he has expertise in selection techniques. On the other hand he is not an expert in the work to be done and has to rely for technical judgment on the prospective superior. There are clear political considerations for the functional superior to make: will the candidate be a threat with potential for taking over the superior's job? Might he reduce his power bases, perhaps by providing an alternative source of technical expertise? Might the candidate be a useful ally in some struggle within or between departments? The selection decision is often complex politically which is why the alert candidate who can detect signs and respond appropriately may be more successful than the 'rational' choice.

For example, a candidate for the production manager post may detect at the interview that the prospective boss is aware of the need for someone with knowledge of robotics but fears his own lack of expertise in this area. If the candidate emphasizes that he is highly competent in the technical aspects but appreciates that his new boss, with his awareness of the people involved, will have to help him tackle the most difficult human problems of change then he presents himself as an ally rather than a threat.

Nowhere is the politics of the selection process more crucial than at the interview stage. The commonest type of interview follows a semi-structured format with some questions prearranged by the interviewers so that they can assess each interviewee against their jobholder specification. If interviews are too tightly structured then discussion tends to remain superficial, so some 'open' questions are included and time is allowed to pursue some issues in depth. Open questions take the form 'What are your views on ...' and it is here that the candidate's ideas on what is wanted are put to the test.

After the interview, information on all the candidates will be sifted, including references, and the selection made. Hopefully the new appointee will not just be dropped into the job and forgotten but personnel should arrange for some sort of induction programme to introduce him to the ways of the company.

Appraisal

A more recent innovation into the systematic side of personnel work is employee appraisal. Employees have always been assessed in order to decide on promotions, training needs, pay increases and so on, but it is arguably much more effective to create a formal assessment system. This should ensure that everyone is appraised with the same care, and should help to facilitate comparisons between people and reduce bias by particular supervisors.

Appraisal systems tend to be used primarily for white-collar employees, the most highly structured systems being used in the armed forces and the civil service. In industry there are many systems flourishing and probably as many just creaking along with supervisors just filling in forms which are not used.

A well-designed and utilized appraisal system provides a useful database for many personnel decisions and can have an important motivating effect on employees, providing feedback on how well they are doing. Recognition and encouragement may make it all seem worthwhile, especially if promotion or a pay rise can result. The system helps to ensure that supervisors perform a coaching role for their subordinates and think about their motivation, ambition, ability, performance, and potential.

Most appraisal systems consist of two related parts, the paperwork and the interview. The paperwork can take a number of forms. Some systems ask supervisors to write a paragraph describing each subordinate, others use 'graphic rating scales' such as:

outstanding/above average/average/below average/unacceptable

in order to help the supervisor evaluate separate characteristics of each subordinate.

The best systems ask direct questions about promotion potential, achievements, ambitions and training needs, forcing the supervisor to consider these vital issues which are too often neglected in favour of the day-to-day task. Often the subordinate will fill in a self-assessment form in which he is asked to outline his own strengths, weaknesses and ambitions, and perhaps to make suggestions about how the organization can help him to perform better.

An appraisal system is more likely to have an impact on job performance if consideration of past achievements and future objectives is built in and given more central importance than less tangible factors such as attitudes and personality. Discussion of objectives is one of the key aspects of the appraisal interview.

The interview is, for many supervisors, the most difficult part of the appraisal process. Often they resent filling in the forms because it is time-consuming and shows no short-term return, but complaints about the appraisal system though directed at the forms, can, in many cases, be traced to nervousness about the interview.

Imagine that you are a supervisor and one of your subordinates, Alison, has just completed a year's service. She is very good at most aspects of her job but in her relationships with her colleagues and occasionally workers from other departments she has shown herself tactless and at times unpleasant. There has been nothing serious enough to warrant action at the time, but now you have to conduct an appraisal interview. Alison's self-assessment shows that she is ambitious and apparently unaware of the effect she has on other people. You are worried about her reaction to your entries in the 'promotion potential' and 'relationships with others' parts of the appraisal form. How would you handle the interview?

Thinking about how you would handle the interview with Alison should make it clear how difficult a task the supervisor faces. Sometimes the supervisor tries to impose his evaluation of the subordinate's inadequacies, and suggests changes in behaviour.

Usually it is more effective to stimulate subordinates to identify their own solutions and better still to encourage them to identify the problem in the first place. It is much easier if the interview centres around more concrete subjects such as the degree of achievement of goals agreed last time, and it looks forward to ways of improving performance for the next period.

From the personnel manager's point of view his problems start when the forms have been completed. What should be done with them? Often they are simply filed in case a promotion or transfer situation arises during the year. Sometimes where special training needs have been identified a course is arranged. The forms may well also provide the basis for the annual salary review.

Disenchantment with appraisal systems chiefly occurs when employees do not see them relating to a considered programme of career development. If a company lacks the will or the ability to build appraisal into its wider systems then it tends to become a pointless procedure. Ideally appraisal is not seen as a separate system but as part of the management way of life.

Selection and appraisal systems are in the scientific/systematic tradition of personnel which originated in the early 1920s. They have been improved over the years by both managerial innovation and contributions from the social sciences. The personnel manager also now has at his disposal a significant body of knowledge about training techniques, payment methods and systems of hours of work. Another well-developed area is that of job evaluation which is the study of procedures for comparing jobs so that they can be put into a logical grading structure. They can then be paid according to a more rational pattern than that which usually arises after years of piecemeal job creation and expedient pay rates. The problem with job evaluation, as with many personnel systems, is that it impinges on our next area of discussion, industrial relations. Pay rates, like selection and promotion, are often as much a result of power and politics as of rationality and system.

The industrial relations phase

Industrial relations is concerned with relationships between management and employees, it tends to focus mainly on the formal relationships between employee representatives and management representatives. In the United Kingdom the term 'industrial relations' conjures up pictures of the beleaguered personnel manager, or in larger organizations, the industrial relations manager, constantly battling against the hardbitten union negotiator. There is undoubtedly a 'them and us' flavour to British industrial relationships which is not matched in many of our western economic competitors. Nevertheless, perhaps we sometimes exaggerate our problems on this score. In Chapter 1 we briefly reviewed trade union history and pointed out the importance to any manager of competence in managing industrial relations. He will need to be aware of the main ways in which unions and management interact and the part he plays. It will also pay him to know something about union structure.

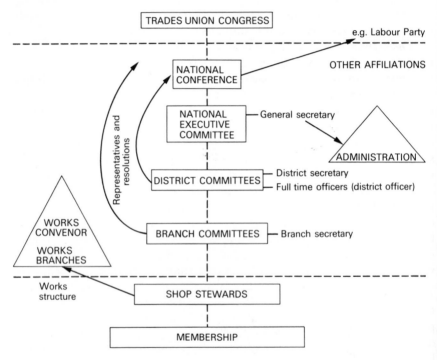

Fig. 8.2   Trade union structure.

Trade union structure

When drawing the structure of a business organisation we start at the top and work down. To understand the trade union, however, we start at the bottom, with the membership (Fig. 8.2). The union is financed by them and is designed to work for their interests.

Shop stewards The next level are the shop stewards. Most unions have great difficulty finding volunteers for these positions. They involve unpaid, hard work, much of it outside working hours. Many shop stewards have been pressed less than willingly into service. Their tasks involve representing their work group to management when local issues arise such as complaints, dismissals, work changes and sometimes pay. As far as the union is concerned one of their major tasks is to recruit new members.

On the positive side there is the challenge and respect to be earned by handling difficult human problems which affect your close colleagues. Many firms allow the shop steward time off to deal with union matters and attend training courses, and there is also perhaps satisfaction to be derived from dealing with high levels of management, making speeches at branch meetings and even attending conferences. The shop steward's life can be far from routine.

More serious or wide-ranging issues are dealt with at higher levels of the union. If an organization is large it may have a works branch or branches and a senior union official known as the convenor. Sometimes he will chair a multiunion committee which deals with company issues of common interest. It is at these higher levels that the more committed union representatives, sometimes politically active and more militant, begin to increase in numbers. The unwilling shop steward learns to step backwards when branch and district elections come up.

Note in Fig. 8.2 the dotted line between the shop stewards and the rest of the hierarchy. This draws attention to the ambiguity and conflict which the shop steward may suffer. Sometimes he is caught between union policy on the one hand, and the wishes of those who elected him on the other; this dilemma can make shop stewardship very stressful.

District officers It is usually at district level that we find the first full time officials of the union. The district officer is probably elected for a period of about five years, he will be called in when disputes are at a difficult stage and he will also be the overseer of all union activity in his district. The district officer answers to the National Executive Committee and in particular the General Secretary. Executive members are elected for fixed terms, sometimes even for life. They are responsible for carrying out union policy and making the strategic decisions which govern union activity. The General Secretary is the most powerful figure, and as well as being the major voice on the Executive he may have, depending on the size of the union, administrators, accountants, lawyers, and researchers, reporting to him.

National conference The highest level of any individual union is the National Conference. This is the *policy*-making body which sets out plans for union activities in key areas such as pay, hours, safety, equal opportunities and so on. It also determines the rules of the union which govern its day-to-day systems and routines such as election of officials, powers of shop stewards and qualifications for membership.

Union policy originates with the membership at branch level. From here, or the District, resolutions concerning important issues are sent for discussion at the Conference by representatives also from these levels. Executive members can speak but often not vote at the Conference; their function is to carry out the members' wishes as the Conference tells them. That is not to overemphasize the democratic nature of union policy-making, resolutions are frequently ambiguous or open-ended, leaving the Executive considerable freedom of interpretation. Many resolutions do not demand specific actions, and if the Executive chooses it can ignore them, regarding them as expressions of attitude or long-term statements of intent. This is particularly true of resolutions on issues such as apartheid in South Africa or political prisoners in Chile, but it can also apply to more parochial matters.

Trades Union Congress (TUC) Most of the major trade unions are affiliated to the Trades Union Congress. The main aim of this organization is to coordinate the activities of individual unions for mutual benefit. The TUC may become involved in industrial disputes and in discussions with the government over individual negotiations, economic policy or legislation. The general direction of all its activities is the pursuit of greater strength for the trade union movement. It has extensive research, advice and education facilities which are available to its members. Note, however, the dotted line on Fig. 8.2. Although the TUC has an annual conference and a General Council to create and oversee policies decided by representatives of all unions, it has only limited powers over its members. Its resolutions are not binding on individual unions.

Union structure today This picture of union structure does not apply precisely to any particular union. Actual structure will depend on size, age, industry, and the way the union has developed over time. Many of the old craft unions representing skilled trades have merged together or into the larger general unions which began to emerge at the turn of the century. In some industries single unions represent particular types of workers; the National Union of Mineworkers and the Postal Workers Union are examples of these industrial unions. The most recent development has been the white-collar unions, which have grown rapidly since the 1950s to represent the growing number of office workers who saw their privileged conditions being eroded as they increased in numbers and as blue-collar unions increased in strength. Draughtsmen (Draughtsmen's and Allied Technicians' Association), local government workers (National and Local Government Officers), and bank employees (Banking, Insurance, Finance Union) are among the vast range of white-collar workers who have flocked to the union banner since the war.

Union recognition

About half the working population are trade union members and three-quarters are covered by trade union negotiated agreements. This bears witness to the degree of acceptance and recognition achieved by the trade union movement since the turn of the century. It has not been an easy road for the unions and there are still employers who reject or at least resist unionization. Why?

Some managements of non-union companies compare their own powers to make decisions about such issues as pay, training, redundancy and dismissals with those of their counterparts in unionized companies. They see the time spent in discussion, participative decision-making and negotiating, and the occasional disruption, and feel they would rather keep the power to themselves if they can. They may argue that it is a managerial right to decide such matters, workers are merely paid to do their job. Often they would claim that in the long run the workers benefit due to increased efficiency. The attitude of non-union managements tends to be paternalistic, 'we will look after our workers, they have no need of a union to protect them'.

Another common attitude in non-unionized companies is that of individualism. They want to motivate employees to compete against each other for wage increases and promotion on the basis of individual ability and effort. Unions are a collective force which tend to encourage feelings of brotherhood and solidarity that may work against the individualist ethic. This helps to explain why even in unionized companies managers are often discouraged from becoming members.

In the United Kingdom most companies now allow their employees a voice in the form of trade union representation. Perhaps this is partly due to the power of trade unions but most managements accept that there are a number of areas in which conflicts of interest exist and consultation and negotiation are the best ways to arrive at compromises. Personnel managers are often particularly positive about the need for trade unions; their lives can be made much easier if formal procedures and channels can be worked out with elected employee representatives. Perhaps a cynic might suggest that personnel managers need unions almost as much as policemen need criminals! It is certainly true to say that in organizations where the unions are strong the personnel department tends to be influential.

Management and unions

Once management has agreed to recognize a union as the legitimate representative of a group of workers they will come together in a number of ways. The industrial relations manager may be directly involved in particular interactions or he may stay in the background, acting as a source of strategic or legal advice to the line manager.

Collective bargaining is the major union–management activity. It simply involves the parties negotiating over any issue of mutual importance. Pay, of course, is central but hours and conditions of work, holidays, overtime, shifts and, too often these days, redundancy are all areas for collective bargains to be reached.

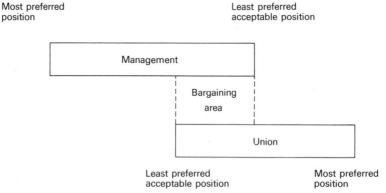

Fig. 8.3   Collective bargaining between two parties.

Figure 8.3 represents a simple bargaining situation. The two parties have to have acceptable positions which overlap to create a 'bargaining area', or conflict is inevitable. The final compromise will depend on the relative power of the two parties and their ability to use it skilfully. The art of negotiation is important to any manager, and differences in ability between the parties can have a significant effect on the outcome. This is why a good industrial relations manager can often command a very high salary; it is also why line managers have to learn negotiating skills.

It is significant that unions rarely become involved in negotiations over matters such as job design, product policy, pricing policy, mergers, purchase of new buildings, appointment of managers and choice of new plant. Their influence on company activity and involvement in decision-making is strictly limited. Management prerogatives are much wider in the United Kingdom than in many of our European neighbours.

In West Germany and in Sweden for example many more managerial decisions are the subject of discussion and negotiation. One positive side to increased worker participation is that implementation of decisions is easier and there is less industrial strife; on the negative side, however, decision-making is slower and management criteria of 'efficiency' may be compromised.

Sometimes unions offer something, or are asked for something, in return for improvements in their conditions; this is known as productivity bargaining. The aim here is to carry out a joint problem solving exercise and share the new gains. In recent years employees have been asked to reduce overtime working, relax job demarcation, work shifts, allow work study teams, work with new technology, reduce manning levels and operate flexible rosters in order to increase productivity in return for better pay or other benefits.

Many companies, even non-union companies, have systems of joint consultation which deal with different types of decision. The common procedure is a system of works committees, with joint union–management representation, at which employees may raise ideas like flexible working hours or new canteen arrangements or make complaints about supervision systems or working conditions. In some cases these committees work well and are given serious decision-making powers. Too often, though, they are caught between management decisions on the one hand and collective bargaining matters on the other to leave fairly low level issues for their consideration. Nevertheless, they serve as a useful communication system in both directions and may fulfil a safety valve function, giving management early warning of trouble brewing.

Other joint committees with specific functions are common. Health and safety, sports and social, and job grading are areas in which unions and management may come together to mutual benefit. On all these committees the personnel manager will be involved, sometimes as a normal participant but often as chairperson. It is he who will undertake much of the 'behind-the-scenes' work, gathering information, carrying out surveys, preparing agendas and minutes, implementing some decisions and taking others to higher authority.

There may also be grievance committees as part of a grievance or disputes procedure to which employees can resort if they have complaints over any aspect of their employment. Such procedures usually start with an approach to the local supervisor by the shop steward. If the dispute is not settled it can continue though a hierarchical system which, for major issues, may have a regional joint or independent committee or even the Advisory Conciliation and Arbitration Service (ACAS) as its pinnacle.

Key issues

Industrial relations is one of the most challenging fields in British industry. Our society and our organizations still have to solve issues such as the closed shop, picketing and the involvement of trade unions in different types of organization decisions. Trade unions themselves are still battling with issues like the role of the shop steward and with their own procedures for ensuring internal democracy.

Industrial relations is an area where power has to be carefully identified and skilfully used. It is here that the 'dynamic coalition of conflicting interests' is at its most fragile, and it is undoubtedly one of the fields in which British management must improve if the economic and technological challenges of the next two decades are to be successfully met.

The systems phase

Most medium and large-sized firms have fairly well-developed personnel functions which would carry out all the activities described so far. Their employees will be recruited, appraised for training and promotion, working on jobs with formal job descriptions that are part of a grading structure and paid on a (probably very complex) system of pay scales. The employees will have the benefit of sports and social, canteen and welfare facilities and a high level of health and safety provision. Those employees who want it will have the protection of union membership and their representatives will work on their behalf to improve pay and conditions in negotiations with an established industrial relations function.

If that all sounds rather neat and tidy then just remember that each of the aspects of personnel work, more so than for any other department, involves the coming together of parties with different points of view. There are almost infinite opportunities for headaches and problems which helps to explain why the systems phase of development is rarely reached. The personnel manager has too much trouble trying to fight the fires which rage daily around the organization without having to find time to integrate the underlying procedures into a coherent 'system'.

The systems phase is characterized by the use of integrated manpower planning and career development programmes.

Manpower planning

Large modern organizations produce a series of short, medium and long-term corporate plans to guide the future direction of the enterprise. Interdisciplinary teams of experts armed with computers and crystal balls try to weigh up the foreseeable changes in the environment and the resources of the company in order to chart a course towards a desirable future. They will plan for new factories, new plant, new markets, new capital, new products and so on but also, increasingly in the current circumstances, for contraction and retrenchment. It should be clear that any corporate plan would not be complete without a corresponding plan for manpower.

Those firms who attempt manpower plans follow roughly similar procedures:

(1) Maintain an inventory of current manpower in terms of skills, grades and locations.
(2) Monitor the labour market for each type of job.
(3) From (1) and (2) make forecasts of the supply of manpower at appropriate times in the future.
(4) From the corporate plan make forecasts of the demand for manpower.
(5) Compare (3) and (4) and take appropriate action.

Where there is an anticipated shortfall in the supply of labour it may be necessary to consider changing the corporate plan or carrying out a training programme. Where there is an anticipated surplus a range of measures such as retraining, redeployment and 'natural wastage' can be considered before resorting to redundancies. If redundancies seem inevitable the use of manpower planning should allow more time for discussions with the unions in order to minimize hardship and strife. The number of emergency redundancy programmes in recent years is a comment on the efficient manpower planning of many British companies or perhaps, more charitably, on the problems of making plans in the face of a hostile and turbulent environment.

By working as closely as possible to a coherent plan which incorporates pay levels and employment levels it is possible to see recruitment, training, appraisal, job grading and payment schemes as an integrated network of systems aimed at long-term goals. Each individual action can be evaluated against the plan. Recruitment of people for one job may be appropriate now, but perhaps it must be kept in mind that in a year they will need to be retrained, so have they the potential for developing new skills? As far as managers are concerned the ideal complement to a manpower planning system is a career development system. A career path for each manager is roughly mapped out. If he comes up to scratch at each appraisal he is given appropriate training and transfers or promotions. Alongside this system will be a succession plan so that if any vacancy arises there are a number of suitable candidates already earmarked.

The practice of personnel management

We started this chapter by identifying two common stereotypes of the personnel manager—the soft, good guy or 'welfarist', and the 'bureaucrat' or 'technicist', carrying out the decisions of others. These stereotypes embody some of the ambiguities and tensions experienced in personnel work. Is the personnel manager primarily pursuing social justice on behalf of employees, a tradition stemming from the welfare phase which often attracts young people to this field, or is he pursuing corporate efficiency as a full member of the management team? In practice the pressures to fulfil both roles can cause considerable strain. The issue of redundancy provides an example of the dilemma.

The decision to make employees redundant may, as we have seen, emerge from a manpower planning exercise. More often, however, it comes as an expedient response to a crisis which has been looming for some time and has not been removed by management action. Such crises may arise from combinations of factors leading to reducing sales; economic changes, tough competition, reduced demand, high costs, and so on.

The personnel manager may not be involved in the initial decision to make people redundant; he is more often called in later to carry out the operation. There are many difficult problems to be tackled, how many should go, from which departments, with how much redundancy pay? The welfare tradition in personnel would tend towards criteria such as employability elsewhere, family or personal need and so on. The commonest compromise here is the last-in–first-out (LIFO) principle. The efficiency tradition on the other hand would point to the choice of inefficient employees, 'slackers', those with poor attendance records, and 'troublemakers'.

The personnel manager is frequently caught between his conscience and trade union pressures on the one hand and his career and management pressures on the other. This dilemma can arise in an only slightly less acute form in pay negotiations, dismissal decisions and a wide range of disputes.

Another feature of personnel is that it is a 'staff' function and this raises a range of problems. In formal terms the personnel manager has no direct authority over line managers, he is there to advise and assist. Nevertheless, in practice, he has a number of very real sources of power. Expertise in the handling of disputes, knowledge about company rules and procedures and government legislation may all be used by the personnel manager to influence the activities of line managers. It may also be that his special relationship with worker representatives will encourage line managers to consult and work through him rather than act independently. The personnel department does not have as powerful a web of systems throughout the organization as the accounting department does but it can sometimes get a grip on the payment and grading system, the hours system, the appraisal and promotion systems, the recruitment and selection systems and the disputes procedure which ensures that line managers have to work with personnel and comply with its wishes.

This relationship with line managers is another of the keys to understanding the personnel department. Line managers tend, by the nature of the forces motivating them, to pursue the best short-term interests of their department as they see them. This may lead them to want to promote a popular subordinate rather than advertise a vacant position, it may mean they want to give a large number of subordinates merit rises or dismiss a troublesome shop steward or neglect the appraisal system. The personnel manager has to consider the wider organizational implications of such actions and take the longer-term view. It is a major part of his job to use his superior knowledge of procedures and the legal position to keep impetuous line managers out of trouble.

How does he get the line manager to comply? The ideal situation is to establish working relationships with line managers so that they respect advice given; often this has to be backed up with occasional recourse to higher levels of management on specific issues and the establishment of company rules and procedures to ensure that personnel policy is practised consistently.

A recent trend in personnel department activities is the push towards management development programmes. There is always a need for further training for managers either because they have been promoted into jobs for which they are not fully qualified, or the organization has changed, or new concepts have emerged which affect them. The personnel manager, by coordinating management development, gains the credibility of line managers and perhaps a measure of prestige which can help him when he needs their confidence in other matters.

Another recent trend is the personnel manager who almost seems to look too hard for problems to solve. This is particularly true in companies where most personnel procedures and negotiating are centralized but there is still a personnel department at each decentralized site. Figure 8.4 represents the tricky staff position of the personnel department.

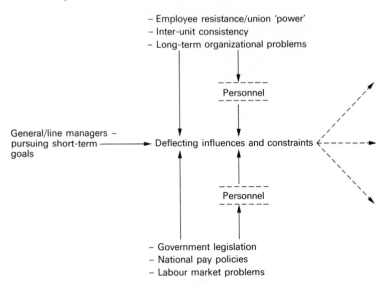

Fig. 8.4   Constraining influences on managers' use of labour, mediated by members of the personnel department. From Watson (1977), reproduced with permission.

The following quotes from conversations with personnel specialists help to convey the flavour of their situation.

The top management in this organization are always happy to admit that the human resource is the most important of all and in principle they recognize that personnel has a major part to play, but when it comes to practice—no way. They make all their decisions on the basis of pounds and pence and they never involve us unless there is a crisis.

I came to X Ltd. from a large company with a full range of sophisticated personnel policies. It was easy to ensure uniform decision-making and procedures throughout the company and personnel was a respected function. Here at X we only have policies in a few areas such as recruitment, wages and conditions of employment. Everybody realizes without systems we are just surviving from day to day with no coherent practices between divisions and sometimes not even observance of our legal obligations. But until a major crisis occurs so that we can justify setting up policies and procedures to prevent it happening again, nobody is going to spend the time. I find it very stressful.

I came to personnel from work study. The thing you have to get used to is that nobody notices when you do a good job. You can't say, 'I sold £10 000 worth last month', or 'my unit's productivity is up 15 per cent'. Who gives credit to personnel for recruiting a good manager or reducing labour turnover or reducing the number of srikes?

The thing I work hardest at is my relationship with the line managers. When I first came they only communicated with personnel through the paperwork systems: requisitions for new staff, requests to go on training courses, recommendations for wage rises or promotion and even formal notification of warnings to problem employees after the event. Now they often ring me before they make major changes of any sort, just to ask my advice. I am always consulted on disciplinary matters and promotions. Perhaps the most rewarding change though has been the number of departmental managers who are now prepared to talk to me about general problems they have with their people. I see the line managers as the major exponents of personnel practice in any company; if we can't get their confidence and cooperation we may as well go home.

Recommended reading

Cuming, M. (1975). *The theory and practice of personnel management*. Heinemann, London.

Legge, K. (1978). *Power, innovation and problem-solving in personnel management*. McGraw-Hill, Maidenhead.

Thomason, G. (1976). *A textbook of personnel management*. Institute of Personnel Management, London.

Watson, T. (1977). *The personnel managers*. Routledge and Kegan Paul, London.

Questions

1. 'Personnel management is best left to line managers, the personnel department should stick to record keeping!' Discuss.
2. What are the factors which prevent organizations from having an integrated personnel function?
3. To what extent can personnel selection be scientific?
4. Outline the main ways on which unions and managements interact in the United Kingdom. What factors are likely to affect these interactions during the next 12 months?
5. What are the major issues in the relationships between personnel and the other main business functions?

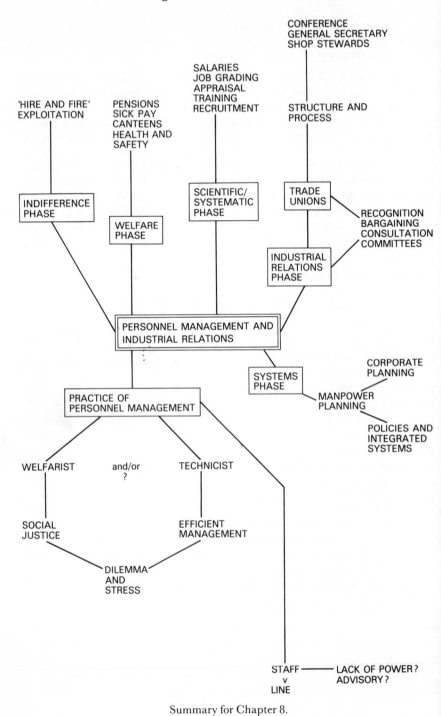

Summary for Chapter 8.

9 Contemporary issues in British industry

Introduction

The modern manager works in a dynamic and challenging environment. Britain in the last decades of the twentieth century is going through a period of rapid economic, social and technological change. This makes it difficult to predict the form our society, and its business organizations, will take as they enter the twenty-first century. At that time many readers of this book may be reaching the height of their organizational careers, some may have moved into new industries which we cannot yet foresee, and others may be happily looking after the home whilst their spouse is earning the family income.

For those of us raised in a time of full employment there is also the sobering prospect that many of today's readers will be trying to make the best of enforced unemployment when the new century dawns. Or perhaps the structure and culture of society will be such by then that not working, or working only a few hours each week, will be a perfectly acceptable position. Or perhaps full employment will have returned, stimulated by the development of a range of new resources, new products and new technologies.

The purpose of this chapter is to focus attention on some issues which are being faced by contemporary managers and whose impact will influence the future of our society. The potential list of subjects is endless but we have chosen just five which are both topical and important:

(1) Unemployment—impact and prospect
(2) Japan—lessons to be learned?
(3) Male/female roles
(4) Management and social responsibility
(5) The impact of new technology.

In dealing briefly with such wide subjects the aim is not to provide comprehensive treatment but to stimulate thought and further investigation. Furthermore, these issues cannot be discussed impartially. Although a reasoned description and analysis will be attempted, it is inevitable that the writers' values will become evident. Let it be recorded here: there are no right answers.

Unemployment—impact and prospect

For over two decades after the Second World War mass unemployment seemed to have been abolished in Britain. The number of people out of work averaged only 1½ per cent of the workforce in the 1950s and 2 per cent in the 1960s. During that time, the labour force had grown due to population increase and a rising number of women workers, and grew from 23.6 million to 25.4 million. In the early 1970s, however, oil prices quadrupled, and the world went into recession. Since then, Britain's unemployment has been climbing rapidly, the percentage unemployed reached double figures around the turn of the decade, and continues to increase.

Different sectors of the population are affected to varying degrees. Almost half the long-term unemployed (longer than six months) are over 60 years of age. School-leavers cause perhaps most concern. A quarter of those under 18 who have left school are without work. The government has tried to help with special 'job creation' and 'work experience schemes'. The quarter of a million young people on the Youth Opportunities Programme (YOP) help to soften only slightly the figures for this age group.

The causes of unemployment

There are many causes of unemployment. It is not possible to identify one specific cause of the current situation; if it were then perhaps a solution would have been found. However, in the opinion of many observers the first statement to make would be that Britain's international competitiveness has declined sharply. This did not lead to unemployment while world trade was still expanding, but the oil crisis and the world recession have meant that our small share of a contracting market has left us with reduced export orders. Furthermore, tough overseas competition on home markets has led to a decline even in those firms which have never sold outside the United Kingdom.

This begs the question, 'Why has Britain failed to compete?' There are many interrelated factors involved. Large wage increases led, in part, to a high rate of inflation which pushed up the prices of British goods. Lower productivity than our major rivals has been a key influence. Unproductive labour practices, inadequate investment in new processes, and poor management skills are in turn all causes of low productivity.

Britain has also failed to adapt its heavy industries, such as steel-making and shipbuilding, to compete effectively in a tight market, and she has been slow to move into the newer, fast-growing industries.

If Britain were to cure these problems, would full employment return? This is a difficult question. It is certain that if international competitiveness is not improved then unemployment will increase as firms continue to go out of business, but it could be that in order to become competitive labour must still be shed.

A related issue when considering the future is that of technical change. New technologies are emerging which are not labour-intensive. Whilst they have not yet had a significant effect on employment it seems likely that firms will increasingly look to new technology as the answer to productivity problems. The impact of this trend will be the final issue examined in this chapter.

The consequence of unemployment

Unemployment has three main undesirable consequences. In economic terms, large numbers out of work represent a drain on resources away from other areas of the economy because they need to be supported. They also represent a waste of the resources used to raise, educate and train them.

In social terms, high unemployment has been linked to greater levels of crime, more divorces, increased racial tension and a higher incidence of cruelty to children.

In psychological terms, on a personal level, unemployment is often associated with a loss of self-esteem, less contact with former workmates and, of course, lower standards of living. This can lead to severe depression and other forms of psychological suffering. A Manpower Services Commission report in 1980 indicated that 44 per cent of those questioned felt that unemployment was the worst thing to have happened to them.

What is it like to be unemployed?

People in our society, especially men, have been brought up with the expectation that they will work and support a family. Social status is often ascribed on the basis of an individual's job and the income which goes with it. Many people derive meaning and fulfilment from their work and satisfaction from the belief that through it they become useful members of society. If unemployment is to be with us permanently it may be that this aspect of our culture will have to change.

Meanwhile, there appear to be many undesirable consequences for the unemployed individual, including:

(1) A loss of self-respect, due partly to having to live on unemployment benefit.

(2) Poisoning of family relationships, as a man may feel inadequate because he is not supporting his family. His image may
suffer in their eyes too, even though his position is no fault of
his own. The large amount of time spent at home when upset
by humiliation, frustration and depression can lead to friction
between family members.

(3) Poverty. Unemployment benefit is likely to be far less than
previous earnings. This can lead to hardship and further
compound the other problems of unemployment.

Interviews with long-term unemployed have identified three phases
of mental state which they tend to experience. 'Novelty'—with
perhaps some redundancy pay or savings the newly unemployed
person may find the change interesting for a short time at first.
Eventually, however, 'apathy' tends to set in as the job-hunting
begins to look hopeless. The last stage, which varies in intensity and
may revert back to the second stage, is 'desperation', the consequences of which can sometimes be violent or unpleasant.

The future

The low death rate and relatively higher birth rate mean that more
jobs must be provided in the future just to maintain current
employment levels. Furthermore the trend for more women to enter
the workforce creates a still greater demand for jobs. It is to be hoped
that some actions can be taken to at least slow down the growth of
unemployment. What actions might be taken?

There are a number of short-term economic actions which might
affect unemployment. Governments will no doubt pursue their
policies of monetarism, protectionism, incomes policy, reflation, etc.;
it is not possible to discuss these subjects here.

In perhaps the more desirable scenario for the future our
established industries will be reorganized and re-equipped to become
competitive in a recovering world market. Even more important may
be the emergence of new industries exploiting the latest technological
developments, providing jobs and exports and 'spinoff' effects such as
orders for other industries.

It seems likely, however, that in the long term less and less hours of
work will be required to meet the needs of our manufacturing
industry. To retain employment levels there will need to be sharing of
work, perhaps by reducing hours, increasing holidays, or earlier
retirement. Or perhaps by extending current experiments with
'job-sharing' in which two or more people carry out a job previously
undertaken by one person. The government is exploring ways of
offsetting the increased costs to employers of such arrangements.

Whilst work will continue to be the central life activity for many people, it may be that leisure, and this would include voluntary work, will increase in prominence. Leisure activities can provide many of the psychological satisfactions of work. Opportunities to interact with others, develop personal identity, structure time, achieve goals and relate to society can all be realized through leisure. Unfortunately, leisure does not in general provide economic returns. This is one of the central problems for the future.

Japan—lessons to be learned?

Japan is an island off China in the Pacific Ocean with a population of 115 million people. She has virtually no physical resources, she imports all her oil and 55 per cent of her food. The effects of the Second World War, including the atomic explosions at Hiroshima and Nagasaki, left a nation in devastation. However, less than 40 years later she leads the world in one industry after another: motorcycles; cars; cameras; steel; watches; shipbuilding; industrial robots, and a host more.

Japan has achieved the fastest post-war rate of economic growth in the world. Partly this must be seen as a catching-up process, but nevertheless she can now boast the highest average GNP per square kilometre of any country, along with very low unemployment and inflation.

The search for remedies to improve the efficiency and competitiveness of British industry has led to a study of Japan as a model for economic prosperity. The key question is: can British management transfer any lessons from Japan to their own circumstances? We shall examine this possibility after a brief description of the major characteristics of Japanese industry.

Japanese industry

A central point of this issue is that Japan has a unique culture and history. Without examining these in detail we can make some simple generalizations about their consequences for Japanese industry.

Consensus Two important strands of Japanese culture are *Gimu* loyalties which stress the repayment of indebtedness, whether to parents or to society or to the company, and *Giri* attitudes which demand that one maintains one's good reputation and honours commitments. Partly due to these norms there is much more concern in Japan than in Britain with the implications of any action for the greater good. Self-interest within organizations tends to be tempered by a consideration of the effects on the company, and self-interest between organizations tends to be offset by a concern with society as a whole.

Furthermore, in all dealings there is a social norm which says the other party must not be dishonoured. There is less tendency to try to defeat the other party and more emphasis on arriving at compromises which both feel are just.

These two cultural patterns make the likelihood of industrial strife much lower in Japan than in the United Kingdom.

Unions A related effect is that 94.2 per cent of all unions in Japan are enterprise unions; there is, for example, a Honda union. There is a national body representing the political aspirations of the labour force but most union activity is at company level. This means that all workers, and usually management too, are in the same union. For this reason demarcation disputes are very rare. There are some, though by European standards few, strikes but in general the unions work *with* management and try to avoid actions which may harm the company. Industrial action often takes the form of publicity campaigns, for example posters and press releases, designed to put pressure on management without striking. There is a much greater feeling of working together rather than 'them and us'.

Decision-making The general Japanese decision-making style, especially where changes are to be made, is discussion. Their organizations may have formal hierarchies, but superimposed on them are many groups, some formal but many informal, which thrash out a wide range of problems. This type of decision-making is known as *Ringisho*. It often involves not just individuals on the same level but superiors and subordinates grouped together in hierarchies of dependence. In British industry this might be considered time-consuming and expensive, as it undoubtedly is, but it has the advantage of getting everyone involved and helping to avoid resistance at a later stage.

A much-publicized example of this aspect of Japanese management are 'quality circles'. A quality circle is a group of people within an organization, usually seven or eight in number, who meet regularly, perhaps once a week, to identify, analyse and solve problems relating to the quality of their daily work. 'Quality' is interpreted in its widest sense and may include the working environment, work systems, productivity, the product itself or almost any aspect of day-to-day work. Usually, members are from the same work area or do similar work, and membership is voluntary.

The quality circles concept, with its emphasis on employee involvement, implies a need for management at all levels to listen to, and act upon, the suggestions which emerge from circle discussions.

This is a distinctive feature of Japanese management which is currently being tried by a number of British companies.

Seniority In most Japanese companies increased rewards result from length of employment. This means that young, highly trained, dynamic people can often find themselves in poorly paid jobs. This is accepted because eventually the worker knows he can expect to move up the hierarchy.

Lifetime employment Acceptability of the seniority principle relates partly to the fact that in large Japanese organizations there is an expectation of lifetime employment. A young person will join an organization straight from college and can continue to be employed in that organization for the rest of his working life. Retirement is often compulsory at between 55 and 57 years of age, although company pensions are high and part-time employment is often offered.

Worker commitment The feeling of security and belonging engendered by the management style outlined partly explains why Japanese workers seem to fear technological change less than their British counterparts. Their commitment is demonstrated by the fact that only 22 per cent of Japanese workers take their full holiday entitlement and they frequently work overtime without payment. In large companies their involvement is shown in the early morning exercise sessions, often followed by recitation of the company creed, inconceivable in British companies.

Industrial policy Finally, in this list of characteristics of Japanese industry, it is important to note the nature of the economic structure within which firms operate. Since the war Japan has singlemindedly pursued economic growth, at the neglect of housing, welfare and social amenities that are enjoyed in Britain. She has maintained a consistent industrial policy by developing continuous dialogue between industry and government using a number of national institutions. These provide guidelines to industry, government, banks and unions on where Japan's future should lie, which industries should expand or decline and which areas of technology should be exploited. Thus the consensus decision-making in individual companies has a parallel at national level.

What can British management learn from Japan?

Japanese companies are embedded in the culture of their country. Nevertheless most of their management techniques were imported from the United States after the Second World War and have been successfully adapted to their situation. The time has now come to ask whether we, in our turn can learn from them. We should not blindly adopt Japanese ideas, but we should examine whether certain of their techniques are appropriate and we might also take a close look at the industrial problems caused by our own culture.

The major difference between the United Kingdom and Japan is that their approach favours agreement and consensus where ours tends to emphasize disagreement and a plurality of views. British governments, managements and unions have all been guilty of creating conflict which is in the long-term interests of no one. It will probably be ineffective to merely exhort all sides to cooperate, so what structural changes are possible?

To start at the top, it might be valuable to create economic institutions with representatives from all sectors, which have more executive power than the present National Economic Development Councils. Governments could increase the involvement of management and union representatives in policy formulation. They could make much more strenuous efforts to influence the quantity and direction of investment in different sectors of industry.

A further government policy issue is education. Japan places a heavy emphasis on all aspects of applied science and engineering. Over half of her 601 universities are dedicated to science and technology. This is matched by correspondingly high salary, status and career prospects for engineering graduates. In Britain there have been some moves in this direction but they are, at best, half-hearted.

Within individual enterprises British managements could learn much about the involvement of employees, and unions, in decision-making. In few developed countries do workers have less say than in Britain. This may stem from the old Taylorian philosophy in which managers manage and workers do routine tasks, but it was not adopted by Japan and seems less and less appropriate to modern business. The *ringisho* decision-making system is a peculiarly Japanese idea but in Britain we might develop industrial participation via worker directors, increasing the power of works committees, disclosing more information to trade unions and perhaps adopting quality circles. It is not suggested that every firm should change in these specific ways, but the advantages of an involved and committed workforce are clear from the Japanese example.

In conclusion, let us not forget that British companies are often dynamic and successful. The energy created by conflict and competition can lead to great achievements. Perhaps few of us would want to see the conformism and relative docility which exists in much of Japanese industrial life. Nevertheless, there is a strong case for pursuing a greater degree of industrial harmony and cooperation in some areas if we are to regain our international competitiveness.

Male and female roles

Women have long been discouraged from pursuing careers and taking up responsible positions in business. There is no doubt, however, that this is gradually changing. In 1951 34.7 per cent of all women worked, by 1961 the figure was 37.4 per cent and by 1971 it was 42.7 per cent—about one-third of these part-time. However, despite their large involvement in the labour force, only 11 per cent of administrators and managers are women.

Women who want to compete in the world of work, as we shall see, often have problems which men do not, but it is important to note also that men may suffer too, not in their work but in their family lives. Men who want to spend time with a growing family are often being pushed to make great efforts in their career and have to make sacrifices in one or the other.

Consider the three sets of views about women described below and decide which conforms most closely to your own:

(1) Mrs Smith sees herself essentially as a housewife and mother—these are her main functions in life and her main source of pleasure. She believes women are weaker both physically and psychologically than men. Her place is to maintain the home which is provided by her husband and to care for the children. She supports him in his work and would pursue no ambitions of her own to the detriment of his. It is unfortunate if she has to work, as ideally a man should provide the financial means of support for his whole family.

(2) Mrs Jones believes that if a woman chooses to be a housewife that is her right and it should be defended. It is appropriate for a woman to work while she is young, leave her job and devote herself to children and home during the years of active motherhood, and then pick up the threads of her occupation when the children are older.

The woman has a greater responsibility for the children, particularly during their earlier years, but she has a right to be given facilities which help her to meet her home responsibilities and also to undertake gainful employment.

(3) Mrs Brown believes that both parents have an equal responsibility for housework and children—indeed for every facet of family life. She believes they have equal responsibility for the financial support of the family and should actively pursue their careers to the full. If this leads to conflict it must be resolved between equals with neither parent assuming obligations or rights by virtue of his or her sex.

Mrs Brown sees the role of 'housewife' as unacceptable; she believes men and women are essentially alike in their needs, feelings and aspirations—both having one main role, that of human being.

If you find yourself most strongly in agreement with Mrs Smith then your views on the role of women are the traditional ones which appear to be on the wane in our society. Mrs Jones on the other hand with her 'senior partner—junior partner' ideas presents the most commonly held attitudes at the moment. Mrs Brown's ideas on equality appear to be growing in popularity, particularly amongst the young, the better educated and the middle class, but as yet they are not reflected in the structure of our society.

The factors hindering women from becoming senior managers and engineers appear to be a complex mixture of company policies and practice, men's attitudes and behaviour and women's own attitudes and behaviour. We must also note the importance of parental and societal influences.

Girls tend to be conditioned from infancy not to be assertive or aggressive, such behaviour being seen as 'not feminine'. They are encouraged to be dependent and submissive rather than competitive and resourceful.

Boys and girls perform equally well at O level, but after that girls tend to be discouraged from taking A levels or college courses. There is no evidence of major intellectual differences between men and women, so the differences in levels of qualification must be attributed to the influences of family and society and the attitudes of women themselves.

Social conditioning is all around us, people, the media, institutions and advertising pushing people towards particular types of behaviour. Boys are usually brought up to expect to have to support their families and themselves. A girl is often brought up to expect that work will only be temporary and that in due course someone will support her. The resulting uncommitted attitude to work is a partial explanation for women's lack of career success.

Women are not only conditioned in terms of the level of their career aspirations but also in the type of work they do. They are rarely encouraged towards scientific or engineering subjects which are seen as 'unfeminine' in some way. One consequence of this situation is that British industry is deprived of an enormous well of potential talent. Despite unemployment there is still an alarming lack of able people to take up senior industrial jobs.

The Equal Pay Act of 1970 and the Sex Discrimination Act of 1975 have made it harder for companies to deliberately discriminate against women. These laws reflect a growing belief that women should have equal opportunity with men. Nevertheless there is still widespread resistance among Britain's predominantly male managers to large-scale female involvement. Discrimination is often impossible to prove and males tend to have control of the all-important recruitment, training, appraisal and promotion systems. Much discrimination is subconscious, men tending to simply regard 'male' qualities as more appropriate for senior tasks. They may also tend to stereotype women, assuming they do not want promotion, will leave work to get married as soon as they can, will probably get pregnant, or will leave their job to follow their husband's career. Such overgeneral assumptions make it hard for women who are genuinely ambitious to gain credibility.

To summarize, we have so far identified a number of explanations for the unequal representation of women in industry. They tend to be conditioned by their families and by society to exhibit the sort of qualities which are often seen as inappropriate in business and also they are encouraged not to be career-oriented. Their education may often be less suitable for management or, more especially, engineering posts. They are likely to meet resistance from male-dominated institutions.

Further problems may exist for women due to the lack of facilities for child care. Even if a mother is prepared to sacrifice five years of her career until her child reaches school age she will find that school hours are so short as to necessitate often difficult arrangements for delivery at school and collection and care in the afternoon not to mention the thirteen or so weeks of school holidays. Britain is very poorly provided with creches for mothers who want to return to work soon after the baby is born.

Note the bias here. The expectation tends to be that it is the woman who should give up work, with consequent damage to career prospects, in order to care for the children. Why should this be so?

The future

More widely held egalitarian beliefs about a woman's right to a career and a man's responsibility for the home are making life difficult for today's young potential managers. Young men increasingly decide to marry girls who they meet at college with similar ability and qualifications to their own. Decisions have to be made about whose career comes first or whether a compromise should be reached—like not moving outside a particular region. When, if at all, should a family be started and how should the offspring be cared for? Even once-simple matters like housework can no longer be assumed as the woman's responsibility.

Perhaps in a society where hours of work are reduced and part-time work, flexible working hours, and job-sharing become more common, it would be easier to settle these new sex role issues. In any event it is

to be hoped that in future men will be able to enjoy more of the
benefits of forming a full relationship with their families, and women
will be able to undertake fulfilling careers and not be unwillingly tied
to the home. This can only happen if society in general and business
organizations in particular start to implement equal opportunities
policies.

Management and social responsibility

What values should managers be guided by? What objectives should
they pursue? In previous chapters they have been variously represented as owner-serving technocrats, as system-serving bureaucrats,
as customer-oriented marketing men, as employee-centred leaders
and as self-serving politicians. These different perspectives on the
manager's role serve to demonstrate the number of conflicting
influences on his behaviour. Which has the greatest influence will
depend, at least in part, on the beliefs management hold about its
social role. In this section we are not concerned with what managers
actually do but with what they *ought* to do.

Managements have an enormous amount of freedom. To some
extent they are limited by laws and to some extent by economic
constraints but this leaves a very wide discretionary band. Much
managerial behaviour is legal and profitable but based on ethical and
moral judgments which may be questioned. For example, asbestos
has been known to be highly dangerous for four decades, the fibres
cause fatal industrial diseases like asbestosis as well as cancers of the
lung and its linings. Yet there is still an asbestos industry in the
United Kingdom, using safety standards which research has shown to
be inadequate. Should they implement stricter safety systems than the
law requires? Should the managements of these companies use other
materials, even if they jeopardize profits? If totally safe work systems
cannot be devised, should they voluntarily close down their companies, even if workers in the industry are prepared to take the risks?

There are basically three schools of thought on managerial social
responsibility. The first may be called the 'social constraints'
perspective.

It is often argued that management should do whatever they want
to so long as it is legal. If society wants protection from pollution,
shoddy products and unsafe working practices, then it will pass laws
to prevent these actions. Management, by this argument, cannot be
expected to make moral judgments on behalf of society which are
against its own interests. It is also pointed out that if one
unscrupulous company can gain a competitive advantage by behav-

ing unethically then others have to follow suit. Only laws, or enforced 'codes of practice', can ensure uniform business policies and thus fairness.

A second point of view on social responsibility is that managements have to maintain high standards of ethical behaviour because in the long run it is sound strategy to do so. This view may be called the 'social expectations' perspective, it involves bringing organizational behaviour up to a level where it is in congruence with currently prevailing societal expectations. Thus, while in the 'constraints' approach managers will only be diverted from their goals by new laws or economic changes, the 'expectations' approach will lead to changes when social norms make previously acceptable behaviours no longer legitimate. By this means managers may hope to avoid attacks by pressure groups and bad publicity from media exposure of their activities.

The third school of thought may be called 'social concern'. This involves organizations in taking ethical stances on a wide range of issues which are based on some long-term view of their role in society, even though they may sometimes harm economic interests or even go against prevailing social norms. An example of this approach is represented by Scott Bader Co. Ltd. whose Code of Practice states:

We recognize that we have a responsibility to society in which we live and believe that where we have some special talent or interest we should offer it to the wider community. We are agreed that our social responsibility extends to:
(1) Limiting the products of our labour to those beneficial to the community, in particular excluding any products, for the specific purpose of manufacturing weapons of war.
(2) Reducing any harmful effect of our work on the natural environment by rigorously avoiding the negligent discharge of pollutants.
(3) Questioning constantly whether any of our activities are unnecessarily wasteful of the earth's resources.

There are relatively few firms in this last category. Most would probably argue that it is undesirable for business to try to do other than reflect social values. This means that their activities may work against social change. An example of this is the relationship between advertising and our previous issue, sex roles. In commercials women are almost universally portrayed as housewives or sex symbols. They are encouraged to believe that achievement involves washing their children's clothes cleaner or providing their husband with a tastier meal. Those who wish to see women in more responsible jobs and men sharing the household chores are fighting a battle against the highly sexist marketing man.

Let us examine another major ethical issue. Cigarettes are killers. In Britain every year thousands of people die or are made seriously ill by lung cancer and other diseases caused by smoking. There is no longer any room to doubt this fact. Why then do companies go on producing them? What is their ethical justification?

The cigarette manufacturers' central argument is individual freedom. Mature adults, who are aware of the risks, should be allowed to smoke if they choose. They maintain that their advertising does not encourage smoking, only smoking of a particular brand. They also note that their industry provides enormous revenue to the exchequer, is an important employer of labour and a major exporter. They salve their social conscience further, and also improve their marketing, by sponsoring a wide variety of sporting and cultural events.

Nevertheless, the tobacco industry has seen the threat to its home market; it has branched out into third world markets where the dangerous side-effects of its products are less well understood and restrictions on its marketing are less severe.

Hence the managers of these companies argue that they have obligations to their shareholders, their employees and the economy which outweigh their ethical obligations to their customers. The government apparently supports their position since it has banned the non-wearing of seat belts on safety grounds, even though this measure will save far fewer lives than a ban on the sale of cigarettes.

Perhaps all this seems far removed from day-to-day management? Yet it is only by junior managers agreeing to implement policies that they become effective. Each manager, at whatever level, has to make ethical judgments almost every time he makes a new decision or agrees to take action. Should self-interest take precedence over company interest? Should company interest take precedence over the interest of society? What balance should be struck in each individual case between the rights of the owners, the employees and the nation?

Let us look at some examples of ethical issues faced by middle management.

A personnel manager is told to make 10 per cent of the labour force redundant. Should he refuse and argue for a cut in dividends or cost savings elsewhere? If he agrees to make the redundancies how should he select those who have to go? Ask for volunteers and risk losing the best staff who are confident of getting work elsewhere? Should he choose those who are least able workers, even if they have many years service or growing families to support?

A purchasing manager is choosing between suppliers for a large order. Should be 'buy British' knowing that if he does not a component manufacturer will close down and jobs will be lost? What if this is more expensive than an overseas supplier, should he decide that the shareholders can take the minor effect on their dividends or the employees the small reduction in wages which will offset the increased costs?

A production manager has become aware that most of his shopfloor workers are not using the guards on their machines because it slows them down and means they make less bonus. He has been told that his job is in jeopardy if he fails to meet production targets and he knows it will be a close thing. His family circumstances make it impossible for him to move and there are no jobs locally. Should he turn a blind eye to the flouting of safety regulations?

A manager has to wrestle with the conflicts caused by competing interests. For most people an ethical decision is one which they intuitively feel is right. We each have our own moral code of conduct, for some it is based on religion but for most it has been ingrained in us by our parents and our experiences and personal value judgments we have made. Frequently, however, we do not do that which we feel is right, we pursue our own self-interests, we respond to pressures from our family or colleagues or we do what our employer expects of us. If an individual compromises his conscience often enough he will find justifications for his actions and probably change his value position so that his conscience is no longer troubled. It is very common for people to believe that serving their own best interest is the morally correct way to behave.

The impact of new technology

There can be few readers who have not heard the phrase 'technological revolution' being used to discuss the changes which science and technology have recently been bringing to the products and processes of industry. The new technologies have been called the 'sunrise' technologies, perhaps because they may lead to the dawning of a new era in which less work is required and amazing new consumer products are available, but also appropriate because Japan is among the world leaders in their development and application.

There are four 'sunrise' technologies:

Biotechnology	concerned with the development of new drugs, chemicals and food products by creating new life-forms to literally ferment them from basic substances.
Laser technology	for example, using optical fibres instead of copper cables to revolutionize communications systems.
Microtechnology	using microprocessors, tiny electronic circuits, as the basis for computers, word

Robotics

processors and a wider range of other devices which can perform tasks or provide services which have previously been impossible or required from human labour.

the development of devices to carry out mechanical tasks. Robots, controlled with microprocessor-based technology, are rapidly becoming more capable and versatile, and they can be easily programmed to perform a variety of different functions. The latest models are equipped with sensory equipment so that they become 'aware' of their environment and can learn to distinguish between colours, avoid obstructions and detect mistakes.

Microprocessors and robots are the developments which will have most impact on British industry in the near future. Their main effect should be to increase productivity. They are cheap to run; they do not object to cramped, unpleasant or dangerous working conditions; there are no supervision or industrial relations problems; they can work 24 hours a day all year round without strikes, lateness, sickness or holidays; they do not tire or make mistakes.

Think of all the routine record-keeping, monitoring, information retrieval, number crunching, data analysis and other paperwork jobs which have to be done in a modern business organization. Microprocessor-based machines are often faster, cheaper, more reliable and more accurate than their human counterparts.

Think of all the laborious materials handling, painting, assembly and welding operations which have to be carried out on the shopfloor. These can often be done much more efficiently by an industrial robot. At Mazak Machine Tools in Japan, an extreme example, the introduction of totally robot-based manufacture reduced the labour force from 220 men to 12. Furthermore throughput time was reduced from three months to two days.

The question of whether or not we should adopt the new technologies is not at issue; if we fail to do so our international competitors will become even more productive and British firms will lose yet more of their markets. The question of their impact on employment is important but if firms go out of business, through either managerial or worker resistance to the changes, then unemployment will certainly be increased. It is not yet clear, however, what effects the new technologies will have.

The optimistic argument is that there will be new though different employment opportunities created, as has been the case with all technological changes since the industrial revolution. Those displaced by computers or robots in one industry will be able to find work in new industries manufacturing microprocessor-based products, or in service industries which will develop to generate new jobs.

The pessimistic argument is that the sunrise industries will enable such large numbers of manual tasks to be carried out by machines that there will be massive unemployment leading to social unrest by the end of the decade if our society remains wedded to the work ethic. Some of those who follow this line talk hopefully of an ordered progression to a 'leisure society', in which machine-created wealth is used to expand education, health, leisure and the social services.

An alternative pessimistic argument is that Britain may fail to adapt quickly enough and thus may lose her markets to more innovative overseas competitiors. In the light of this very real danger, perhaps the most important question we should ask concerns the actions which should be taken to stimulate adoption of the new technologies and ensure that Britain is in the forefront of world development.

The first robot to start work in a factory was installed in 1961 at a General Motors plant in the United States to unload hot pieces of metal from a die-casting machine. By 1970 there were still only 700 robots operating worldwide. From there on the market has expanded rapidly. By 1974 the figure was 3500, in 1978 it was 8000, and in 1981 about 20 000. Japan is the world leader in robot use, with the United States second. Britain is sixth with only about 400, behind Sweden, West Germany and Italy.

In computers too Britain is lagging behind. Japan has launched a massive national campaign to try to wrest market dominance from the United States. Her powerful Ministry of International Trade and Industry has spent over £100 million in supporting and restructuring the country's electronics industry. It now plans to spend a further £200 million developing a new generation of computers.

Japan's investment in new technologies of all kinds is striking. Between 1953 and 1971 her manufacturing sector invested 23 per cent of their sales income on new plant and equipment. In Britain the figure was just 13 per cent. Use of outdated machinery is one of the reasons why it takes something like two-and-a-half British workers to produce the same value of output as a single Japanese.

The government is not entirely unaware of the situation. Money has been set aside to encourage high technology research and investment but this is small in comparison to the scale of the problem.

What is needed are widely available cheap loans for technological improvements, support for small firms trying to use the new developments and, equally important, a large-scale education programme to inform managers about what is available.

Discussion

In all the previous chapters we have attempted to show how the dynamic nature of management can keep the practitioner always interested and stretched. Not only are the jobs changing, but the individual too is developing, striving to do his or her job better and to achieve personal goals.

In this chapter the frame of reference has been broadened still further to show that a wide range of issues are relevant to a manager's role. We have not, of course, attempted to deal with all the major contemporary issues. The treatment given to each has been only brief but, hopefully, provocative.

This book is intended to be of use to those who are learning management now and consequently will be managing business organizations into the twenty-first century. Undoubtedly by that time many of its ideas and concepts will appear dated and, hopefully, will have been developed much further. Management is one of the fastest changing occupations, which makes it extremely challenging. It demands that the practising manager always keeps himself up to date with the latest techniques and systems. More than this, it demands that he be always abreast of social, economic and technological changes which are taking place in the society in which his organization exists. Managers need to be much more than technical specialists; to do their jobs well they need to be socially aware.

Recommended reading

Aldred, C. (1981). *Women at work*. Pan Books, London.
Beesley, M. and Evans, T. (1978). *Corporate social responsibility*. Croom Helm, London.
Hawkins, K. (1979). *Unemployment*. Penguin, Harmondsworth.
Jenkins, C. and Sherman, B. (1979). *The leisure shock*. Methuen, London.
Large, P. (1980). *The micro revolution*. Fontana, London.
Marsh, P. (1982). *The robot age*. Abacus, London.
Pascale, R. T. and Athos, A. G. (1982). *The art of Japanese management*. Allen Lane, London.
Rapoport, R. and Rapoport, R. (1978). *Working couples*. Routledge and Kegan Paul, London.
Sato, K. (1980). *Industry and business in Japan*. Croom Helm, London.

Questions

1. What are the major causes and consequences of unemployment in Britain? Which of these can be overcome and what can the government do to help?
2. Compare and contrast Japanese and British management. What might British managers learn from their Japanese counterparts? What are the obstacles to directly transferring Japanese methods?
3. Outline the problems which may be faced by women trying to make a career in management. Present the cases for and against women achieving equal representation in British management.
4. What obligations do business organizations have to the society in which they operate? What values should guide the managers who work within these organizations?
5. What impact would the large-scale use of microprocessor and robot technologies have on British industry and society? How should government policy be influenced by this scenario?

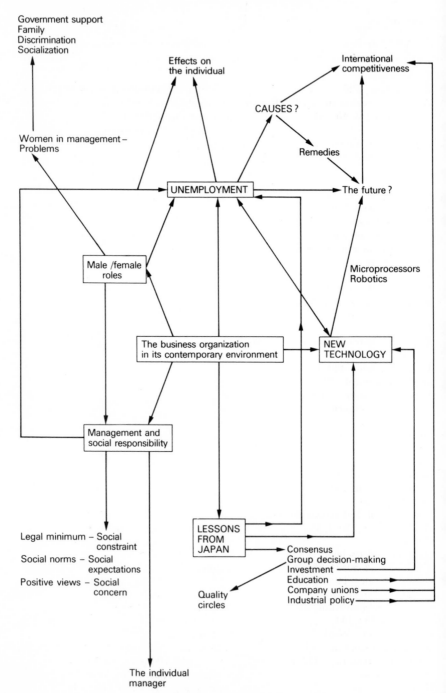

Government support
Family
Discrimination
Socialization

Effects on
the individual

International
competitiveness

CAUSES ?

Women in management –
Problems

Remedies

UNEMPLOYMENT

The future ?

Male /female
roles

Microprocessors
Robotics

The business organization
in its contemporary environment

NEW
TECHNOLOGY

Management and
social responsibility

Legal minimum – Social
constraint
Social norms – Social
expectations
Positive views – Social
concern

LESSONS
FROM
JAPAN

Consensus
Group decision-making
Investment
Education
Company unions
Industrial policy

Quality
circles

The individual
manager

Summary for Chapter 9.

INDEX

absenteeism   120
Advisory Conciliation and Arbitration
    Service (ACAS)   13
Air Ministry   40
appraisal (personnel)   161–3, 177
Arkwright, Richard   15

BP   148
balance sheet   43, 44
Battle of Britain   39
Bessemer, Sir Henry   17
big company buying   110–12, 115
Blake and Mouton   67–9, 70, 72
Board of Directors   10, 27, 79, 80
Boots   147
Borden, N. H.   136, 151
bought-out parts   43, 90, 91, 92, 101,
    115, 116, 133
Brazil   98
British Institute of Management   90,
    93, 114
British Leyland   143, 148
budgetary control   34
Burns and Stalker   39–42
business environment, changes
    in   11–21
business policy   46, 131

Cadbury   155
call-off rate   105
Cartwright, Edmund   15
cash flow   104
Chancellor of the Exchequer   148
chief executive   30–1, 36
China   181
classical model/school/structure/
    view   48–50, 74, 87, 88
closing the sale   149–50, 153
Common Market   7
competition/competitors   2, 3, 24, 75,
    79, 89, 134, 144
Complex Man   59–61, 72
consignment stocking   98
control of purchasing   112–13
corporation tax   43
Cort, Henry   17

cost and management accounting   44–5
credit control   44
Crompton, Samuel   15
Crozier, M.   85
customers   2, 3, 31, 73, 75, 89, 97, 99,
    101, 109, 110, 118, 122, 131, 134,
    135, 148, 153, 188
Customs and Excise   112

Darby, Abraham   17
delivery, delivery performance, delivery
    punctuality   80, 100, 113, 115, 133
Department of Employment   13
design   10, 77, 93, 95, 113, 117, 118–19,
    127, 133
deskilling   12
de-stocking   25
directors' report   43
distribution   10, 124, 134, 136, 152
Dun and Bradstreet   142

engineering (function)   10, 27, 32, 34,
    93, 95, 107
environment of business
    organization   1–3
Equal Opportunities Commission
    (EOC)   13
Equal Pay Act 1970   186
Equipment Process Technology
    (EPT)   131
expectancy theory   61–2

factory system   5–6, 26, 155
Farrington and Woodmansey   90, 114
Fayol, Henri   52, 72
finance   2, 3, 10, 32, 42–5, 75, 93, 95,
    117, 122, 127, 128, 133
financial accounting   42–4
financial ratios   45
First World War   9, 11, 12, 23, 155, 156
Ford   21
foreman   9, 28, 29, 30, 33, 34, 35, 36, 50,
    117, 119, 122, 126, 146
formal organization   51–4, 72
Four Ps   134, 136–7, 148, 151, 152

France   22
French and Raven   83–4

General Motors   193
General Strike   12, 25
Germany (West)   22, 23, 96, 97, 138,
   148, 169 193
GKN   98
Gilchrist, Percy   18
Gill and Lockyer   118, 132
goods inwards section   118, 133

Hargreaves, James   15
head office   29, 36
Hersey and Blanchard   69–70, 72
Herzberg, Frederick   58–9, 60, 63, 72
Honda   182
human relations   54–9, 63, 66, 71, 72,
   74, 78, 89
Huntsman, Benjamin   17
Husband and Barker   121

IBM   21, 146
ICI   92
industrial democracy   20
industrial relations   25, 34, 128–30,
   154–76
Industrial Revolution   5, 7, 22, 26, 117
inflation   24, 25, 178
Institute of Personnel Managers   156
Ireland   23
Italy   193

Japan   23, 177, 181–5, 191, 192
   industry   181–3
   learning from   183–5, 196
job design   62–6, 72

Kay, John   15
Kompass   97, 142

leadership   66–71, 72, 87, 160
lead time   101
Lewin, Lippit, and White   66–7
Limited Liability Statutes   8
Lockyer and Jones   121, 126, 132
Lombe, Thomas   5
London Weekend Television   145

McCarthy, Jerome   136, 148, 151
McGregor, Douglas   56, 72

maintenance   10, 28, 30, 32, 34, 35,
   37, 91, 93, 117, 121, 127, 133
male and female roles   185–8, 196
MAN   145, 153
management and social
   responsibility   188–91, 196
Management Today   143
managerial class, emergence of   20–1,
   26, 48
managing director   10, 32, 33–4, 82, 93,
   117, 121, 146, 147
manpower planning   171–2, 176
Manpower Services Commission   179
manufacturing policy   130–2, 133
marketing   2, 3, 10, 24, 28, 33, 74, 75,
   77, 124, 127, 134, 135, 148, 188, 189
Marketing Mix   134, 136, 137, 138
market research   9
Maslow, Abraham   56–9, 60, 71, 72
mass production   37, 38, 39, 120
materials control (controller)   31, 94
Mazak Machine Tools   192
Mechanic, David   84–5
mechanistic structure(s)   39–42
Mexico   97
motivation and behaviour   56–9
Motor Show   143
multinational companies,
   multinationals   8, 22, 33, 105

Nasmyth, James   17
National Insurance   13
Neilson, J. B.   17
new products, manufacture   118–19
new technology(ies)   65–6, 177, 179,
   196
   impact of   191–4
North Sea Oil   23

organic structure(s)   39–42
organization chart(s)   27, 34, 40, 41,
   117, 135
overtime   120, 129

personnel   2, 3, 9, 10, 32, 34, 42, 74, 75,
   77, 93, 117, 127, 133, 154–76
personnel management, practice
   of   172–5, 176
Philips   21
planning, financial   34
pluralist model   80–1

political view (of organizational behaviour)   78–87, 89
power   81–7, 89
pre-industrial production   3–5
pricing policy   30
process costing   44
process production   38, 39
production   1, 3, 4, 6, 10, 32, 34, 35, 36, 42, 74, 75, 80, 94, 102, 107, 113, 116–33, 142
production control (controller)   28, 31, 32, 93, 94, 113, 116, 117, 124, 127, 138
production engineer (engineering)   29, 55, 93, 116, 119
production management   36, 93, 116
production manager(s)   32, 45, 94, 96, 100, 103, 114, 117, 118, 119, 122, 123, 124, 125, 126, 128, 129, 130, 158, 159, 161
productivity   9, 24, 55, 90, 169, 178
profit and loss account   43, 44
puppydog close   150
purchasing   2, 3, 10, 24, 31, 74, 75, 77, 90–115, 116, 127, 133
purchasing, when difficult   105–8, 115

quality circles   131, 182–3, 198
quality control   34, 93, 101–3, 107, 117, 133

RAF   40
recession   24, 25, 99, 141, 178
Red Star parcel service   98
research and development, R & D   9, 10, 32, 35, 36, 77, 93, 95, 111, 120, 127
Revlon   147
Rolls Royce   109
Rowntree   135, 156

sales (function)   30, 31, 33, 42, 93, 107, 117, 127, 128, 131, 133, 134–53
salesman(men)   131, 134, 135, 137, 138, 139, 140, 141, 142, 143, 144, 145, 146, 147, 148, 149, 150
salesman, background and qualifications   140–2
Schein, Edgar   59, 72
Scott Bader   189

Second World War   7, 12, 19, 21, 178, 183
selection (personnel)   157–61
Sex Discrimination Act 1975   186
shop floor management   50–1
shop loading   116
shop steward(s)   164, 165, 166, 170, 173, 176
Skinner, Wickham   131, 132
small company buying   108–10, 115
statement of the sources and uses of funds   43
Stock Exchange   8, 9, 20
stockist(s)   108, 136
structure and technology   36–9
structure of business organization nineteenth century   7–8
twentieth century   9–10
Sweden   169, 193
superintendent   29, 30, 33, 34, 116, 117, 137
supplier(s)   2, 3, 24, 73, 75, 79, 80, 95, 96, 97, 98, 99, 100, 101, 102, 103, 104, 105, 106, 107, 108, 109, 110, 111, 112, 114, 115, 123, 140
systems model approach   73–8, 87

Taylor, Frederick   50–1, 53, 62, 63, 72
Telecoms Gold   139
Third World   141
Thomas, Sidney   18
time study   51
Trades Union Congress (TUC)   164, 166
training   35, 81, 117, 154, 171, 173, 175

unemployment   24, 25, 65, 177, 186, 196
causes   178–9
consequences   179
and the future   180–1
how it feels   179–80
union(s) (trade)   2, 6, 7, 11, 13, 21, 25, 26, 75, 79, 164, 165, 166, 167, 168, 169, 170, 176, 182
United States   14, 22–3, 33, 183, 193
unit production   37, 38, 39
USSR   141

Value Added Tax 13
value engineering 116
vendor analysis 105, 115
vertical integration 92
Volkswagen 97–8
Volvo 148

Walker, Samuel 17
Watt, James 15, 17
Woodward 37–9
worker participation 20
workforce size 120
works manager 28, 32, 35

The FODMAP Friendly Kitchen

The
FODMAP
Friendly
Kitchen

100 easy, delicious recipes for
a healthy gut and a happy life

Emma Hatcher

yellow
kite

I dedicate this book to my readers, without whom this would never have been possible. We're in this together, you brilliant bunch, and I hope this book gives back just some of the inspiration and support you've given me.

Contents

FOREWORD – FODMAP FRIENDLY 8

My story – Emma Hatcher 11

IBS AND FOOD INTOLERANCES 18

GETTING FODMAP FRIENDLY 20

A CLOSER LOOK AT FODMAPS 22

A new way of cooking 29

MY STORE CUPBOARD 32

A FEW NOTES ON USING THIS BOOK 39

ESSENTIALS 42

Recipes 47

GOOD MORNING SUNSHINE 49

WHOLESOME LUNCHES AND NUTRITIOUS SUPPERS 73

MID-AFTERNOON SLUMP 119

SOMETHING SPECIAL 135

SWEET TREATS 171

DELICIOUS DESSERTS 197

SAMPLE MENUS 220

STRESS, FREQUENTLY ASKED QUESTIONS AND TOP TIPS 226

RESOURCES AND REFERENCES 230

INDEX 232

Dear readers,

I wanted to start by saying that I am like so many of you. Busy, active, happy and yet somebody with a gut that just does not want to play by the rules.

But thankfully now I love my gut and it loves me. Sure we have our ups and downs, sometimes we fight – mainly when there's milk chocolate involved – but for the majority of the time we live in harmony, chilling out with delish food that's low in a thing called FODMAPs.

Cutting out foods that are high in FODMAPs doesn't have to be hard. In this book I'll explain how FODMAP friendly living works, and share my favourite recipes with you. Gut health can have such a huge impact on your life, and I hope that this book will change yours in the same way it has mine. Enjoy!

Lots of love,

Emma x

FOREWORD

Emma's blog caught our eye some time ago. Not only are her photographs bright, positive and beautifully presented, but her personality shone through in the content she was creating. Her passion for helping those with food intolerances was paramount, and we could feel it was the start of something big.

We first met up with Emma in London, when working on FODMAP Friendly during a trip over from Melbourne in 2015. Since then our relationship has blossomed with the objective of spreading the FODMAP word, sparking both a close friendship and opportunities to work together.

Emma knows first-hand just how nasty suffering from IBS, or even just some of its symptoms can be, and we're sure many of you reading this will too.

Irritable Bowel Syndrome (IBS) currently affects 1 in 7 individuals on a daily basis. Medically, it's defined as a syndrome affecting the large colon and a chronic condition that requires long-term management. Symptoms include cramping, abdominal pain, bloating, diarrhoea and constipation. Charming, right? Even if you haven't been diagnosed with IBS, chances are that you have experienced some of these symptoms after eating.

The good news is, a management plan has been found – one that sees results for over 70 per cent of sufferers.

Research from the last two decades has shown that FODMAP sugars (full low-down on what these are on page 20) are known to cause IBS type symptoms, due to the body's inability to break them down during the first stages of digestion. These sugars are poorly absorbed in the small intestine, so move into the large intestine, where they're fed on by bacteria, a process known as fermentation. This in turn leads to the production of gas, and can result in many unpleasant gastrointestinal symptoms, such as those mentioned.

Numerous studies have consistently proven the efficiency of a low FODMAP approach to managing IBS on a global scale. Prominent examples include:

– A study in Australia that showed 85 per cent of patients reported experiencing improved symptoms with the implementation of a Low FODMAP Diet to manage their IBS symptoms (Shepherd et al, 2006).

– A King's College London clinical study (Staudacher, 2011) into IBS management, that showed the adoption of a Low FODMAP Diet for six weeks to show an improvement in 78 per cent of patients.

– A 2016 clinical trial conducted by doctors at the University of Michigan Health System that concluded at four weeks, the proportion of patients with a meaningful improvement in IBS severity and quality of life was significantly higher in the low FODMAP group compared to the control group – 61 per cent versus 27 per cent.

Consequently, the adoption of a diet low in FODMAPs is now regarded as the recommended treatment for IBS worldwide. This approach is now endorsed by health professionals around the globe, and was recently written into the National Institute for Health and Care Excellence (NICE) guidelines: evidence-based recommendations for health and care in the UK.

Adopting a diet low in FODMAPs requires commitment, but this book will make it simple and easy to follow. The diet itself is comprised of three phases – elimination, reintroduction and maintenance – which were devised from original research into managing IBS through a reduction in FODMAPs, and the findings that were produced. By progressing through the three phases, and reducing the amount of FODMAPs in your diet, your gut wall has a chance to repair and heal. The end aim is to eat and live as freely as possible with the least restrictions you can get away with - the more FODMAPs you can return to your diet, after giving your gut wall a chance to repair and without triggering symptoms, the healthier (and happier) your gut is likely to be.

Alongside diet, stress plays a big part in IBS too. Its associated symptoms can be embarrassing to manage, which can increase stress levels as a result. Unfortunately, stress is then associated with an increase in symptoms, which can exacerbate the condition overall. The shame and awkwardness associated with gastrointestinal symptoms can be socially isolating – social situations involving food and drink can start to feel like a nightmare and sometimes it's just easier to avoid them for fear of inducing symptoms.

Research is also emerging about the link between gut health overall and depression, due to the interaction of the central nervous system function in the brain with the body's digestive processes. This link is known as the 'gut brain axis', and is an area of research that is constantly expanding, giving us a greater insight into the relationships between emotions, life situations and the gut immune system.

Therefore along with allowing the gut wall to repair and heal, adopting a Low FODMAP Diet, may also have the ability to reduce such symptoms of stress and anxiety.

So who are we? FODMAP Friendly is the only registered Certification Trademark worldwide certifying FODMAP levels in packaged foods. Our job is to have foods tested and certified for their FODMAP status. All foods are independently tested in an approved scientific laboratory, by a team of qualified scientists and technicians. The FODMAP thresholds have been set in accordance to the original research into FODMAPs. Foods which fall below the set thresholds are deemed eligible for certification, and are eligible to carry the FODMAP Friendly approved green logo. This logo is displayed on product packaging and is designed to take

the guesswork out of supermarket shopping, label reading and ingredient confusion! The FODMAP Friendly green logo allows you to select products, knowing that the food has been independently tested for FODMAP levels, so that you can eat with confidence.

Our aim is to continually increase public awareness and understanding about IBS management, and make adopting a diet low in FODMAPs an easier prospect. When approached by Emma and Hodder & Stoughton to co-author this cookbook, we were thrilled with the prospect of working together – and even more excited for the recipes! Emma's personal story, tips and life-hacks, along with information provided by ourselves, within *The FODMAP Friendly Kitchen*, will show you that you're not alone, gut health is important, your symptoms can be managed, and you can still eat some downright delicious food!

We hope you enjoy it.

The FODMAP Friendly team

My story

I'm going to put it out there. Being diagnosed with food intolerances, irritable bowel syndrome or any digestive disorder, SUCKS. A sensitive gut isn't sexy, and I – like so many of you – have had one for as long as I can remember.

We don't really talk about it, because it's just not cool. No one likes bowels. The word alone makes me shudder a little bit and even though I was diagnosed with irritable bowel syndrome at the age of fourteen, I still find myself referring to it when asked, as 'IBS' in a hushed whisper. It's as if shortening and saying it quickly makes it a bit more acceptable in public, a little more PC.

But, sadly, you can't make leaving a friend's birthday early because your stomach has expanded a good eight inches and you're doubled over in pain, or a night spent in a restaurant bathroom – instead of at the table – because you didn't know your innocuous-sounding meal was going to wreak havoc on your insides, more socially acceptable. 'I was up all night – my gut's really suffering' doesn't quite have the same ring to it as 'I've got a terrible cold/an awful migraine – I just don't think I'm going to make it today'.

If you're like me, when symptoms were debilitating – and out-and-out embarrassing – I didn't want to go to work; or venture far. I hated being invited to my lovely friends' homes for dinner and having to explain why I couldn't eat this or that, and I was always wary of going to a festival or party when my gut was playing up, just in case. Even just feeling bloated and sluggish after every meal was getting frustrating. Sound familiar?

When, at the age of fifteen, my doctor at the time first suggested cutting out wheat, I jumped at the chance – anything to help the pain. But while it helped for a year or so, it wasn't long before symptoms started creeping up again. I'd go back to my doctor and each time they would suggest a new food to remove, and each time the restriction was met with only varying degrees of success. I'd go through phases of good and bad weeks and quickly noticed that stress played a huge part too. I tried everything, from changing what times of day I ate, to portion sizes, but nothing helped long term.

It wasn't until I was twenty-one and still suffering horrendous symptoms that repeated hospital visits confirmed for a second time, that a gluten intolerance and IBS were the main culprits of my illness, and a dietician suggested the Low FODMAP Diet.

Within two weeks my life had completely changed.

Gone were the nasty stomach aches and bloating and the constant thoughts of 'oh man, what caused it this time?' I felt less stressed, I had more energy, and I was happier because I wasn't constantly frustrated at my gut! I hadn't realised before just how much it had affected my life, ever since I was young.

The only issue was that although the diet was incredible, it seemed still relatively unknown. The information I was given by my dietician at the time filled no more than an uninspiring four-page leaflet and alongside my research I quickly noticed that there was a huge lack of easy, nourishing recipes available that were both genuinely healthy and low FODMAP.

The traditionally healthy recipes I came across were often high in FODMAP-containing foods such as dates and nuts. And on the other hand, the (few) existing low FODMAP recipes were high in fat, contained lots of processed ingredients, and all really meat-heavy. As well as wanting to avoid symptoms, I wanted a healthy and nourished gut too – along with stand-out, delicious food - and refused to believe that you couldn't marry all three.

So I shut myself in the kitchen and started cooking. I encouraged (gently forced) my family and friends to try my creations, and the great response I got, along with the way I was feeling, was amazing.

I started a blog called 'She Can't Eat What?!' and filled it with my experiences, along with the easy, healthy, low FODMAP recipes that I was eating. Determined to share my knowledge on all things FODMAP friendly – and my love of food – I wanted to help others and, while I was at it, help create a better understanding of digestive disorders and food intolerances in the UK.

I never appreciated the scale of how many people were affected by a sensitive gut, IBS or other digestive disorders, until I started talking. I received messages from people all over the world telling me how great it was for more information to be out there, along with easy, realistic recipes. People are so powerful, hilarious and genuine, I think because we can relate to what each other have been through.

A NEW FOOD PHILOSOPHY

I love to eat. A lot. I often joke that I learnt how to cook delicious FODMAP friendly meals because I'm greedy and couldn't bear a life without tasty food. But in an increasingly busy world, with growing pressures and stress, there's never been a more important time to think about what we eat – and how it affects our health. While there are so many aspects that come into play for a healthy gut, food is paramount.

IBS or a sensitive gut affects so many of you lovely lot, throughout the world. Yet from blogging, meeting and talking to people, I've realised just how many of us ignore our symptoms. We're so busy and they've become so normalised, so routine, that we forget they're there. We're so cut off from our bodies and our bellies – myself included – and if I'm busy at work then out in the evening, a whole twenty-four hours can have passed and I won't have had a moment to think about what I actually ate or how my gut is feeling.

Many of us eat the same convenience food industry staples week in and week out and have incredibly busy lives. But along with what you eat, how you eat and cook is without doubt one of the most important things we can do for our health. Developing a good relationship with food is crucial, and I want to banish the idea that cooking has to be complicated, bland or time consuming, especially if catering for a sensitive gut.

Our digestion determines the health of each cell in our body. Strong, effective digestion can result in great energy, glowing skin, deep sleep and good mood, while bad digestion and an unhappy gut can lead to low energy, breakouts, poor sleep, mood swings, anxiety and a lack of confidence to boot. You could be eating the most nutrient-packed diet around, full of leafy greens and fresh fruit, but if your body isn't absorbing that goodness it all goes to waste.

THIS BOOK

Whether you've recently been diagnosed with IBS or a similar digestive disorder, have struggled with a sensitive gut for many years and are running out of ideas, or are now realising your tum just needs a bit of TLC, this book will give you all the information you need to know about the Low FODMAP Diet, along with over 100 low FODMAP recipes, for healthy, everyday, real-life living.

From breakfast to dinner and everything in between, I've written this book not only to teach you how to create delicious

meals with the foods you can eat (which are still a lot, by the way!), but to show you a new stress-free and modern-day way to cook for your sensitive gut that is both simple and inclusive.

The FODMAP Friendly Kitchen is divided into lifestyle chapters to make it easier to navigate in everyday cooking, and I've created recipes that are all designed to be flexible and adaptable. Although this approach is backed by scientific research, it's important to remember that everybody and everybody's gut is unique, so although I can tell you what foods I can now tolerate after completing the three phases, your tolerance levels might be different. You'll know your body and gut better than anyone else and we ask you to listen to it and how it reacts to certain foods. Play, adapt and amend recipes to suit you.

This way of eating is not about deprivation but about taking back control so that you can manage those nasty symptoms. My hope is that this book will provide you with an arsenal of healthy, simple FODMAP friendly recipes that you can amend and build from, because if you do have food intolerances, allergies, or a delicate gut, you shouldn't have to feel restricted in what you eat! Everybody deserves to be healthy and happy – and eat doughnuts (page 190).

Now it's not going to be easy. You've got to be really committed to nurturing your gut and giving it a chance to heal. You might make mistakes and some days suffer from a few symptoms – but I promise you the crap's not going to hit the fan if you mess up, you'll feel better and you'll be more confident as a result. Once you get your digestive system back on track and it's had a chance to heal, you can then reintroduce foods back into your diet and you might even find you can tolerate more than you could before.

So it's time to listen to your body and your gut and learn what foods are best for you! The kind of food that makes you smile and leaves you with a very happy belly.

Welcome to my kitchen x

IBS AND FOOD INTOLERANCES

In the past decade, IBS has become one of the most common health conditions to date, and 1 in 3 people suffer from bloating on a regular basis.

SO WHAT ACTUALLY IS IBS?

The medical definition of IBS states that it's a common disorder that affects the large intestine (colon). Commonly causing cramping, abdominal pain, bloating, diarrhoea and constipation (told you it was sexy), IBS is a chronic condition that needs to be managed long term. In the majority of people, no single cause has been identified to explain IBS or a sensitive gut. Instead, gut sensitivity may have been triggered by an emotion, or in some cases a crisis, either in the gut such as gastroenteritis or a traumatic life event.

WHAT CAUSES IBS SYMPTOMS AND WHY ARE THEY SO COMMON?

Research spanning across the last two decades has shown that FODMAP sugars, found in a variety of foods, are known to cause IBS type symptoms. This is due to the body's inability to break them down, creating these symptoms as a response.

After passing through the stomach, these sugars aren't properly digested in the small intestine, and move into the large intestine, where a large colony of bacteria reside. These bacteria 'feed' on the malabsorbed sugar, resulting in fermentation. Fermentation leads to the production of gas, which can in turn result in an onslaught of uncomfortable symptoms, such as bloating, stomach distension – aka when it feels like somebody's trying to wring out your insides – general stomach pain and constipation. Because your gut is kindly trying to balance things out for you, there's also often increased water delivery to the large bowel in an effort by the body to help the digestive process, which may inspire diarrhoea as a result. Lovely.

Severity of symptoms differs largely between people, and also within an individual's lifespan. IBS isn't characterised as an immune-related response, it's categorised as a food intolerance rather than an allergy. This means it can manifest itself as a physiological reaction to stress, alcohol, and other life influences too.

THE LINK BETWEEN THE BRAIN AND THE GUT

Research shows that stress levels and emotional health can impact us IBS sufferers, due to a phenomenon known as the 'gut brain axis'. Put simply, it's been recognised that there's a link between our central nervous system function in the brain and the digestive process happening in the gastrointestinal tract. A fascinating research area that is constantly growing, I talk more about mindfulness and stress reduction on page 226.

CROHN'S DISEASE, COELIAC DISEASE AND OTHER DIGESTIVE DISORDERS

Recently, research has emerged regarding the link between FODMAPs and it's ability to help those with inflammatory bowel disease (IBD) conditions such as Crohn's and ulcerative colitis. Although both of these conditions require a specific management plan and are generally nastier than IBS, studies show that a diet low in FODMAPs can also be used to help soothe unresolved digestive issues.

Contrary to IBS, coeliac disease is an auto-immune condition (an allergy), where damage to the intestinal lining and the body's antibody production requires a sufferer to remove all gluten-containing foods from their diet. It affects 1 in 120 people and a number of coeliacs find that a diet low in FODMAPs is helpful in reducing ongoing digestive issues they may still be experiencing, despite their adoption of a fully gluten-free diet also.

BREAKING THE TABOO AROUND SYMPTOMS

For many people there is a still a great deal of stigma around discussions of digestive health. Toilet chat is still pretty taboo – I'm OK with that, I'm not saying we should give everyone a detailed low-down each time we go, but we still shy away from talking about IBS, and often allow our unhappy guts and their effects to become so habitual, that we start to ignore them.

It's time to start making gut health a priority! You know your body better than anybody and not only is this book about YOU taking control of your sensitive, dodgy gut (using health care professionals for advice and reassurance where necessary obviously) with the aim of lessening symptoms, but also being comfortable and confident talking about them with others.

GETTING FODMAP FRIENDLY

WTF ARE FODMAPS?

FODMAP is an acronym that stands for:

Fermentable – meaning they are quickly broken down (fermented) by bacteria in the large bowel

Oligosaccharides – fructans and galacto-oligosaccharides (GOS) (wheat, onion, garlic, beans)

Disaccharides – lactose (milk, ice cream)

Monosaccharides – fructose (apples, pears, honey)

And

Polyols – sugar alcohols, such as sorbitol and mannitol (mushrooms, apricots, gum)

I know – it's a lot to take in. But really the above words are just complex names for a collection of molecules (more specifically short-chain carbohydrates and sugar alcohols), found in foods naturally and in food additives. Just remember, saccharide is basically another word for sugar. A monosaccharide has one sugar, a disaccharide has two, an oligosaccharide has a few and a polysaccharide has more than ten. Polyols are just sugar molecules with an alcohol side-chain (don't worry – there won't be a test on whether you remember all of this).

SO WHAT DOES THE DIET DO?

A diet low in FODMAPs is now recommended internationally as the most effective dietary therapy for IBS and other nasty disorders. A Low FODMAP Diet has also been proven, with solid scientific research, to reduce symptoms of fatigue, lethargy and poor concentration.

The principle of a Low FODMAP Diet for IBS is to restrict the foods high in FODMAPs causing chaos in the gut, before working out an individual's own personal tolerance thresholds. This means it can be tailored to you specifically and as a result improve the gut symptoms associated with IBS.

What you have to remember is that it's not about being incredibly restrictive long term. The ultimate goal is to eat and live as freely as possible with the least restrictions you can get away with – the more FODMAPs you can return to your diet without triggering symptoms, the healthier yout gut is likely to be.

EVERYBODY'S DIFFERENT

The short-chain carbs/FODMAPs are in everyday foods and are always poorly absorbed, but it comes down to you and your gut on whether, and how much, you can tolerate them. People who have IBS have very sensitive intestines, and the stretching of the gut that comes from the poor absorption contributes to a lot of pain. Many can tolerate some FODMAPs, while others may find that all FODMAPs can be symptom triggers. Not everyone has a problem with all the different FODMAP groups, which is why it's important to work with a nutritionist or dietician to figure out what exactly your specific trigger foods are. By controlling and managing the consumption of foods that contain the FODMAPs triggering your symptoms you should then be able to significantly reduce or even say goodbye to your IBS type symptoms. Hurrah!

IS A FODMAP FRIENDLY LIFESTYLE SUITED TO ME?

The elimination and reintroduction phases of the diet are quite complex approaches and so it's fully recommended that you consult a healthcare professional to help guide you through the diet and to make sure you've ruled out associated digestive conditions such as coeliac and inflammatory bowel disease and have undertaken all relevant tests.

After ruling out other health conditions, you can also get a breath test, to identify and pinpoint the offending sugars in your diet. From here, you will have a base as to which sugars are the most malabsorbed, and can begin your low FODMAP journey to improve your symptoms.

IS A FODMAP FRIENDLY DIET A GLUTEN-FREE DIET?

Contrary to popular belief, no. Gluten is not a FODMAP. Many health professionals, prior to the discovery of FODMAPs, recommended a fully gluten-free diet to non-coeliac IBS sufferers to decrease their symptoms – I was instructed to do so myself.

Many assumed it was the gluten portion of grains causing IBS type symptoms, due to the similarities between gluten (a protein found in grains) and wheat (a carbohydrate in grains which contains FODMAP fructan sugars). But by removing these grains from their diet, people weren't consuming the fructans in the wheat either! And it's more likely that that is what was helping people.

To break it down a bit:

Grains containing GLUTEN (a protein) include:

- wheat
- rye
- barley
- spelt
- triticale (wheat + rye)

Grains containing WHEAT (a carbohydrate containing the FODMAP fructan sugarss) include:

- wheat
- rye
- barley
- spelt
- triticale (wheat + rye)

Both wheat and gluten are therefore tightly interwoven, but many studies suggest that gluten is a very uncommon trigger for symptoms of IBS – instead it is the fructans, a type of FODMAP, found in wheat that could be causing the chaos.

A CLOSER LOOK AT FODMAPS

SUITABLE FOODS AND FOODS TO AVOID

This list is by no means conclusive but hopefully gives you an overview of the FODMAP amounts in various foods, so that you can have an understanding of why particular ingredients are used, and the amounts in which they are used, in the recipes in ths book. The chart is just a guide - everybody has different tolerance levels and just because a food is listed as high in FODMAPs it might not mean that you can never eat it, likewise if it's low in FODMAPs it might not mean that your gut always loves it – so experiment (safely!) to find out what's best for you and don't be afraid to adapt the recipes to suit.

FRUIT

Generally, stoned fruits are high in FODMAPs, along with watermelons and other fruits such as blackberries - but there are still plenty of others to eat. Dried fruit often means an increased concentration of FODMAPs, so it's often best to keep these in small portions.

VEGETABLES AND PULSES

Veggies and pulses are a mixed bag when it comes to the FODMAP diet, but there is a huge variety low in FODMAPs. The green parts of leeks and spring onions are low FODMAP and great for adding flavour. Unfortunately most legumes aren't low FODMAP – but tinned lentils and chickpeas can be easier on the gut because the FODMAPs leach out into the liquid, which you can then remove, by draining and rinsing before eating. Just make sure you stick to recommended portion sizes.

GRAINS, CEREALS AND FLOURS

Many assume that a Low FODMAP Diet means no grains, cereals or flours, but there are tonnes of options out there. Unless Ceoliac, don't write off wheat, barley and rye entirely – small amounts may be tolerated by some people with a sensitive gut: one slice of toast or a small bit of wheat flour coating on fish for example. However lots of other options are listed and are used in the recipes in this book that contain lower amounts of FODMAPs which means eating them in bigger amounts shouldn't affect your gut. Gluten-free bread is now readily available, but check for high FODMAP additives such as high-fructose corn syrup, honey and chicory root/inulin, which is often added by food companies to boost the fiber content of their products.

DAIRY AND NON-DAIRY SUBSTITUTES

You might be pleased to know that a Low FODMAP Diet isn't a dairy free diet! It's the lactose you might need to watch out for. Most hard cheeses contain very little lactose so are suitable and although butter is a dairy product, it's considered low FODMAP in small amounts as it contains very little lactose too. If you can tolerate it, sub in regular butter anywhere I've specified lactose-free. Watch out for yoghurts labelled dairy or lactose free; they often contain chicory root or inulin and can be sweetened with honey or apple juice.

NUTS AND SEEDS

Most nuts and seeds can be eaten in small portions without causing symptoms, but some are lower in FODMAPs than others. Alternate in recipes, adapting to suit your tolerances.

SWEETENERS

Beware of an excess of fructose when it comes to sweeteners – I find maple syrup and brown sugar great options for sweet recipes.

A QUICK NOTE ON...

Fish, eggs and meat: Any plain fish or meat, along with eggs should be FODMAP friendly. Try to avoid fatty cuts of meat, or

	Low in FODMAPs	Medium in FODMAPs	High in FODMAPs
	Suggested to eat as part of your normal diet	Suggested to be eaten in medium amounts	Suggested to be eaten only in very small amounts
FRUIT	Bananas (ripe, but not overripe), blueberries, clementines, grapes, kiwi fruits, lemons, limes, melons (cantelope and honeydew), oranges, papayas, passion fruits, pineapples, raspberries, rhubarb, strawberries	Avocados, cranberries, dessicated coconut, grapefruits, raisins	Apples, apricots, blackberries, cherries, dates, figs, mangos, nectarines, peaches, pears, plums, prunes, sultanas, watermelons
VEGETABLES AND PULSES	Alfalfa, aubergines, blueberries, broccoli, cabbage, carrots, celeriac, chard, chillies, chives, courgettes, cucumbers, ginger, kale, leeks (green leaves only), lettuces, okra, olives (green and black), parsnips, peppers, potatos, radishes, spinach, tomatoes, turnips, watercress	Beetroots, brussel sprouts, butternut squashes, celery, pumpkin, sweet potatoes, chickpeas (canned), green beans, lentils (canned)	Asparagus, cauliflowers, garlic, mushrooms, onions, peas, sweetcorn, baked beans, black beans, borlotti beans, broad beans, butter beans, cannellini beans
GRAINS, CEREALS AND FLOURS	Buckwheat flour, corn flour, maize flour, potato starch, rice flour, sorghum flour, tapioca flour, quinoa flour, rice (white, brown, red or wild), polenta, quinoa and quinoa flakes	100% spelt bread, oats	Wheat flour, barley flour, wholegrain/wholemeal flour, rye flour
DAIRY AND NON-DAIRY SUBSTITUTES	Almond milk, lactose-free milk, lactose-free yoghurt, rice milk, brie, camembert, cheddar cheese, cottage cheese, feta cheese, goats' cheese, mozzerella cheese, parmesan, pecorino, swiss cheese	Butter, coconut milk, yoghurt (greek, full fat), sour cream, cream cheese, halloumi, ricotta	Custard, cows' milk, kefi
NUTS AND SEEDS	Brazil nuts, macadamia nuts, peanuts, pecans, pine nuts, walnuts	Almonds, chia seeds, hazelnuts, linseeds, pumpkin seeds, sesame seeds, sunflower seeds	Cashews, pistachios
SWEETENERS	Golden syrup, maple syrup, sugar (brown, caster, icing, raw, white)	Coconut sugar	Agave syrup, artificial sweeteners ending with 'ol' such as sorbitol, mannitol, xylitol, fructose, golden syrup, honey, inulin

eat in small portions, as fat can aggravate symptoms. Watch out for sausages and other processed meats as they often contain wheat, garlic and/or onions, all of which can upset a sensitive gut.

Herbs and spices: Almost all fresh and dried herbs and spices are suitable – just watch out for too much chilli and foods that are very spicy, as these can cause symptoms for some.

Oils: All oils are low FODMAP as they are carbohydrate free. However, just like with fatty cuts of meat, some people with IBS struggle to tolerate fats in large amounts (and we shouldn't be having too much anyway!), so it's been suggested to eat these in moderation.

SO WHAT NEXT?

Following a Low FODMAP Diet is a three-phase process. The first is the elimination phase, where you remove all high FODMAP foods from your diet. After that, each subgroup is slowly introduced back into the diet, one at a time. That way, you know if it's the lactose group that's a problem, the fructans group, or one of the others. Finally, phase three allows you to eat what you want, whilst avoiding the high FODMAP foods or groups that were a trigger during phase two.

ELIMINATION PHASE

The elimination phase is the first in the series of three phases to get your gut back dancing and to its optimum health. In these 8 weeks, you're going to remove all the foods that are known to be high in FODMAPS from your diet and that could be irritating your gut.

The elimination phase should be implemented for 8 weeks in order to establish the role of FODMAPs in triggering symptoms. It's likely you'll see a big improvement in symptoms after 3–5 days but you should stick with it for the full 8 weeks for the best results. It's important to remember that FODMAPs aren't all bad. They are good for gut health, producing short-chain fatty acids which are partly used as food for beneficial bacteria. So after 8 weeks it is time to move on to the next phase and reintroduce some FODMAPs into your diet.

REINTRODUCTION PHASE

Once you have followed the diet for 8 weeks and you know your gut is happier, it's time for you to reintroduce FODMAPs, listen to your own body and establish your own tolerance levels by identifying the type and amount of FODMAPs that trigger symptoms. Once you understand your own FODMAP triggers, you can then move on to the maintenance phase.

The goal is to systematically reintroduce each FODMAP one at a time to establish your thresholds. The reintroduction phase should last for roughly 5 weeks, during which time you should trial a FODMAP each week. Eat the challenge food three times during the test week, in normal portion sizes and evenly spaced out (or until symptoms are triggered). Continue to restrict all other FODMAPs until your tolerance level is confirmed.

Keep track of what you eat, monitor your symptoms and record how you feel.

If you get symptoms, make sure your gut has had a chance to settle before trying again with a smaller portion size, or assume the FODMAP is a problem for you and come back to it in the future, as your sensitivity to that particular FODMAP might change over time. If you don't get symptoms, continue to eat the amount and type of food you have tested and move on to trying the next FODMAP challenge.

This phase isn't easy, I know. It is likely at some stage your IBS symptoms will reappear when you find a trigger food and these symptoms could last for a few days – I know mine did. But when this happened I tried to focus on the positive – that I now had identified a trigger and could manage the bastard! And it might be you can still reintroduce this food into your diet but at a lower level – baked beans used to kill my stomach but now a couple of mouthfuls and I'm fine.

It's known that people may have varying degrees of thresholds for each FODMAP, however. This means that for some of us certain FODMAPs may never be well tolerated, while for others they might be OK. I have friends that follow the diet and can tolerate avocados for example (lucky things), while avocados for me, along with other foods containing polyols such as mushrooms and sweet potato, cause me agony.

On the other hand I can now tolerate medium amounts of honey and eat an apple (yes!), both of which contain excess fructose, whereas my friends still have to steer clear. Ingredients such as onions, however, are off the food list for all of us for a while.

But that's why it's so important to slowly reintroduce some FODMAPs into the diet, to establish these thresholds and gauge personal tolerance levels. Since FODMAPs are found in so many healthy foods, you don't want to overly restrict the diet if you don't have to. Restricting dietary intake of a wide array of foods may lead to nutritional deficiencies – and we don't want any of that. Furthermore, FODMAPs contain key prebiotic fibres which are important for establishing and maintaining optimal gut health, long term, so make sure you go through this phase – it's worth it, I promise!

MAINTENANCE PHASE

Congratulations for getting this far! Here you can be much more chilled with your ingredients and portion sizes (so amazing). That's not to say you can go back to what you were eating before. But now you're aware both of your key triggers and of the FODMAPs that don't cause you symptoms, you can experiment a bit more. I hope that, like me at this point, you feel so empowered to be back in control of what you eat and, most importantly, how you feel. Understanding what and why your trigger foods are causing havoc and being able to manage them is the most incredible thing.

So celebrate! A variety of foods is important both nutritionally and just for pure enjoyment. All fresh and packaged foods which are low in FODMAPS (look out for the FODMAP Friendly logo) are allowed here, along with any foods that contain FODMAPs that were OK for you during testing. Ultimately, you can 'FODMAP-up' your diet as tolerated. It's all about what you can eat – not what you can't.

Just a quick note: as FODMAP tolerance levels do vary between people, sometimes it might not always be the best idea to 'push' your tolerances continually. If symptoms begin to re-emerge, don't worry – simply scale it back, focus on only low FODMAP foods for a few days and give your gut a chance to 'reset'.

One thing to watch out for: it's not just the amount of a single FODMAP that counts but the total amounts of FODMAPs in a meal. For example, you can eat a small piece of food containing FODMAPs on its own but if you whack it in a salad with ten other things higher in FODMAPs it might cause your gut havoc.

BEING FLEXIBLE

Just like these recipes can be adapted to your personal tolerances, they can also be adapted to suit which phase of the diet you are on.

Elimination phase: Be as strict as you can with the portion sizes we've recommended and keep using a food diary to note down exactly what you've eaten, how those foods made you feel and any other events or big stresses that are going on at the time. Stay as close to the recipes as you can, only altering if you know the sub ingredient is suitable and don't be reluctant to keep referring to this book and other resources like a mad person, to build on your knowledge of what foods contain what FODMAPs – it takes time to learn!

Reintroduction phase: Follow the recipes in this book but do so alongside reintroducing the food groups as explained on page 25, adapting recipes if needed. Your food diary is really important for this phase.

Maintenance phase: Now you're aware both of your key triggers and the FODMAPs that don't cause you symptoms, you can experiment. For example, if sweet potato is fine for you, try adding it in my creamy green coconut curry – it's delicious. If apples made it through to your OK list, grate one on top of the bircher muesli right before serving for a lovely texture and extra bit of goodness. You won't know how your gut reacts to every food out there and it's likely there'll be some mistakes and symptoms, but if you have a bad episode don't worry – just revert to using the recipes as if you were in the elimination phase for a couple of days and give your gut a break.

A new way
of cooking

Cooking on a FODMAP friendly diet can be quite a different experience. I remember the first time I stood in my kitchen, opened my fridge, gazed down at the long list of foods I'd been told not to eat and *panicked*.

So I could eat green lentils from a tin but not from a carton? And the tops of spring onions but not the bottom? How does that work? I couldn't use onion *or* garlic to flavour my meal? And it had to be wheat free *and* low in lactose?

It was so incredibly daunting and this was only dinner – what was I going to eat for breakfast and lunch the next day?

So I embarked on the journey the only way I knew how: start simple. I'm sure that for lunch for the first two weeks all I did was eat soup that I made by blending cooked vegetables with hot water. It may well have been verging on baby food but actually it tasted pretty damn good and I had forgotten how delicious veggies can taste on their own. It turned out that with a bit of planning I didn't actually need lots of added ingredients to have a delicious meal and I soon noticed that when the quality of the veg I used was better, the better the soup tasted.

So that's the approach I've taken with the recipes in this book. I want to show you that it is possible to cook delicious varied and balanced FODMAP friendly dishes, with simple methods and ingredients, alongside giving you real, manageable tips that can be applied to daily cooking and weekly shopping.

If you're a newbie in the kitchen, to the Low FODMAP Diet, or if your gut just needs a bit of TLC, my hope is that this book will arm you with a foundation of recipes – joyful, flavoursome ones – so that when you too first look in your fridge and think what on earth do I eat, you can pick up this book and get cooking. If you're a confident cook, or are now well versed in the Low FODMAP Diet, I hope they'll add some more simple dishes to your repertoire and might inspire you to try something new. Either way, I hope to share just a few of the recipes I've created and use regularly in my kitchen at home, influenced both by my own experiences and working with FODMAP Friendly. I want to take the pressure and stress out of cooking FODMAP friendly food, so that both you and your gut are chilled and you not only enjoy cooking for yourself but are confident cooking for others too.

You have to be prepared for the fact that recipes may not act exactly the same as the original versions – cakes may not rise as dramatically as a wheat flour sponge and fruit-based ice cream may not hold the same texture as its milk and cream-based counterpart – but they offer a new way to eat. These ingredients not only work for those with a sensitive gut, but they taste amazing and are often full of nutrients too.

I've given a list of my favourite food essentials on the next pages but although they suit me, you might find you have other favourites, that your gut loves better.

It's your responsibility to take care of your body and learn how it reacts to different foods. Working with a dietician when on the Low FODMAP Diet, especially throughout the elimination and reintroduction phases, is crucial – but at the end of the day it's you that's going to know what works for your body and what doesn't. Some FODMAPS cause more trouble for some people than others – it depends on the proportions in the diet, how sensitive you are to each FODMAP, how well or poorly you absorb fructose or lactose. So take the time to listen to your body and use it as an excuse to try lots of foods in the meantime.

MY STORE CUPBOARD

Many of the following ingredients have become staples in my kitchen. In addition to cooking with fresh ingredients it helps to have some delicious essentials on hand to make everything that bit easier.

One of the first things I did when starting the diet was go food shopping and fill my cupboard and fridge full of as many low FODMAP gut-friendly ingredients as possible. I'd love to say that my kitchen cupboards are tidy and perfectly organised, but as my housemates well know there is no order; just chaos. Every space is crammed full of ingredients, but one of the things I love most is being able to reach in and pull something out to help transform a dish.

I've tried to make sure that many of the same ingredients filter through the recipes so that you don't have to buy a million and one things, although some ingredients are a little different. All should be possible to find in large supermarkets and high-street grocers however, but if not head online. I've listed my go to places at the back of this book (page 230).

GRAINS

There are so many incredible grains out there – it's never been easier, cheaper or tastier to include them in your diet. Some of my FODMAP friendly staples include: quinoa, buckwheat, rice, oats and millet. It should be noted, however, that some of these do contain medium amounts of FODMAPS in large quantities, so do watch portion sizes.

Quinoa I love this stuff. Pronounced 'keen-wah' not 'quin-oah', this grain-like seed is actually from the same family as chard, spinach and beetroot, and it's been a staple food in its homeland South America for hundreds of years. It's full of protein and includes all nine essential amino acids, plus it's jam-packed full of dietary fibre – meaning it's slowly digested keeping you fuller for longer. Use as a FODMAP friendly alternative in place of bulgur wheat or couscous or try it in

breakfast dishes instead of oats, such as quinoa porridge (page 58). For baking, try quinoa flakes, which, like oats, are made from steaming the grain and then rolling to create a thin flake.

Buckwheat Derived from the seeds of a flowering plant, buckwheat isn't a grain or a cereal (you may hear it being called a pseudo-cereal but don't let that scare you!). It's got a rich, nutty, wholesome flavour and is low FODMAP and fructose friendly, which makes it a perfect alternative for IBS or allergy sufferers to use in both savoury and sweet recipes when made into flour. Buckwheat groats, which recipes such as buckwheat risotto (page 142) call for, are the buckwheat kernels that have been crushed.

Brown and white rice Rice often gets a bad rap but I think it's actually a great budget-friendly addition to a low FODMAP diet. Brown rice does have more nutritional value and is a good source of fibre, but it can cause stomach upset for some people with IBS. Try both and work out your own tolerance. Rice noodles are great in stir-fries too (page 98); you can get them in most supermarkets.

Oats Oats are incredibly versatile and full of fibre. I love rolled oats not only in porridge but in chewy cookies, crunchy granola and filling smoothies too. They're naturally gluten-free, but like some other grains can get 'contaminated' with gluten if they're grown and processed close to wheat. If you're coeliac, make sure you purchase certified gluten-free oats, but otherwise normal oats should be fine to digest for those with a sensitive gut – just be mindful of serving sizes, however, as they are moderate in FODMAPs.

Millet Although it might often be the main ingredient in birdseed, millet is delicious for humans too! With a creamy texture, it's an easy to digest, gluten-free grain that can accompany many foods. It's also a good source of important nutrients such as copper, manganese, phosphorus and magnesium.

BEANS, LEGUMES, NUTS AND SEEDS

Lentils Low in calories, high in nutrition. Lentils are one of the few pulses that are suitable on the low FODMAP diet – but make sure you use lentils from a tin and stick to the recommended portion sizes. The FODMAPS found in lentils are water soluble so leach out of the lentils and into the water surrounding them. Just make sure you give them a good rinse before using.

Hemp seeds and sunflower seeds Two of my favourite seeds to use when cooking, most notably in baking, or sprinkled on top of salads to give an extra crunch. Hemp is a soft seed, full of flavor, with a rich, nutty texture. Sunflower seeds are mild and rich in healthy fats. Inexpensive and easy to get hold of, they're also a good source of potassium and iron.

Peanuts, macadamia nuts, walnuts and pecans Some of my favourite FODMAP friendly nuts to use when cooking (or just for munching on as a snack). Packed with protein, fibre and essential fats, all have their own characteristics and in moderation are great additions to a FODMAP friendly diet. Macadamia nuts can be used to make velvety creams and desserts due to their higher fat content, while peanuts (technically a legume – but let's not be fussy) are delish used in savoury dressings and tossed on top of noodle dishes.

Chia seeds I love cooking with chia seeds, they're a really versatile ingredient that add easily to recipes. Use them as an egg replacer in cakes, to enhance the texture of creamy bircher muesli or even to thicken jam. They are really high in fibre, however, which can cause symptoms for some people with a sensitive gut. The best idea is to include a small quantity of chia seeds in your diet and, over a couple of days, monitor symptoms.

HERBS AND SPICES

As soon as you tell people you can't eat garlic or onion, they panic and think 'how on earth is she going to eat anything with flavour?'. But actually, almost all herbs and spices are low FODMAP and can transform even the humblest ingredients into something really beautiful.

My favourite fresh and dried, herbs and spices to use when cooking include basil, mint, coriander, rosemary, thyme, sage, oregano, cinnamon, turmeric, sumac, cloves and cardamom. From robust and lemony to evocative and earthy, when used cleverly herbs and spices can add a delicious depth of flavour to dishes.

For extra punch, spice mixes such as dukkah (page 150), advieh (page 156), or Chinese five-spice (page 166) bring big, bold flavours to any dish.

DAIRY, FATS AND OILS

Coconut oil The popularity of coconut oil has boomed over the last couple of years and for good reason too. It's a very stable and versatile fat that you can use for roasting, frying or baking. Glossy white and solid at room temperature, it melts easily into a clear oil – plus nearly every big supermarket stocks or has brought out their own branded version, so it's now cheaper and easier to get hold of. Coconut oil is a wonderful fat for baking since it behaves very much like butter.

Olive oil Delicious as a salad dressing and for drizzling over rich dishes. A staple in the much praised Mediterranean diet, I've also used olive oil in a couple of sweet dishes – like hazelnut and banana muffins (page 122).

ALL THINGS SWEET

Brown sugar I often choose to bake with soft brown sugar, which is less refined and processed than white. The molasses in brown sugar give it a slightly richer, more distinctive caramel flavor, which I think works better in most of the recipes in this book.

Maple syrup Lower in fructose than many other liquid sweeteners such as honey, maple syrup is brilliantly versatile and FODMAP friendly, giving a warm sweetness to recipes. It can be expensive so is a great one to order in bulk online if you know you're going to be doing lots of baking.

FLOURS

Quinoa, buckwheat and oats can all be made into gluten-free flours that add a variety of texture and tastes to bakes. Quinoa flour works especially well in savoury recipes while buckwheat and oat flour each offer different properties and textures to baked goods.

Potato starch Potato starch is a very fine white powder starch, with a texture much like cornflour, made from the dried starch component of peeled potatoes. It has no potato flavour, so works well in most recipes, and as part of the starch component of a gluten-free flour blend (page 45) it

lends a light, fluffy texture to baked goods. Note – not to be confused with potato flour

Tapioca flour Tapioca flour is made from the dried starch of the cassava root. It has little flavour but is great in gluten-free flour blends.

Rice flour You can buy both brown and white rice flour, however I've used mostly brown throughout this book, for its denser nutritional value and similarities to whole wheat flour. Rice flour works best in recipes when it's combined with other flours, to balance texture and build structure.

MY GO-TO EXTRAS

Baking powder A raising agent, that I find essential to use in wheat-free baking. It contains bicarbonate of soda and tartaric acid, which, when they become moist and warm, react and give off carbon dioxide, giving food a lovely lift. Some brands of baking powder do contain wheat flour, so just make sure you double check the label.

Tamari A Japanese condiment brewed from soy beans and a wheat-free alternative to soy sauce; tamari is dark in colour and has a stronger, more intense flavor. It's especially good in marinades and dressings. Soy sauce has been classified low FODMAP in smaller amounts, however, so please feel free to mix and match if you like.

Vanilla extract Vanilla is a delicious way to add depth and flavour to baking and sweet dishes, without the FODMAPs. I've referred to pure vanilla extract in my recipes because anything labelled vanilla flavouring or essence won't contain much real stuff. It's a quicker and cheaper way to get the vanilla flavour, without whole vanilla pods – but by all means if you would like to sub, please do.

ADDING FLAVOUR WITHOUT GARLIC OR ONION

Red and white onions, shallots, garlic and the white part of spring onions and leeks all contain high amounts of fructooligosaccharides (FOS) and therefore aren't suitable on the Low FODMAP Diet.

Being the base of so many recipes, and with many store-bought stocks out the window too (keep an eye out for onion in packaged foods such as stocks, sauces, crisps and soups), it can sometimes feel like you can only ever eat bland food. But don't fear! I've got some tricks below for great substitutes I've learnt over the years.

Try the following for that depth of flavour:

For an onion flavour Green leaves of spring onions and leeks can be used when a recipe calls for onion. Amazingly the green leaves break down the fructans present in the bulbs of onions, leeks and garlic, making them tolerable for most people with a sensitive gut. Chives are delicious for adding flavour too, and are most powerful when added to dishes right before serving.

For a garlic flavour Garlic-infused olive oil is amazing. FOS in garlic are soluble in water, whereas the allicin and other bits that give garlic its delicious aroma aren't soluble in oil. Now readily available in most big supermarkets, it's inexpensive, lasts a long time and is perfect for adding to hot dishes or quick dinners if you don't usually have garlic bulbs lying around.

If you have the time and are up for making your own garlic-infused oil, however, as and when you need it, rest assured it's incredibly simple to do.

When heating up your oil for a recipe, simply add one or two sliced cloves of garlic. Fry for a couple of minutes and then remove and discard the garlic, before continuing with the recipe. Just remember, the fructans in garlic are soluble in water – so never use it to flavour stocks or soups – only oil!

A FEW NOTES ON USING THIS BOOK

MEASUREMENTS

When I first started cooking, I was much more slapdash and used to use cups/throw things in a bowl. However, I soon learnt that weighing ingredients and getting your measurements right in recipes – especially when it comes to FODMAP friendly baking – really does matter. Portion sizes are also important when it comes to FODMAP friendly meals too, so you'll find everything measured in grams . If you prefer using cups, however, I've placed a conversion table at the back of the book (page 231) with converted measurements where possible – just make sure to stick to those recommended portions if you're in the elimination phase.

EQUIPMENT

If you're new to home cooking and haven't spent much time in a kitchen, don't worry! None of the recipes in this book are particularly labour intensive – nor do they call for obscure apparatus. The only items I would really recommend investing in are a high-speed blender and a food processor. These range vastly in cost so purchase one in a price range best suited to you. At the moment I use a food processor with a high-speed blender attachment – I bought it for about £40 and it's fantastic.

MILK

Throughout this book I've often called for lactose- or dairy-free milk in a recipe. I've given the option because almost all are interchangeable – and I want you to adapt the recipes to suit your tastes and tolerances. If I've specifically called for one milk in particular then it's just because I think it tastes the best in that recipe.

INGREDIENTS

Eggs Delicious scrambled for breakfast, incorporated in cakes, or baked in a quiche, eggs are a versatile and inexpensive FODMAP friendly food to see you through the week. When eggs are called for, always use large, preferably free-range eggs – especially when it comes to baked goods. I store my eggs at room temperature – I find they're better for baking with and are less likely to crack when boiling

Lemons and limes The juice of one lemon or lime refers to the measurements below. If a savoury recipe calls for either however, I find it always best to have extra on hand so that you can adjust to taste if you want to.

Juice of 1 lemon – roughly 3 tablespoons
Juice of 1 lime – roughly 2–3 tablespoons

OVEN

All of these recipes have been tested in a conventional, electric oven. If you are using a fan oven, simply lower the temperature by 20 °C.

EATING WITH THE SEASONS

Eating seasonally, and eating a variety of foods, is not only a great way to keep a healthy and happy gut, but is great for sustainability, is cheaper and tastes better too. Many years ago we used to eat rotationally naturally because we only had access to the food in season. Now, because we can get hold of the same foods almost every single day of the year, we tend to eat very similar meals and many would argue our diet has become a lot more limited.

Use the charts to see what FODMAP friendly foods are in season when, and adapt your shopping and cooking to suit. That's not to say that you need to completely avoid foods that aren't in season – if you can get a certain food all year round and you love it, then by all means do – but maybe think about whether there might be a seasonal or local alternative that's just as good and might taste even more delicious.

Fruit

SPRING *March–May*	SUMMER *June–August*	AUTUMN *September–November*	WINTER *December–February*
Bananas	Bananas	Bananas	Bananas
Blueberries	Blueberries	Grapes	Clementines
Kiwi Fruit	Kiwi Fruit	Oranges: valencia, navel	Kiwi Fruit
Oranges: blood, seville, valencia	Melons	Passionfruit	Oranges: blood, navel
Papayas	Passionfruit	Tomatoes	Passionfruit
Pineapples	Raspberries		Pineapples
	Strawberries		
	Tomatoes		

Vegetables

SPRING *March–May*	SUMMER *June–August*	AUTUMN *September–November*	WINTER *December–February*
Cabbage	Aubergines	Aubergines	Celeriac
Carrots	Beetroot (small serving size)	Beetroot (small serving size)	Celery
Chillies	Broccoli	Broccoli	Fennel
Courgettes	Cabbage	Cabbage	Kale
Cucumbers	Carrots	Carrots	Olives
Lettuce	Celery	Celariac	Parsnips
Peppers	Chillies	Celery	Potatoes
Potatoes	Courgettes	Courgettes	Pumpkins
Purple sprouting broccoli	Cucumbers	Cucumber	Rhubarb
Rhubarb	Fennel	Fennel	Spinach
Spinach	Green beans	Ginger	Swedes
Spring greens	Lettuce	Kale	Sweet potatoes (small serving size)
Spring onions (eat tops only)	Peppers	Lettuce	Turnips
Watercress	Potatoes; new potatoes	Parsnips	
	Radishes	Peppers	
	Rocket	Poatoes	
	Spring onions (eat tops only)	Pumpkins	
	Watercress	Spinach	
		Squash	
		Sweet potatoes (small serving size)	
		Turnips	

ESSENTIALS

Have these elements nailed and you're already halfway there with most of the recipes in this book. Together, they will form a big chunk of the foundation of your new FODMAP lifestyle. I use them all the time and having them in the back of my mind helps make life just a little easier.

NUT MILK

Makes 1 litre

Nut milks are a great lactose-free alternative to cows' milk if you suspect your body isn't tolerating lactose well. As long as you stick to FODMAP friendly nuts and portion sizes, nut milks can be easier on digestion, some more environmentally sustainable, simple to make, affordable, and most importantly taste great. Making them yourself means you know exactly what's in them.
Nut milks are delicious by themselves but they can also be used as a great base for smoothies and desserts, or poured over freshly made granola for breakfast (page 56). The only thing you must, must do is soak your nuts! They'll get plump, double in size ready for blending and will become easier to digest. You'll thank me for it, I promise! Use the basic recipe below, pick that flavour you've always wanted to try and get milking.

GATHER
120g brazil nuts, almonds, macadamia nuts, walnuts or pecans
1 litre cold, filtered water
2–3 tbsp maple syrup
1 tsp pure vanilla extract
1/4 tsp sea salt

MAKE
Place the nuts in a bowl or jar and add cold water, making sure to cover the nuts completely. Let soak in a cool place (but not in the fridge) overnight. Drain, discard the soaking water and rinse with fresh water.

Add the nuts, filtered water and maple syrup to a high-speed blender and whizz for a minute or so until smooth. Prepare a large jug with a cheesecloth (or coffee filter) over the top and pour out the nut milk into the jug. Squeeze the excess bits of milk out of the pulp that is compressed into the cheesecloth. Remove the cheesecloth and then stir in the vanilla along with the salt and one of the flavour combos, if you like.

Store in a covered glass jar or bottle in the fridge and use within 3 days. Separation is totally natural with homemade nut milks, just be sure to shake it up before serving.

Feel free to use the pulp in other recipes such as smoothies or cakes, to add more texture and flavour. Just be mindful of FODMAP friendly portion sizes.

FLAVOUR COMBOS
Rose and cardamom – 1 tbsp rose water and 1 tsp ground cardamom powder

Lavender – 1 tsp dried lavender

Chocolate – 2 tbsp cacao or cocoa

Vanilla chai – 1/2 tsp cinnamon

SIMPLE VEGETABLE STOCK

Makes 2 litres

Most ready-prepared stock powders or granules contain onion and many contain high amounts of salt or sneaky additives and fillers too. Making your own stock from vegetables and herbs will not only make you feel like a domestic goddess, but means you can control exactly what goes in.

Store any leftovers in freezer bags in the freezer so that you can have it on hand whenever you need it.

GATHER
4 large carrots
2 celery stalks
2 leeks, green leaves only
1 fennel bulb
2 bay leaves
10 black peppercorns
2.5 litres cold water

MAKE
Peel the carrots and wash and roughly chop along with the rest of the veg. Place all in a large saucepan, along with the bay leaves and peppercorns. Add the water and bring to the boil. Reduce the heat and allow to simmer gently for 1 hour.

Remove from the heat and allow to cool. If you have time, place in the fridge and allow the veg to continue to infuse for another couple of hours. If not, strain the liquid into another saucepan and discard the veg.

Use fresh within 3 days or freeze portions in freezer bags and use within 2 months.

Top tip

Throughout this book I've given the option of veggie stock or hot water in many of the recipes. While vegetable stock adds an extra depth of flavour to dishes, I don't want you to stress if you haven't got any on hand – if the ingredients you use are good then the recipes will still be full of flavour.

QUINOA

Makes about 400g

Here's how to cook great quinoa that's not mushy or bitter, but delicate and perfectly fluffy.

GATHER
190g quinoa
420ml water or vegetable stock
1/2 tsp salt, to taste

MAKE
Wash the quinoa thoroughly under cold water. Heat a drizzle of olive oil in a saucepan over a medium-high heat, and add the drained quinoa. Cook, for 1 minute, stirring throughout – you want to let the water evaporate and the quinoa to lightly toast. Add water or stock and salt and bring to a boil. Reduce the heat to low, cover and simmer until tender and most of the liquid has been absorbed, roughly 12–15 minutes. Leave to rest for 10 minutes, with a paper towel under the lid. Fluff with a fork before serving. The grains should have white 'halos'.

NUTTY BUCKWHEAT

Makes 500g

Raw buckwheat groats are very light tan, slightly green in colour and are almost pyramid-shaped. I prefer cooking with raw buckwheat but you can also buy your buckwheat groats pre-toasted, they are called kasha. Darker brown in colour, kasha has a stronger flavour and can work well in some recipes.

GATHER
170g raw buckwheat groats
420ml water
1/2 tsp salt

MAKE:
Wash the buckwheat thoroughly under cold water. Bring the buckwheat, salt and water to a boil in a medium saucepan. Reduce the heat to low, cover and simmer until tender and most of the liquid has been absorbed, 10–12 minutes.

FLUFFY RICE

Makes 500–750g

I like to boil rice in ample water, before straining and letting it steam in the pot's residual liquid. I think this method yields fully cooked rice with the perfect texture.

GATHER
250g brown or white rice
500ml boiling water
1 tsp salt

MAKE
Wash the rice thoroughly under cold water, until the water runs clear. Place a saucepan over a medium heat and add the rice. Cover with boiling water – make sure the water is about 2 cm above the rice – and add the salt. Stir and bring back to the boil, then reduce the heat to low and cover the pan. Cook white rice for 15 minutes, brown for 30–40. Keep an eye on the water and add more if necessary. Once tender, strain the rice and discard the cooking liquid then add the rice back to the pot. Cover and let it rest for 10 more minutes. Fluff with a fork and serve.

GLUTEN-FREE FLOUR BLEND

Gluten-free flour blends differ from brand to brand so you never quite know how they're going to work in a recipe. I find it much easier to make up my own blend so I know exactly what's in it and have more of an idea of how it's going to behave. This is my easy gluten-free flour blend, perfect to use in place of plain flour in most recipes.

For extra binding (since there is no gluten) I often add a teaspoon of xanthan gum. It's a vegetable gum that helps to improve the elasticity and crumb structure of baked goods and you can buy it in health food stores and most large supermarkets, along with the flours.

GATHER
240g brown rice flour
100g potato starch
30g tapioca flour
1 tsp xanthan gum (optional, but does help to bind)

MAKE
Whisk the flours and gum, if using, together in a large mixing bowl and store in an airtight container in a dry place.

Top tip

Feel free to pair with other flours such as buckwheat or oat in recipes for extra texture and flavour.

VEGETABLE NOODLES

I'm partial to a bit of spiralising, if I do say so myself. It's such a wonderful alternative to pastas containing gluten and another way to get some extra nutrients into a plate of food. Courgette, butternut squash and carrots are three of the low FODMAP vegetables that work extra well when spiralised. Eat raw or steam for a few minutes before serving.

If you haven't got a spiraliser, just use a box grater! To create lovely long ribbons of courgette instead of short shreds, hold the grater on its side like a mandolin. Make sure the thickest grater is facing up, and move the courgette along it in long strokes to create the ribbons. Super easy and you have less fear of hand slicing!

Recipes

← 50

**Lazy baked eggs
with spicy tomatoes
& feta**

57 ↑

**Tropical overnight
bircher**

↑ 60

**Griddle pan waffle
with orange &
rhubarb compote**

← 64

**Raspberry & coconut
oat porridge**

← 54

**Spinach smoothie
pancakes with home-
made hazelnut spread
& fresh strawberries**

↑ 70

**Good morning
sunshine juice or
Sunday detox juice**

Good morning sunshine

I've never been one of those people that can skip breakfast and not eat until lunch. It's by far my favourite meal of the day and I'm truly convinced everything tastes better first thing. What you eat in the morning really does set you – and your gut – up for the rest of the day.

When you think of a typical breakfast, what comes into your mind? Packaged cereals, white bread, fruit juice from a carton? All foods often highly processed and high in FODMAPs that can wreak havoc with your digestive system – even if you purchase the 'free from' versions. I know that if I've started the day with sugary packaged granola or two slices of store-bought wheat-free white bread laden with fructose-filled jam, I soon feel crappy, unsettled and lethargic later on. It's likely my gut will also feel on high alert every time I eat something else.

But breakfast doesn't have to make you feel like this and it certainly doesn't have to be based on wheat and dairy products or their 'free from' substitutes! If there's one thing I'd love for you to take away from this chapter, for breakfast – and all food on the low FODMAP diet – it would be: make it yourself!

It's all about naturally low FODMAP, energising and delicious ingredients that are full of goodness and, along with a little pre-planning, I guarantee you'll start your day feeling more nourished and satisfied. And I know you're probably thinking 'Who does she think I am – I don't have time for that' but, I promise – you really do.

In this chapter, you'll find recipes that can be whipped up in ten minutes or less for a healthy, delicious, gut-friendly breakfast mid-week, through to those recipes that take a little longer and feed a crowd, for when you've got more time to spare at the weekend.

A delicious bowl of overnight bircher (page 57) is an incredibly easy way to start your week on a gut high; simply bung all of the ingredients in a clean jar the night before and you'll wake up to the best tummy-loving breakfast.

Whip up a big batch of banana granola (page 56) on a Sunday morning baking sesh, so that you can just pour it into a bowl and sloosh over your favourite milk. It's so much easier to find a wonderful range of plant-based and lactose-free cows' milks now, which can be more gentle on the gut. Or you can make your own milk (page 42) so you know exactly what's in it.

For a filling, savoury breakfast that eschews high FODMAP ingredients such as mushrooms and baked beans, the dukkah poached egg, buckwheat and brekky greens bowl (page 66) has your name on it.

Of course there are some mornings when you find yourself rushing out the door and even ten minutes spare is a luxury – that's when smoothies come into their own. Strawberry milk, pina colada, breakfast powerhouse (all pages 67 and 68), you name it, I've got you covered. Throw into a blender, pour into a flask for later and off you go.

Fast forward to the weekend and a huge griddle pan waffle (page 60), served with thick yoghurt and fruit compote, is one of my favourites for feeding a crowd, along with my lazy baked eggs with spicy tomatoes and feta (page 50). Supplement with cups of peppermint tea and hot lemon waters all round and all guts are going to love you.

So start small. Have a few healthy FODMAP friendly breakfast staples on rotation and work your way up to trying other things. Eat the foods that make you feel energised, happy and ready to rule the day and you'll wonder why you never did before.

Lazy baked eggs with spicy tomatoes & feta

SERVES 4

GATHER
1 tbsp coconut oil

1 red pepper, deseeded and chopped into small chunks

1 tin (400g) chopped tomatoes

1/2 tsp red chilli flakes

1/4 tsp paprika

1 tsp dried mixed herbs

150g spinach

4 eggs

100g feta cheese

1 big handful of fresh herbs, such as parsley or coriander, finely chopped

Seriously easy, wholesome, belly-warming food. Serve with gluten-free crusty bread if you're feeling naughty, smoked salmon if you're feeling fancy, or on its own if you're just hungry and want to keep it simple. With only a few ingredients that you're bound to have lying around, this easy baked eggs recipe is fail-proof – and not to mention cheap to make, which is always welcome.

MAKE
Preheat the oven to 200°C (gas 6) and deseed and chop the pepper into small chunks.

Heat a little coconut oil in a pan and fry the chopped pepper for 2–3 minutes, before adding the tomatoes, spices and dried mixed herbs. Let the tomato mixture bubble and cook down for 5 minutes or so, then add the spinach and stir until it wilts. Take the pan off the heat and pour the spinach and tomato mixture into a medium oven dish.

Using the back of a large spoon, make four wells in the mixture, then crack an egg into each one. Sprinkle the feta on top before baking in the oven for 15 minutes, or until the egg whites are set but the yolks are still runny. Serve immediately, topped with fresh herbs.

Buckwheat crêpes with smoked salmon & goats' cheese smash

SERVES 4

GATHER

Crêpes

125g buckwheat flour

1/4 teaspoon fine salt

1 egg

300ml water

1 tbsp coconut oil

400g smoked salmon, sliced into pieces

Juice of 1 lemon

Goats' cheese smash

200g goats' cheese

Juice and zest of 1 lemon

2 tbsp fresh coriander, roughly chopped

3 spring onions, green tops only, finely sliced

Sea salt and freshly ground black pepper

Top tip

If you have any leftover batter, make mini pancakes and store them in the fridge for easy-to-transport snacks on the go. I like mine with a little blueberry chia jam (page 63) . . .

Many a time have I been on holiday and struggled to find somewhere suitable to eat – whether for breakfast, lunch or dinner. Crêperies have become my fail-safe – which is just as well because crêpes are delicious. My take on the savoury and naturally gluten-free delight are deliciously thin and full of fibre, topped with smoked salmon and creamy goats' cheese smash. So easy to make – say goodbye to the morning bloat and hello to those skinny jeans.

MAKE

Sieve the flour into a large bowl and add the salt. In a separate bowl, whisk the egg with the water, and then pour slowly into the flour, whisking constantly to ensure you get a smooth, thin batter. Leave to rest for 10 minutes (I promise it's worth the wait) and then whisk again.

Heat a large non-stick frying pan over a high heat and add a little coconut oil. Pour a large ladleful of the mixture into the pan and tilt it quickly, spreading the mixture out to a thin circle. Cook for 2–3 minutes, until the edges begin to curl, and then flip over and cook for another minute. When the crêpe has turned a lovely golden colour, transfer it to a warm plate or very low oven while you repeat with the rest of the mixture (give the batter a stir every so often, to avoid lumps).

In a small bowl, roughly mash the goats' cheese with a fork. Don't worry about getting it totally smooth – it's better a little chunky. Add the rest of the ingredients and stir to combine. Taste, and add more seasoning and lemon juice if needed.

Serve the crêpes with the smoked salmon, a big dollop of goats' cheese smash and an extra squeeze of lemon juice.

Use the goats' cheese smash immediately or store, covered, in the fridge. Leftovers will keep for the rest of the day.

Spinach smoothie pancakes with homemade hazelnut spread & fresh strawberries

SERVES 4

GATHER
125g buckwheat flour
1 large egg
1/4 teaspoon fine salt
300ml lactose- or dairy-free milk of choice
2 big handfuls of spinach
1 tbsp coconut oil
8 tbsp hazelnut and pecan spread (page 184)
300g strawberries, hulled and sliced

These are a different, sweet and delicious way to enjoy the basic crêpe mixture on page 53, while getting in some extra greens and a healthy chocolate fix. The batter needs to be refrigerated for a while, so I like to make it first thing in the morning then jump in the shower while I'm waiting.

MAKE
Place the buckwheat flour, egg, salt, milk and spinach in a blender and whizz until smooth. Refrigerate the batter for 20 minutes.

Heat a large non-stick frying pan over a high heat and add a little coconut oil. Pour a large ladleful of the mixture and tilt the pan, spreading the mixture out to a circle. Cook for 2–3 minutes, until golden and then flip over and cook for another minute. When the crêpe has darkened in colour, transfer it to a warm plate or very low oven while you repeat with the rest of the mixture (make sure to keep stirring the batter often for the best results).

Serve with hazelnut spread and sliced strawberries.

Banana granola

SERVES 6

GATHER

270g rolled oats
80g raw almonds
4 tbsp pumpkin seeds
½ tsp sea salt
2 bananas
3 tbsp coconut oil, melted
3 tbsp maple syrup
1 tsp pure vanilla extract

So much store-bought, pre-packed granola contains wheat, refined sugars and preservative-filled dried fruit, which can wreak havoc on a FODMAP friendly diet. Making your own granola not only makes you feel like a domestic goddess, but is delicious and allows you to change the flavour and amount of sweetness to suit you, whilst omitting FODMAPs. Using mashed bananas in the recipe encourages lovely crunchy clusters to form and also means you can use less sweetener and oil to bind the ingredients, keeping the recipe healthier too.

MAKE

Preheat the oven to 200°C (gas 6) and line a tray with baking parchment.

Add the oats, almonds, pumpkin seeds and salt to a large bowl and stir with a wooden spoon to combine. In a separate bowl, mash the bananas and pour over the coconut oil, maple syrup and vanilla extract and mix together. Add the dry mix to the wet mix and give them a stir or use your hands to fully combine.

Spoon the mixture onto the baking tray, spreading out in an even layer. Bake for 15–20 minutes, or until golden brown, giving a quick mix after 10 minutes.

Serve with cold lactose-free or dairy-free milk or yoghurt of choice.

Store any leftovers in an airtight container for up to a month.

Top tip

Don't skip the salt here, it's imperative for flavourful granola. Just half a teaspoon makes the flavours sing.

Tropical overnight bircher

SERVES 1

GATHER
50g rolled oats
125ml lactose- or dairy-free milk of choice
1 tbsp flaked almonds
1 tbsp sunflower seeds
1/4 tsp of sea salt
1 tbsp lactose-free yoghurt
1 tbsp maple syrup
1 kiwi fruit, skin removed and sliced
1/2 passionfruit

Soaking the oats and seeds in this recipe, not only gives the bircher a delicious creamy texture but speeds up the digestion process.
All you need to do is bung everything in a jar or bowl, cover and place overnight in the fridge. Crawl out of bed, stir, top with fresh fruit and you're ready to go. Multiply the recipe to prepare a large batch to see you through a couple of mornings a week – just store it in an airtight container in the fridge and add the fresh fruit each morning.

MAKE
Combine the oats, milk, nuts, seeds and salt in a bowl and cover with a plate or clingfilm, leaving to soak overnight in the fridge.

In the morning, give the mixture a stir and top with a dollop of yoghurt, a drizzle of maple syrup, slices of kiwi fruit and a spoonful of passionfruit seeds.

Top tip

If your gut doesn't love oats, try quinoa flakes instead, which, like oats, are made from steaming the grain and then rolling to create a thin flake.
If you know you can tolerate chia seeds, stir in 1 teaspoon before you put the mixture in the fridge, for an extra boost of fibre and an even creamier and thicker result.

Vanilla quinoa porridge, with lavender strawberries

SERVES 2

GATHER
150g strawberries
1½ tbsp maple syrup (plus extra for serving if you like)
1–2 tsp lavender buds
100g quinoa
375ml water
120ml almond milk
1 tsp cinnamon
1 tsp pure vanilla extract

This is a killer recipe if you want to mix up your breakfast routine or if you struggle to tolerate oats. A great source of fibre and high in protein, quinoa is an awesome grain to have for brekky, and will keep you full, energised and satisfied throughout the day. Simmered to creamy dreamy perfection and topped with lavender strawberries, don't be put off by the quinoa – this is one you need to try.

MAKE
Dice the strawberries and place them in a small bowl. Add ½ tablespoon maple syrup and the lavender buds, lightly crushing them with your hands as you go. Stir and set aside.

Rinse the quinoa under cold water until the water runs clear. Add the quinoa to a medium saucepan, followed by the water. Bring to the boil, then reduce the heat and simmer, covered, for 10 minutes. Add in the milk, cinnamon, 1 tablespoon maple syrup and vanilla, then pop the lid back on and cook for another 5 minutes, stirring every few minutes or until the quinoa is cooked through and most of the liquid has been absorbed.

Remove from the heat, and divide the quinoa porridge between two bowls. Top with the lavender strawberries and extra milk or maple syrup if you like.

Top tip
Rinsing the quinoa helps to remove any of the remaining outer coating, which can be difficult to digest and can taste bitter too.

Griddle pan waffle with orange & rhubarb compote

SERVES 6

GATHER

For the waffle

225g gluten-free flour blend (page 45)

2¹/₂ tsp baking powder

2 eggs

300ml lactose- or dairy-free milk of choice

1 tsp pure vanilla extract

50g lactose-free butter, plus a little extra,
for greasing

For the compote

400g rhubarb

5cm chunk of fresh ginger, peeled and
finely sliced

Juice of 1 navel orange

50g brown sugar

Lactose- or dairy-free yoghurt to serve

This is an awesome show-stopping dish for the weekend. Made with a griddle pan, you don't need a waffle maker (who has one anyway?), it's bright and full of sunshine. Think soft on the inside and crispy on the outside, with golden grooves that effortlessly fill with fruity compote and creamy yoghurt. A non-stick griddle pan is favourable here, but if you have a cast iron one and the waffle gets a little stuck, it will still taste good.

MAKE

To make the compote, wash and trim the rhubarb and chop into 2.5cm pieces. Gently cook the rhubarb, orange juice, ginger and sugar in a covered saucepan for 8–10 minutes, or until the rhubarb is just turning soft.

To make the waffle, sift the flour and baking powder into a large bowl and make a well in the centre. In a separate bowl or jug, beat together the eggs, milk, vanilla and butter. Slowly pour the milk mixture into the flour, stirring with a wooden spoon.

Grease a 25cm square, ridged griddle pan with butter and place on a medium heat. Pour in the batter and cook gently for 6–8 minutes then carefully turn over and cook the other side for a further 2–3 minutes, until both are golden and the waffle is cooked through.

Slide the waffle onto a chopping board and cut into six rectangles. Top each with a dollop of thick yoghurt and spoon over the fruit compote.

Keep any leftover compote in an airtight container, in the fridge, for up to 3 days.

Fluffy banana cinnamon pancakes

SERVES 1

GATHER

1 banana

2 eggs

1/2 tsp baking powder

1/4 tsp salt

1 tsp pure vanilla extract

1/2 tsp cinnamon

2 tbsp oats

1 tsp coconut oil

Maple syrup and FODMAP friendly toppings of choice to serve

These two-ingredient banana pancakes seem to have become a staple in many FODMAP followers' diets and as soon as you try them you'll know why. I've given my own spin on them below with a few added extras such as cinnamon, oats and maple syrup, which I think takes them to the next level.

MAKE

Add the banana to a bowl and give it a mash. Crack the eggs into the bowl and mix to combine. Add the baking powder, salt, vanilla, cinnamon and oats and stir once more.

Place a frying pan over a medium heat and add the coconut oil. Allow to warm before adding 2 tablespoons of batter into the hot pan per pancake – it should sizzle lightly when dropped. Cook for about a minute, or until the bottoms look golden brown when you lift a corner. Flip the pancakes gently and cook for another minute until the other side is also golden brown. Transfer any cooked pancakes to a serving plate and continue cooking the rest of the batter. Keep the finished pancakes warm in the oven if cooking more than a single batch.

Best served immediately, still warm. Drizzle with maple syrup or add a dollop of blueberry chia jam (page 63) and lactose-free yoghurt.

Top tip

Stick to small pancakes. It's more difficult to flip larger pancakes because they're delicate, so stay with 2 tablespoons of mixture per pancake and make a taller stack instead.

Blueberry chia jam

MAKES ABOUT 200g

GATHER
230g blueberries
2-4 tbsp maple syrup, depending on
desired sweetness
1 tbsp lemon juice
1 tsp pure vanilla extract
½ tsp sea salt
2 tbsp chia seeds

This jam is made with real fruit, natural sweeteners and chia seeds. All the hard (easy) work is done in 5 minutes and then you just need to sit back and let the chia seeds do their thing. This is delicious with strawberries or raspberries in place of the blueberries too.

MAKE

Add the blueberries to a saucepan and set over a medium heat. Cook until the berries break down and become syrupy, roughly 7–10 minutes, then mash them with the back of a spatula, or a fork, leaving them as smooth or as lumpy as you like.

Take the pan off the heat and stir in the maple syrup, lemon juice, vanilla extract and salt. Taste and add a little more maple syrup or lemon juice, if required. Stir in the chia seeds and let stand for 5 minutes until thickened – this won't quite reach the firm consistency of regular jam, but it will noticeably thicken.

Allow to cool to room temperature, then transfer to a sterilised jar or other storage container. The jam will become more set once completely chilled. *Store in the fridge for up to 1 week.*

Top tip

Chia seeds are packed with omega-3 fatty acids, are rich in fibre and protein, and — most important for this lovely jam recipe — they turn any liquid into a thick gel, with the ability to absorb up to nine times their volume in water. Although one tablespoon has been identified as low FODMAP they can cause issues for some people with a sensitive gut however, so try depending on your own tolerances.

Raspberry & coconut oat porridge

SERVES 1

GATHER

50g rolled oats

250ml lactose- or dairy-free milk of choice

½ tsp sea salt

1 tbsp peanut butter (optional)

1 handful of raspberries

1 handful of coconut flakes

I know I've already mentioned quinoa porridge on page 58, but I feel like it would be a crime for me not to include an oat porridge recipe too, when I eat it as often as I do. Put simply, this is velvety and delicious and a great way to start the day.

MAKE

Put the oats in a saucepan, pour in the milk and sprinkle in a pinch of salt. Bring to the boil and simmer for 4–5 minutes, stirring from time to time to prevent sticking. Take off the heat and stir in the peanut butter, if using.

Spoon into a bowl and top with a handful of fresh raspberries and a showering of coconut flakes.

Dukkah poached egg, buckwheat & brekky greens bowl

SERVES 1

GATHER

For the buckwheat and brekky greens bowl

4 tbsp buckwheat groats
2 spring onions, green tops only, finely sliced
½ medium chilli, seeds removed, finely sliced
2 large handfuls of kale, torn
1 tbsp coconut oil
1 small handful of fresh mint, finely chopped
1 small handful of fresh parsley
Juice of ½ a lemon

For the dukkah poached egg

1 tbsp apple cider vinegar or white wine vinegar
1 egg
1 tbsp dukkah (page 152)

Top tip

*This is lovely cold for lunch too –
just top with a hard-boiled egg instead.
Quinoa also works beautifully in place
of the buckwheat.
More people at the breakfast table? Just
multiply up the ingredient amounts.*

This is a delicious savoury breakfast alternative made with naturally gluten-free buckwheat groats, whose nutty texture pairs amazingly with the sautéed kale and spicy chilli. Dukkah, the traditional Persian combination of nuts, seeds and spices, is usually served in a small dish, alongside a bowl of olive oil and chunky bread. But it's also delicious here on top of a plump poached egg.

MAKE

Fill a small saucepan with water two-thirds of the way up and bring to the boil. Add the buckwheat groats and simmer for 10 minutes or until tender (you still want them to have a bit of a bite). Drain and set aside.

Heat a little coconut oil in a frying pan over medium heat. Fry the spring onion and chilli for around 2 minutes, or until fragrant.

Add the kale and cooked buckwheat. Sauté until the kale begins to wilt, around 2–3 minutes. Add the fresh herbs and cook for a further minute. Season with sea salt and stir in a squeeze of lemon juice.

To poach the egg, fill a saucepan about two-thirds full with water and bring to the boil. Take the water down to a low simmer and add the vinegar, this helps the egg cook in a more compact shape.

Crack the egg into a mug. Carefully lower the mug into the water and then tip out the egg. The final cooking time for a poached egg is very much up to you, but 4 minutes, give or take, should give you a firm white and runny yolk. Use a slotted spoon to remove the egg from the water .

Spoon the buckwheat and greens mix into a bowl, top with the poached egg and then sprinkle over the dukkah. Enjoy immediately.

FODMAP friendly smoothies

Most store-bought smoothies are full of high FODMAP fruits, sugar and fructose – it's often better (and cheaper) to make them yourself! As a general rule for FODMAP friendly smoothies: keep them simple. Use no more than two fruits, and one or two veggies or leafy greens in each smoothie and experiment with small amounts first, using various foods from the safe category to see how your body reacts. Once you have gauged your tolerance levels they are an amazing way to get loads of goodness in your body first thing and can be easier on the gut than bigger brekkies. If any of the smoothies are too thick for your liking, simply add some more liquid and blitz again.

Strawberry milk smoothie

SERVES 1

This might be the oldest smoothie recipe out there, but it never fails and it's low FODMAP. If you're new to smoothies, berry and banana flavour combinations are great; not only do they look very pretty, but taste like pudding too.

GATHER

150g strawberries (roughly 2 big handfuls)
1/2 a banana, peeled, chopped and frozen
125ml almond milk

MAKE

Wash and chop the strawberries and add into a blender with the banana and milk. Whizz on high until perfectly smooth.

Cucumber & honeydew smoothie

SERVES 2

The lightest of the four smoothie recipes – this is truly green. Refreshing and hydrating, the honeydew melon base is a superb low FODMAP ingredient that's naturally sweet.

GATHER

150g cucumber
320g honeydew melon
12 (or around about) fresh mint leaves
2–4 tbsp fresh lime juice, to taste
1 tsp maple syrup (optional – if your melon is super ripe and sweet, omit)

MAKE

Wash the cucumber and chop into small chunks along with the melon. Add all of the ingredients into a blender and whizz on high until lovely and smooth.

Ginger pina colada smoothie

SERVES 1

Banish the grey clouds and damp drizzle from your morning commute or journey with this baby and replace with sunny skies and palm trees. Pineapple has been said to aid digestion, while ginger has long been used to soothe the gut – a perfect smoothie to start the day.

GATHER
Juice of ½ a lime
1cm piece of fresh ginger, peeled and grated
225g pineapple, in chunks, frozen
240ml lactose- or dairy-free milk of choice

MAKE
Add all of the ingredients into a blender and whizz on high until lovely and smooth.

Top tip

This is delicious frozen in ice lolly moulds too.

Breakfast powerhouse smoothie

SERVES 1

Oats are a great addition to this smoothie to make it more filling when you've got a busy day ahead.

GATHER
1 banana, frozen
2 tbsp rolled oats
½ tsp cinnamon
1 tsp maple syrup
240ml lactose- or dairy-free milk of choice

MAKE
Add all of the ingredients into a blender and whizz on high until smooth and creamy.

Good morning sunshine juice

SERVES 3–4

When I think of all the juices I've ever made, this one's still my favourite. Imagine a virtuous version of your classic morning carton orange juice, with anti-inflammatory properties thanks to turmeric, digestion-boosting benefits from the ginger and an immune boost from carrots and oranges.

GATHER

6 large carrots, peeled
2 large oranges, peeled
2.5cm piece of fresh ginger, peeled
1/2 tsp turmeric

MAKE

Put all the ingredients except the turmeric through a juicer and pour into a jug. Add the turmeric, stir and serve chilled.

Top tip

If you don't have a juicer you can make this using a blender too. Just blitz the carrots, oranges and ginger with 240ml water and then push through a fine-mesh strainer (or with a bit of patience a coffee filter would do the trick) to remove the pulp. Stir through the turmeric and serve chilled.

Sunday detox juice

SERVES 2

This juice is great after a busy weekend. Fresh and hydrating, it instantly makes me feel that bit more alive. Worth leaving bed for – really.

GATHER

1 cucumber
225g pineapple, de-skinned, chopped into wedges
150g kale
2.5cm piece of fresh ginger, peeled
1 lemon, peeled

MAKE

Put all the ingredients through a juicer, pour into glasses and serve chilled.

Soothing ginger tea

SERVES 1

Ginger tea is a diaphoretic tea, meaning it will warm you up from the inside. I like to drink buckets of this when I feel a cold coming on, and I find it great for improving digestion after I've been greedy and eaten too much or am suffering from nasty symptoms.

GATHER

1 tsp grated fresh ginger
1 tbsp lemon juice
2 tsp maple syrup
3–4 mint leaves (optional but delish)
240ml boiling water

MAKE

Add all ingredients into a mug or small pitcher, stir to combine and let sit for 3 minutes to infuse. Strain the mixture, or drink as is, munching on the ginger and mint leaves when you reach them.

← 74

Strawberry & hemp seed millet salad

76 →

Courgette noodles topped with one-pot lentil chilli

↑ 80

Baba ganoush

← 90

Cheat's buckwheat pizza with lemony basil pesto & goats' cheese

Prawn, courgette & chilli linguine

↓ 106

96 →

Roast pumpkin salad with whipped feta cream

Wholesome lunches & nutritious suppers

Easy, delicious lunches and healthy post-work dinners were two of the things I struggled with most when beginning a Low FODMAP Diet. Starting work early in the morning, I would manage to munch a healthy FODMAP friendly breakfast quickly at home, but by lunchtime I would be starving, and heading to the only supermarket or café close by, would end up spending a fortune or eating crap, due to the exceedingly limited options available.

I quickly learnt that prep was everything and making my own lunch every day made all the difference. Putting that hour aside on a Sunday or Monday evening to make your own meals means you can still eat pizza (page 90), roast pumpkin salad with whipped feta cream (page 96) and vibrant soups (pages 84, 86 and 88) and have a happy gut. Which might not be the case if you eat their ready-made, high FODMAP counterparts.

Over 75 per cent of the recipes in this chapter are veggie, and although that wasn't on purpose, making veg the centre of a dish instead of meat every now and then can not only be healthier, but cheaper and easier on the environment too. One of my favourite veggie pairings in the book is the quinoa and pomegranate tabbouleh (page 78) with baba ganoush (page 80). Both are incredibly easy to make and you can whip up big batches on the weekend for lunches and quick dinners for the next few days – prepping ahead so that you're not spending hours in the kitchen mid-week (unless you want to!) is something I fully advocate. Using green spring onion tops only, garlic-infused olive oil instead of garlic bulbs, and peanut butter instead of tahini, ensures both are low in FODMAPs but taste just as good.

Two of the most delicious FODMAP friendly curries, chock-full of flavour, feature on pages 92 and 94 – tomato, turmeric and coconut dahl is my ultimate fail-safe weeknight dinner, and just like my mellow green coconut curry, is naturally vegan. Best served hot on top of a scoop of nutty brown rice.

Fish- and meat-eaters don't fear, however – it's not all veg. My much-loved prawn, courgette and chilli linguine makes an appearance on page 106 and a recent discovery – laid-back parchment-baked chicken with coriander and lime veg – is on page 108. Just throw everything into a parcel, bung it in the oven and 20 minutes later you've got one hell of a feast.

Fancy noodles? Sticky salmon-topped soba noodles with greens (page 102) make a perfect quick and easy weeknight dinner, while my smoked mackerel salad with cucumber, orange, fennel and radish (page 104) and veggie sushi rolls (page 113) are ideal make-ahead lunchbox fodder, perfect to transport.

Variety, ever more so in the maintenance phase, is important for your gut and health, so once you've nailed a few favourite dishes, adapt them to suit your tolerances and tastes. And always remember a little prep goes a long way – even if that means making sure you're always stocked with a few cupboard essentials for an I'm-too-tired-to-think, throw-in-the-pan FODMAP friendly stir-fry (page 98).

Strawberry & hemp seed millet salad

SERVES 4

GATHER
250g millet

470ml water

Juice and zest of ½ a lemon

25g flaked almonds, toasted

200g rocket

180g strawberries, hulled, sliced or quartered

1 small bunch of fresh mint, finely chopped

1 small bunch of fresh basil, finely chopped

3 tbsp olive oil

50g hemp seeds

Sea salt and freshly ground black pepper

This is a fresh, summery salad, with undervalued millet brought alive by juicy strawberries, zesty lemon and fragrant herbs. The almonds add a great crunch and it's lovely topped with a sprinkle of feta too.

MAKE
Add the millet to a medium saucepan and toast on a medium heat for about 5 minutes. Once slightly golden, add the water and bring to a boil. Simmer for about 15 minutes until all the water has evaporated and the millet is cooked. Leave to stand for 10 minutes, covered. Fluff up with a fork and stir in both the lemon zest and toasted flaked almonds.

Put the rocket in a bowl along with the strawberries, mint and basil. Stir to combine.

Add the millet to a plate or big bowl and top with the salad. Drizzle with olive oil and lemon juice, season to taste and then sprinkle over hemp seeds.

Top tip
To toast almond flakes, simply toss them in a pan on a medium heat for a few minutes until golden.

Courgette noodles topped with one-pot lentil chilli

SERVES 4

GATHER

2 carrots, peeled and chopped
2 red peppers, seeds removed and chopped
1 red chilli, deseeded and finely chopped
2 tbsp garlic-infused oil or coconut oil
2 tsp ground cumin
1 tsp smoked paprika
1 tsp dried oregano
1 tin (300g) lentils, drained and rinsed
1 tin (400g) chopped tomatoes
250ml vegetable stock or water
4 medium courgettes
Sea salt and freshly ground black pepper

Chilli reminds me of my family when I was younger; my mum always had a great recipe up her sleeve. You won't miss the standard garlic or onion in this lovely lentil chilli though. Simple, healthy and hearty, it's great for feeding a crowd or for a nutritious weeknight dinner.

MAKE

Heat the oil in a large saucepan and throw in half the chilli, along with the cumin, smoked paprika and oregano. Cook for a few minutes and add the carrots and peppers; sauté for a few more. Add the lentils to the pot followed by the tomatoes and stock and simmer for 45 minutes, or until the vegetables are tender and the liquid slightly reduced.

Just before serving spiralise the courgettes into ribbons and steam for 2 minutes. Divide between four bowls. Remove the lentil chilli from the heat and season to taste. Spoon over the courgette noodles and top with the rest of the freshly chopped chilli.

Top tip

The chilli freezes really well and is great to have on hand in the freezer for a nutritious FODMAP friendly dinner when you're strapped for time. Just double the recipe and portion out into suitable plastic containers.

Quinoa & pomegranate tabbouleh

SERVES 4–6

GATHER

235ml water
190g quinoa
½ tsp salt
1 large cucumber
3 spring onions, green tops only
1 pomegranate
Zest and juice of 1 lemon
1 small bunch of mint, finely chopped
1 bunch of parsley, finely chopped
60ml extra virgin olive oil

This dish has become a staple in the summer. Light and nutritious, I've subbed the usual bulgar wheat for quinoa, which is naturally gluten-free and low FODMAP. Using only the green tops of spring onions gives you the flavour without any of the nasty symptoms, while cucumber is great for a healthy digestion.

MAKE

Add the water to a saucepan and bring to the boil. Rinse the quinoa under cold water until it runs clear and add to the pan along with the salt. Bring the water back to the boil, reduce the heat to low, cover and simmer for 15 minutes, or until the quinoa is tender (be careful not to overcook as you don't want it mushy). Remove from the heat, leave for 10 minutes, and then fluff up using a fork. Set aside to cool.

Meanwhile, dice the cucumber and finely slice the spring onions, and add both to a large mixing bowl. Add the cooled quinoa and stir, before adding the pomegranate seeds, lemon zest, mint and parsley and stirring again. Drizzle over the lemon juice and olive oil, season to taste and then serve.

Baba ganoush

SERVES 4

GATHER

2 large aubergines
2 tbsp olive oil
Juice of 1 lemon
2 tbsp garlic-infused olive oil
2 tbsp smooth peanut butter
¼ tsp sea salt
2 tbsp coriander, finely chopped

Give me a spoon and I could eat this all in one go. Creamy, smoky and delicious, it's free from garlic and tahini (high in oligos), which are found in most versions, and instead subs in garlic-infused olive oil and peanut butter for a result just as good – if not better.

MAKE

Preheat the oven to 200°C (gas 6). Pierce the aubergines in several places with a fork then cut in half lengthwise and brush the cut sides lightly with olive oil. Place on a baking sheet, cut side down, and roast until very tender, about 35–40 minutes. Remove from the oven and allow to cool for 15 minutes.

Peel the skin off the aubergines and add the flesh to a food processor – it should be soft and the skin should come away easily. Add the lemon juice, garlic oil, peanut butter and the salt and blend until creamy. Add two-thirds of the coriander and pulse to incorporate. Taste and adjust seasonings as needed.

Serve topped with the remaining coriander. Delicious with quinoa and pomegranate tabbouleh (page 78), chopped veggie sticks or gluten-free pitta.

This will keep, covered, in the fridge for several days.

Top tip

For this recipe, the aubergines cook well on a barbecue too. Grill until the skins are wrinkled and black, and the aubergines shrivelled and soft, turning often.

Aubergine quinoa rolls

MAKES ROUGHLY 16 ROLLS

GATHER

240g quinoa
2 tbsp olive oil
1 tsp ground coriander
$1/2$ tsp turmeric
600ml boiling water
1 carrot, peeled and grated
1 handful of parsley, finely chopped
1 handful of coriander, finely chopped
100g feta cheese
Juice and zest of 1 lemon
2 large aubergines

The filling of these summery rolls is made with a mixture of quinoa, grated carrot, feta cheese, fresh herbs and lemon; it is delicious on its own, but tastes (and looks) so much better when stuffed into grilled aubergine tubes. These are delicious hot but also great cold for a picnic – pop a cocktail stick through the centre of each one to keep them together if transporting somewhere and remove just before eating.

MAKE

Rinse the quinoa under cold water until the water runs clear. Heat the oil in a large pan over a medium heat. Add the spices and fry for a minute or so, until fragrant. Add the quinoa, and continue to fry for a further minute, or until you can hear gentle popping sounds. Stir in the boiling water, then gently simmer for 10–15 minutes until the water has evaporated and the quinoa grains have a white 'halo'. Leave to cool, covered, for 10 minutes.

Add the grated carrot, parsley and coriander to the pan and stir through the quinoa. Crumble in the feta cheese and add the lemon juice and zest. Leave to one side.

Cut the aubergines into thin slices lengthways and spread them out on a tray or plate. Heat a griddle pan or you can pop these under a grill. Brush each aubergine slice with a little olive oil and cook in batches for 2–3 minutes, turning once, until softened and lightly charred. Pile each aubergine slice with some of the quinoa mix, then roll up and enjoy.

Carrot, ginger & coconut soup

SERVES 4–6

GATHER

8 large carrots

4 large parsnips

4cm chunk of fresh ginger

1 litre vegetable stock or boiling water

1 tsp turmeric

1 tbsp paprika

Sea salt and freshly ground black pepper

4 tbsp coconut milk

1 tbsp apple cider vinegar

Toppings of choice, such as sunflower seeds (keep to 4 tbsp to stay FODMAP friendly)

A reader favourite from my blog, which I hope you'll love. I promise you won't miss the onion, or other common high FODMAP soup ingredients such as leek, in this – the amazing flavour comes from the veggies themselves, the coconut milk and the turmeric and paprika. Creamy, nutritious and bold – top with an extra swirl of coconut milk, cooked quinoa, or a few chunks of fresh bread and get cosy.

MAKE

Peel the carrots, parsnips and ginger and chop into small chunks. Place the vegetables and ginger in a large saucepan and add the vegetable stock or boiling water. Toss in the turmeric, paprika, and salt and pepper and allow to simmer, covered, for 15-20 minutes, or until the vegetables are tender.

Once cooked, allow the mixture to cool slightly, before transferring into a blender.

Add the coconut milk and apple cider vinegar and blitz until smooth. Pour into bowls and top with an extra swirl of coconut milk and your toppings of choice.

Top tip

This soup freezes really well and I love to have it in the freezer for those days when you have nothing in the fridge. If you are freezing it, leave out the vinegar and coconut milk and add to the soup when reheating.

Raw salad with carrot, orange & ginger dressing

SERVES 2–3

GATHER

For the salad

½ head of broccoli

2 large carrots

100g spinach

2 tbsp sultanas

2 tbsp pumpkin seeds

For the dressing

1 large carrot, peeled and chopped

2 tbsp chopped fresh ginger

2 tbsp toasted sesame oil

1 tsp tamari

1 tbsp apple cider vinegar

½ large orange

1 tbsp neutral oil, such as sunflower

I'm not very good with lettuce in a salad, I like lots of 'stuff' – seeds, veggies, fruit – with bold flavours and great texture instead. This salad recipe provides both in abundance. The dressing is inspired by a salad I repeatedly had in Miami a few years ago and I was determined to try and recreate it when I got home.

MAKE

To make the dressing, steam the carrot until soft. Let cool and add with the rest of the ingredients to a food processor. Blend until smooth. Taste and adjust ingredients as necessary.

To make the salad, chop the broccoli into small florets and grate the carrots. Combine in a large bowl with the spinach, sultanas and pumpkin seeds. Top with 2 big spoonfuls of the dressing.

Keep leftover dressing covered in the fridge for up to 3 days.

Roasted red pepper & Greek basil soup

SERVES 4–6

GATHER

500g plum tomatoes

3 large red peppers

2 large parsnips, peeled

3 tbsp basil-infused olive oil

1 bunch of fresh Greek basil

1 litre vegetable stock or boiling water

This soup tastes like pizza, in a good way. Greek basil has small green, oval, pointed leaves, which pair deliciously well with tomatoes for all the flavour without the FODMAPs. You can use regular basil too, but Greek is more robust and holds up better in the oven for extra flavour – buy in the fresh herbs aisle from any big supermarket.

MAKE

Preheat the oven to 200°C (gas 6). Halve the plum tomatoes, deseed and quarter the peppers and cut the parsnips into small chunks. Place in a roasting tin, drizzle with the basil-infused oil and sprinkle with a handful of basil. Roast for 40 minutes, turning halfway through.

Add the roasted veg to a large saucepan, along with the vegetable stock. Simmer on a low heat for 10 minutes, then season, add 2 handfuls of basil and blitz with a hand-held blender or pour carefully into a blender or food processor and blitz. Adjust seasoning to taste and serve.

Top tip

Just like garlic-infused olive oil, you can buy basil-infused olive oil from most supermarkets. It's inexpensive and another great way to add flavour to low FODMAP dishes.

Happy belly green soup

SERVES 4–6

GATHER

3 medium parsnips, peeled
1 large baking potato
1 tbsp butter or coconut oil
2 large courgettes
1 litre vegetable stock or boiling water
80g watercress
1 big handful of coriander
1 tbsp lemon juice, or more to taste

This is a beautifully mellow soup, with simple ingredients and a lift from the coriander and lemon. A great way to use up any leftovers, sub in any greens on hand. Adjust the amount of liquid to make the soup thinner or thicker, depending on your preference.

MAKE

Chop the parsnips and potato into small pieces. Melt the butter in a large saucepan over a medium heat. Add the potato and parsnips to the saucepan and gently cook for 5 minutes. Meanwhile, chop the courgettes and add them into the pan too, with the stock or hot water. Bring back to the boil and then simmer until the veg is tender, roughly 15–20 minutes. Add the watercress, coriander and lemon juice and blitz with a hand-held blender or pour carefully into a blender or food processor and blitz.. Season and add more lemon or coriander to taste.

Coconut kale

SERVES 2

GATHER

1 bunch of kale (roughly 160g)

1 tbsp coconut oil

1 tbsp garlic-infused olive oil

180ml vegetable stock or water

120ml full-fat coconut milk

Sea salt and cracked black pepper

Toasted flaked almonds, for topping

This is a great way to use up the rest of a can of coconut milk. It's delicious as a side or serve with a generous bowl of brown rice or buckwheat (page 44) and some toasted nuts for a really simple dinner during the week.

MAKE

If not already chopped, prepare the kale by removing the stems and cutting the leaves into 1cm strips. Heat both the coconut oil and garlic-infused olive oil in a medium saucepan and add the chopped kale, stirring to coat. Add in the vegetable stock or water, cover, and let the kale cook for 5 minutes, stirring occasionally. Pour over the coconut milk and continue to cook, covered, until tender, roughly another 3–5 minutes. Taste and season. Serve topped with toasted flaked almonds.

Cheat's buckwheat pizza with lemony basil pesto & goats' cheese

MAKES 3 MEDIUM PIZZAS

GATHER

For the base

125g buckwheat flour

70g brown rice flour

1 tbsp dried Italian mixed herbs

½ tsp sea salt

½ tsp black pepper

1 egg

1 tsp maple syrup

180ml almond milk

3 tbsp olive oil

For the lemon basil pesto

4 large handfuls of fresh basil leaves

50g pine nuts

50g freshly grated pecorino cheese

1 tsp lemon zest

1 tbsp fresh lemon juice

90ml extra virgin olive oil

1 tbsp garlic-infused olive oil

Sea salt and freshly ground black pepper

For the topping

1 courgette, thinly sliced with a V slicer

4 big handfuls of fresh spinach or spring greens

125g firm goats' cheese, sliced

30g grated pecorino cheese

The texture of this pizza base resembles something similar to cake mix before it's cooked, but I hope you'll be surprised at how delicious it turns out. A cheat's way to create a delicious gluten-free pizza base, nobody can ever believe the ingredients. Think thin, delicious, herby dough covered in lemony basil pesto and piled high with spring greens.

MAKE

Preheat the oven to 180°C (gas 4) and prepare three baking trays, splashing a generous tablespoon of olive oil on top of each and spreading to cover.

Make the pesto first by combining the basil, pine nuts, cheese, lemon zest and juice in a food processor and pulsing until coarsely combined. Add the olive oil and garlic-infused oil and process until fully incorporated and smooth. Season with salt and pepper. Leave to one side.

To make the base, put the dry ingredients into a large bowl and mix to combine. Make a well in the centre and break in the egg. Beat into the mix along with the maple syrup and then slowly add the milk, mixing until combined. Put spoonfuls of the mixture onto the prepared trays to create three pizzas, and use a spatula to spread the mixture into circle or square shapes, approximately 1cm thick.

Bake for approximately 10 minutes until very light golden brown (the mixture should be cooked but still not quite crisp). Spread the pesto over the cooked base (you might not need all of it) and top with the greens, courgette and cheeses. Bake for approximately 7–10 minutes until golden brown at the edges and the cheese has melted.

Three-tin tomato, turmeric & coconut dahl

SERVES 4

GATHER

300g brown rice
1 tbsp coconut oil
1 tbsp garlic-infused olive oil
2 tsp cumin
2 tsp turmeric
1 tsp ground coriander
1 tin (300g) green lentils, drained and rinsed
1 tin (400g) chopped tomatoes
1 tin (400ml) coconut milk
Sea salt and freshly ground black pepper
2 tbsp coriander, finely chopped
140g kale, chopped

This dahl is my go-to recipe for evenings when there is almost nothing in the kitchen, the shops seem too far away, and I spent too much money the weekend before. Fresh herbs and spices transform the simple ingredients and take something quite humble to the next level. Serve with steamed kale and a hefty scoop of brown rice.

MAKE

Start by boiling your rice in a pan on a medium heat until soft but still al dente, as instructed on the packet. It should take about the same time as the dahl. Once done, drain and set aside.

To prepare the dahl, add the coconut oil and garlic oil to a large saucepan and heat for 1 minute. Next, add the spices and fry for another minute or so until nice and golden. Finally, add the drained lentils along with the tomatoes and coconut milk and cover. Cook for 20 minutes or until slightly reduced, stirring regularly and adding a small amount of water if you like a thinner consistency.

Remove from the heat, add salt and pepper to season and a handful of coriander. Serve with the rice and lightly steamed kale (cook this just before serving).

Creamy green coconut curry

SERVES 4

GATHER

1 tbsp coconut oil

1 tbsp garlic-infused olive oil

2.5cm chunk of fresh ginger, peeled and finely chopped

1 tsp turmeric

1 tsp cumin

2 potatoes, cut into cubes

1 head of broccoli broken into florets

1 medium courgette cut into small chunks

1 tin (400ml) coconut milk

1 'tin' (400ml) water

150g of spinach

½ tsp chilli flakes

Juice of ½ a lime

Fresh coriander, a small handful of peanuts (lower in FODMAPs than cashews) and lactose-free plain yoghurt, to serve

This was the first curry I made when I started this diet and there were no words for how happy I was when it worked. I ate it cold for breakfast the next day. Two days in a row. With a base of ginger and spices, tonne of fresh veg and a creamy coconut milk sauce it requires barely any prep time and you can leave it alone on the hob while you get on with other things. Come back 20 minutes later and you've got a comforting one pot dinner, full of nutritious veg.

MAKE

Heat the oils in a large saucepan on a medium heat. Peel and chop the ginger and add to the pan along with the turmeric and cumin. Stir and cook for a minute or until the ginger has softened slightly.

Add the potatoes to the pan and sauté for a few minutes. Add a splash of water or more oil if the spices or potato start to stick to the bottom of the pan and add the broccoli and courgette to the pan, together with the coconut milk and the equivalent amount of water. Cook until the potato is soft and the liquid creamy and slightly reduced (this should take roughly 20 minutes depending on size).

Remove the curry from the heat, add in the spinach, chilli flakes and a squeeze of lime and give it a stir. Add more salt and spices if needed before topping with the peanuts, yoghurt and fresh coriander.

Roast pumpkin salad with whipped feta cream

SERVES 4

GATHER
½ kabocha pumpkin
2 tbsp olive oil
1 tsp dried chilli flakes
Sea salt and cracked black pepper
2 tbsp lemon juice
400g wild rocket leaves
75g flaked almonds, toasted
Extra virgin olive oil, to serve (optional)

For the whipped feta cream
85g feta cheese
125g lactose- or dairy-free plain yoghurt
Juice of ½ a lemon
1 tsp oregano

This is just dreamy. Sweet roasted pumpkin wedges, topped with light, whipped feta cream. What's not to love.

MAKE
Preheat the oven to 200°C (gas 6) and line two baking trays with foil.

Remove the skin and cut the pumpkin into 2cm-thick wedges. Arrange in a single layer on the baking trays and drizzle with the oil; scatter over the chilli flakes and season. Bake for 20–25 minutes until tender and lightly golden. Set aside to cool.

To make the whipped feta cream, place the feta cheese, yoghurt, lemon juice and oregano into the bowl of a food processor and blitz until creamy. Season to taste. Place the cream in a serving dish, cover and refrigerate until ready to use.

To serve, divide the rocket between four plates, top with the roasted pumpkin, whipped feta cream and flaked almonds. Drizzle with a little olive oil, if you wish.

Top tip
Feel free to add in any gluten-free grain to bulk out the recipe. You can make the cream in a bowl instead of a food processor too; just make sure to give the mixing a bit of oomph.

Leftover veg & pineapple stir-fry

SERVES 2

GATHER

For the sauce

2 tbsp tamari or soy sauce

1 tbsp maple syrup

Juice of 1 lime

For the noodles

170g (two dried nests) rice noodles

1 red pepper sliced into thin strips

2 carrots peeled and chopped into matchsticks

150g pineapple chopped into small chunks

2 tbsp toasted sesame oil

2 tbsp sesame seeds

A delicious and simple one-pan dish that's full of flavour and good for you too. Keep a packet of dried rice noodles in your cupboard and a bottle of tamari in your fridge and you've got a simple base on which to add any veg, fish or meat you've got to hand. I love adding pineapple to this for a sweet, caramelised tang. It's a satisfying, quick dinner, that will leave you feeling light and full of goodness.

MAKE

Put the rice noodles in a large bowl and cover completely with boiling water. Let cook for 2–3 minutes (or according to packet instructions), stirring occasionally to prevent sticking. Drain and set aside.

Make the sauce by adding the tamari or soy sauce, maple syrup and lime juice to a small mixing bowl. Whisk to combine, then taste and adjust seasonings as needed.

Heat a large frying pan over medium-high heat. Once hot, add the toasted sesame oil, the red pepper, carrots and pineapple. Sauté for 3–4 minutes, stirring frequently, or until the veg is browning and the pineapple fragrant and sticky. Add in the sauce, stir, then add the noodles and toss to combine. Cook for 1–2 minutes more, then remove from the heat. Delicious as is or topped with a handful of sesame seeds and a showering of lime zest.

Goats' cheese-stuffed peppers

SERVES 6

GATHER

6 red peppers

3 tbsp garlic-infused olive oil

200g goats' cheese, sliced into 12

Sea salt and freshly ground black pepper

½ a bunch of basil

This might be the simplest recipe in the book, but I've lost count of the amount of times this dish has graced my family table. Sweet and juicy, creamy and rich, and fresh and fragrant all at once, these stuffed peppers are whipped out on weeknights, at barbeques, for dinner parties – you name it. Sub in any FODMAP-friendly cheese you like and add a cooked grain for a more filling meal.

MAKE

Preheat the oven to 200°C (gas 6) and halve and deseed the peppers, keeping the stalk – this helps the pepper keep its shape when cooking.

Arrange the peppers on a baking tray, cut side up. Drizzle each pepper with a little oil and roast for 30 minutes. Remove from the oven and wedge a slice of cheese into each pepper. Return to the oven and cook for another 5 minutes or until the cheese is lightly golden and beginning to melt. Drizzle with a little extra oil, season and top with torn basil leaves.

Sticky salmon-topped soba noodles

SERVES 2

GATHER

180g gluten-free soba noodles (check all
ingredients are FODMAP friendly)

2 tbsp garlic-infused olive oil

2 salmon fillets

2 tbsp tamari or soy sauce

1 tbsp maple syrup

2 tbsp rice wine vinegar

½ a head of broccoli, broken into florets

150g green beans, ends removed and
roughly chopped

2.5cm piece of fresh ginger, peeled
and grated

This is best served with thick noodles and good quality salmon.
It contains just a handful of ingredients but is bursting with flavour and
a lovely subtle sweetness from the maple syrup. If you can't find gluten-
free soba noodles, rice noodles work just fine too.

MAKE

Cook the noodles according to packet instructions – should take roughly
5–6 minutes. Drain, refresh with cold water and set aside.

Heat the garlic oil in a frying pan over a medium heat and cook the
salmon fillets for 3–4 minutes each side, or until cooked through.

Meanwhile, whisk the tamari, maple syrup and rice wine vinegar in a small
bowl and put to one side. Remove the salmon from the pan and add in
the broccoli and green beans. Cook for a few minutes then pour over the
tamari mix and add in the noodles. Stir to combine and cook for another
minute or until all heated through.

Split the noodles between two bowls and serve with the salmon fillets
nestled on top, coated with a showering of fresh ginger.

Smoked mackerel salad with cucumber, orange, fennel & radish

SERVES 2

GATHER

2 large navel oranges

½ small fennel bulb

4–5 radishes

1 cucumber

1 tsp extra virgin olive oil

1 tbsp apple cider vinegar

1 tbsp chopped dill

2 large smoked mackerel fillets, broken into pieces

This is a classic salad combination that's naturally low in FODMAPs and also delicious. Full of good fats and omega-3 oils from the smoked mackerel, it feels indulgent, despite being very healthy. It's a firm favourite.

MAKE

Zest the oranges. Cut into segments and remove the skin and pith. Trim the fennel and slice very finely along with the radishes before mixing both with the oranges in a medium bowl. Peel the cucumber into ribbons with a peeler or mandolin and mix with the rest of the ingredients.

To make the dressing, put the olive oil, apple cider vinegar and chopped dill into a small bowl or mug. Give it a good stir until combined.

Divide the salad between two plates and top with the smoked mackerel. Drizzle the dressing over the top, sprinkle over the orange zest and serve.

Prawn, courgette & chilli linguine

SERVES 2

GATHER

1 large courgette

½ tsp sea salt

½ a red chilli, deseeded and finely sliced

180g gluten-free linguine (check all ingredients are FODMAP friendly)

2 tbsp garlic-infused olive oil

200g cooked prawns

Zest of ½ a lemon

Grated parmesan, to serve

Each time I serve up this pasta recipe it's been demolished in seconds. It uses really lovely fresh, simple and nutritious ingredients and is ready in just 15 minutes. Cook as much or as little pasta as you like and make up the rest with courgette. White crab meat works beautifully in place of the prawns too.

MAKE

Spiralise the courgette or use a box grater in long swoops (page 45) for thin strands. Place in a colander and sprinkle with a little salt to draw out some of the moisture.

Meanwhile, cook the pasta according to packet instructions, until al dente. Drain and tip back into the pan (a little cooking water leftover is good). Add the garlic-infused oil, courgette, prawns and chilli and warm through over a low heat. Season to taste, top with lemon zest and split between two bowls. Serve with a grating of parmesan, if you like.

Parchment-baked chicken with coriander & lime veg

SERVES 2

GATHER
6 baby new potatoes, thinly sliced
2 chicken breasts, scored
50g green beans
1/2 red pepper, chopped into thin strips

For the sauce
2 tbsp olive oil
1cm chunk of fresh ginger, peeled and finely chopped
2 tbsp coriander, finely chopped (stems are good too)
Juice of 1 lime
1/4 tsp dried chilli flakes (optional)
1/2 tsp salt or more to taste

Say no to dry and boring chicken! A FODMAP friendly dinner doesn't have to mean no sauce or just mayonnaise in its place (as much as I love the stuff.) You deserve to be able to eat a silky sauce, like everybody else, that's full of flavour. To make the parcles throw in whatever veg you have to hand and pop in the oven as soon as you get home. Thirty-five minutes later, you've got yourself a light, nutritious and delicious dinner – with minimal washing up.

MAKE
Preheat the oven to 200°C (gas 6) and cut two large squares of baking parchment. To make the sauce, simply add all the ingredients to a bowl and combine.

Place the potatoes in the centre of the parchment squares and top with the chicken. Scatter over the vegetables and the sauce. Fold over two sides of the paper and then fold over the other sides to enclose, creating a lovely little envelope. Place on a baking tray and bake for 35 minutes, or until the chicken is white and cooked through. Serve in the parchment or spoon onto plates.

Spinach pesto pasta with chicken

SERVES 4

GATHER

For the pasta

300g gluten-free pasta of choice (check all ingredients are FODMAP friendly)
2 chicken breasts, cooked

For the spinach pesto

125g baby spinach
4 tbsp hazelnuts
35g parmesan cheese, plus extra to serve
60 ml extra virgin olive oil
2 tbsp lemon juice
Sea salt and freshly ground black pepper

Top tip

To make this recipe vegan, swap the chicken for veg and use nutritional yeast in place of the parmesan cheese.

Who can say no to a bowl of creamy pesto pasta? Wheat- and gluten-free pastas have really upped their game in recent years so try with any variety you like – just check the ingredients to ensure they are FODMAP friendly. The pesto is made with spinach and a small amount of hazelnuts instead of pine nuts, making it slightly easier on your wallet midweek.

MAKE

To make the pesto, add all of the ingredients, bar the olive oil, into the bowl of a food processor and pulse until combined. With the machine still running, slowly pour in the olive oil and blend until smooth. Taste and adjust the flavours with extra olive oil, lemon juice, or sea salt if needed. If the pesto needs to be thinned down slightly, add 1–2 tablespoons of extra olive oil or water.

Bring a large saucepan of water to the boil with a pinch of salt. Add the pasta, return to the boil then reduce the heat to a simmer and cook until the pasta is tender, roughly 8–10 minutes. Remove pan from the heat and drain, reserving a mugful of the starchy cooking water. Return the pasta to the pan, pour in the pesto from the food processor and stir together, loosening with splashes of cooking water until silky. Slice the chicken breasts and fold into the pasta. Divide between bowls and top with an extra grating of cheese.

Green bean & potato pesto salad

SERVES 6–8 AS A SIDE

GATHER
750g new potatoes

250g green beans, ends removed, roughly chopped

1 tsp sea salt

For the pesto
50g (roughly 1 large handful) rocket

50g (roughly 1 large handful) basil

50g freshly grated parmesan

3 tbsp pine nuts

Juice of 1/2 a lemon

1/4 tsp salt

60 ml olive oil, plus extra, to bring it all together to a thick but pourable consistency

An easy and delicious side dish, this is a zesty potato salad recipe that shouts summer barbeque. Simply boil the potatoes and beans, blend the pesto and fold together to create the magic.

MAKE
Bring a saucepan of water to the boil. Add the potatoes and the salt and cook until the potatoes are tender, adding the green beans for the last 5 minutes of cooking.

To make the pesto, add the rocket, basil, parmesan, pine nuts, salt and lemon juice into the bowl of a food processor and pulse until evenly ground. With the machine still running, slowly pour the olive oil in and blend until smooth.

While the potatoes and beans are still warm, pour the pesto over the top, then toss gently to combine, being careful to break up the potatoes as little as possible.

Delicious served hot or cold.

Top tip

Freeze any leftover pesto in ice cube trays for next time.

Veggie sushi rolls

SERVES 2

GATHER

190g brown or sushi rice
240ml water
4 tbsp white wine vinegar
1 tbsp brown sugar
1/4 tsp sea salt
4 dried nori sheets
1 carrot, peeled and cut into thin strips
1 red pepper, cut into thin strips
1 cucumber, cut into thin strips
1 handful of fresh coriander, finely chopped
2 tsp tamari or soy sauce

I think a lot of people believe making your own sushi is time consuming – I too was under that impression, until my sister came back from university for Easter once and started whipping it up left, right and centre. It turns out that it's not hard to make at all – it's actually foolproof. All you need is some gorgeous sticky rice, a sheet or two of nori, some thinly sliced raw veggies and a little white wine vinegar, sugar and salt. Make when you're after something wholesome and easy on the stomach, but filling and energising too.

MAKE

Rinse the rice in a fine-mesh strainer until the water runs clear, then add to a medium saucepan with the water and bring to the boil. Reduce the heat to low, then cover and cook until the water is completely absorbed, about 15 minutes.

In the meantime, add the vinegar, sugar and salt to a small saucepan and heat gently, stirring occasionally, until the sugar and salt are dissolved. Place in a jar or dish and cool until the rice is ready. Once the rice is done, stir in the vinegar mixture with a rubber spatula or fork (be careful not to over-mix – it should be sticky but completely dry once ready).

Lay a nori sheet on a flat surface. Spread a thin layer of rice over the nori, leaving a 1cm border at the top of the sheet. Lay the sliced veggies and coriander over the top in layers, parallel to the edge of the nori sheet (horizontally), covering about a quarter of the rice. Dampen your fingers with water and, with a steady hand, take the edge with the veggies and roll back over onto the nori sheet, continuing this rolling action until you reach the other end. Wet your index finger with water and touch along the far edge of the nori sheet until damp and press the wet edge onto the rest of the roll to complete! Lightly dampen your hands with water again and run alongside the whole nori roll (this makes it easier to cut). Slice with a sharp knife and repeat with the rest of the nori, rice, veg and coriander. Serve with tamari or soy sauce.

Sweet & spicy peanut noodle salad

SERVES 2

GATHER

For the noodles

150g gluten-free soba noodles

2 carrots, peeled and spiralised or grated

2 tsp sesame seeds

1 tbsp peanuts, crushed

1 tbsp chopped fresh coriander, to serve

For the sauce

3 tbsp peanut butter, softened

2 tbsp maple syrup

2 tbsp white wine vinegar

1 tbsp tamari or soy sauce

½ tsp garlic infused olive oil

1 tsp toasted sesame oil

½ tsp grated peeled fresh ginger

60ml – 120ml lactose- or dairy-free milk

Fancy something a bit different in your lunchbox? This salad packs a punch and is lovely served cold. Add in any veggie additions you like; I think courgette would work well.

MAKE

Bring a large saucepan of salted water to a boil. Add the noodles and cook to the packet instructions, or until tender, about 5 minutes. Drain and rinse the noodles under cold water to refresh, then transfer to a bowl and refrigerate until ready to use.

To make the sauce, add the ingredients into the bowl of a food processor and process until smooth, adding the milk last, a bit at a time until you reach a consistency you like. Taste and adjust flavours as necessary – you may need to add a touch more tamari or a little extra vinegar.

Pour the sauce over the chilled noodles and toss with the carrots and sesame seeds. Sprinkle with the peanuts and coriander to serve.

Five FODMAP friendly dressings

A simple olive oil and lemon dressing is my normal go-to – but these five are great alternatives when I'm after something a little more jazzy.

Lemon & hemp dressing

GATHER
50g shelled hemp seeds
80ml lemon juice
80ml water
2 tbsp extra virgin olive oil
2 tsp maple syrup
1 tsp lemon zest
1 pinch of sea salt
1 pinch of freshly ground black pepper
1 small handful of fresh basil

MAKE
Place all of the ingredients except the basil into a high-powered blender and blend until smooth (you may need to stop and scrape down the sides every now and then). Taste and adjust the flavours as necessary. Add the basil and blitz once more.

Store in an airtight jar in the fridge for 4–5 days. Stir before using and thin out with a bit of water or lemon juice if needed.

Creamy green goddess dressing

GATHER
2 handfuls of spinach
1 tbsp fresh tarragon, finely chopped
1/2 an avocado
2 tbsp apple cider vinegar
120ml lactose-free plain yoghurt or mayonnaise
Salt and freshly ground pepper

MAKE
Place all of the ingredients into a high-powered blender and blitz until smooth. Taste and adjust the flavours as necessary. Store in an airtight jar in the fridge for 1–2 days.

Top tip
Avocados are delicious, but they're also high in FODMAPs, so make sure you stick to one-quarter serving size max of this dressing to keep it FODMAP friendly.

Apple cider vinegar dressing

GATHER

60ml apple cider vinegar

80ml extra virgin olive oil

2 tbsp fresh lemon juice

1–2 tbsp maple syrup

1 tsp Dijon mustard (optional)

Salt and pepper, to taste

MAKE

Whisk all the ingredients together until well combined. Adjust the flavour to taste, if necessary.

Peanut dressing

GATHER

135g salted smooth peanut butter

2 tbsp tamari or soy sauce

3 tbsp maple syrup

Juice of 1 lime

Hot water

MAKE

Whisk all the ingredients together except the water. Add in 1 tablespoon very hot water a little at a time until it forms a pouring consistency. Taste and adjust the flavours as necessary.

Creamy yoghurt dressing

GATHER

80g lactose-free plain yoghurt

2 tbsp white wine vinegar

1 tbsp extra virgin olive oil

1 pinch of sea salt

1 pinch of cracked black pepper

MAKE

Whisk all the ingredients together until well combined. Adjust the flavour to taste, if necessary.

← 128

Seedy quinoa crackers and carrot & cumin dip

↑ 133

Miso soup

↑ 122

Toasted nori chips

130 ↑

Rosemary, black pepper & parmesan popcorn and Tequila Popcorn

124 →

Banana & hazelnut muffins

↑ 120

Baked veggie crisps

Mid-afternoon slump

Gathering at the dinner table, a big, fragrant dish emerging from the oven, chatter just beginning. Big sit-down meals are the dream, but I have to admit I also have great affection for SNACKS. Glorious, never-ending, gut-irritating, snacks. We all love them (at least I'm hoping it's not just me) – but they can be so bad for us and it doesn't matter how FODMAP friendly your breakfast, lunch and dinners are, if you're also filling your gut with high FODMAP nibbles, you're likely to suffer the consequences.

Snacks have become a huge part of our daily eating schedule – and that's totally OK – but when it comes to eating snacks on the low FODMAP diet, I know many of us still reach for cereal bars or smoothies that often contain FODMAPs such as honey, or are forced to eat plain rice cakes and bland veggies because we struggle to find anything else suitable.

Alongside arming you with mind-blowing breakfast, lunch and dinner recipes I want to show you in this chapter that there are super simple FODMAP friendly snacks out there that are healthy and just as – if not more – delicious.

My one-bowl nut butter and seed oat chewies (page 132) have seen me through many a hunger pang at all hours of the day and I can't recommend them enough for a foolproof, adaptable snack. Minimal effort and washing up and they keep well for a few days in an airtight container too, so you can make a batch up at the weekend and have them on

hand. Stick to my recipe or throw in any flavour additions you like; raspberries or blueberries are especially good.

I'm a huge crisp fan, but they're often ridiculously high in fat and I can easily munch my way through an entire big bag before I notice. I rarely come across flavours other than ready-salted that are low FODMAP too, which can get a bit repetitive. Two much healthier crisp options are the baked veggie crisps on page 120 and the toasted nori chips (page 122), both of which are packed with flavour and the latter a bit of a kick.

Banana and hazelnut muffins (page 124) and raspberry and hemp flapjacks (page 126) are two other delicious options that are perfect for a mid-afternoon pick me up and are great on the go. Full of healthy fats and fibre from ingredients such as oats, they're sweet but not too sweet and will help get rid of those cravings for sugary snacks, as well as boosting your energy levels so that you can keep going until dinner time.

Miso is a staple in Japanese cooking thanks to its versatility and suggested health benefits. Make a steaming bowl of soup (page 133) packed with powerful umami flavours, and bulk the recipe up or down depending on hunger levels. Finally, if you needed any more persuasion to make your own gut-friendly snacks, homemade savoury popcorn is the perfect way to stave off hunger with natural flavours such as rosemary and black pepper (page 130). Yum.

Baked veggie crisps

SERVES 4–6

GATHER

2–3 tbsp olive oil

1 tsp sea salt

3 large carrots, peeled or scrubbed

3 large parsnips, peeled or scrubbed

1 turnip, peeled or scrubbed

Please don't think I'm mad when you've got three big trays of sliced veg to go in the oven – these shrivel up to crispy, salty morsels and because they taste so good, they're eaten quickly, and you want lots! Slicing the veg takes a little bit of time to do, but grab a friend, put some music on and have a chat – more hands make light work.

MAKE

Preheat the oven to 150°C (gas 2) and line three trays with baking parchment. Lightly coat the paper with oil and sprinkle with flaky sea salt. Using a mandolin or V slicer, cut the carrots, parsnips and turnip lengthways into paper-thin slices. Place the veg in a single layer on the trays, brush with a little more oil, add a sprinkle of sea salt and bake, for 1½ hours, or until crisp.

Top tip

For extra flavour drizzle over 2 tablespoons of maple syrup and add a good pinch of cracked black pepper, or sprinkle over a handful of fennel seeds before baking.

Toasted nori chips

MAKES 60

GATHER
10 dried nori sheets
2 tbsp sesame oil

For the topping
1 tbsp finely grated orange rind
2 tsp cracked black pepper
1/2–1 tsp chilli flakes, depending on how
much you like your spice
4 tsp sesame seeds

Once in the pan this nutrient-rich dense sea vegetable dries out and performs a lovely puckering display, becoming beautifully crisp. Aside from the kitchen entertainment, they're also delicious – and a great alternative to crisps when you want something healthier to munch on, with big bold flavours.

MAKE
Line two trays with baking parchment. To make the topping, dry-fry the orange rind in a small frying pan for 4–5 minutes or until dry and crispy. Combine with the black pepper, chilli flakes and sesame seeds in a small bowl and set aside.

Cut each nori sheet into triangles or squares and place on the trays in a single layer. Lightly brush with sesame oil. Heat a large non-stick frying pan on a medium heat and toast the nori in batches, roughly 2 minutes each side. Return to the trays and sprinkle immediately with the chilli and orange mix. Repeat until all the nori has been toasted.

Banana & hazelnut muffins

MAKES 12

GATHER

60g hazelnuts

80ml extra virgin olive oil

120ml maple syrup

2 eggs

250g bananas (roughly 2½ large bananas)

60ml lactose- or dairy-free milk of choice

1 tsp bicarbonate of soda

1 tsp pure vanilla extract

½ tsp salt

½ tsp cinnamon

230g gluten-free plain flour mix (page 45)

30g oats

1 tsp brown sugar, for sprinkling on top

Packed full of sweet gooey bananas and studded with crunchy hazelnuts, brought together with savoury olive oil for a delicious twist. These muffins are sweet but not too sweet, and ideal for an afternoon pick-me-up. Made in one bowl, they save on the washing up too.

MAKE

Preheat the oven to 180°C (gas 4) and line a twelve-hole muffin pan with paper cases. Add the hazelnuts to a mortar and crush lightly with a pestle. Set to one side.

Add the oil and maple syrup to a large bowl and beat together with a whisk until fully combined. Add the eggs and beat again. Mash the bananas and then stir them into the mix along with the milk, then stir in the baking powder, vanilla extract, salt and cinnamon using a wooden spoon.

Sieve in the flour, add the oats and hazelnuts and mix throughly until combined.

Divide the batter evenly among the paper cases and sprinkle with brown sugar. Bake for 25–30 minutes, or until a skewer inserted into a muffin comes out clean. Leave to stand in the tray for 2 minutes before turning out onto a wire rack to cool.

Top tip

If you don't have a pestle and mortar, simple pop the hazelnuts into a sandwich bag, seal and bash (carefully) with a rolling pin until crushed.

Raspberry & hemp flapjacks

MAKES 10 BARS

GATHER
375g oats
50g hemp seeds
60g lactose-free butter
60g coconut oil
60g maple syrup
250g raspberries
1 tbsp oat flour

Hemp seeds have a lovely nutty flavour that blends easily into baked goods and slyly increases the protein, fibre and healthy fats. To my knowledge, they haven't yet been tested for FODMAPs, but there's nothing to suggest that in small amounts they wouldn't be suitable. You can buy them from any good health store or online – but if you don't fancy them, these still taste delicious without.

MAKE

Preheat the oven to 180°C (gas 4) and line a medium sized tray with baking parchment.

Add the oats to the bowl of a food processor and pulse a few times, until at least half of the oats have a sand-like consistency. These flapjacks can be a bit crumbly as they are lower in fat, so this will help them stick together – and make the oats easier on your gut at the same time. Place the oats in a large bowl along with the hemp seeds.

Melt the butter, coconut oil and maple syrup in a saucepan over a medium heat, stirring to combine. Grab your bowl of dry ingredients and slowly pour in your wet mix, stirring well to make sure all is incorporated. Spoon two thirds of the mixture onto your baking tray, pressing it down firmly into the edges. Ideally you want the mixture at least 1 cm deep. Pop the flapjack base in the oven and bake for 5-6 minutes, or until lightly golden.

While it's baking, toss your raspberries into the food processor and blitz (no need to clean it), or mash with a fork. Add the oat flour and give it one final blitz.

Remove the base from the oven and spread the raspberry mixture over the top. Sprinkle the remaining third of the oat mixture on top of the raspberries, pressing it down slightly so that it sticks. Return to the oven for a further 10 minutes, or until golden on top.

Leave to cool before cutting into bars.

Carrot & cumin dip

SERVES 4–6

Finding a tasty FODMAP friendly dip can be a little tricky. Most recipes or store-bought dips use either large quantities of beans or dairy as a base, which makes them less than ideal. They almost all contain onion and garlic too but this recipe is here for the rescue. Because the ingredients are simple, good quality carrots and olive oil make all the difference.

GATHER

500g carrots, peeled and chopped
100g tinned chickpeas, drained and rinsed
3 tbsp olive oil
1 tsp ground cumin
Sea salt and freshly ground black pepper
1 tbsp garlic-infused olive oil (optional)

MAKE

Add the carrots to a large saucepan of salted boiling water. Cook for 30 minutes or until tender, and then drain. Place the carrot, chickpeas, oil and cumin into the bowl of a food processor, and pulse until smooth. Season to taste and transfer to a serving bowl. Drizzle with garlic-infused oil, if you like.

Top tip

Chickpeas do contain medium amounts of FODMAPs, so make sure you stick to ¼ serving size max and use chickpeas from a tin, draining and rinsing them thoroughly. If you know you can't tolerate chickpeas at all, simply leave them out and reduce the amount of olive oil to 2 tablespoons. The dip will be as equally delicious.

Seedy quinoa crackers

MAKES ROUGHLY 30 CRACKERS

Along with dips, FODMAP friendly cracker options are often limited or pretty unhealthy. These crackers are really easy to make and use quinoa flakes, for a wholesome twist on the standard baked cracker. Deliciously moreish eaten on their own or paired with the carrot and cumin dip.

GATHER

130g quinoa flakes
30g sunflower seeds
½ tsp sea salt
1 tbsp olive oil
1 tbsp maple syrup
6–7 tablespoons cold water (more if needed)
2 tbsp sesame seeds, for topping (optional)
2 tbsp caraway seeds, for topping (optional)

MAKE

Preheat the oven to 180°C (gas 4). Place all the dry ingredients into the bowl of a food processor and pulse until fine. Transfer the mixture to a large bowl and set aside.

In a small bowl, whisk together the olive oil, maple syrup and 1 tablespoon of water. Slowly add the wet ingredients to the dry ingredients and mix with a wooden spoon. Add the remaining water 1 tablespoon at a time until you have a thick, pliable dough.

Shape the dough into a rectangle (it doesn't have to be perfect) and place it between two pieces of baking parchment. Roll the dough between the two pieces of paper until it's roughly 3mm thick. Remove the top layer of paper and transfer the other piece to a baking sheet. With a pizza cutter, slice the dough into small squares and sprinkle over the seeds, if you like.

Bake the crackers for 12–15 minutes, or until they start to brown. The outer crackers can cook faster, so make sure to keep an eye on these. Once golden, allow to cool and serve with carrot and cumin dip.

Rosemary, black pepper & parmesan popcorn

SERVES 6 AS A SNACK

There's something incredibly satisfying about popping your own corn, rather than putting a bag in the microwave. It's said that fragrant ingredients and recipes can take you places and every time I eat this I'm transported to a chilly autumn afternoon in front of the telly, post-walk, roast dinner cooking in the oven.

GATHER

4 tbsp extra virgin olive oil

3–4 tsp chopped fresh rosemary

2 tbsp lactose-free butter

180g popcorn kernels

50g grated parmesan

Sea salt and freshly ground black pepper

MAKE

In a small bowl, whisk together the olive oil and chopped rosemary.

Heat up the butter in a large, lidded, heavy-bottomed pot, over a medium heat. Add the kernels and close the lid. Give the pot a quick shake so they cover the pot evenly. Within a few minutes the kernels should start popping. Cook until the popping sound slows to about one pop every few seconds. Remove the popcorn from the heat and transfer it to a large bowl.

Evenly sprinkle the hot popcorn with the grated parmesan and toss, using two spoons is a good way to make sure everything is coated thoroughly. Drizzle with the rosemary olive oil, stir and season generously.

Tequila popcorn

SERVES 6 AS A SNACK

You can't go wrong with anything that contains a little tequila in my books. This is fun, quirky and I love serving it at the start of the evening with drinks, or saving it until the end of a meal for an informal dessert. It takes a bit of time to make as the popcorn does need some love from the oven, but prep is over in a matter of minutes.

GATHER

2 tbsp coconut oil

180g popcorn kernels

50g brown sugar

75g butter

1 tsp salt

1 1/2 tbsp tequila

Zest and juice of 1/2 a lime

1 tsp paprika

MAKE

Preheat the oven to 150°C (gas 2) and line two baking trays with baking parchment.

To pop the corn, heat the coconut oil in a large, lidded, heavy-bottomed pot over a medium heat. Add the kernels and close the lid. Give the pot a quick shake so they cover the pot evenly. Within a few minutes the kernels should start popping. Cook until the popping sound slows to about one pop every few seconds. Remove the popcorn from the heat and transfer it to a large bowl.

To make the coating, combine the brown sugar with the butter and salt in a large saucepan and bring to the boil, stirring until the sugar is completely dissolved. Remove from the heat and, using a wooden spoon, stir in the tequila, lime juice and zest and paprika – be careful, the mixture will be incredibly hot. Immediately pour the syrup over the popcorn and toss with two spoons to coat thoroughly.

Spread the popcorn onto the baking trays and bake for 40 minutes or so, stirring occasionally and swapping the trays over halfway through. You're looking for the popcorn to be golden and almost dry. Remove from the oven and let cool before serving.

Leftover popcorn can be kept in an airtight container for up to 3 days.

One-bowl nut butter & seed oat chewies

MAKES 8–10

GATHER

1 tbsp coconut oil

1¹/₂ bananas

2 tbsp peanut butter

3 tbsp maple syrup

2 tbsp lactose- or dairy-free milk of choice

1 tsp pure vanilla extract

180g rolled oats

4 tbsp pumpkin seeds

¹/₄ tsp sea salt

¹/₂ tsp bicarbonate of soda

A cup of tea and one of these babies – any time of day – and the world can be set to rights, I'm sure. These got me through exam time at university, when I had to keep working through the night, needed a boost and didn't want to eat junk food. They've been mustered up in emergencies ever since. One-bowl nut butter and seed oat chewies. Late night snacking game changers.

MAKE

Preheat the oven to 180°C (gas 4). Line a tray with baking parchment and lightly grease with coconut oil.

Place the bananas in a large bowl and mash, then add the peanut butter, maple syrup, milk and vanilla and mix together with a wooden spoon. Add the oats, pumpkin seeds, salt and bicarbonate of soda and stir again until combined.

Spoon the mixture onto your tray in small mounds (aim for 2 tablespoons of mixture per chewie). Press down each chewie with the back of your spoon to flatten slightly and bake for 15–20 minutes or until golden brown. Let cool slightly and get munching.

Leftovers will keep in an airtight container for up to 3 days.

Top tip

Sub the pumpkin seeds for any other suitable seed or nut or go for dark chocolate chunks if you fancy. Slather on some extra nut butter, layer with some slices of banana and top with another chewie, and you've got yourself a pretty damn good sandwich . . .

Miso soup

SERVES 2

GATHER

750ml water
2 spring onions, green tops only,
finely sliced
2 handfuls of kale, shredded
2 dried nori sheets, cut into strips
1 tbsp tamari
1–2 tbsp miso paste

Miso soup can be an amazing option on the low FODMAP diet, because it's so full of flavour without containing any garlic or onions. Although it's made from soya beans (which normally contain GOS), miso is fermented which reduces the FODMAP content, and 2 tablespoons of paste per serving is classed as low FODMAP. A steaming pot of this soothing, flavourful soup always makes you feel good – especially when you're under the weather.

MAKE

Add the water to a large saucepan, place on a medium heat and bring to the boil.

Toss the spring onions into the water, along with the kale, nori and tamari. Simmer for 2 minutes, then take the pan off the heat and stir through 1 tablespoon of miso paste. Taste and decide if you'd like to add a little more miso before serving.

Top tip

To turn this into a delicious dinner, pour over cooked gluten-free soba or rice noodles and top with some grilled tofu or prawns. Mmmm.

← 166

Sticky maple, lime and ginger pulled pork

144 →

Quinoa, feta & kale patties & rainbow slaw

↑ 162

Prawn tortillas with sweet & spicy pineapple salsa

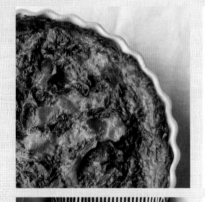

← 150

Bacon & spinach quiche

← 158

Tray-baked cod & advieh-spiced veggies

↑ 140

Spicy potato & carrot chips with sweet yoghurt dressing

Something special

Some days you want to make a little more effort. You've got some more time, you're feeling fancy or you might be having some friends over. Music's on in the background, you've got a glass of something chilled and you're ready to make some mess in the kitchen. These recipes are for you.

From buckwheat risotto with macadamia cream (page 142) to maple, lime and ginger pulled pork (page 166), my hope is that these recipes inspire you to be confident cooking not only for yourself but for others too.

Whether that's for two – haddock fishcakes with celeriac and squash mash and wilted greens (page 156) and cheesy polenta with mozzarella and tomatoes (page 138 – halve the recipes) are favourite Friday night dinner eats – or twelve – grilled spicy prawn tortillas with sweet and spicy pineapple salsa (page 162) are extra great enjoyed in the sun with a crowd – cooking should be fun and make you feel good.

If you're after more prep time, but less cooking time, my gluten-free gnocchi (page 146) has a couple of stages – but I swear rolling the dough is so therapeutic and the result so rewarding you won't once check the clock. My two quiche recipes (pages 148 and 150) take a bit longer to make too, but are perfect for a weekend lunchtime gathering with friends or family, and leftovers taste even better cold the next day.

A few dinner classics have been given a FODMAP friendly, healthier twist – homemade meatballs with tomato sauce are topped with butternut squash spaghetti on page 154, instead of pasta; along with my lightened-up lasagne (page 164). Great recipes for feeding a crowd, they're informal and cooked in one dish, perfect for everyone digging in and serving themselves, with a crisp leafy salad.

I used to be terrified cooking a FODMAP friendly meal for people, convinced it would be boring and bland. I soon learnt that practice really does make perfect when trying new flavours without onion or garlic, so get in that kitchen and have a go!

If you are nervous about cooking for others for the first time, bold flavours nobody can question are abundant in my tray-baked cod with advieh-spiced vegetables (page 158) and dukkah-crusted salmon with samphire and garlic minted yoghurt (page 152). Both aromatic and different, I promise you that no one will think about the fact they're eating food from a FODMAP friendly kitchen or even notice their dinner is missing foods high in FODMAPs. Put garlic in the title and they'll really be thrown – my pumpkin mac and cheese with a crispy garlic and thyme crumb (page 136) is not only warm, satisfying and full of creamy goodness, but vegan, gluten-free and low FODMAP too.

Vegan pumpkin mac & cheese with a garlic & thyme crumb

SERVES 4

GATHER

1 small pumpkin

300g gluten-free pasta (check all ingredients are FODMAP friendly)

350ml lactose- or dairy-free milk of choice

3 tbsp lactose- or dairy-free butter

40g brown rice flour

2 tsp Dijon mustard

½ tsp turmeric

½ tsp sea salt

½ tsp black pepper

30g nutritional yeast, or 115g grated cheddar cheese

2 slices gluten-free bread

1 tbsp garlic-infused olive oil

1 tsp fresh or dried thyme

Top tip

Sub in butternut squash if pumpkins aren't in season, just note FODMAP content will be slightly higher, so adjust portion sizes to suit. Add in spinach or kale if you like your food to contain some greens too.

Some say love conquers all, but I'm pretty sure mac and cheese does. Creamy, comforting and perfect for autumn, here it's finished off with a crispy garlic and thyme crumb. Nutritious pumpkin subs in for some of the butter and cheese more commonly found in recipes and turmeric also makes an appearance, enhancing a healthed-up version of the classic that'll become a new staple.

MAKE

Preheat the oven to 200°C (gas 6). Slice the pumpkin in half, scoop out the seeds and place both halves cut side down in a baking dish. Pour enough water into the dish to cover 5mm of the pumpkin, this helps to steam the veg, stop it from drying out and cook it quicker. Place the dish in the oven and roast until the pumpkin is tender, roughly 45–55 minutes. Let it cool slightly and scoop out the flesh. Measure 240ml (1 cup) and set aside – keep the rest for adding to salads or quiches.

Bring a large saucepan of water to the boil, add the pasta and cook according to packet instructions or until just tender. Strain and set aside.

In a blender, combine the reserved pumpkin and milk, blending until smooth. In a large saucepan, heat the butter until melted and then whisk in the flour, Dijon mustard, turmeric, salt and pepper. Cook and whisk for another minute. Pour the pumpkin purée mixture into the saucepan and whisk until well combined. Cook, stirring frequently, until the sauce thickens, 3–4 minutes. Remove from the heat and add in the nutritional yeast or cheese, stirring until combined. Combine the pasta and sauce mixture and place into a medium baking dish.

In a food processor, pulse the slices of bread and, with the food processor running, pour in the garlic-infused oil and add the thyme. Sprinkle the mixture over the pasta. Bake in the oven at the same temperature for 20–25 minutes until the top is brown and golden Serve warm.

Creamy polenta with mozzarella & burst tomatoes

SERVES 4

GATHER

300g cherry tomatoes, on the vine
if you can
1 tbsp olive oil
Sea salt and freshly ground black pepper
Small bunch of basil
700ml water
160g instant polenta
40g grated parmesan
2 tbsp lactose-free butter
250g mozzarella cheese

Ever since I tried polenta, I've had a bit of an obsession. An amazing FODMAP friendly base for dishes, it takes on any flavour you give it. You can set it into pieces and fry it, or use it in cakes like my rhubarb and polenta cake on page 204. Here, however, we're serving it creamy, with mozzerella and burst tomatoes.

MAKE

Preheat the oven to 200°C (gas 6). Arrange the cherry tomatoes in an even layer on a large baking sheet. Toss with the olive oil and a couple of generous pinches of salt and pepper. Roast for 10 minutes, or until glistening and starting to pop. Remove from the oven and toss with the basil.

Meanwhile, make the polenta. In a medium saucepan, bring the water to a gentle boil. Slowly pour in the polenta whisking as you go. Add a good pinch of salt and pepper and continue to whisk until the mixture thickens – this should only take a few minutes. Take off the heat, stir through the parmesan and butter and spoon into bowls. Top with torn mozzarella cheese, piles of tomatoes and a few extra basil leaves.

Spicy potato & carrot chips with sweet yoghurt dressing

SERVES 6

GATHER

4 large potatoes

4 large carrots

1 tbsp coconut oil, melted

2 tbsp garlic-infused olive oil (can use more coconut oil instead)

1 tsp mustard seeds

1/2 tsp cumin powder

1/2 tsp turmeric powder

1 tsp chilli flakes

A couple of handfuls of coriander, finely chopped

2 tbsp lactose- or dairy-free yoghurt

1 tsp maple syrup

1 pomegranate

This recipe is great when you've got friends over – toss on a serving plate and everyone can just dig in. The Middle Eastern inspired flavours are of course divine, and although best enjoyed immediately it's delicious when cooled and served as a cold salad too.

MAKE

Preheat your oven to 180°C (gas 4) and line a baking tray with baking parchment.

Cut the potatoes and carrot into wedges. Toss the wedges in the coconut oil and place them on the baking tray in a single layer. Roast for 40–45 minutes, or until golden and crispy.

About 5 minutes before your potatoes are ready, heat the garlic-infused olive oil in a frying pan over a high heat. Once the oil is hot, add the whole mustard seeds and cook for 1 minute or so, until the seeds start gently spluttering. Turn the heat down to medium and add the other spices, toasting for another 3 minutes, or until fragrant. Take off the heat. Remove the potato and carrot wedges from the oven and transfer them to the frying pan. Toss well to combine.

Put the yoghurt and maple syrup in a small bowl and mix together. Add 1 tablespoon of water to the mix, just to thin it out slightly. Pile the chips onto a serving dish and dollop with the yoghurt. Sprinkle over the coriander and the seeds of one pomegranate.

Buckwheat risotto with macadamia cream

SERVES 4

GATHER

1 large aubergine, chopped into small chunks

2 tbsp garlic-infused oil

255g buckwheat groats

80ml dry white wine

470ml vegetable stock or hot water

150g spring greens

Juice and zest of 1 lemon

1/2 small bunch of fresh parsley, finely chopped

Grated parmesan, to serve (optional)

For the macadamia cream

40g macadamia nuts, soaked for 5 hours or overnight

35g sunflower seeds

160ml water

1/2 tsp sea salt

1 tbsp lemon juice

Mushroom risotto used to be one of my favourites and the aubergines here are a great substitute that provide a very similar texture. Warming and satisfying, this is real 'bowl' food. The buckwheat groats cook in a third of the time of a standard rice risotto, so that you can get more time away from the stove. Plus, its creaminess comes from the macadamia nuts, instead of the butter, offering a different texture and a lovely richness.

MAKE

To make the macadamia cream, add all of the ingredients apart from the water into the bowl of a food processor and pulse to combine. While the processor is still running, pour in the water bit by bit, until you reach a thick, cream-like consistency. Leave to one side whilst preparing the rest of the dish.

To make the risotto, heat the garlic-infused oil in a saucepan over a medium heat. Add the aubergine and sauté for about 10 minutes or until softened and starting to brown. Add the buckwheat groats to the pan. Toss and let cook, 'toasting' the buckwheat, for about 1–2 minutes. Add the wine, stir and let cook until completely absorbed. Ladle in the vegetable stock, a little bit at a time, keeping the mixture at a low simmer. Each time the liquid is absorbed by the buckwheat, add a bit more, until you've used up all the stock and it's been absorbed fully by the buckwheat. Have a quick taste. The buckwheat should be tender at this point, but not mushy. Add in the spring greens and lemon juice and cook for another couple of minutes. Take the pan off the heat and stir the macadamia cream.

Divide into bowls and serve topped with parsley, lemon zest, and a little parmesan, if you like.

Quinoa, feta & kale patties with rainbow slaw

SERVES 4

GATHER

For the patties

1 small courgette

150g quinoa

300ml water

3 eggs

2 big handfuls of shredded curly kale (roughly 35g)

Small bunch parsley, finely chopped

35g day-old gluten-free breadcrumbs

120g feta cheese, crumbled

75g grated parmesan

1 tbsp garlic-infused oil

2 tsp lemon zest

60ml olive oil

Sea salt and cracked black pepper

For the rainbow slaw

1/2 red cabbage, grated

2 large carrots, grated

3 tbsp mint leaves, finely chopped

1 tbsp olive oil

1 tsp sesame oil

2 tbsp apple cider vinegar

1 tbsp maple syrup

Pinch of salt

Protein-packed and delicious, these patties exceeded all my expectations. Serve in warm gluten-free wraps, piled high with crunchy slaw, a dollop of creamy yoghurt and fresh herbs and you've got yourself a cracking veggie meal. There are a couple of stages involved, but both the patty mix and slaw can be made up ahead of time and kept in the fridge.

MAKE

Grate the courgette and place in a sieve with the salt over a small bowl. Stand for 30 minutes.

Rinse the quinoa under cold water until the water runs clear. Add to a medium saucepan and lightly toast on a medium heat for 1–2 minutes. Add the water and bring to the boil. Reduce the heat to low and cook, covered, for 15 minutes or until the quinoa is cooked through. Remove from the heat and leave to stand, covered, for 10 minutes. Fluff up with a fork and spread out on a plate or tray to cool.

Meanwhile, make the rainbow slaw by adding the cabbage, carrots and mint to a small bowl. In a small, separate bowl, make the dressing by combining the rest of the ingredients. Pour over the slaw and mix thoroughly. Set to one side.

Squeeze the courgette in a paper towel to remove any excess liquid. Combine the courgette, cooked quinoa, eggs, kale, parsley, breadcrumbs, feta, parmesan, garlic infused oil and lemon zest in a large bowl; season. Cover and refrigerate the mix for 1 hour.

Preheat the oven to 150°C (gas 2) and line an oven tray with baking parchment.

Shape small handfuls of the mixture into patties – think slightly flattened golf-ball. Heat half the olive oil in a large frying pan over a medium heat. Cook half the patties for 3–5 minutes each side, or until golden and cooked through. Take care when turning the patties as the mixture can be quite delicate. Transfer to the oven tray and keep warm in the oven while you repeat with the remaining oil and patties.

Serve with rainbow slaw, wraps, yoghurt and chunky lemon wedges.

Gnocchi with butter & crispy sage

SERVES 4

GATHER

2 medium baking potatoes

1 egg

150g gluten-free flour blend (page 45)

Juice and zest of 1 lemon

1/2 nutmeg, grated

Sea salt and freshly ground black pepper

20g butter

Small bunch of sage leaves

40g parmesan cheese

1 tbsp olive oil

Top tip

Sub the sage butter mix with one of the pesto recipes in this book for a delicious, fresh alternative. Or you can try adding in 160g cooked lardons to the sage and butter mix, for a decadent salty dish.

Gnocchi is one of my favourite foods and there's nothing I don't love about this dish. Making your own gnocchi doesn't have to be a difficult or time consuming task, and with this recipe I hope you'll agree. Buttery, rich, delicate pieces. Race you to the table.

MAKE

Bring a large pan of salted water to the boil. Add the potatoes and cook until tender, 10 minutes or so. Remove the potatoes, leaving the water in the pan. Let the potatoes cool and then peel off the skin.

Crack the egg into a bowl and whisk. Grate the potatoes then add to a bowl along with the flour, egg, lemon zest and grated nutmeg. Season and mix together with your hands – you're aiming for a delicate ball of dough. Carefully divide into four, then roll each quarter into a sausage shape, about 2.5cm wide. Cut into roughly 2cm pieces, press the edges to soften them into rounded shapes and make an indent with a fork on top of each one. Bring the water in the pan back to the boil and add the gnocchi. Cook for 2 minutes, or until they start floating to the surface.

Melt the butter in a frying pan over low heat. Add the sage leaves and cook for a couple of minutes until crisp – but don't let them burn. Using a slotted spoon, carefully remove the gnocchi and transfer to the frying pan. Take the pan off the heat and toss everything together. Grate in most of the cheese and toss again. Divide the gnocchi among 4 plates and finish with more parmesan, a drizzle of olive oil, a squeeze of lemon juice and the crispy sage leaves.

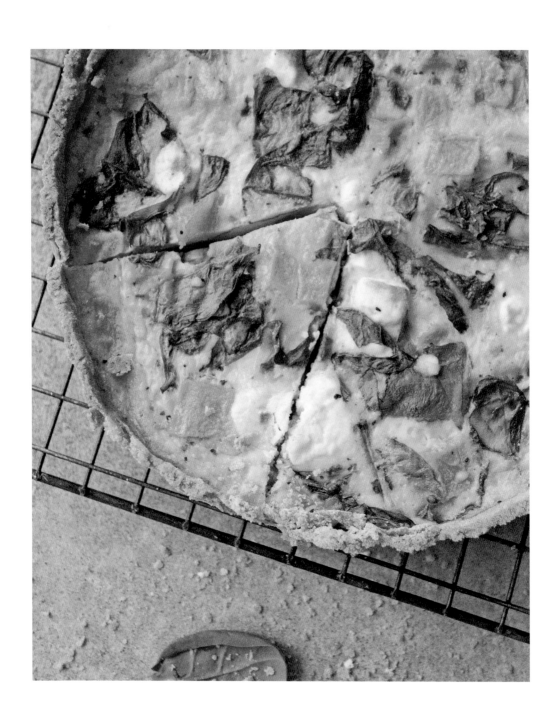

Butternut squash, spinach & feta buckwheat quiche

SERVES 10

GATHER

125g buckwheat flour

1/2 tsp sea salt

60g coconut oil, must be really cold or
Lactose-free butter

3 tbsp water

For the filling

4 eggs

250g roasted butternut squash, peeled
and chopped

100g feta cheese

120ml lactose- or dairy-free milk

3 tbsp brown rice flour

1/2 tsp baking powder

1/2 tsp dried basil

1/2 tsp salt

1 small handful of chopped basil

1/4 tsp black pepper

2 large handfuls of spinach

This is a lighter, yet gloriously flavoursome and robust veggie quiche, thanks to the sweet butternut squash and salty feta. The crust can be a little crumblier thanks to the buckwheat flour, but it offers a really delicious texture in return.

MAKE

Preheat the oven to 180°C (gas 4) and grease a 26cm tart tin with a little butter. Make the crust by mixing the flour and salt in a bowl. With a fork, cut the butter or coconut oil if using, into the flour until the butter is the size of peas. Add the water in 1 tablespoon at a time and mix to combine. The dough should start to come together, but if too dry, add an additional tablespoon of water. When you can form the dough into a ball, roll out into a circle gently with a rolling pin, and transfer to the tart tin, pressing the dough into the bottom and the sides until it resembles a crust. Poke a few holes in the crust with a fork and bake for 10 minutes.

In a mixing bowl, beat all of your filling ingredients together. Pour the egg mixture over the crust and bake for 40–45 minutes or until the centre is set and no longer jiggles when you move it. Allow to cool for a few minutes before serving and enjoy hot or cold.

Bacon & spinach quiche

SERVES 10

GATHER

3 large potatoes

1 egg

1 tsp dried basil

Sea salt and cracked black pepper

For the filling

4 rashers of bacon

120ml lactose- or dairy-free milk of choice

4 eggs

3 tbsp brown rice flour

½ tsp baking powder

½ tsp dried basil

½ tsp salt

1 small handful of chopped basil

¼ teaspoon black pepper

2 large handfuls of spinach

Spinach and bacon is a classic quiche combination, but I've lightened this recipe up, eschewing the normal fillers of cream and cheese for extra eggs and a bit of milk, and changing the typical pastry crust to one made from crispy potatoes. Lovely for brunch the next day too.

MAKE

Preheat the oven to 180°C (gas 4) and grease a 26cm tart tin with a little coconut oil. Grate the potatoes onto a clean tea towel or fresh paper towel. Squeeze out as much liquid as you can – this bit's important. In a large bowl, mix with the egg, herbs, salt and pepper. Press onto the greased tart tin to form a crust and poke a few holes with a fork. Bake for 20 minutes or until golden and lightly crisp.

While the crust is baking, fry your bacon for a couple of minutes until cooked, allow to cool slightly and then chop into small pieces. In a mixing bowl, beat all of your remaining ingredients together. Pour the egg mixture over the crust and bake for 40–45 minutes or until the centre is set. There should be only the slightest hint of a jiggle at the centre of the quiche. Allow to cool for a few minutes before serving and enjoy hot or cold.

Dukkah-crusted salmon with samphire & garlic minted yoghurt

SERVES 2

GATHER

2 salmon fillets

1 tsp olive oil

70g samphire

For the dukkah mix

4 tbsp hazelnuts

4 tbsp sesame seeds

2 tbsp coriander seeds

1 tbsp cumin seeds

1 tsp fennel seeds

1 1/2 tsp black peppercorns

1/2 tsp fine sea salt

For the garlic minted yoghurt

240ml lactose- or dairy-free yoghurt

1 tbsp garlic-infused olive oil

1 tbsp finely grated lemon zest

2 tbsp mint, finely chopped

1 tbsp lemon juice

As I've mentioned a sprinkle of dukkah is a great way to add instant flavour to any dish. Here I've used it to boost two delicious fillets of salmon. The warm, aromatic blend paired with the cool minted yoghurt is just fab and the samphire tops it all off, creating something a little bit different.

MAKE

Preheat the oven to 180°C (gas 4). Make the dukkah mix by adding all ingredients to a pestle and mortar and crushing together.

Place the salmon fillets on a baking tray and rub with the olive oil. Spoon 1 tablespoon of dukkah over each, pressing down lightly to make a crust. Bake for 20 minutes, or until the fish is golden and cooked through.

Meanwhile, whisk the ingredients for the garlic minted yoghurt together in a small bowl, and lightly fry the samphire for 2–3 minutes. Serve the salmon with the samphire and a drizzle of minted yoghurt.

The dukkah mix will keep for a couple of weeks in an airtight jar.

Top tip

Samphire is a type of seaweed with a distinctively crisp and salty taste, at its best in July and August. If you can't get hold of it, any robust greens will work perfectly in its place.

Spicy meatballs with butternut squash spaghetti

SERVES 6

GATHER

150g carrots, peeled and diced

1 red pepper, diced

3 spring onions, green tops only, finely sliced

450g minced beef

4 tbsp peeled and grated fresh ginger

1 egg

½ red chilli, deseeded and finely chopped

2 tbsp olive oil

1 butternut squash, peeled

1 tin (400g) chopped tomatoes

½ bunch of fresh herbs, such as basil and parsley, finely chopped

100g mozzarella cheese (optional)

Meatballs seem to have gone a little out of fashion as of late, but when done well, they can be both incredibly delicious and nutritious and a great crowd pleaser. Full of flavour without the FODMAPs and packed with extra goodness, thanks to the butternut squash noodles in place of normal pasta. I tried baking these for the health conscious but frying does taste so much better. Just go easy on the oil and they'll be so worth it.

MAKE

Combine the carrots, pepper, spring onion, beef, ginger, egg and chilli in a large bowl. Season generously. Get your hands dirty and mix all of the ingredients together. Form meatballs – you're aiming for roughly the size of golf balls.

Place a large frying pan over a medium heat, add a little oil and fry off the meatballs until cooked in the middle. Meanwhile, spiralise the squash into lovely noodles. Add the tomatoes and herbs to the pan and simmer for 5 minutes. Add the squash noodles, and cook for a further 2 minutes.

Delicious topped with fresh basil and a handful of cheese and placed under the grill for 5 minutes before serving, if you're feeling decadent.

Haddock fishcakes with celeriac & squash mash & wilted greens

SERVES 4 – MAKES 4 LARGE OR 6 SMALLER FISHCAKES

GATHER
½ butternut squash
½ celeriac
2 tbsp lactose-free butter
2 large haddock fillets (roughly 350g)
1 tbsp Dijon mustard
1 tbsp chopped dill
1 tbsp chopped lemon thyme
Sea salt and freshly ground black pepper
150g of spinach

These are so easy to make and healthy to boot. Delicious served with a little mayonnaise or plain lactose-free yoghurt, speckled with a few chilli flakes.

MAKE
To make the mash, peel the butternut squash and celeriac, cut into small chunks and boil for 8–10 minutes or until tender. Drain and mash with the butter, seasoning to taste.

In a food processor, blend the haddock (make sure the skin is off) with the mustard, dill, thyme and a pinch of salt and pepper. Process until the fish is minced and mixed well with the herbs. Roll into 4–6 small patties.

Heat the oil in a frying pan on a medium heat. Sear the fish cakes for 3 minutes on each side or until cooked through. In the last minute, add the spinach to the pan and wilt.

Spoon onto plates, followed by a dollop of mash and a haddock fishcake.

Tray-baked cod & advieh-spiced veggies

SERVES 2

GATHER
4 parsnips, peeled
6 carrots, peeled
2 large baking potatoes
2 tbsp olive oil
2 cod fillets
Juice of 1 lemon, to serve

For the advieh spice mix
2 tsp dried rose petals
1 tsp ground nutmeg
1 tsp cinnamon
1 tsp ground cardamom
1 tsp caraway seeds
1/2 tsp ground cumin

This is a gorgeous, fragrant dish that always receives compliments (lucky thing). Easy to scale up and down, it's cooked in one tray so you can just bung it in the oven and get on and enjoy your evening. Advieh spice is a warm, aromatic blend with Persian roots, that can be used with all kinds of rice dishes, meats and vegetables. It's an amazing way to add huge flavour without FODMAPs and pairs beautifully here with the flaky white fish.

MAKE
Preheat the oven to 180°C (gas 4). Make the spice mix by adding all of the ingredients to a pestle and mortar and crushing together. Place to one side.

Cut the carrots and parsnips into quarters and the potatoes into wedges and place in a roasting tray. Drizzle over the olive oil and sprinkle with 3 tablespoons of the spice mix. Toss to combine and bake for 20 minutes.

Remove the tray from the oven and give the veg a stir. Place the cod fillets on top of the veg and cook for another 15 minutes or until the fish is white, flaky and cooked through. Season with salt and pepper, add another drizzle of olive oil and the juice from the lemon. A final scattering of dried rose petals is a nice touch.

Store leftover spice mix in an airtight container.

Lamb kofta salad with creamy tzatziki

SERVES 4

Each of these three recipe elements are so brilliantly simple, yet you end up with a cracking meal. I love the way they marry so effortlessly and I hope you do too. If you're feeling especially peckish, serve with flatbreads.

GATHER

For the koftas

500g lamb mince
1 small bunch of parsley, finely chopped
1 tbsp chilli flakes
1 tbsp sumac
1 tsp paprika
2 tsp cumin
1 tsp coriander
Sea salt and freshly ground black pepper

For the salad

1/2 cucumber
200g cherry tomatoes
1 handful of fresh coriander
200g cooked quinoa (page 64)
Juice of 1 lemon
2 tbsp extra virgin olive oil

For the tzatziki

1 cucumber
1 small bunch of mint, finely chopped
200g lactose- or dairy-free plain yoghurt
Juice of 1/2 lemon
1 tbsp garlic-infused olive oil
Sea salt and freshly ground black pepper

MAKE

To make the koftas, place the lamb mince, chilli, parsley, sumac, paprika, cumin and coriander in a bow. Season and stir to combine. Using your hands, shape the mixture into four sausages.

Thread a skewer into each sausage. Place the lamb koftas over a medium grill or barbecue and cook, turning occasionally, for 15 minutes, or until cooked through.

For the salad, dice the cucumber and quarter the tomatoes; finely chop the fresh coriander. Add to a bowl along with the quinoa, lemon juice and olive oil and stir to combine.

To make the tzatziki, peel and dice the cucumber. Combine with the yoghurt, cucumber, mint, lemon juice and garlic-infused oil in a bowl. Season to taste.

Once cooked, transfer the koftas to a plate and cover with foil. Allow to rest for 5 minutes. Serve with the salad and a drizzle of tzatziki.

Easy flatbreads

MAKES 4

Simple and enjoyable to make. Best devoured straight away with a liberal drizzle of olive oil. Perfect as a pillowy bed for the aromatic lamb kofta, or also very good served with the dahl on page 92.

GATHER

200g gluten-free flour blend (page 45)
1 1/2 tsp baking powder
1 tbsp cumin seeds, toasted
1 tbsp ground coriander
150ml lactose-free plain yoghurt
50ml water
2 tbsp olive oil

MAKE

Heat the grill to medium, line a baking sheet with baking parchment and dust with a little flour.

Mix the flour blend, baking powder, cumin seeds and coriander in a bowl, then season. Stir in the lactose-free yoghurt and the water, then mix well to form a soft dough – don't be afraid to use your hands!

Divide the dough into four equal pieces, then shape into circles about 5mm thick. Dust each lightly with a little extra flour. Place on the prepared baking sheet and grill for 3–5 minutes on each side or until puffy and golden.

Prawn tortillas with sweet & spicy pineapple salsa

SERVES 4

GATHER

For the prawn tortillas

1 tbsp coconut oil

500g raw, peeled king prawns

8 corn tortillas

Lactose- or dairy-free plain yoghurt or sour cream, to serve

1 bunch of fresh coriander, finely chopped, to serve

1 lime, to serve

For the pineapple salsa

1/2 red or green pepper,

1 green chilli, deseeded and finely diced

100g cherry tomatoes

200g pineapple, roughly chopped

Juice and zest of half a lime

1 tbsp extra virgin olive oil

1 tbsp maple syrup

4 tbsp chopped coriander

Sea salt and freshly ground black pepper

These prawn tortillas are so quick and easy to prepare but look and feel like a real treat. Perfect for sharing; everyone can get stuck in. Take a warm tortilla, load with prawns, spoon over the pineapple salsa and finish it off with a dollop of yoghurt. Recommended served with a glass of crisp white wine, in the sun, for ultimate enjoyment.

MAKE

Heat the oil in a frying pan over a medium heat and add the prawns. Fry, in a single layer, for 2 minutes each side – you'll know they're cooked when they turn pink and feel firm to the touch.

Next, make the salsa. Cut the tomatoes into quarters and dice the pepper, and add to a medium bowl along with the rest of the ingredients. Mix together and season to taste.

Heat the corn tortillas in a pan for a minute or so each side, or until they start to crisp. Serve warm, with the grilled prawns, a big spoonful of pineapple salsa, a dollop of yoghurt or sour cream, some freshly chopped coriander and an extra wedge of lime.

The salsa can be made up to a day in advance and stored in the fridge. This encourages the flavours to develop too.

Top tip

Make into quesadillas instead – heat the coconut oil in a frying pan and add a corn tortilla. Sprinkle over a handful of grated cheddar cheese and layer on the cooked prawns and pineapple salsa. Add a little more cheese and top with a second tortilla. Cook on both sides until golden. Flip onto a board and slice into wedges. Repeat with the rest of the tortillas and filling ingredients.

Lightened-up lasagne

SERVES 6–8

GATHER

1 parsnip, peeled and diced

3 carrots, peeled and diced

1 red pepper, diced

2 tbsp olive oil

1kg minced beef

2 tins (each 400g) chopped tomatoes

120ml water

2 tsp dried oregano

2 bay leaves

20g basil

Sea salt and freshly ground black pepper

2 butternut squash

200g spinach

100g grated mozzarella

I had reservations of calling this 'lightened-up lasagne', for fear of how many of you would quickly turn the page. But there's no better way to describe this dish that replaces wheat pasta with silky layers of butternut squash, making it gluten-free and lighter on the gut. Delicious served alongside a kale based green salad.

MAKE

In a large saucepan, heat 1 tablespoon of the oil and sauté the parsnip, carrot and pepper until soft. Add the mince and cook until browned. Pour in the tomatoes and water and stir in the oregano, bay leaves and basil. Simmer for roughly 1 hour until the meat is tender and saucy. Taste and season.

Preheat the oven to 180°C (gas 4). Peel and cut the squash into thin slices, as if lasagne sheets. Bake in the oven with a drizzle of olive oil for 15 minutes. Once tender, you can get to work on layering the lasagne, just quickly fish out your bay leaves from your meat first. In a baking dish, add one layer of the mince mixture, one layer of spinach and one layer of squash, repeating until all of the ingredients are used up. Sprinkle with the cheese and bake in the oven at the same temperature for 30 minutes, or until the top is golden and crispy.

Top tip:

This keeps really well. Store any leftovers covered in the fridge for up to 3 days.

Sticky maple, lime & ginger pulled pork

SERVES 6

GATHER

1.5kg pork shoulder

1 tbsp olive oil

Sea salt and freshly ground black pepper

120ml maple syrup

60ml tamari

1 tbsp Worcestershire sauce

Juice of 1 lime

1 ½ tbsp Chinese five-spice powder

1 tbsp cornstarch

Lime wedges, to serve

Chopped coriander, to serve

6–8 gluten-free buns, toasted, to serve

Top tip:

Make your own Chinese five-spice by combining 1 tsp ground cinnamon, 1 tsp ground cloves, 1 tsp ground star anise, 1 tsp fennel seed and 1 tsp szechuan peppercorns, both toasted and ground.

Set this pork up in the morning and let it cook slowly all day. Come dinnertime, you'll have tender, delicious meat that effortlessly falls apart, all covered in a sweet, tangy marinade. Pile in to toasted buns with the rainbow slaw on page 144 and enjoy. Bring on the food coma.

MAKE

Heat the oil in a large pan, over medium high heat. Season the pork and add to the pan, browning the meat on all sides. Place the pork into the bottom of a slow cooker.

In a small bowl, whisk together the maple syrup, tamari, Worcestershire sauce, lime juice and five-spice powder. Pour the marinade over the pork. Slow cook on low for 6–8 hours, or until the pork is lovely and tender and falls apart.

Once the pork is cooked, lay the meat onto a serving dish and pour the juices from the slow cooker into a medium saucepan. Cook the marinade over medium high heat and slowly whisk in the cornstarch. Within a few minutes it should start to thicken. Pour the sauce over the pork and pull the meat apart with a fork. Garnish with lime wedges and freshly chopped corriander. Serve with warm, toasted buns and crispy rainbow slaw.

Fennel and potato bake

SERVES 2–4

GATHER

1 small fennel bulb, trimmed and thinly sliced lengthways
1 tbsp chives, finely chopped
2 medium floury potatoes
Sea salt and freshly ground black pepper
200ml lactose- or dairy-free milk of choice
1 tbsp lactose-free butter
A handful of cheese of choice, such as parmesan, cheddar or gruyere

This dish is a great accompaniment to fish or meat for four or delicious for two on its own with a green salad. Although free from garlic, onion and lactose it still tastes decadent and creamy. Don't be put off by the fennel if you're not a fan; I served this to somebody who swore they hated the stuff and they loved it - it's not overpowering at all, but instead a subtle and dreamy addition to the bake.

MAKE

Preheat the oven to 200°C (gas 6) and lightly butter a small baking dish.

Place a saucepan of lightly salted water over a medium heat and boil the fennel for 5 minutes or until tender. Drain and put to one side.

Thinly slice the potatoes. Layer the potato slices and fennel in the dish, seasoning each layer with a little salt, pepper and sprinkling of chives as you go. Finish with potato as the last layer. Pour the milk over the potatoes and fennel, dot the top with a little butter and cover with foil.

Bake for 35 minutes. Remove the foil, sprinkle with the cheese and return to the oven for 10 minutes or until golden brown on top and the veggies tender.

Top tip

Substitute the parmesan with another hard lactose-free cheese to keep this vegetarian.

← 174

Nutty chocolate
truffles

180 ←

Glazed blood orange
doughnuts

↑ 194

Vanilla bean
glazed scones

← 182

Hippie bars

Peanut &
caramel bars

↓ 176

← 192

Dark chocolate chip
banana bread

Sweet treats

FODMAPs or not, when it comes to food, balance is absolutely key. Naturally this chapter along with the following, Delicious Desserts, are the most naughty of the bunch – but I think everybody deserves an indulgence every now and then.

I've found that, like most savoury recipes, most sweet and dessert recipes readily available are either incredibly unhealthy and low FODMAP, or healthier and really high in FODMAPs. I've tried to create a balance across the next two chapters as a result – they're no doubt called sweet treats and delicious desserts for a reason – but I really believe such recipes can often taste better and make you feel better with less processed ingredients. I've tried to use the least refined sugars and most wholesome low FODMAP options to keep the recipes as nutritious as possible. That's not to say I've banned all sugar – and I hope you're not surprised to see that most recipes in this chapter do contain it. I don't think we should be eating tonnes of the stuff and in all of the sweet recipes here my aim has been to add the minimum amount necessary – but it's important that the finished article still tastes good. If you're going to indulge, it better be worth it. My main problem with sugar is when it appears in places it doesn't need to be – drinks, pasta sauces and cereals, to name a few. And it's when those products try to market themselves as 'healthy', that I get really mad! So although the low FODMAP diet can be complicated, one thing I'm not going to say is that I think you should be avoiding all sugar too – just take it easy. Recipes like my glazed blood orange doughnuts (page 190) and my favourite passionfruit cupcakes with whipped coconut cream icing (page 172) are definitely not for every day, but every so often they are really delicious.

For someone who's always picked vanilla and fruit flavours over chocolate, a sneaky amount has appeared in this chapter – most notably in the name of gooey sea salt pecan brownies (page 178), chocolate chip banana bread (page 192), and hazelnut and pecan chocolate spread (page 184); the latter I have to say is perfect with just about everything.

Inulin is a sneaky FODMAP that's found in many store-bought dairy-free chocolates – so I've created a recipe for raw rose chocolate bark on page 180 so you can make your own, with fragrant, dried rose petals and light, crunchy rice puffs.

Finally, the lavender shortbread cookies (page 188) are a joy to make and are great for summer picnics, parties and birthdays alike. Fragrant, light and buttery they're a great gift wrapped up in parchment too, and like many other recipes in this chapter are easily adapted to be vegan.

So when a sweet craving strikes and fruit just won't do – don't reach for the processed sugary sweets. Step away from those jelly beans and try one of these homemade gut-friendly sweet treats instead.

Passionfruit cupcakes with whipped coconut cream icing

MAKES 10

GATHER

70g ground almonds

75g brown rice flour

40g potato starch

¼ tsp sea salt

2 tsp baking powder

75g brown sugar

Zest of 1 lemon

1 egg

60ml almond milk

60ml passionfruit pulp (from roughly 2 passionfruit), plus extra to top

2 tbsp coconut oil, melted and cooled

1 tsp pure vanilla extract

For the whipped coconut cream icing

1 tin (400ml) full-fat coconut milk, refrigerated for 24 hours

2 tbsp maple syrup

1 tsp pure vanilla extract or 1 vanilla pod, seeds scraped

1 tsp cinnamon

Top tip

The coconut cream icing is best served immediately, but can be stored in an airtight container in the fridge for up to 3 days.

These cupcakes are light and delicate with a charming, tropical tang. Every few bites you get a little crunch from the passionfruit pulp, and when topped with the rich whipped coconut cream icing you've got a stunning flavour and texture combination, if I do say so myself. Don't skip chilling the coconut milk. It is this process that allows the coconut fat to separate out and solidify, giving you creamier, thicker icing at the end.

MAKE

Preheat the oven to 180°C (gas 4) and line a cupcake tin with ten paper cases. Place the ground almonds in a medium bowl and sieve over the rice flour, potato starch, salt and baking powder. Add the sugar and lemon zest and whisk to combine.

In another bowl combine the egg, almond milk, passionfruit pulp, coconut oil and vanilla, whisking thoroughly. Add the wet mix to the dry mix and stir until just combined. Spoon into the paper cases and bake for 25–30 minutes, or until a skewer comes out clean when inserted into the centre. Remove the cakes from the oven and set aside for 5 minutes before transferring to a wire rack to cool.

Meanwhile, make the icing. Open the can of coconut milk and scoop the top layer of white, creamy goodness into a mixing bowl, discarding the water. Blend the thick coconut milk with a hand mixer on a high speed for 15–20 seconds, just until the mixture softens. Add the maple syrup and vanilla extract and mix again for 1–2 minutes, until light and creamy. Finally add the cinnamon and stir to incorporate. I like to place in the fridge for a few minutes to solidify again before using.

When the cakes are cool, pipe or spoon the whipped coconut cream on top of each and drizzle over a little passionfruit pulp to finish.

These cupcakes are best eaten on the day of baking, however any uniced leftovers will store in an airtight container for 2–3 days or can be frozen for longer.

Nutty chocolate truffles

MAKES 16

GATHER
100g hazelnuts, roasted
100g walnuts
3 tbsp raw cacao or cocoa powder
¼ tsp sea salt
2 tbsp coconut oil
4 tbsp maple syrup
1 tsp pure vanilla extract
4 tbsp chopped hazelnuts, to coat

With a gorgeous nutty chocolate inside, a roasted hazelnut centre, and a crunchy chopped hazelnut coating, these little balls are gluten-free, dairy-free, and FODMAP friendly, ensuring that dietary restrictions need not get in the way of taste, or the ability to enjoy a cheeky treat with friends.

MAKE
Set aside roughly sixteen roasted hazelnuts for the centres of the truffles. Add the rest of the hazelnuts and walnuts into a food processor and blend until chopped into small pieces. Add the cacao and sea salt and blend again. Add the coconut oil, maple syrup and vanilla extract and blend until the ingredients start to stick together. Every so often you might have to scrape down the sides of your processor.

Shape the mixture into 16 small balls and pop a hazelnut in the centre of each one. Roll the balls in chopped hazelnuts to cover and place in the freezer for 20–30 minutes to harden. Store in the fridge.

Peanut & caramel bars

MAKES 12 SMALL SQUARES

GATHER

For the base

70g almonds

90g oats

2 tbsp coconut oil, melted

2 tbsp maple syrup

For the caramel layer

135g peanut butter

80ml maple syrup

1/4 tsp sea salt

1 tsp pure vanilla extract

30g peanuts

For the chocolate top

3 tbsp cacao or cocoa powder

50g coconut oil, melted

4 tbsp maple syrup

1/2 tsp flaky sea salt

Top tip

*If you don't fancy making the raw
chocolate layer yourself, melted dark
chocolate (70%) will work just as well.
Simply pour over as described and
place in the freezer to set.*

This recipe is decadent and isn't shy with its use of sweet maple syrup. But vegan, FODMAP friendly and, most importantly, delicious; these bars are good for the soul. With a base layer of almonds and oats and a top layer of raw dark chocolate – all sandwiched together with a gooey peanut caramel – you just can't go wrong.

MAKE

To make the base, add the almonds and oats to a food processor and pulse until the mixture resembles fine breadcrumbs. While the motor is still running, pour in the coconut oil and maple syrup, until the mixture starts to come together. Add a little more coconut oil if needed. Line a small baking tin with clingfilm, ensuring a little juts over the sides (this makes it much easier to get the bars out at the end), and spoon the mixture on top, pressing down with clean hands. Place in the freezer while you prepare the other layers.

To make the caramel layer, add the peanut butter, maple syrup, sea salt, and vanilla extract to the food processor (don't worry about cleaning it) and blitz until silky smooth. Toss in the peanuts and pulse for 30 seconds, leaving small peanut chunks. Spoon the mixture on top of the base and return it to the freezer.

To make the chocolate layer, mix together the cacao or cocoa powder, coconut oil and maple syrup in a small bowl until completely combined and smooth. Once the caramel layer has set, pour the chocolate on top and sprinkle with the sea salt. Place back in the freezer for a final hour.

Once set, remove from the tin, slice into squares and store in an airtight container in the fridge.

Sea salt pecan brownies

MAKES 16

GATHER

200g dark chocolate (aim for 70–80%)
100g coconut oil
100g brown rice flour
75g buckwheat flour
1 tsp baking powder
1 tsp sea salt
2 eggs
150g soft brown sugar
1 tsp pure vanilla extract
75g pecans

It took *a lot* of testing to get these babies right, although my housemates didn't seem to mind! Made with rich dark chocolate and coconut oil, these brownies are gluten-free and dairy-free but, dotted with silky pecans and topped with an extra sprinkle of flaky sea salt, they're also irresistible – and nobody will notice the difference.

MAKE

Preheat the oven to 180°C (gas 4). Line a 20cm square baking tin with baking parchment and grease with a little coconut oil.

Break up the chocolate and place, along with the coconut oil, in a heatproof bowl. Set the bowl over a pan of simmering water over a very low heat (careful the bowl doesn't touch the water) and melt slowly, stirring occasionally. Take off the heat and leave to one side to cool until barely warm.

Sift together the rice flour and buckwheat flour, baking powder and salt; set to one side. Whisk the eggs, sugar and vanilla together until fully combined and frothy (roughly 1 minute with an electric whisk or 2 minutes by hand with a balloon whisk should do the trick). Make a well in the centre of the dry ingredients and pour the wet mixture in, followed by the chocolate mix. Slowly mix with a wooden spoon until fully combined, then add the pecans and stir once more.

Scrape the mixture into the tin, spreading out with a spatula and bake for 20 minutes, or until the top looks firm. Insert a skewer and check the brownies are cooked – a few sticky crumbs are allowed. Sprinkle with an extra pinch of sea salt if you like, before letting the brownies cool in the tin completely and then cutting into squares.

Top tip

Place the brownies in the fridge if you like them a little fudgier.

Raw rose chocolate bark

MAKES 18–20 PIECES

GATHER

100g coconut oil

60g raw cacao or cocoa powder

60ml maple syrup

1 tsp pure vanilla extract

1 tsp sea salt

15g puffed rice

3 tbsp dried rose petals

Get your apron on and swap that store-bought chocolate bar for making your own. This is the perfect way to end an evening with guests. It is naturally lactose- and dairy-free and takes just five minutes. You can adapt the recipe to suit you – top with any suitable fruit, nuts or seeds you like or add in mint or orange extract, for a completely different vibe. In this recipe, the puffed rice naturally rises to the top so you get a satisfyingly thick, chocolate layer base, followed by a puffed rice crunch, topped off with fragrant rose.

MAKE

Line a small tin with baking parchment or cling film and put to one side.

In a medium saucepan, melt the coconut oil over a low heat. Remove from the heat and whisk in the cacao (or cocoa) powder, maple syrup and vanilla extract until smooth. Add a pinch of sea salt to taste before stirring in the puffed rice.

With a spatula, spoon the chocolate mixture into the prepared tin and smooth out until roughly 1cm thick. Sprinkle on the rose petals and an extra pinch of salt if you fancy. Place into the freezer on a flat surface for about 20 minutes, or until frozen solid.

Once frozen, use a knife to break apart into bark. Store in the fridge until ready to eat – because of the natural coconut oil it melts fast.

Hippie bars

MAKES 16

GATHER

240ml maple syrup
125g peanut butter
175g dark (70%) chocolate, chopped
4 tbsp coconut oil
1/4 tsp sea salt
100g gluten-free crisp rice cereal
4 tbsp sunflower seeds

These bars were inspired by a family friend's insanely delicious recipe, with a few subs to make them FODMAP friendly. A glorified chocolate rice crispy cake (rightly so), with extra dark chocolate on top and a speckle of vitamin- and mineral-dense sunflower seeds, they make both kid and adult devourers very happy.

MAKE

Line a 20cm square tin with baking parchment.

In a large saucepan, bring the maple syrup to a rolling boil for 1 minute, stirring frequently with a heatproof spatula or wooden spoon. Remove from the heat and stir in the peanut butter, half the chocolate, 2 tablespoons coconut oil and the 1/4 teaspoon fine salt until the chocolate is melted and the mixture glossy and smooth. Fold in the rice cereal and sunflower seeds and pack the mixture firmly and evenly into the lined pan.

In a small saucepan (or the same big one, if you've scraped it clean!), melt the remaining chocolate and 2 tablespoons coconut oil together over very low heat, stirring constantly just until melted. Pour the chocolate mixture over the rice mixture, spreading it smooth with a spatula or the back of a spoon. Sprinkle the flaky salt over the top. Pop in the fridge for about 1 hour, until firm.

Lift out of the tin and cut into sixteen squares. Best kept in the fridge.

Hazelnut & pecan chocolate spread

MAKES ROUGHLY 250g
(STICK TO 2 TABLESPOONS AT A TIME TO STAY LOW FODMAP)

GATHER

210g hazelnuts and pecans, roasted
4 tbsp cacao or cocoa powder
¼ tsp sea salt
120ml almond milk
80ml maple syrup
1 tbsp pure vanilla extract
1 tbsp coconut oil

This creamy, rich chocolaty spread is wonderful spread on fresh fruit, toast, crêpes (page 53) or eaten straight out of the jar with a spoon! With just a handful of ingredients and a few minutes in the food processor, it's easier to make it yourself than it would be to drive to the store and buy it. The milk bulks out the recipe, adding both a lovely creaminess and decreasing the amount of nuts to ensure it's FODMAP friendly.

MAKE

Add the nuts, cacao and salt into a food processor and pulse until starting to form a paste. Continue to blend and drizzle in the milk, maple syrup, vanilla and coconut oil. Once deliciously smooth and creamy, spoon into a sterilised airtight jar and pop it in the fridge.

Keeps for 3–4 days.

Peanut butter cups two ways

MAKES 10

GATHER
200g dark (70–80%) chocolate
10 tsp peanut butter
½ banana
5 tsp raspberry chia jam (page 63)

Made with healthier fats – such as coconut oil and raw cacao – than their store-bought counterparts, these peanut butter cups are decadent bites of hard dark chocolate and oozy sweet goodness. Go on treat yourself. Great fun to make with kids too.

MAKE
Line a cupcake tin with ten paper cases. In a medium saucepan, melt the chocolate over a low heat and spoon 1 heaped teaspoon into the bottom of each paper case. Place in the freezer until the chocolate is solid – it only takes a few minutes.

For the peanut butter and banana filling, spoon a teaspoon of peanut butter in each of the cups – try to make sure it doesn't touch the sides of the cups. Top with one thin slice of ripe banana in each. Pour more of the chocolate on top until it covers the peanut banana centre. Place back in the freezer and let it solidify completely before devouring.

For the peanut butter and jam cups, repeat the above, subbing the banana slices with a teaspoon of chia jam.

Top tip

If you like, you can swap the dark chocolate with the basic raw chocolate mix on page 180, made from coconut oil, cacao or cocoa and maple syrup.

Lavender shortbread cookies

MAKES ROUGHLY 20 SMALL COOKIES

GATHER

90g lactose-free butter, at room temp

120ml maple syrup

1/2 tsp pure vanilla extract

1/4 tsp sea salt

280g gluten-free flour blend (page 45)

Zest of 1 lemon

1/2 tbsp dried lavender flowers

One of my favourite recipes in the book, these shortbread cookies are gloriously buttery, with a rich sandy texture and a subtly floral lavender flavour. Great with a cuppa (Earl Grey is a winner) and an afternoon gossip. You can use coconut oil in place of the butter to make these vegan. Just note you'll get shortbread cookies with a more biscuit-like texture. Still absolutely delicious though.

MAKE

Preheat the oven to 180°C (gas 4) and line two baking sheets with baking parchment. Prepare a rolling area with two additional sheets of baking parchment and have your cookie cutter(s) handy.

Place the butter in a large mixing bowl and whip it until creamy. Add the maple syrup, vanilla and salt and mix once again to combine. Sieve in the flour, then add the lemon zest and lavender, and use a wooden spoon to mix until just starting to come together. Use your hands and work the dough, mixing until fully combined and you can shape it into a ball.

Cut the ball into two (this just makes it easier to manage) and roll out one of the dough balls between two sheets of baking parchment to about 1cm thickness. Use a cookie cutter to cut out the cookies. Carefully transfer to the prepared baking sheets, spacing them 1cm apart – they won't spread as they bake. Gather up any dough scraps and repeat until all the dough is used up. Repeat the process with the second dough ball.

Bake for 12–15 minutes, or until the edges just begin to turn golden. Remove from the oven and place on a cooling rack – the cookies will harden in a few minutes so 'undercooked' is better than 'overcooked' here.

Glazed blood orange doughnuts

MAKES 6 LARGE OR 12 MINI DOUGHNUTS

GATHER

100g white rice flour

4 tbsp tapioca flour

70g brown sugar

1 tsp baking powder

¼ tsp xanthan gum

¼ tsp salt

60ml lactose- or dairy-free milk of choice

4 tbsp oil

2 eggs

2 tsp pure vanilla extract

For the blood orange glaze

200g icing sugar, sifted

Zest of ½ a blood orange

3–4 tbsp fresh squeezed blood orange juice, depending on desired consistency

Edible flowers to decorate

I've reworked this classic so that the words 'doughnut' and 'low FODMAP' can exist in the same sentence (imagine the hands up 'ahh' emoji inserted here). Baking them instead of frying makes them slightly healthier, and covered in a sweet, seasonal blood orange pink glaze, they not only look beautiful but finish with a light citrus taste.

MAKE

Preheat the oven to 180°C (gas 4) and lightly grease a doughnut pan.

In a mixing bowl, whisk together the rice flour, tapioca flour, sugar, baking powder, xanthan gum and salt. Set aside. In a separate mixing bowl, whisk together the milk, oil, eggs and vanilla extract. Pour this mixture into the dry ingredients, and stir to combine.

Spoon the batter into a piping bag or a large resealable sandwich bag with a hole cut in one of the corners. Pipe the batter evenly into the prepared doughnut pan. Bake for 10–12 minutes, or until the top of the doughnuts bounce back when gently pressed. Let the doughnuts sit in the pan for 5 minutes, before popping them on a wire rack and leaving to cool.

To make the blood orange glaze, add the icing sugar, orange zest and 3 tablespoons of blood orange juice to a bowl and whisk together. Adjust the icing thickness by adding additional orange juice, 1 teaspoon at a time. Dip the cooled doughnuts into the glaze and then decorate with the flowers. Place the doughnuts on a wire rack and allow the glaze to set.

Top tip

You can buy doughnut pans designed for six medium doughnuts or twelve mini doughnuts. This recipe will work with mini doughnuts too, just reduce the cooking time.

Dark chocolate chip banana bread

MAKES 1 LOAF

GATHER

70g coconut oil, melted
120ml maple syrup
2 eggs
3 large bananas
60ml almond milk
1 tsp pure vanilla extract
1 tsp bicarbonate of soda
½ teaspoon salt
1 tsp cinnamon
215g gluten-free flour blend (page 45)
100g dark chocolate chunks

There's something magical and comforting about warm banana bread, even more so when it contains chocolate. I'm not sure I'll ever tire of baking this on a weekend, and if you're new to gluten-free or FODMAP freindly baking, this recipe is a great place to start. Feel free to replace the chocolate chips with walnuts or any other add-in and serve spread with your favourite topping or devour a slice on its own.

MAKE

Preheat the oven to 165°C (gas 3) and grease a 900g/2lb loaf tin (approx. 23 x 13 x 7 cm).

In a large bowl, beat the coconut oil and maple syrup together with a whisk. Add the eggs and beat well. Mash two of the bananas then add them to the bowl along with the milk, whisking until combined. (If your coconut oil solidifies on contact with cold ingredients, just let the bowl rest in a warm place, such as on top of the stove, for a few minutes). Add the vanilla, bicarbonate of soda, salt and cinnamon, and whisk to blend once more. Sift the flour into the bowl and with a wooden spoon stir until just combined. Add the chocolate chunks and stir again. Pour the batter into your greased loaf tin. Slice the remaining banana in half lengthways and place on top of the batter with another sprinkle of cinnamon.

Bake for 60–65 minutes, or until a skewer inserted into the centre comes out clean. Let the bread cool in the loaf tin for 10 minutes, then transfer it to a wire rack to cool for 20 minutes or so before slicing.

This loaf is best eaten the day it's made, but will keep for 2 or 3 days at room temperature, or in the freezer for up to 3 months or so. When popping in the freezer, slice beforehand – then you can defrost individual slices, either by lightly toasting or leaving out at room temperature.

Vanilla bean glazed scones

MAKES 10–12

GATHER

For the scones

240g gluten free flour blend (page 45)

2 tsp baking powder

1 tsp bicarbonate of soda

1/2 teaspoon sea salt

50g brown sugar

1 vanilla bean, seeds scraped

1/2 tsp pure vanilla extract

115g cold butter, cut into small cubes

2 eggs, plus 1 for egg wash

120g lactose-free yoghurt

1 tsp pure vanilla extract

For the vanilla bean glaze

1 vanilla bean, seeds scraped or 1 tbsp

Vanilla bean paste

100g icing sugar, plus more if needed

2 tbsp lactose- or dairy-free milk of choice

1/2 tsp vanilla extract

Scones were never something I jumped at the chance to make. They can be temperamental when they want to be, tough or too cake-like in texture. I think this recipe and method is pretty good at getting a lovely textured gluten-free scone however and the smell of vanilla is just irresistible – they're worth making for that alone. Alternatively, you can cut back on the vanilla, skip the glaze and these are the perfect backdrop for beautifully tangy, sharp lemon curd.

MAKE

Preheat the oven to 210°C (gas 6). Line a baking sheet with parchment paper and sprinkle scantly with gluten-free flour. Set aside.

Place all of the dry ingredients and the seeds scraped from the vanilla bean, into the bowl of a food processor. Pulse to mix the ingredients.

Add the cold butter, and pulse in short bursts until the butter is the size of peas. Add the eggs, yoghurt and vanilla extract. Pulse again, just until the dough comes together in a ball. Tip the dough onto your parchment lined baking sheet.

Dusting your hands with flour, form the dough into a disk, about 2.5 cm thick. Dust a circle cutter with flour and carefully cut out the scones, or alternatively, cut the disk into eight even wedges, and give each one a little space. This will allow them to all bake up evenly. Brush the tops of the scones with an egg wash, and sprinkle with a little extra sugar, if you like.

Bake for 15-16 minutes, or until the tops are a nice golden brown and a skewer inserted comes out clean. Place the scones on a wire cooling rack for 15 minutes to cool, before topping with the vanilla bean glaze.

To make the glaze, stir together the seeds from the scraped vanilla bean, the icing sugar and milk in a small bowl. You want the glaze stiff enough that it won't run off the sides of the scones, but runny enough to drizzle. Place the vanilla icing into a small zipper bag, seal it and cut a small corner off. With a back-and-forth motion, drizzle the vanilla icing onto the scones. You can do this bit with a spoon too.

Allow the glaze a few minutes to set, then devour immediately, or store in an air-tight container once the scones are completely cool.

← 202

Strawberries & cream cheesecake

214 ↓

Papaya, macadamia & lime salad

↑ 204

Rhubarb & polenta cake

← 210

Cardamom rice pudding

Best ever carrot cake with cream cheese icing

↓ 218

200 →

Lemon & mint loaf

Delicious desserts

There's nothing better than finishing off a meal with a dreamy dessert. Especially one you've whipped up yourself. It's a lot easier to buy a wheat-free cake or 'free from' dessert in the supermarkets now – but they're often not only insanely expensive, but full of many artificial ingredients and sneaky FODMAPs too.

Homemade FODMAP friendly desserts don't have to be complicated or time consuming – many in this chapter contain just a small amount of ingredients and for those that contain a few more, such as the cakes, hopefully you should have many of the store cupboard items on hand already.

When cooking and baking without high FODMAP ingredients, such as wheat flour and certain dairy products, I've had to learn how to use alternative fats and flours to make delicious treats. The recipes that follow therefore focus not only on delicious flavours, but contain a bit more goodness too, using unrefined, natural fats such as coconut oil and naturally gluten-free flours such as buckwheat.

A true crowd-pleaser is my best ever carrot cake (page 218). Serve with pillows of icing adorned with edible flowers and I'll be damned if you don't receive a heartening chorus of 'ooohs' and 'aaahs' from those at the table. A good crumble (page 206) can do great things. A beautiful, staple recipe requiring very little finesse – adapt it as your own.

An old school classic is brought up to date on page 210: creamy cardamom rice pudding that captures an evocative essence of the exotic – serve hot or cold with a showering of toasted coconut flakes for a delightful treat.

When the weather turns warmer, look no further than the refreshing melon sorbet on page 212. Made with just a handful of ingredients and topped off with a sprinkle of edible flowers it's a gorgeous and simple dessert that tastes as good as it looks. Juicy papaya boats (page 214) stuffed with yoghurt, nuts and lime are great for sunny days.

If you're in the mood for cake, my rhubarb and polenta cake (page 204) brightens up any table top and always goes down a storm with a splash of lactose-free cream. Lastly, I've made sure the cheesecake (page 202) keeps nut amounts to FODMAP friendly levels so you can make a decadent raw dessert, bursting with strawberries and 'cream' and needn't worry about ending your night with an unhappy gut.

As long as you're up for a little experimenting, low FODMAP desserts don't have to be dull. For those that do contain nuts or nut meal, such as almond, simply make sure you stick to portion sizes suggested or eat the amount you know you can tolerate – even though you might want to go back for seconds.

Mixed berry & rosemary galette

SERVES 6

GATHER

For the crust

90g rolled oats

60g buckwheat flour

1/4 tsp sea salt

Lactose-free butter, very cold

2 tbsp maple syrup

60ml iced water

For the filling

125g raspberries

125g blueberries

2 tbsp rice flour

2 tbsp maple syrup

1 tsp pure vanilla extract

Zest of 1 lemon

1 tsp fresh rosemary leaves or 1/2 tsp dried

The food processor does all the work here, so you're only required to do the fun bit of rolling the dough and bringing the galette together. Adapt the fruit filling to what is in season (page 41) and play around with different herbs and spices for some delicious flavour combinations. Sweet, aromatic, and slightly spicy, basil is delicious with strawberries. If you're after a big showstopper of a dessert, double the pastry and filling ingredients.

MAKE

Add the oats to the bowl of a food processor and pulse until finely ground – you want it to resemble flour. Add the buckwheat flour and sea salt and pulse briefly to combine. Roughly chop the butter and add piece by piece, pulsing until the mix has a sandy consistency. Add the maple syrup, pulse, then slowly dribble in the water 1 tablespoon at a time, just until the dough starts coming together (you may not need to use all the water – so be patient and don't over process). Empty the mix onto a piece of clingfilm and knead until it barely comes together. Roughly form a disc, wrap with the clingfilm and place in the refrigerator to chill for at least 30 minutes.

While the dough is chilling, make the filling. Place the fruit in a bowl with the rice flour, maple syrup, vanilla, lemon zest and rosemary. Gently toss, coating all the fruit. Set aside.

Preheat the oven to 180°C (gas 4) and have a baking tray to hand.

Remove the dough from the fridge, unwrap, and place on a large piece of baking parchment. Roll out the dough to about 3mm thickness (try and keep it as circular as possible – you can use a knife to cut the dough but I like leaving the edges messy). Place the fruit in a single layer on top, overlapping slightly. Fold the edges up around the fruit in any shape you fancy. Transfer to the baking tray, still on the baking parchment and place in the oven. Bake for 30–35 minutes, or until the crust is golden brown and crispy and the fruit bubbling. Let cool slightly before slicing.

Lemon & mint loaf

SERVES 8–10

GATHER

3 eggs

160g brown sugar

80ml olive oil, plus a little for greasing

Juice and zest of 2 lemons

190g polenta

45g ground almonds

30g buckwheat flour

$\frac{1}{2}$ tsp salt

1 $\frac{1}{2}$ tsp baking powder

Leaves from 3 sprigs of mint, finely chopped

For the syrup

50g brown sugar

Juice of 1 lemon

35ml water

Light, fresh and zingy, the mint lifts this lemon loaf to give another level of flavour. The buckwheat flour addition reduces the amount of almonds, making it lower in FODMAPs and I've used olive oil instead of the usual butter too. Drizzle over the sticky syrup when the cake is still warm, to let it really soak in.

MAKE

Preheat the oven to 150°C (gas 2) and line and grease a 900g/2 lb loaf tin (approx. 23 x 13 x 7 cm) with a little olive oil.

Crack the eggs into a large bowl and pour in the sugar. Beat together until light and creamy (keep going for about 4 minutes or so). Continue to whisk and slowly pour in the olive oil, until all of the oil is combined. Whisk in the lemon zest.

In a separate bowl, stir together the polenta, ground almonds, buckwheat flour, baking powder and salt. Sieve this mixture over the eggs and sugar in stages, alternating with the lemon juice and folding until just combined.

Coat the mint leaves in a little buckwheat flour (this stops them from rising to the top as much) and add them to the bowl, gently folding once more until incorporated.

Pour the mixture into the prepared cake tin (the batter should come roughly half way up the side of the tin) and bake for 40-45 minutes, or until a skewer comes out clean.

To make the syrup, place the sugar in a small saucepan along with the lemon juice and water. Heat over a medium heat, stirring occasionally, until the sugar has dissolved. Increase the heat, boil for 4 minutes until slightly reduced and syrupy, then remove from the heat. Remove the loaf from the oven and let it cool briefly in the tin. While it is still warm, turn it out of the tin, peel off the lining paper and put the loaf on a wire rack set over a baking tray or similar. Use a skewer, or a cocktail stick, to poke holes all over the surface of the warm cake. Pour the lemon syrup over the cake, letting it sink in.

Decorate with lemon slices, lemon zest and mint leaves.

Strawberries & cream cheesecake

SERVES 12

GATHER

For the base

100g oats

125g brazil nuts (soaked overnight or for at least 5 hours)

¼ small ripe banana

½ tsp sea salt

2 tbsp coconut oil, melted

2 tbsp maple syrup

For the filling

450g strawberries, hulled

240g raw macadamia nuts (soaked overnight or for at least 5 hours)

100g coconut oil, melted

1 banana

240g thick dairy- or lactose-free plain yoghurt

120ml lemon juice

150ml maple syrup

2 tsp pure vanilla extract or 1 vanilla pod, seeds scraped

Extra chopped strawberries, nuts and dried rose petals (optional), to serve

Every raw vegan cheesecake recipe I've come across looks amazing, but they all use cashew nuts in the filling, which, with high amounts of oligos (GOS) and fructans in large quantities, are seriously high up on the FODMAP scale. I've made this cheesecake with FODMAP friendly macadamia nuts instead, which give just as creamy a texture and I think, an even more indulgent flavour. Sneaky banana helps to bind the base and filling, so there are no high FODMAP dates in sight and the end result is gorgeous.

MAKE

Line an 8-inch cake tin with baking parchment or clingfilm – this makes it much easier to remove the cheesecake once 'set'.

To make the base, place all the ingredients into a food processor and pulse until a sticky, crumbly mixture starts to form. Spread the mixture into the prepared tin and press down firmly with the back of a spoon or your fingers to form the base. Place in the freezer while preparing the next layer.

To make the cream layer of the cheesecake, drain and wash the soaked macadamia nuts and place them in the bowl of a food processor with the coconut oil, banana, yoghurt, lemon juice and maple syrup. Blitz until smooth and creamy. Pour half of the mixture on top of the crust and spread evenly. Sprinkle half the strawberries over the top and slightly push into the mixture. Place into the freezer for at least 30 minutes while preparing the final layer.

Place the remaining strawberries and the vanilla in the food processor with the remaining cream filling. Blitz until combined and you're looking at a smooth pink cream.

Take your cheesecake out of the freezer. Place the strawberry mixture on top of the cream layer and then pop the cheesecake back into the freezer for at least 2 hours, or until set.

For serving, remove the cheesecake from the freezer and allow to sit at room temperature for 5–10 minutes to make it easier to slice. Top with extra strawberries, nuts and dried rose petals, if you like. Cut into slices and enjoy.

Rhubarb & polenta cake

SERVES 8–10

GATHER
120g polenta
65g ground almonds
55g brown rice flour
2 tsp baking soda
½ tsp bicarbonate of soda
½ tsp sea salt
150g brown sugar
120ml extra virgin olive oil
2 eggs
1 tsp pure vanilla extract
150g rhubarb, chopped

For the vegan 'buttermilk'
120ml almond milk
½ tsp apple cider vinegar

This is a cake to win hearts. Great for a pudding, add some fresh lactose-free cream or a dollop of lactose- or dairy-free yoghurt – which lend themselves well to the slight tartness from the rhubarb.

MAKE
Preheat the oven to 180°C (gas 4), line an 8-inch cake tin with baking parchment and grease with a little coconut oil.

First, make the vegan buttermilk by combining the almond milk with the vinegar; leave for 5 minutes.

In a large bowl, lightly whisk together the polenta, ground almonds, flour, baking powder, bicarbonate of soda and salt. In another bowl, combine the sugar, olive oil, vegan buttermilk, eggs and vanilla. Pour the wet ingredients over the dry and gently fold a couple of times. Coat the chopped rhubarb in a little extra flour to prevent sinking, and fold into the mixture until the streaks of flour just disappear.

Spoon the batter into the cake tin and bake for 30–35 minutes or until risen and firm to the touch. Allow to cool in the tin for 10 minutes or so before removing.

Because of the rhubarb, this cake stays fairly moist and is best eaten quickly.

Top tip
To make muffins instead, simply divide the cake batter among paper cases and bake for 15–20 minutes.

Individual strawberry & rhubarb quinoa crumbles

MAKES 4–6, DEPENDING ON SIZE OF DISHES

GATHER

200g rhubarb

400g strawberries, hulled

Juice of 1/2 a lime

6 tbsp maple syrup

140g gluten-free oats

45g quinoa flakes

65g walnuts, chopped

2 tsp cinnamon

3 tbsp coconut oil, melted

1 tsp pure vanilla extract

1 tbsp brown sugar to top (optional)

Lactose-free cream to serve (optional)

This dish is as delicious as it is simple (and vegan and gluten-free). Crumbles are a brilliant way to enjoy low FODMAP fruit, and the strawberries and rhubarb in this make a delicious pairing. It requires no equipment and very little prep – alter the fruit depending on what's in season (page 41) and you've got a fail-safe, delicious dessert. It's healthy enough for brunch and the other elements are so easy to customise too. If you haven't got quinoa flakes to hand, no worries – just sub in more oats.

MAKE

Preheat the oven to 180°C (gas 4). Grease individual tins or ramekins with a little coconut oil and put to one side.

Chop the rhubarb, slice the strawberries, and place in a large bowl. Add the lime juice and 2 tablespoons of the maple syrup and stir to combine. Divide the fruit among the ramekins.

To make the crumble, put the oats, quinoa flakes, walnuts and cinnamon in a large bowl and stir to combine. Add the coconut oil, remaining 4 tablespoons of maple syrup and vanilla extract and stir once more. Spoon the crumble mixture on top of the fruit in each dish and sprinkle with a little brown sugar if desired.

Bake for 25–30 minutes, or until the crumble is golden brown and the fruit is bubbling. Serve warm with a generous dollop of lactose-free cream.

Rich chocolate tart with a chia seed base

SERVES 12

GATHER

For the tart case

150g gluten-free flour blend (page 45)

100g buckwheat flour

40g chia seeds

1/2 tsp sea salt

1 egg

30g lactose-free butter, melted

A little extra butter or coconut oil, for greasing

For the filling

150ml almond milk

200ml water

75g brown sugar

1 tbsp tapioca flour

250g dark (70%) chocolate

1 tsp pure vanilla extract

I'm a bit of a pastry fiend and I think this tart is sublime. Chia seeds act as a binding agent, along with the egg, marrying everything together in this dinner party worthy dessert. Nothing about it looks or tastes 'free-from', but you can dig in too knowing your gut won't make you pay later. The tart needs to chill for at least 5 hours before serving, so make ahead of time and have a few hours to relax before guests arrive.

MAKE

Preheat the oven to 180°C (gas 4) and lightly grease a 20cm round tart tin.

In a mixing bowl, combine the flours, chia seeds and sea salt. Stir to combine. Whisk the egg and add to the dry ingredients along with the melted butter. Stir with a wooden spoon, then using your hands, knead the dough until it comes together. Push the dough into the tart tin base until roughly 5mm thick. Prick the base all over with a fork and place in the oven. Bake for 15 minutes, or until lightly golden. Remove from the oven and allow to cool slightly.

To make the filling, place the milk in a small saucepan with the water and sugar. Warm over a low heat. Put the tapioca flour in a small bowl with a few tablespoons of the warm milk mixture and stir until smooth. Add the mixture to the pan, stir and bring to the boil, before taking off the heat.

Break the chocolate into a bowl and pour over the hot milk mixture; stir until smooth and creamy. Add the vanilla extract and a pinch of sea salt, then pour into the tart case and chill for 5–6 hours before serving.

Cardamom rice pudding

SERVES 4–6

GATHER

150g pudding rice

10 cardamom pods, lightly crushed

50g brown sugar

1 litre lactose- or dairy-free milk of choice
(I like rice for a natural sweetness)

20g lactose-free butter, plus extra for
greasing

Toasted coconut, to serve

Rice pudding is so underrated. Humble ingredients and minimal fuss, this recipe creates an amazing dessert – creamy perfection so charming no one will question you if you have it for breakfast too.

MAKE

Preheat the oven to 150°C (gas 2) and lightly butter a 1.5 litre ovenproof dish. Into the dish toss the rice, cardamom pods and sugar. Stir in the milk, dot with the butter and put in the oven.

Cook the pudding for 30 minutes then give it a stir. Return to the oven for a further 30 minutes before stirring again. Return to the oven for a final hour; by this time the rice should be tender and creamy. Serve hot with a handful of toasted nuts or coconut.

Melon sorbet

SERVES 6

GATHER

700g honeydew melon (roughly 1 large
melon), chopped and frozen
1 tbsp lime juice
4 tbsp maple syrup
4 tbsp water
Dried edible flowers, to decorate

Marvellously simple and refreshing, this melon sorbet is ready to serve straight away just like the banana-based ice cream (page 217). All you need to do is freeze the melon in chunks and throw into the food processor, with lime juice, maple syrup and a little water. Pulse until thick and smooth. Serve immediately, topped with a sprinkle of dried flowers, or spoon into a freezable container for scooping later. If you can find dried cornflowers, the blue colour contrasts with the melon sorbet beautifully.

MAKE

Add all of the ingredients into a food processor and whizz until smooth. Spoon into bowls and decorate with dried edible flowers. Keep any leftovers back in the freezer for subsequent munching.

Papaya, macadamia & lime salad

SERVES 4

GATHER
2 small papayas
50g macadamia nuts
450g lactose- or dairy-free yoghurt
The zest of 1 lime, plus 2 limes to serve

High in fibre, water and naturally occurring digestive enzymes, papayas are one of my top fruits for promoting optimal and healthy digestion – and they're low FODMAP! This fruit salad is very simple, but looks beautiful and is a pleasure to eat.

MAKE
Cut the papayas in half lengthways and scoop out the seeds. Lightly crush the macadamia nuts in a pestle and mortar. Spoon yoghurt into the papaya hollows, and sprinkle over the nuts and lime zest. Serve immediately with extra lime wedges.

Campfire baked bananas with caramel sauce

SERVES 6

GATHER

60g pecans, chopped

120g dark chocolate, broken

6 bananas

60g coconut shreds

For the caramel sauce

3 tbsp maple syrup

2 tbsp brown sugar

2 tbsp lactose- or dairy-free butter

3 tbsp lactose- or dairy-free cream

Top tip

If you don't fancy using the barbecue, you can bake them in the oven instead. Pre-heat the oven to 200°C (gas 6). Repeat the steps above, but transfer the foil wrapped bananas to a baking sheet and cook for 25 mins until the banana skins are black and the flesh soft and sticky.

Let me introduce you to your new favourite summer pud. I can't count how many times I've made these; they're such a great laid-back dessert for when you've got friends or family over. Just supply a big bowl of bananas, smaller bowls filled with the different toppings and some foil, and let your guests self-assemble their own. Whack the bananas on the barbecue and cook on the residual heat. I think you're going to enjoy making them.

MAKE

Slice the bananas down the middle, without cutting through the skin furthest away from you. Stuff the bananas with your fillings of choice – pecans, chocolate or coconut – and then wrap them individually in foil. Roast them on the barbecue, turning occasionally. Depending how hot your barbecue is, it should take about 10–15 minutes for any chocolate to melt and the bananas to soften (check by opening the foil and carefully stabbing with a fork).

To make the caramel sauce, melt the maple syrup, sugar, butter and cream together in a small saucepan; set aside.

Once the bananas are cooked, transfer to plates, unwrap from the foil and either eat out of the skin or remove the skin and tip onto the plate. Serve with a generous drizzle of caramel sauce.

Salted peanut butter ice cream

SERVES 3–4

GATHER
4 ripe bananas
2 tbsp maple syrup
3 tbsp peanut butter
60ml almond milk
1/2 tsp flaky sea salt

I had an incredible trip to Miami a couple of years ago and came across a dairy-free ice-cream shop of dreams. After spending far too long determining which flavour to choose, I went for peanut butter. The best decision I ever made, I ate it curled up on a bench with my boyfriend (well, unattractively sprawled – it's so hot out there!), watching the world go by. This is my simple, and I imagine healthier, take on their decadent ice cream.

MAKE

Peel and roughly chop up the bananas. Freeze overnight.

In a blender, whizz the bananas up with the maple syrup, peanut butter, almond milk and salt. Serve straight away or spoon into a freezable container for scooping at a later date.

Top tip

Remove the peanut butter and add 1 teaspoon pure vanilla extract for equally delicious banana ice cream.

Best ever carrot cake with cream cheese icing

MAKES 1 LAYER CAKE

GATHER

For the cake

4 carrots, grated

75g pecans, chopped

410g gluten free flour blend (page 45)

2 ½ tsp baking powder

1 tsp bicarbonate soda

4 tsp ground cinnamon

1 tsp ground nutmeg

½ tsp salt

4 eggs

320ml olive oil

1 tsp pure vanilla extract

175g brown sugar

85g pineapple, crushed

50g desiccated coconut

For the icing

500g lactose-free cream cheese, room temperature

6 tbsp lactose-free yoghurt (thickest you can find)

80ml maple syrup or 100g icing sugar

2 tsp pure vanilla extract

This is the cake that gets whipped up for birthdays and all manner of celebrations. I don't think I've ever met somebody who doesn't like carrot cake and for those you know that have – I think this recipe might just change their mind. Packed with spice and brimming with extras such as crushed pineapple and desiccated coconut, this healthier take on the classic is a FODMAP friendly showstopper.

MAKE

Preheat the oven to 180°C (gas 4) and grease 2 round 8-inch cake tins with a little coconut oil. Peel and grate the carrots and place on a paper towel. In a large bowl combine the flour, baking powder, soda, cinnamon, nutmeg and salt. In a separate bowl, whisk the eggs, olive oil, vanilla extract and brown sugar until creamy. Slowly add the flour mixture and whisk until smooth. Squeeze the carrots in the paper towel to remove any excess water and add to the bowl; stir to combine. Add the pineapple, pecans and coconut, stirring after each addition. Pour the mixture evenly into the prepared tins. Bake for 35–40 minutes or until springy to the touch and an inserted skewer comes out clean. Allow cakes to cool before removing from the tins.

To make the icing, mix together the cream cheese, yoghurt, maple syrup and vanilla until smooth. Keep in the fridge until ready to use – this allows it to thicken slightly. Once the cakes are cool, sandwich them together with half of the icing, then spread the remaining icing over the top. Finish with an extra handful of chopped pecans.

Store refrigerated.

Top tip

If you're feeling extra fancy, edible flowers on top to decorate look lovely.

Sample menus

I hope that the recipes you've just seen have not only shown you that food can be healthy, delicious and low FODMAP (it really does exist!) but that they've also inspired you to see FODMAP friendly living in a different way. It doesn't have to be complicated or time consuming and I wanted to show you some examples of just how easy it is to embrace these recipes in your everyday life.

Having to eat differently from others, and suffering from food intolerances, can often make you feel like you're missing out. In the past, friends might have been cooking a big dinner to share but often I'd cook for myself because I didn't want to restrict them from the 'good stuff' – flavour and texture. I couldn't have been more wrong.

So to get you started in embracing and adapting these recipes as your own, I've shared some of my favourite recipe collections on the next couple of pages, so you don't have to worry about a thing. Packed with flavour, these recipes will instantly bust the myth that low FODMAP food is bland, and I hope these ideas inspire you to invite your friends and family over and show them the joys of low FODMAP food. Not only will they soon realise that food for a sensitive gut can be easy, inclusive and delicious, they might pick up some inspiration and tips for cooking recipes for themselves or for other sufferers they know of too!

Sharing the love is good. Even better when it's topped with whipped coconut cream icing (page 170).

← 122

128 →

Summery Al Fresco Feast

TOASTED NORI CHIPS WITH
CARROT AND CUMIN DIP
(PAGES 122 AND 128)

VEGGIE SUSHI ROLLS
(PAGE 113)

LAVENDER SHORTBREAD COOKIES
(PAGE 188)

Friends, fresh air, sun (or drizzle), a game of rounders and this spread – I'm a happy girl. But whilst picnics can be long and wonderful affairs, they can also be a last-minute simple supper taken to the park on a weeknight, armed with a blanket and a book.

Toasted nori chips can be whipped up in no time and are great to transport, studded with really punchy flavours. Pile them high with silky carrot and cumin dip for a delicious pairing. Adapt the sushi roll fillings to whatever you have on hand at home and cut them into bigger pieces so they're even easier to eat, if you are likely to have a rounders bat in hand.

End the meal by munching away on melt-in-your-mouth lavender shortbread cookies; buttery, crumbly and perfect to share.

← 142

202 →

Girls get together

BUCKWHEAT RISOTTO WITH
MACADAMIA CREAM
(PAGE 142)

STRAWBERRIES AND CREAM
CHEESECAKE
(PAGE 202)

I love serving this healthy risotto when the girls are round – because it's made with buckwheat it only takes ten minutes instead of the normal thirty, allowing all the more time out of the kitchen for catch-ups. Decadent and comforting, people are always surprised to hear the creaminess comes from nuts instead of butter. Blend the macadamia cream up beforehand if you want to save on time, so you've got it on hand to stir through the dish towards the end of cooking.

Follow the risotto with a strawberries and cream cheesecake and you're on to a winner. Prepare the cheesecake earlier that day, or even the night before and embellish with fresh strawberries, chopped nuts and rose petals just before serving. It not only looks picture-worthy in the middle of the table, but tastes delicious too. You're all invited!

Friday night in

CHEAT'S BUCKWHEAT PIZZA
WITH LEMONY BASIL PESTO
AND GOATS' CHEESE
(PAGE 90)

GOOEY SEA SALT PECAN BROWNIES
(PAGE 178)

You can't go wrong with pizza on a Friday night. You can't go wrong with pizza anytime, let's be honest – especially when it's full of green goodness and easy on the gut - but there's something about settling down with a slice in hand after a long day at work.

I've eschewed starters here to minimise the faff, but the pudding makes up for their absence. Once your pizzas are cooked, take them out of the oven and turn the heat down to low. Pop a couple of sea salt pecan brownies on an oven tray and place on a shelf to warm. When you've finished your pizza, the brownies will be hot, gooey and perfect to eat on their own, or to serve with some deliciously creamy, cold banana ice cream (page 217 – top tip).

← 130

↓ 210

166 →

Sunday lunch

ROSEMARY, BLACK PEPPER
AND PARMESAN POPCORN
(PAGE 130)

STICKY MAPLE, LIME AND GINGER
PULLED PORK
(PAGE 166)

CARDAMOM RICE PUDDING
(PAGE 210)

For me, Sunday lunch has always been a relaxed affair, served closer to 6pm after a long walk. This is a lovely menu to cook for a family get together – especially if family members are new to or sceptical about this way of eating.

The rosemary, black pepper and parmesan popcorn is a delicious snack to have on the table for people to nibble on while they are waiting for dinner. The pulled pork can be prepped and put on to cook first thing in the morning, so you can just forget about it and let it do its thing while you look after everything else. Using the juices for a sauce means that nobody will miss the standard gravy too, which normally contains wheat and onion.

Finish lunch with a steaming dish of creamy cardamom rice pudding, bowls piled high with generous scoops, topped off with shards of toasted coconut.

Laid-back cooking for a crowd

SPICY POTATO AND CARROT CHIPS
WITH SWEET YOGURT DRESSING
(PAGE 140)

LAMB KOFTAS WITH SALAD
AND TZATZIKI AND EASY FLATBREADS
(PAGE 160)

RHUBARB AND POLENTA CAKE
(PAGE 204)

This menu is all about informal, help-yourself dishes. Having grown up with an incredible bunch of family friends, big gatherings are a common occurrence. A menu like this is great to serve, because people won't even think about their dinner being FODMAP friendly.

If it's a special occasion, pop the chips in individual cones and then let people help themselves to the sweet yoghurt dressing, pomegranate seeds and chopped coriander for a nice touch. Cook the koftas in either the oven or on a grill outside depending on the weather - a crowd gathered around the BBQ is always a nice sight. Spoon the tzatziki into small dishes, the salad into bowls and pile the flatbreads under a tea towel to keep them warm. Grab a plate, fill it with a bit of everything, if you like, and then plomp a delicious kofta on top. Finish with rhubarb and polenta cake and generous lashings of cream (lactose-free). Aromatic, warm and delicious, this is real Middle-Eastern inspired, bringing people together food.

STRESS, FREQUENTLY ASKED QUESTIONS AND TOP TIPS

Remember how I chirped on at the start of this book about how closely our gut is linked to everything? There's still so much to be explored and researched when it comes to the gut–brain connection, but alongside food, we do know that other lifestyle and emotional factors can play a huge part in managing IBS symptoms and having a sensitive gut.

Unsurprisingly, stress and anxiety are right up there. And hands up, I can be terrible when it comes to both.

Life is hard. Jobs, interests, exercise, friends, family, relationships, wellbeing. I want everything – I want to excel in what I do, be able to eat what I want but also look the way I want, have the best relationship and see my friends and family all the time. But you just can't do everything. Stress produces a hormone, called cortisol, which when chronically elevated can have big effects on weight, immune function, and, you've got it – IBS. So before we delve further into this chapter, if any of you lovely lot feel the same, I want you to take a deep breath and STOP COMPARING YOURSELF TO OTHERS. You are you and there's only one of you. You're bloody fantastic and you're smashing life. So don't be so hard on yourself.

Over time I've tried to change the way I think about my gut and symptom flare-ups and I'd love for you to do so too. Think of them as a warning system, telling you to ease up when you're trying to do all these things at once, or have eaten something it can't tolerate at that moment. It's not your body attacking you but helping you instead, so listen to it!

Everybody is different, but to help manage a sensitive gut, some other tips and practices that I've found useful include:

- Try to avoid overeating. You hear the word 'mindfulness' a lot, and it gets a lot of flack, but I have to admit it is a great concept to apply to eating. Try and eat at a table, turn off any distractions and chew your food. I'm greedy, so sometimes I like the good old trick of eating off smaller plates too – often portion sizes are much, much bigger than they need to be. Eating a big amount, quickly, really does have an impact on the gut.

- Try to avoid excessive intake of fats and caffeine. I love a coffee but I can feel the effects on my gut if I drink too much, and it doesn't help me with feeling anxious either.

- Get a good night's sleep! It's something I've always been terrible at and have had to work hard at over the years. Step away from screens for a while before bed too. I really do believe sleep is the key to a healthy gut and mind.

- Doing yoga or going for a long walk is great to help get your digestion moving. I find absurdly leaping and dancing around the kitchen with my mum and sister helps too.

- When anxiety is rearing its unhelpful head, something that I find really helps to chill me out is focusing on my breathing for a few minutes. Breathe out 1-2-3-4 seconds, hold 1-2-3-4 seconds, breathe in 1-2-3-4, hold 1-2-3-4, and repeat.

- Talk to others. Know that you're not alone. I remember skimming Facebook groups and couldn't believe some of the posts from people suffering in silence, only able to talk about it online. It's time to make gut health a priority!

Many people find that a combination of the above, along with a FODMAP friendly diet, are a good strategy for dealing with their individual symptoms and triggers – but if you're doing something else that's working for you and your doctor says it's OK, please carry on.

FAQS

I've tried to answer some of the questions I receive most from my lovely blog readers here.

What happens if I slip up and eat something I shouldn't?

Don't beat yourself up about it. It happens. If you're suffering from crappy symptoms as a result, take it easy and be extra good with the food you eat for the next few days. And if you've eaten something that you thought was a no-go, but actually you're feeling all right – it may turn out to be something you can look at reintroducing back into your diet.

Eating out has become a minefield and I dread explaining my intolerances to restaurant staff. Do you have any advice on what to look for or how to avoid any issues?

It's the worst feeling when you're out having dinner with friends and you look down at the menu only to think '. . . crap, I can't eat one item on here'. But if you generally try to avoid the more extravagant and ingredient-packed dishes, and instead opt for those that are simpler, you'll most likely be OK. Choosing like this may minimise the risk of the overall dish containing too many FODMAP rich foods for your gut in one sitting.

I'll often speak to a chef before I eat at a restaurant about my intolerances. It's not always easy, and patience and compromise is required – but you deserve a delicious, nutritious meal the same as everybody else, so don't feel bad about asking questions and explaining your situation! A gluten-free meal with no onion or garlic is a simplistic description of the low FODMAP diet, but I often find it's the easiest way to explain. If you don't want to do it in front of everyone on the day, phoning ahead is a great idea and not only gives you more time to speak to the chef or restaurant staff, but allows them to note that somebody with intolerances is coming and possibly prepare ahead, depending on the food. Restaurants are becoming more and more accepting of intolerances and most are more than happy to help.

As a rule, try to avoid cuisines that have a lot of rich sauces and bold flavours such as Chinese and Indian. Instead go for something like Middle Eastern or Italian, which is often a great option as many restaurants now serve gluten-free pizza bases (just make sure you ask for low FODMAP toppings). Japanese food is delicious and healthy too – I just stick with simple sushi such as cucumber or salmon rolls.

I can eat a food containing a medium amount of FODMAPs one day and be absolutely fine, but another day I could be in agony. Why does this happen?

One of the most frustrating things about IBS, sensitive tummies and food intolerances is that they affect everybody differently and, just as I've mentioned, stress and anxiety play a huge role and vice-versa. Some days I can eat dried fruit for example and be absolutely fine, but if I'm tired or run-down another day it might really mess up my stomach. The trick for me has been learning to acknowledge when I'm run-down and stressed.

Take 10 minutes to think about and list down what you've been stressing about today. Boyfriends, girlfriends, jobs, weight, an upcoming event – I bet it doesn't take long to identify those triggers. Then think about what food you've eaten or are going to eat for the rest of the day – for example, if you know your breakfast contained a few medium FODMAP foods and you are run-down or have had a bad night's sleep, make sure you stick to all low FODMAP foods for the rest of the day and be mindful of your body and how you eat.

Help! I've accidentally eaten a large amount of high FODMAP foods – is there anything I can do to lessen or prevent the symptoms?

Unfortunately it's not easy to avoid symptoms once high FODMAP foods have been accidentally eaten – trust me, I wish I could give you a miracle cure! But a cheeky (if somewhat embarrassing) action that always helps me is massaging my stomach. You might look like a bit of a lunatic and get a sore arm but it really does help to stimulate your digestion – especially if you're suffering from bloating.

Why do food lists sometimes offer differing and conflicting information?

There are some discrepancies between FODMAP data that exist in the literature. This is largely due to seasonal variances in food quality. For example, a tomato grown in a warmer climate may have slightly different fructose levels to one sourced elsewhere. Like anything, if you're unsure, try a small amount at a time and see how it affects you, or speak to a dietician.

I seem to spend a fortune buying gluten-free flours and other FODMAP friendly ingredients – how can I save money?

Processed wheat- and gluten-free store-bought goods can be so expensive and quite often unnecessary. Making your own meals from naturally low FODMAP ingredients and buying less processed foods can be a great way to save money.

If you can, pick up a few bits every couple of days so that you don't waste food, and try to shop both locally and seasonally (see page 41) where you can.

FODMAP friendly baking is generally more expensive and this is hard to avoid. But you've got to think about it as investing in nutritious ingredients that are not only better for your body, but also cheaper in the long run when you're no longer spending money on pretend-healthy crisps, chocolate and snacks when you're out. A good trick is to buy wheat- and gluten-free flours in bulk online – and note that many supermarkets now have their own versions of flours and oils, like coconut.

Does organic matter to FODMAP?

No, the FODMAP levels of the food are not affected by the origin of the food (i.e. organic or non-organic). The FODMAP sugars are contained in and around the food, but are not impacted by the sourcing/method of food harvesting overall. As mentioned, there may be some differences between foods of the same nature due to seasonal changes.

Is alcohol FODMAP friendly?

Anybody who knows me well, knows I'm partial to a few G&Ts with friends and family so I would love to say yes, however alcohol in excess is a known gut irritant. Stick to one or two drinks every now and then if you do drink, and don't mix, to help reduce the chance of symptoms. The most common potential problem with alcohol is the fructose load of drinks, most notably mixers such as fruit juice; rum and sweet, sparkling and dessert wines, so make sure to avoid those.

Do you take any daily supplements?

I don't personally take any supplements for my IBS specifically but do have some little rituals. I always try and start my day with a mug of hot water and lemon in the morning – it helps stimulate and wake up the digestive system when it's snoozing from the night before – and I drink peppermint tea throughout the day. Peppermint oil and peppermint tea have been used for thousands of years to help soothe a variety of digestive and gastrointestinal conditions and I love the stuff. Reducing the associated pain of cramps, bloating and indigestion, it helps to calm the intestines and muscles of the digestive tract, while giving your entire digestive system a boost for optimal activity levels.

I've been following the diet for a while now but it still doesn't seem to be helping. What should I do?

Firstly know that you're not alone! It can be so frustrating when you feel like it's not working but everybody really is different and it takes time for our bodies and digestive systems to balance and heal. Life can be so stressful and it's often hard to find balance, so don't be too hard on yourself. Being happy as well as healthy is the most important thing. Make sure you've followed the elimination phase accurately, for at least 8 weeks, and if you're still suffering, please go back to your GP and ask for help or a further diagnosis.

RESOURCES AND REFERENCES

RESOURCES

While I hope it's been a valuable resource, this book has only just scratched the surface of all things FODMAP.

There's a lot of brilliant information out there, but as I've mentioned a couple of times throughout the book, I reccomend you seek the advice of a registered dietician when starting the diet. Ask your GP about seeing a dietician with expertise in or who specialises in the Low FODMAP Diet. They can help tailor elements specifically to you and assess and advise on your individual tolerances.

USEFUL WEBSITES

There are too many wonderful blogs out there to name.
FODMAP Friendly: **www.fodmapfriendly.com**
FODMAP Friendly App: **http://fodmapfriendly.com/app**
IBS Network: **www.theibsnetwork.org**
Coeliac UK: **www.coeliac.org.uk**
Crohn's and colitis UK: **www.crohnsandcolitis.org.uk**

GREAT SHOPS FOR FODMAP FRIENDLY STAPLES

A good health food shop is normally my first go-to when buying ingredients, but a number of supermarkets and high street grocers now stock great options too.

Holland and Barrett are often my go-to for a variety of wheat-free flours. They're really good value and have a lot of stores around the UK for easy access too.
www.hollandandbarrett.com

Goodness Direct are a great online supplier for a plethora of gluten-free, wheat-free and lactose-free products delivered to your door. If I can't locate an ingredient or product in the shops, they're often my first point of call. They have a list of low FODMAP products, but just be mindful of your own tolerances.
www.goodnessdirect.co.uk

LOW FODMAP RESEARCH REFERENCES

Shanti L. Eswaran, William D. Chey, Kenya Jackson, Sivaram G. Pillai, Samuel W. Chey, Theresa Han-Markey. 821 A Low FODMAP Diet Improves Quality of Life, Reduces Activity Impairment, and Improves Sleep Quality in Patients With Irritable Bowel Syndrome and Diarrhea: Results From a U.S. Randomized, Controlled Trial. Gastroenterology, 2016; 150(4): S172.

Shepherd SJ and Gibson PR: Fructose malabsorption and symptoms of irritable bowel syndrome: guidelines for effective dietary management, J. Am. Diet. Assoc. 2006; 106(10): 1631–9.

Staudacher, H. M., et al. Comparison of symptom response following advice for a diet low in fermentable carbohydrates (FODMAPs) versus standard dietary advice in patients with irritable bowel syndrome." J Human Nutr Diet 2011; 24(5): 487–495.

UK NICE guidelines: Evidence-Based Recommendations for Health and Care in England **www.nice.org.uk**

The data for high, moderate and low FODMAP lists and tables throughout has been derived from:
The Monash University Low FODMAP App for smartphones. July 28, 2016. Version 2.0.1
FODMAP Friendly App for smartphones. June 6, 2016. Version 2.0
All data is correct at time of publication.

MEASUREMENT CONVERSION TABLE

Different ingredients will vary in weight, but this measurement
conversion table is a handy guide to get you started.

Ingredient	1 cup
Flour	120g
Brown sugar	180g
Pasta, uncooked	140g
Rice, uncooked	190g
Oats, uncooked	90g
Butter	240g
Nuts, chopped	125g
Liquids	240ml

Index

A

advieh spice: Tray-baked cod &
advieh-spiced veggies 158
almonds: Banana granola 56
Peanut & caramel bars 176
Tropical overnight bircher 57
Apple cider vinegar dressing 117
aubergines: Aubergine quinoa rolls 82
Baba ganoush 80
Buckwheat risotto with macadamia
cream 142
avocado: Creamy green goddess
dressing 116

B

Baba ganoush 80
Bacon & spinach quiche 150
baking powder 34
bananas: Banana & hazelnut muffins
124
Banana granola 56
Breakfast powerhouse smoothie 68
Campfire baked bananas with
caramel sauce 216
Dark chocolate chip banana bread
192
Fluffy banana cinnamon pancakes
62
One-bowl nut butter & seed oat
chewies 132
Peanut butter cups two ways 187
Salted peanut butter ice cream 217
Strawberries & cream cheesecake
202
Strawberry milk smoothie 67
basil: Cheat's buckwheat pizza with
lemony basil pesto & goats' cheese
90
Green bean & potato pesto salad
112

Roasted red pepper & Greek basil
soup 86
beans see green beans
beef: Spicy meatballs with butternut
squash spaghetti 154
blueberries: Blueberry chia jam 63
Mixed berry & rosemary galette 198
bread: Easy flatbreads 160
Breakfast powerhouse smoothie 68
broccoli: Creamy green coconut curry
95
Raw salad with carrot, orange &
ginger dressing 85
Sticky salmon-topped soba noodles
102
brownies: Sea salt pecan brownies
178
buckwheat flour 32, 34
Buckwheat crêpes with smoked
salmon & goats' cheese smash
53
Butternut squash, spinach & feta
buckwheat quiche 149
Cheat's buckwheat pizza with
lemony basil pesto & goats'
cheese 90
Spinach smoothie pancakes with
homemade hazelnut spread &
fresh strawberries 54
buckwheat groats 32, 44
Buckwheat risotto with macadamia
cream 142
Dukkah poached egg buckwheat &
brekky greens bowl 66
butternut squash: Butternut squash,
spinach & feta buckwheat quiche
149
Haddock fishcakes with celeriac &
squash mash & wilted greens 157

Lightened-up lasagne 165
Spicy meatballs with butternut
squash spaghetti 154
Vegetable noodles 45

C

cabbage: Quinoa, feta & kale patties
with rainbow slaw 144
cakes: Best ever carrot cake with
cream cheese icing 218
Dark chocolate chip banana bread
192
Lemon & mint loaf 200
Passionfruit cupcakes with whipped
coconut cream icing 172
Rhubarb & polenta cake 204
Strawberries & cream cheesecake
202
Campfire baked bananas with caramel
sauce 216
caramel: Campfire baked bananas with
caramel sauce 216
Peanut & caramel bars 176
cardamom: Cardamom rice pudding
210
Rose and cardamom nut milk 42
carrots: Baked veggie crisps 120
Best ever carrot cake with cream
cheese icing 218
Carrot & cumin dip 128
Carrot, ginger & coconut soup 84
Courgette noodles topped with
one-pot lentil chilli 76
Good morning sunshine juice 70
Leftover veg & pineapple stir-fry 98
Quinoa, feta & kale patties with
rainbow slaw 144
Raw salad with carrot, orange &
ginger dressing 85

Spicy potato & carrot chips with sweet yoghurt dressing 140

Sweet & spicy peanut noodle salad 115

Tray-baked cod & advieh-spiced veggies 158

Vegetable noodles 45

Veggie sushi rolls 113

celeriac: Haddock fishcakes with celeriac & squash mash & wilted greens 157

cereals 22, 23

cheese: Aubergine quinoa rolls 82

Best ever carrot cake with cream cheese icing 218

Buckwheat crêpes with smoked salmon & goats' cheese smash 53

Butternut squash, spinach & feta buckwheat quiche 149

Cheat's buckwheat pizza with lemony basil pesto & goats' cheese 90

Creamy polenta with mozzarella & burst tomatoes 139

Goats' cheese-stuffed peppers 101

Lazy baked eggs with spicy tomatoes & feta 50

Quinoa, feta & kale patties with rainbow slaw 144

Roast pumpkin salad with whipped feta cream 96

Rosemary, black pepper & parmesan popcorn 130

Vegan pumpkin mac & cheese with a garlic & thyme crumb 136

cheesecake: Strawberries & cream cheesecake 202

chia seeds 33, 63

Blueberry chia jam 63

Rich chocolate tart with a chia seed base 208

chicken: Parchment-baked chicken with coriander & lime veg 108

Spinach pesto pasta with chicken 110

chickpeas: Carrot & cumin dip 128

chilli: Courgette noodles topped with one-pot lentil chilli 76

chillies: Prawn, courgette & chilli linguine 107

chips: Spicy potato & carrot chips with sweet yoghurt dressing 140

chives 36

chocolate: Campfire baked bananas with caramel sauce 216

Chocolate nut milk 42

Dark chocolate chip banana bread 192

Hazelnut & pecan chocolate spread 184

Hippie bars 183

Nutty chocolate truffles 174

Peanut & caramel bars 176

Peanut butter cups two ways 187

Raw rose chocolate bark 180

Rich chocolate tart with a chia seed base 208

Sea salt pecan brownies 178

cinnamon: Fluffy banana cinnamon pancakes 62

coconut: Raspberry & coconut oat porridge 64

coconut milk: Carrot, ginger & coconut soup 84

Coconut kale 89

Creamy green coconut curry 95

Passionfruit cupcakes with whipped coconut cream icing 172

Three-tin tomato, turmeric & coconut dahl 92

coconut oil 34

cod: Tray-baked cod & advieh-spiced veggies 158

coeliac disease 19

coriander: Parchment-baked chicken with coriander & lime veg 108

courgettes: Cheat's buckwheat pizza with lemony basil pesto & goats' cheese 90

Courgette noodles topped with one-pot lentil chilli 76

Creamy green coconut curry 95

Happy belly green soup 88

Prawn, courgette & chilli linguine 107

Vegetable noodles 45

crackers: Herby quinoa crackers 128

cream cheese: Best ever carrot cake with cream cheese icing 218

crêpes: Buckwheat crêpes with smoked salmon & goats' cheese smash 53

crisps: Baked veggie crisps 120

Toasted nori chips 122

Crohn's disease 19

crumbles: Individual strawberry & rhubarb quinoa crumbles 207

cucumber: Cucumber & honeydew smoothie 67

Lamb kofta salad with creamy tzatziki 160

Quinoa & pomegranate tabbouleh 78

Smoked mackerel salad with cucumber, orange, fennel & radish 104

Sunday detox juice 70

Veggie sushi rolls 113

cumin: Carrot & cumin dip 128

cupcakes: Passionfruit cupcakes with whipped coconut cream icing 172

curry: Creamy green coconut curry 95

D

dahl: Three-tin tomato, turmeric & coconut dahl 92

dairy 22, 23, 34

dips: Carrot & cumin dip 128

doughnuts: Glazed blood orange doughnuts 190

dressings 116
   Apple cider vinegar dressing 117
   Creamy green goddess dressing 116
   Creamy yoghurt dressing 117
   Lemon & hemp dressing 116
   Peanut dressing 117

dukkah: Dukkah poached egg buckwheat & brekky greens bowl 66
   Dukkah-crusted salmon with samphire & garlic minted yoghurt 152

E

eggs 22, 39
   Bacon & spinach quiche 150
   Buckwheat crêpes with smoked salmon & goats' cheese smash 53
   Butternut squash, spinach & feta buckwheat quiche 149
   Dukkah poached egg buckwheat & brekky greens bowl 66
   Fluffy banana cinnamon pancakes 62
   Griddle pan waffle with orange & rhubarb compote 60
   Lazy baked eggs with spicy tomatoes & feta 50
   Spinach smoothie pancakes with homemade hazelnut spread & fresh strawberries 54

F

fennel: Fennel & potato bake 168
   Smoked mackerel salad with cucumber, orange, fennel & radish 104

feta cheese: Aubergine quinoa rolls 82
   Butternut squash, spinach & feta buckwheat quiche 149
   Lazy baked eggs with spicy tomatoes & feta 50
   Quinoa, feta & kale patties with rainbow slaw 144
   Roast pumpkin salad with whipped feta cream 96

fish 22
   Buckwheat crêpes with smoked salmon & goats' cheese smash 53
   Dukkah-crusted salmon with samphire & garlic minted yoghurt 152
   Haddock fishcakes with celeriac & squash mash & wilted greens 157
   Smoked mackerel salad with cucumber, orange, fennel & radish 104
   Tray-baked cod & advieh-spiced veggies 158
   see also shellfish

flapjacks: Raspberry & hemp flapjacks 127

Flatbreads 160

flours 22, 23, 34
   gluten-free flour blend 45

Fluffy banana cinnamon pancakes 62

FODMAPs 8–9, 12–21, 30
   eating with the seasons 40–1
   elimination phase 25, 26
   FAQs 228–9
   maintenance phase 26
   reintroduction phase 25–6
   resources and references 230–1
   sample menus 220–5
   store cupboard 32–8
   suitable foods and foods to avoid 22–5

fruit 22, 23

eating with the seasons 40–1
   see also specific fruits

G

galette: Mixed berry & rosemary galette 198

garlic 36

garlic-infused oil 36
   Dukkah-crusted salmon with samphire & garlic minted yoghurt 152
   Vegan pumpkin mac & cheese with a garlic & thyme crumb 136

ginger: Carrot, ginger & coconut soup 84
   Ginger pina colada smoothie 68
   Good morning sunshine juice 70
   Raw salad with carrot, orange & ginger dressing 85
   Soothing ginger tea 70
   Sticky maple, lime & ginger pulled pork 166
   Sunday detox juice 70

gluten 21

gluten-free flour blend 45

Gnocchi with butter & crispy sage 146

Good morning sunshine juice 70

grains 22, 23, 32
   cooking 44–5

granola: Banana granola 56

green beans: Green bean & potato pesto salad 112
   Parchment-baked chicken with coriander & lime veg 108
   Sticky salmon-topped soba noodles 102

Green goddess dressing 116

Griddle pan waffle with orange & rhubarb compote 60

H

Haddock fishcakes with celeriac & squash mash & wilted greens 157

Happy belly green soup 88
hazelnuts: Banana & hazelnut muffins 124
   Hazelnut & pecan chocolate spread 184
   Nutty chocolate truffles 174
   Spinach smoothie pancakes with homemade hazelnut spread & fresh strawberries 54
hemp seeds 33
   Lemon & hemp dressing 116
   Raspberry & hemp flapjacks 127
   Strawberry & hemp seed millet salad 74
herbs 25, 33, 36
Herby quinoa crackers 128
Hippie bars 183

I
ice cream: Salted peanut butter ice cream 217
inflammatory bowel disease (IBD) 19
irritable bowel syndrome (IBS) 12, 18–19
   FAQs 228–9
   FODMAP friendly diet 8–9, 12–16, 20–6, 30–8
   and stress 9, 19, 226

J
jam: Blueberry chia jam 63
juices: Good morning sunshine juice 70
   Sunday detox juice 70

K
kale: Coconut kale 89
   Dukkah poached egg buckwheat & brekky greens bowl 66
   Miso soup 133
   Quinoa, feta & kale patties with rainbow slaw 144
   Sunday detox juice 70
kiwi fruit: Tropical overnight bircher 57

koftas: Lamb kofta salad with creamy tzatziki 160

L
lactose 22
Lamb kofta salad with creamy tzatziki 160
Lasagne 165
lavender: Lavender nut milk 42
   Lavender shortbread cookies 188
   Vanilla quinoa porridge with lavender strawberries 58
leeks 36
lemons 39
   Lemon & hemp dressing 116
   Lemon & mint loaf 200
lentils 33
   Courgette noodles topped with one-pot lentil chilli 76
   Three-tin tomato, turmeric & coconut dahl 92
limes 39
   Papaya, macadamia & lime salad 214
   Parchment-baked chicken with coriander & lime veg 108
   Sticky maple, lime & ginger pulled pork 166
linguine: Prawn, courgette & chilli linguine 107

M
macadamia nuts 33
   Buckwheat risotto with macadamia cream 142
   Papaya, macadamia & lime salad 214
   Strawberries & cream cheesecake 202
mackerel: Smoked mackerel salad with cucumber, orange, fennel & radish 104
maple syrup 34

Sticky maple, lime & ginger pulled pork 166
meat 22, 25
meatballs: Spicy meatballs with butternut squash spaghetti 154
melon: Cucumber & honeydew smoothie 67
   Melon sorbet 213
milk 34
   nut milk 42
millet 32
   Strawberry & hemp seed millet salad 74
mint: Dukkah-crusted salmon with samphire & garlic minted yoghurt 152
   Lemon & mint loaf 200
Miso soup 133
Mixed berry & rosemary galette 198
mozzarella cheese: Creamy polenta with mozzarella & burst tomatoes 139
muffins: Banana & hazelnut muffins 124

N
noodles: Sticky salmon-topped soba noodles 102
   Sweet & spicy peanut noodle salad 115
   Vegetable noodles 45
nori: Miso soup 133
   Toasted nori chips 122
   Veggie sushi rolls 113
nuts 22, 23, 33
nut milk 42
   see also specific nuts

O
oats 32
   Banana granola 56
   Breakfast powerhouse smoothie 68

One-bowl nut butter & seed oat chewies 132

Peanut & caramel bars 176

Raspberry & coconut oat porridge 64

Raspberry & hemp flapjacks 127

Tropical overnight bircher 57

oils 25, 34

olive oil 34

onions 36

see also spring onions

oranges: Glazed blood orange doughnuts 190

Good morning sunshine juice 70

Griddle pan waffle with orange & rhubarb compote 60

Raw salad with carrot, orange & ginger dressing 85

Smoked mackerel salad with cucumber, orange, fennel & radish 104

P

pancakes: Buckwheat crêpes with smoked salmon & goats' cheese smash 53

Fluffy banana cinnamon pancakes 62

Mixed berry & rosemary galette 198

Spinach smoothie pancakes with homemade hazelnut spread & fresh strawberries 54

Papaya, macadamia & lime salad 214

parmesan: Rosemary, black pepper & parmesan popcorn 130

parsnips: Baked veggie crisps 120

Carrot, ginger & coconut soup 84

Happy belly green soup 88

Roasted red pepper & Greek basil soup 86

Tray-baked cod & advieh-spiced veggies 158

passionfruit: Passionfruit cupcakes with whipped coconut cream icing 172

Tropical overnight bircher 57

pasta: Lightened-up lasagne 165

Prawn, courgette & chilli linguine 107

Spinach pesto pasta with chicken 110

Vegan pumpkin mac & cheese with a garlic & thyme crumb 136

peanut butter: One-bowl nut butter & seed oat chewies 132

Peanut & caramel bars 176

Peanut butter cups two ways 187

Peanut dressing 117

Salted peanut butter ice cream 217

Sweet & spicy peanut noodle salad 115

peanuts 33

Peanut & caramel bars 176

pecans 33

Hazelnut & pecan chocolate spread 184

Sea salt pecan brownies 178

pesto: Cheat's buckwheat pizza with lemony basil pesto & goats' cheese 90

Green bean & potato pesto salad 112

Spinach pesto pasta with chicken 110

pineapple: Ginger pina colada smoothie 68

Leftover veg & pineapple stir-fry 98

Prawn tortillas with sweet & spicy pineapple salsa 162

Sunday detox juice 70

pizza: Cheat's buckwheat pizza with lemony basil pesto & goats' cheese 90

polenta: Creamy polenta with mozzarella & burst tomatoes 139

Rhubarb & polenta cake 204

pomegranate: Quinoa & pomegranate tabbouleh 78

popcorn: Rosemary, black pepper & parmesan popcorn 130

Tequila popcorn 130

pork: Sticky maple, lime & ginger pulled pork 166

porridge: Raspberry & coconut oat porridge 64

Vanilla quinoa porridge with lavender strawberries 58

potato starch 34

potatoes: Fennel & potato bake 168

Gnocchi with butter & crispy sage 146

Green bean & potato pesto salad 112

Happy belly green soup 88

Parchment-baked chicken with coriander & lime veg 108

Spicy potato & carrot chips with sweet yoghurt dressing 140

Tray-baked cod & advieh-spiced veggies 158

prawns: Prawn, courgette & chilli linguine 107

Prawn tortillas with sweet & spicy pineapple salsa 162

pulses 22, 23, 33

see also chickpeas; green beans; lentils

pumpkin: Roast pumpkin salad with whipped feta cream 96

Vegan pumpkin mac & cheese with a garlic & thyme crumb 136

pumpkin seeds: Banana granola 56

One-bowl nut butter & seed oat chewies 132

Q

quesadillas: Prawn tortillas with sweet & spicy pineapple salsa 162

quiche: Bacon & spinach quiche 150

Butternut squash, spinach & feta
buckwheat quiche 149
quinoa 32, 34, 44
Aubergine quinoa rolls 82
Herby quinoa crackers 12
Individual strawberry & rhubarb
quinoa crumbles 207
Lamb kofta salad with creamy
tzatziki 160
Quinoa & pomegranate tabbouleh 78
Quinoa, feta & kale patties with
rainbow slaw 144
Vanilla quinoa porridge with
lavender strawberries 58

R
radishes: Smoked mackerel salad with
cucumber, orange, fennel & radish
104
raspberries: Mixed berry & rosemary
galette 198
Raspberry & coconut oat porridge
64
Raspberry & hemp flapjacks 127
Raw rose chocolate bark 180
Raw salad with carrot, orange & ginger
dressing 85
red peppers: Courgette noodles
topped with one-pot lentil chilli 76
Goats' cheese-stuffed peppers 101
Leftover veg & pineapple stir-fry 98
Roasted red pepper & Greek basil
soup 86
Veggie sushi rolls 113
rhubarb: Griddle pan waffle with
orange & rhubarb compote 60
Individual strawberry & rhubarb
quinoa crumbles 207
Rhubarb & polenta cake 204
rice 32, 44
Cardamom rice pudding 210
Veggie sushi rolls 113
rice cereal: Hippie bars 183

rice flour 34
Cheat's buckwheat pizza with
lemony basil pesto & goats'
cheese 90
risotto: Buckwheat risotto with
macadamia cream 142
rocket: Green bean & potato pesto
salad 112
Roast pumpkin salad with whipped
feta cream 96
Strawberry & hemp seed millet
salad 74
rose: Raw rose chocolate bark 180
Rose and cardamom nut milk 42
rosemary: Mixed berry & rosemary
galette 198
Rosemary, black pepper &
parmesan popcorn 130

S
sage: Gnocchi with butter & crispy
sage 146
salads: dressings 116–17
Green bean & potato pesto salad
112
Lamb kofta salad with creamy
tzatziki 160
Raw salad with carrot, orange &
ginger dressing 85
Roast pumpkin salad with whipped
feta cream 96
Smoked mackerel salad with
cucumber, orange, fennel & radish
104
Strawberry & hemp seed millet
salad 74
Sweet & spicy peanut noodle salad
115
salmon: Buckwheat crêpes with
smoked salmon & goats' cheese
smash 53
Dukkah-crusted salmon with
samphire & garlic minted yoghurt
152

Sticky salmon-topped soba noodles
102
salsa: Prawn tortillas with sweet & spicy
pineapple salsa 162
salt: Sea salt pecan brownies 178
Salted peanut butter ice cream 217
samphire: Dukkah-crusted salmon with
samphire & garlic minted yoghurt
152
scones: Vanilla bean glazed scones
194
Sea salt pecan brownies 178
seeds 22, 23, 33
see also specific seeds
shellfish: Prawn, courgette & chilli
linguine 107
Prawn tortillas with sweet & spicy
pineapple salsa 162
shortbread: Lavender shortbread
cookies 188
slaw: Quinoa, feta & kale patties with
rainbow slaw 144
smoothies 67
Breakfast powerhouse smoothie 68
Cucumber & honeydew smoothie
67
Ginger pina colada smoothie 68
Strawberry milk smoothie 67
soba noodles: Sticky salmon-topped
soba noodles 102
Sweet & spicy peanut noodle salad
115
sorbets: Melon sorbet 213
soups: Carrot, ginger & coconut soup
84
Happy belly green soup 88
Miso soup 133
Roasted red pepper & Greek basil
soup 86
spices 25, 33, 36
spinach: Bacon & spinach quiche 150
Butternut squash, spinach & feta
buckwheat quiche 149

Cheat's buckwheat pizza with lemony basil pesto & goats' cheese 90

Creamy green coconut curry 95

Creamy green goddess dressing 116

Haddock fishcakes with celeriac & squash mash & wilted greens 157

Raw salad with carrot, orange & ginger dressing 85

Spinach pesto pasta with chicken 110

Spinach smoothie pancakes with homemade hazelnut spread & fresh strawberries 54

spring greens: Buckwheat risotto with macadamia cream 142

spring onions 36
  Dukkah poached egg buckwheat & brekky greens bowl 66
  Miso soup 133
  Quinoa & pomegranate tabbouleh 78

stir-fry: Leftover veg & pineapple stir-fry 98

stock: vegetable stock 43

strawberries: Individual strawberry & rhubarb quinoa crumbles 207
  Spinach smoothie pancakes with homemade hazelnut spread & fresh strawberries 54
  Strawberries & cream cheesecake 202
  Strawberry & hemp seed millet salad 74
  Strawberry milk smoothie 67
  Vanilla quinoa porridge with avender strawberries 58

stress 9, 19, 226

sugar 22, 23, 34

Sunday detox juice 70

sunflower seeds 33
  Tropical overnight bircher 57

sushi: Veggie sushi rolls 113

sweeteners 22, 23, 34

T

tabbouleh: Quinoa & pomegranate tabbouleh 78

tamari 34

tapioca flour 34

tea: Soothing ginger tea 70

Tequila popcorn 130

thyme: Vegan pumpkin mac & cheese with a garlic & thyme crumb 136

tomatoes: Courgette noodles topped with one-pot lentil chilli 76
  Creamy polenta with mozzarella & burst tomatoes 139
  Lamb kofta salad with creamy tzatziki 160
  Lazy baked eggs with spicy tomatoes & feta 50
  Roasted red pepper & Greek basil soup 86
  Three-tin tomato, turmeric & coconut dahl 92

tortillas: Prawn tortillas with sweet & spicy pineapple salsa 162

Tropical overnight bircher 57

turmeric: Three-tin tomato, turmeric & coconut dahl 92

turnip: Baked veggie crisps 120

tzatziki: Lamb kofta salad with creamy tzatziki 160

V

vanilla 34
  Vanilla bean glazed scones 194
  Vanilla chai 42
  Vanilla quinoa porridge with lavender strawberries 58

vegetables 22, 23
  eating with the seasons 40–1
  noodles 45
  stock 43
  see also specific vegetables

W

waffles: Griddle pan waffle with orange & rhubarb compote 60

walnuts 33
  Nutty chocolate truffles 174

watercress: Happy belly green soup 88

wheat 21

Y

yoghurt: Creamy yoghurt dressing 117
  Dukkah-crusted salmon with samphire & garlic minted yoghurt 152
  Lamb kofta salad with creamy tzatziki 160
  Spicy potato & carrot chips with sweet yoghurt dressing 140

Acknowledgements

There's no way not to sound like a ball of cheese in this bit and the words that follow will never be as eloquently written as I would like – so I'm just going to go for it.

Writing this book has been empowering, inspiring and emotional all at the same time and it's only here because of a team of brilliant people supporting me behind the scenes.

The actual idea that people take the time to follow one of my recipes and read my writing and that they both might make somebody's life suffering from a sensitive gut a little easier, is just mind blowing. Thank you to every single one of you for purchasing this book and for all your support along the way. I promise every message, comment and email I receive is read, cherished and endlessly appreciated.

Rob, no words will suffice to explain just how lucky I am. Thank you for the constant laughter and love, even when I'm being a nightmare (which happens rarely obviously...) Thank you for never thinking my ideas are too crazy, never too big and for being there every step of the way. I simply couldn't do it without you – and I hope I never have to.

To my wonderful housemates and friends, Dorothy and Ruth, for never ever complaining when I take up all the cupboard space in the kitchen with ingredients or when there are no clean spoons to be found because I've used them all up recipe testing. You've helped make this whole thing easier; thank you for keeping me sane.

Thank you to the amazing team at Hodder, for welcoming me into the Yellow Kite family with open arms. A special thank you to Maddy, my fantastic editor, for taking that initial chance on me and for the constant enthusiasm and patience that has since followed. Becca, Caitriona, Aimee, I'm so grateful for all your hard work.

Louise, thank you for just getting it – right from the beginning. Your vision, design and energy has been amazing. Malou, I'm so thrilled you chose to take on this project. For tirelessly working until that perfect shot was captured; you've brought even the simplest recipes to life. Thank you to you both, for executing it all so beautifully – you make it look easy.

To the rest of the shoot crew – Henrietta, I could watch you work your magic all day. Thank you for making sure the food always looked as good as it tastes. Megan, Alex, Suzie, Charlotte and Lydia. Thank you for all your hard work, patience and energy throughout. You're all fab and it was an absolute pleasure to work with you. A huge thank you Sarah for your time and invaluable input and to Ruth, for bringing such a fantastic team together.

Luke, your work is stunning and the patient photography lessons along the way have been so appreciated. Thank you to both you and Allison and to Gillian and Kevin, for letting me cause chaos in your kitchens when mine got too small.

Annika, Jules, and my 'Strong Independent Women' (yes I really did just write that here; you know who you are) – thank you for being the best friends a girl could ask for. To my family friends, thank you for always making us 'kids' feel like we were invincible in life. To the family friend kids for being 'invincible' with me; I couldn't have done it without you.

Last but by no means least, my family. For the endless enthusiasm, support and for being my biggest cheerleaders right from the beginning. Mum, Dad and Eve; I wrote a book! There will never be words, sentences, chapters, great enough for the support and love you give me every day. Best family ever. Love you x

Follow She Can't Eat What?!
www.shecanteatwhat.com
instagram.com/shecanteatwhat
facebook.com/shecanteatwhat
twitter.com/shecanteatwhat

First published in Great Britain in 2017 by Yellow Kite
An imprint of Hodder & Stoughton
An Hachette UK company

1

Text © Emma Hatcher 2017
Foreword © Fodmap Friendly Pty Limited 2017
Photography pages 2, 4, 17, 24, 27, 31, 35, 45, 50, 52, 59, 60, 65,
69, 75, 77, 81, 83, 93, 97, 103, 105, 106, 109, 111, 125, 131, 137,
141, 143, 145, 147, 153, 159, 161, 163, 173, 177, 191, 198, 205,
209, 211, 215, 219, 231 © Malou Burger 2017
Photography pages 7, 13, bottom-right 28, 37, 38, 55, 63, 79,
83, 87, 94, 121, 129, 156, 164, 167, 182, 185, 212, 227, 240
© Luke Fullalove 2017
Photograph page 36 © Dorothy Cross 2017
All other photography © Emma Hatcher 2017
Images pages 3, 10, 11, 18, 19, 20, 21, 23, 28, 29, 41, 46, 47, 48,
72, 118, 134, 170, 198, 221–225 © Shutterstock.com

A CIP catalogue record for this title is available from the British
Library

Hardback ISBN 978 1 473 64146 4
Ebook ISBN 978 1 473 64148 8

Publisher: Liz Gough
Editor: Maddy Price
Design and art direction: Louise Leffler
Shoot photography: Malou Burger
Food Styling: Henrietta Clancy
Prop styling: Lydia Brun
Hair and makeup: Charlotte Gaskell
Shoot production: Ruth Ferrier

Printed and bound in Germany by Firmengruppe APPL

Hodder & Stoughton Ltd
Carmelite House
50 Victoria Embankment
London EC4Y 0DZ

www.hodder.co.uk